EARLY DEISM IN FRANCE

ARCHIVES INTERNATIONALES D'HISTOIRE DES IDEES

INTERNATIONAL ARCHIVES OF THE HISTORY OF IDEAS

104

C.J. BETTS

EARLY DEISM IN FRANCE

From the so-called 'déistes' of Lyon (1564)
to Voltaire's 'Lettres philosophiques' (1734)

C.J. BETTS

EARLY DEISM IN FRANCE

*From the so-called 'déistes' of Lyon (1564)
to Voltaire's 'Lettres philosophiques' (1734)*

1984 **MARTINUS NIJHOFF PUBLISHERS**
a member of the KLUWER ACADEMIC PUBLISHERS GROUP
THE HAGUE / BOSTON / LANCASTER

Distributors

for the United States and Canada: Kluwer Academic Publishers, 190 Old Derby Street, Hingham, MA 02043, USA
for the UK and Ireland: Kluwer Academic Publishers, MTP Press Limited, Falcon House, Queen Square, Lancaster LA1 1RN, England
for all other countries: Kluwer Academic Publishers Group, Distribution Center, P.O. Box 322, 3300 AH Dordrecht, The Netherlands

Library of Congress Cataloging in Publication Data

```
Betts, C. J.
  Early deism in France.

  (Archives internationales d'histoire des idées ; 104)
  Bibliography: p.
  Includes index.
  1. Deism--France--History. 2. France--Religion.
I. Title, II. Series.
BL2765.F8B47 1984      211'.5'0944      83-27504
ISBN 90-247-2923-8
```

ISBN 90-247-2923-8 (this volume)
ISBN 90-247-2433-3 (series)

Copyright

PRINTED IN THE NETHERLANDS

MAIORIBVS

CONTENTS

viii

ACKNOWLEDGEMENTS

This study originated many years ago in a thesis supervised by Mr, now Professor, Robert Shackleton. The subject developed from his suggestion, and I am deeply indebted to his advice and the example of his scholarship. It is also a pleasure to acknowledge subsequent debts of gratitude: to the administrators of the Zaharoff Travelling Fund, Oxford, for a grant which enabled much of the basic research to be done; to the Provost and Fellows of Queen's College, Oxford, for a research fellowship, and many incidental kindnesses; to Professor E. R. Briggs and Dr Denys Potts, who examined and advised me on my thesis; to the Vice-Chancellor and Senate of the University of Warwick for grants of sabbatical leave and of a subsidy towards the cost of publication, and to my colleagues there, especially Professor Donald Charlton, Professor Richard Coe, Dr Gaston Hall and Dr Marian Hobson, for varied information and encouragement; to the librarians of the Bibliothèque nationale, the Bibliothèque Mazarine and the Bibliothèque de l'Arsenal, Paris; of the British Museum; of the Bodleian Library and the Taylorian Institute, Oxford, especially Dr Giles Barber, and of the library of the University of Warwick, especially Miss Alison Marsh, Mr Jolyon Hall and Mr Peter Larkin; to the staff of the Inter-Library Loans Service; to Mrs Barbara Smith, of Manchester College, Oxford, for much assistance in consulting early Unitarian works; and to Mrs Margaret Haynes for her competence and patience with the typescript; and to the staff of Martinus Nijhoff for their courtesy and helpfulness.

I am particularly glad to be able to thank those who have read earlier drafts, especially Dr Denys Potts, again, for advice concerning Saint-Evremond, Professor Anthony Levi, for valuable help with a version of the first chapter, and Professor Ralph Leigh, for general and specific advice on the whole of a previous version.

My debt to my wife Ann is beyond acknowledgement.

Royal Leamington Spa
September 1981

ABBREVIATIONS AND QUOTATIONS

Besterman D. followed by number: the number of the letter in the definitive
edition of Voltaire's correspondence by Theodore Besterman; see Bibliography, section 2

BHR: Bibliothèque d'Humanisme et de Renaissance
JHI: Journal of the History of Ideas
PMLA: Publications of the Modern Language Association of America
RHLF: Revue d'histoire littéraire de la France
RLC: Revue de littérature comparée
SVEC: Studies on Voltaire and the Eighteenth Century

The titles of some authorities to which reference is often made are abbreviated as stated in the first of the relevant notes.

In quotations from early French sources the spelling is usually modernized,
but titles of books are given in the original spelling. Latin quotations, given
in the notes, are translated or paraphrased in the text.

Part I

Prehistory, from 1564 to about 1670

CHAPTER 1

INTRODUCTORY; PIERRE VIRET'S 'DÉISTES' AT LYON,
AND TWO CHARACTERS IN BODIN

Deism, the religious attitude typical of the Enlightenment in France, England and elsewhere, was never a religion in the usual sense, although for a short time in the French Revolution the worship of the Supreme Being was officially instituted. It was a religion for individuals, especially the educated laity, and was most often presented as the result of the individual's unaided reflections on God and man. Its monuments are literary and philosophical, the greatest of them being, in France, Voltaire's *Dictionnaire philosophique* and Rousseau's *Profession de foi du vicaire savoyard*, in *Emile*.[1] Both date from the apogee of the French Enlightenment, the 1760s. Together with numerous other works they are the culmination of a movement which had reached maturity less than thirty years previously, with Voltaire's *Lettres philosophiques*. Until then the story of deism is one of clandestinity, sporadic appearances and false starts, going back as far as the middle of the sixteenth century as regards the word itself, but lacking any sort of continuity until the last decades of the seventeenth.

There is no adequate brief definition of the substance of deism. It is convenient to follow the usage of distinguishing two complementary aspects, called 'positive' and 'negative' or 'constructive' and 'critical'.[2] The pattern can be perceived as early as 1690, in the definition given by Furetière: 'Déiste. s.m. Homme qui n'a point de religion particulière, mais qui reconnaît seulement un Dieu, sans lui rendre aucun culte extérieur'.[3] The positive aspect includes – necessarily, because of the etymology – the belief in God, and possibly other tenets; it was often synonymous with so-called natural religion. This tended, however, to have a moral element also, and was not automatically incompatible with Christianity. In Furetière's definition the negative side is constituted by the rejection of Christian worship and

---

[1] The *Dictionnaire philosophique*, first published in 1764 as the *Dictionnaire philosophique portatif*, went through many revisions, a number of articles being revised or adapted for the *Questions sur l'Encyclopédie* (1770–1774). See *Dictionnaire philosophique*, edited by Raymond Naves, Classiques Garnier (Paris, 1954 edition), pp. xv–xvi. The *Profession de foi du vicaire savoyard* is in Livre IV of *Emile, ou de l'éducation* (1762).

[2] The terms are used by Paul Hazard, *La Crise de la conscience européenne (1680–1715)*, 3 vols. (Paris, 1935), Vol. II, pp. 26–27, and in the titles of Chapters III and IV of Sir Leslie Stephen's *History of English Thought in the Eighteenth Century*, 2 vols. (London, 1876).

[3] Antoine Furetière, *Dictionnaire universel* (1690).

allegiance to a church. In later texts, critical deism covered many different forms and degrees of opposition to Christianity, ranging from respectful doubt to violent denunciation. Insofar, then, as there is a standard modern definition (since much writing on the subject is regrettably vague over defining the term),[4] it is that deism is a religious attitude based on the belief in God and, on this basis, implicitly or explicitly rejecting Christian belief. This sense, consecrated by the article in Diderot's and d'Alembert's *Encyclopédie*, is usually intended in what follows.[5] The word 'theism' will be reserved for the belief in God when there is no implied opposition to Christianity; with this word it is opposition to atheism that is commonly meant.

To define a movement of thought thus is inevitably somewhat arbitrary and has its drawbacks, but they are outweighed by the advantages. It is a matter of history that, roughly at the beginning of the eighteenth century, large numbers of individuals were in the process of detaching themselves from Christian belief and replacing it by a religious attitude in which the belief in God was independent, at least outwardly, of Church or Bible. This movement requires a name. The main advantage of the standard definition is that it distinguishes deism from Christianity on the one hand (which would not be possible with a definition lacking the negative aspect, and thus identifying deism with natural religion) and atheism on the other, atheism being also well attested at the time. There may be considerable doubt whether particular writers are Christians tending to deism or deists sympathetic to Christianity, but in such cases the definition incorporating both positive and negative aspects is an essential instrument of discussion.[6] One

---

[4]   This seems to me an important defect in Henri Busson's studies: *Le rationalisme dans la littérature française de la Renaissance (1533–1601)* (Paris, 1957; cited henceforth as *Rationalisme*; a revised and enlarged version of his *Les sources et le développement du rationalisme dans la littérature française de la Renaissance (1533–1601)* (Paris, 1922)), and *La pensée religieuse française de Charron à Pascal* (Paris, 1933) (cited henceforth as *Charron à Pascal*).

[5]   The Abbé Mallet, the author of the article, connects deism with English free-thought, and remarks that 'Le nom de *Déistes* est donné surtout à ces sortes de personnes qui, n'étant ni athées ni chrétiennes, ne sont point absolument sans religion (à prendre ce mot dans son sens le plus général), mais qui rejettent toute révélation comme une pure fiction, et ne croyent que ce qu'ils reconnaissent par les lumières naturelles, et que ce qui est cru dans toute religion, un Dieu, une providence, une vie future, des récompenses et des châtiments pour les bons et pour les méchants; qu'il faut honorer Dieu et accomplir sa volonté connue par les lumières de la raison et la voix de la conscience, le plus parfaitement qu'il est possible; mais que du reste chacun peut vivre à son gré, et suivant ce que lui dicte sa conscience' (*Encyclopédie ou Dictionnaire raisonné des arts, des sciences et des métiers*, 35 vols. (1751–1780), Vol. IV (1754), p. 773, col. b). I follow the usage of Mario M. Rossi, in his study of Lord Herbert, which is also the best general study of deism in recent decades: 'userò (...) la parola "teismo" solo per indicare il contrario di "ateismo", cioè tanto il deismo che dottrine ad esso opposte. Indicherò come "deismo" che neghi il valore religioso della Rivelazione' (*La vita, le opere e i tempi di Eduardo, Lord Herbert di Chirbury* (sic), 3 vols. (Florence, 1947), Vol. I, p. 493, n. 1).

[6]   Thus Bernard Tocanne apparently has no means of distinguishing the rational Christianity of Abbadie, in 1684, from deism: 'Abbadie n'est pas déiste, et il attaque les déistes (...) Malgré ses attaques contre le déisme, Abbadie tend à identifier la substance du christianisme avec une religion naturelle qui est une forme de déisme' (*L'Idée de nature en France dans la seconde moitié du XVIIe siècle* (Paris, 1978), Pt. II, Ch. VI, p. 265; cf. pp. 267 on Huet, 273 on Régis). However, what Abbadie meant by the deism which he attacked is not a straightforward matter; see Chapter 6.

of the best examples is Saint-Evremond, who seems to go to the brink of deism, but remains a Catholic, although a worldly and free-thinking one; the examination of his opinions reveals what was involved in the opposition between deism and Christianity.

With writers who, like the 'Militaire philosophe', obviously conform to the standard definition, the disadvantage of using it is that it reduces all to the same low level. To say that one believes in God but does not accept Christianity is not in itself an interesting religious position, however great its significance for the person concerned, and it is not the purpose of this study, even if it were possible, to provide a survey of all the individuals whose views merely conform to a definition. Deism becomes worthy of analysis when the questions inherent in the deist's basic position (the attitude to be taken towards Christianity above all, but also the relation of religion and morality) are faced by writers determined to apply their principles to all the main areas of contemporary religious concern. No doubt because of the period's general tendency to methodological exposition, deists attempted, like others, to create all-embracing religious philosophies. Some of them, apart from their historical importance, have an intrinsic interest which has not been entirely nullified by the subsequent development of deist ideas by greater thinkers such as Rousseau.

The problem of origins virtually solves itself once the work of writers tending to deism and those who are unequivocally deists has been fully described. The situation is not the same as that which inspired Fontenelle's admirable dictum, 'Assurons-nous bien du fait, avant que de nous inquiéter de la cause', but it is true that when the fact of deism is examined in detail there is little mystery about its causes.[7] The essential was said many years ago by Gustave Lanson in his pioneering series of lectures on the origins of the 'esprit philosophique', when he observed that in about 1715 deism comprised a combination of Christianity and rationalism.[8]

What follows, then, is principally a study of the development, between about 1675 and 1715, of more or less complete systems of deistic thought, resembling in both their positive and negative aspects the deism of the great Enlightenment writers. After 1715, the early works of Montesquieu and Voltaire represent both a conclusion of this first period of French deism and the beginning of the Enlightenment proper. However, long before 1675 there are the early references to 'déistes' which have given rise to the view that deism had a continuous history from the later sixteenth century.

---

[7] Fontenelle, *Histoire des oracles* (1686), Dissertation I, Ch. 4; the famous story of the golden tooth.

[8] 'De sorte que le déisme apparaît en somme comme la combinaison du rationalisme et du christianisme' (*Origines et premières manifestations de l'esprit philosophique dans la littérature française de 1675 à 1748*, lectures printed in *Revue des cours et conférences*, 16–18 (December 1907–December 1910), reprinted New York, 1973 (p. 239). Cited henceforth as *Origines de l'esprit philosophique*; references to the 1973 edition). Lanson's remark remains valid, paradoxically perhaps, for deism regarded as anti-Christian by definition.

VIRET'S 'DÉISTES': ANTI-CHRISTIAN OR ANTI-TRINITARIAN?

Throughout the sixteenth and seventeenth centuries the history of terms referring to deism presents much greater problems than is generally realized, and perhaps the most difficult concerns the interpretation of the passage in which Pierre Viret, the reformer of Lausanne, reported in 1564 on the deists about whom he had heard. The passage occurs in his *Instruction chrétienne*, as part of the dedicatory epistle, addressed to the faithful at Montpellier, of the second volume. The epistle is dated 12th December 1563. Viret was a close colleague of Calvin's. After leaving Lausanne, he went for reasons of health to Nîmes and Montpellier. At the outset of the Wars of Religion he was called to Lyon where the Reformers were temporarily in control.[9] The *Instruction chrétienne* is a work of apologetics, and it is in describing various free-thinkers whom the apologist has to combat that Viret mentions those 'qui s'appellent déistes, d'un mot tout nouveau'. His description of their opinions heavily emphasizes their lack of religion. At one point, following, he says, the usage of St Paul, he calls them atheists. According to him, they 'se moquent de toute religion, (. . .) nonobstant qu'ils s'accommodent quant à l'apparence extérieure à la religion de ceux avec lesquels il leur faut vivre'.[10]

It is largely on this report that is based the prevalent but misleading view that deism was from the very beginning a form of unbelief consciously hostile to the Christian faith and therefore fundamentally akin to the aggressive deism typical of the eighteenth century. Such a view was almost certainly held by Pierre Bayle, who in 1702 made Viret's remarks known in his *Dictionnaire*, in the index to which the entry 'Déistes' gives a cross-reference to 'Incrédulité'.[11] Henri Busson, whose studies of rationalism contain the only modern treatment of the early history of deism, makes

---

[9]   See Jean Barnaud, *Pierre Viret, sa vie et son œuvre (1511–1571)* (Saint-Amans (Tarn), 1911), especially Pt. III, Ch. 2, on Viret's stay at Lyon. (Cited henceforth as *Pierre Viret*.) See also Barnaud's article 'Pierre Viret à Lyon (1562–1565)', *Bulletin de la société de l'histoire du Protestantisme français* 60 (1911), 7–43.

[10]   *Instruction chrestienne en la doctrine de la loy et de l'Evangile*, 2 vols. (Geneva, 1564); it is an expanded version of several previous works (Barnaud, *Pierre Viret*, pp. 605–606, 694). A third volume, mentioned on the title-page, failed to appear (ibid., p. 606). The passage on the deists is on unnumbered pages 7–9 of the 18-page dedicatory epistle of Vol. II, 'Aux fidèles qui font profession de la vraie doctrine chrétienne en l'église de Montpellier', and has often been reprinted, first by Bayle (see next note), and more recently by Busson, *Rationalisme*, pp. 517–518; also in *Pierre Viret par lui-même*, Pages extraites des œuvres du Réformateur, edited by C. Schnetzler, H. Vuilleumier and A. Schroeder (Lausanne, 1911), pp. 233–236, and Günter Gawlick, Vorwort, pp. VIII–X, to reprint (Hildesheim, 1965) of G. V. Lechler's *Geschichte des englischen Deismus*.

[11]   *Dictionnaire historique et critique*, 'Viret', Note D; the article did not appear in the first edition (1697). Leland, the first historian of English deism, also seems to have thought that the deism described by Viret was the same in nature as eighteenth-century deism; see his *A View of the Principal Deistical Writers* (London, 1754), Vol. I, pp. 2–3.

similar assumptions.[12] The question is related to the wider and continuing debate about all forms of free-thought or *libertinage* in the sixteenth century. Busson's view that free-thinking rationalist opposition to Christian belief was widespread at the time was denied by Lucien Febvre, in an influential study which seeks to show that speculation outside a Christian framework was virtually inconceivable.[13] In recent scholarship, neither of the extreme views, that anti-Christian free thought was dominant or that it scarcely existed, has found favour; yet in dealing with Viret's account of the deists it would seem that there is no middle way: we must either accept it as truthful, or explain it away.

There is at least one good reason for doubting Viret's accuracy, which is the paucity of supporting testimony. For almost a hundred years after the publication of the *Instruction chrétienne*, it is very difficult to find any reliable evidence for the existence of an attitude called 'déisme' and comprising, as in the standard modern definition, belief in God combined with criticism of Christianity. During this lengthy period the only overt profession of faith from a self-confessed deist is an anonymous poem, *L'Anti-bigot*, or *Quatrains du déiste*, of about 1620, which is a protest against the doctrine of hellfire and seems to have no connection whatever with the 'déistes' of Lyon. Occasional references to deism in other works, up to and including Pascal's *Pensées*, almost always fail to identify deists by name and are often merely hostile or vague.[14] Either, therefore, the attitude of Viret's deists was an ephemeral affair, or it was well concealed after 1564, and whichever may have been the case it seems to have been an anomaly in the history of thought.

The passage from the *Instruction chrétienne* is therefore of crucial interest. Apart from the pathetic figure of Geoffroy Vallée, burnt in 1574 for professing beliefs with Anabaptist connotations, and at the end of the century Jean Bodin's characters Toralba and Senamus, Viret's description is the only evidence in the sixteenth century for a form of anti-Christian free-thought going under the name of deism. Neither in Bodin's *Colloquium heptaplomeres*

[12]   See Busson, 'Question préliminaire', *Rationalisme*, pp. 7–13, and his 'Les noms des incrédules au XVIe siècle', BHR 16 (1954), 273–283 (cited henceforth as *Les noms des incrédules*).
[13]   Lucien Febvre, *Le problème de l'incroyance au XVIe siècle: la religion de Rabelais* (Paris, 1942). See also Gerhard Schneider, *Der Libertin: Zur Geistes- und Sozialgeschichte des Bürgertums im 16. und 17. Jahrhundert* (Stuttgart, 1970); J. C. Margolin, 'Libertins, libertinisme et "libertinage" au XVIe siècle', in *Aspects du libertinisme au XVIe siècle*, Exposés de M. Bataillon (and others) (Actes du colloque international de Sommières) (Paris, 1974), pp. 1–33 (volume cited henceforth as *Aspects du libertinisme*); P. O. Kristeller, 'Le mythe de l'athéisme de la Renaissance et la tradition française de la libre pensée', BHR 37 (1975), 337–348 (cited henceforth as *Le mythe de l'athéisme*); Jean Wirth, '"Libertins" et "épicuriens": aspects de l'irréligion au XVIe siècle', BHR 39 (1977), 601–627, especially 'Etat de la question', pp. 601–607.
[14]   This is more fully discussed in Chapters 2 and 3.

nor in Vallée's *Fléo de la foy* is there any reference to deism.[15] The question is, then whether Viret's 'déistes' can be identified.

Viret was writing to Montpellier from Lyon, which was near the centre of things, while Montpellier was a somewhat distant outpost of the Reformation. He does not say that he is referring specifically to unbelief in Lyon; writing to the faithful of Montpellier, he could well have been telling them of something which he had heard from colleagues in Switzerland, or knew from previous experience or from visitors to Lyon. In the passage about deists he also mentions 'ceux qui font profession des bonnes lettres et de la philosophie humaine', which suggests humanist scholars such as Etienne Dolet. But Dolet's execution for irreligion had taken place in 1546. Another remark about these humanists, who 'sont non seulement infectés de cet exécrable athéisme, mais aussi en font profession et tiennent école' might if taken literally point to another victim of intolerance, Barthélemy Aneau, a professor and for some years the principal of the Collège de la Trinité at Lyon. He was lynched by a Catholic mob in June 1561.[16] He was suspected of being a Huguenot, but the Reformers did not claim him as one of their number. Théodore de Bèze regarded him as impious, and as with Dolet the manner in which he refers to the classical gods in his works might imply pagan scepticism.[17] Viret, who arrived in Lyon in June 1562, must have known of Aneau's death, and may well have had the same view of him as Bèze. He may also have had more information than we have. At about the same time, a young man who was to play an important part in the Reformation, François du Jon, went through a phase of disbelief while at Lyon. He had been reading Cicero and listening to objections to the idea of providence.[18]

[15] On Vallée, see Busson, *Rationalisme*, pp. 523–534 (Ch. XVI, 3). Apparently on the basis of a remark in La Monnoye's *Menagiana* (1700), Vol. IV, p. 131 ('Le fond de la doctrine de G. Vallée n'est pas l'athéisme proprement dit, mais un déisme commode qui consiste à reconnaître Dieu sans le craindre et sans appréhender aucune peine après la mort'), Busson includes Vallée in a chapter on atheists and deists, but decides that he ought to be described as a 'libertin spirituel' (pp. 530–534). However, the 'libertins spirituels' or Anabaptists attacked by Calvin seem to have very little in common with any form of deism (the *Menagiana* probably meant 'theism'). Vallée's *La Béatitude des chrestiens ou le fleo de la foy* (the spelling is for anagrammatic reasons) has been published in a modern paraphrase by Frédéric Lachèvre, *Mélanges* (*Le libertinage au XVIIe siècle*, VIII) (Paris, 1920), pp. 23–29. Lachèvre's opinion on Vallée ('C'est un déiste, adversaire des religions révélées', etc., ibid., p. 18) is an extreme example of the view that sixteenth-century 'deism' is intrinsically the same as in the eighteenth century.

[16] See Georgette Brasart-de Groër, 'Le Collège, agent d'infiltration de la Réforme: Barthélemy Aneau au Collège de la Trinité', in *Aspects de la propagande religieuse*, Etudes publiées par G. Berthoud (and others) (Geneva, 1957), pp. 167–175.

[17] Henri Meylan, in the preface, pp. xiii–xiv, to the volume *Aspects de la propagande religieuse* cited in the preceding note, quotes Bèze's letter to Bullinger, 15 June 1651, on Aneau: 'homo prorsus impius, et quovis supplicio dignus' (see *Correspondance de Théodore de Bèze*, Vol. III (1559–1561) (Geneva, 1963), p. 112), and considers that Aneau's last work, *Alector ou le coq* (1560) would have suggested deism to the Genevan Reformers had they read it.

[18] See Busson, *Rationalisme*, pp. 522–523, who refers to Bayle's article 'Junius' in the *Dictionnaire historique et critique*.

We may therefore read Viret's description as a hostile account of classicizing theists: 'pour autant qu'athéiste signifie celui qui est sans Dieu, ils veulent donner à entendre qu'ils ne sont pas du tout sans Dieu, à cause qu'ils croyent bien qu'il y a quelque Dieu, lequel ils reconnaissent même pour créateur de ciel et de la terre, comme les Turcs, mais de Jésus-Christ ils ne savent que c'est, et ne tiennent rien de lui, ni de sa doctrine'. In a later work mentioning deists, *L'Intérim fait par dialogues* (1565), Viret made the same point.[19] The dedication of the *Instruction chrétienne* adds that while some believe in the immortality of the soul, others do not, 'comme les épicuriens'; and similarly with divine providence. (The denial of providence was commonly assimilated to the Epicurean conception of gods who were indifferent to human affairs.)[20]

The reference to Epicureans would support the hypothesis that the 'déistes' were humanists whose classical reading had detached them from Christian belief and who had invented a word to denote simply the belief in God. If no other evidence were available, this hypothesis would be the most plausible. There are, however, slightly later accounts of deists at Lyon, to which Busson does not give sufficient weight.[21] They strongly suggest quite a different interpretation, namely that the origin of the term 'deism' lies in the anti-trinitarian movement which was then an important, if scattered, phenomenon in the religious life of Europe. It developed in the 1550s and 1560s largely through a cross-fertilization of ideas between Italy and Poland; many Italian exiles sympathetic to the Reformation found at least temporary refuge with educated Polish patrons during a period of religious tolerance.[22]

A few years after Viret's *Instruction chrétienne*, the earliest reference to deism from the Catholic side is found in a catalogue of heresies by Prateolus

[19] The third section of *L'Intérim* is on different sorts of unbeliever, 'libertins', and in it Viret gives free rein to his fondness for classifying and sub-classifying. The passage on deists is pp. 199f. Viret says that mockery of religion is found especially among those privileged enough not to fear reprimand, but it is not clear whether the mockers include deists or not. See H. Meylan, 'Pierre Viret et les libertins, d'après *L'Intérim* (1565)', in *Aspects du libertinisme*, pp. 191–198.

[20] This conception, occurring frequently in the literature of unorthodoxy, was derived in particular from Lucretius, *De rerum natura* (e.g. V, 165–167), and Cicero, *De natura deorum* (e.g. I, xx).

[21] Busson refers to these reports (*Rationalisme*, p. 541, n. 1, apparently following Bayle, *Dictionnaire*, 'Viret', Note F) but separately from his treatment (pp. 517f.) of Viret, although Saint-Julien, Castelnau and Du Préau must have meant the same group as Viret; on Castelnau's report, Busson refers to Socinianism, which is an anachronism, since this movement was not so named until after 1580 (see n. 39 below). In his article *Les noms des incrédules*, Busson dismisses the evidence from Du Préau without giving reasons (p. 279).

[22] Only in recent decades has this movement been subjected to serious scholarly investigation. The works on which I rely most are: Earl Morse Wilbur, *Socinianism and its Antecedents* (cited henceforth as *Socinianism*), the first volume of two entitled *A History of Unitarianism* (Boston, 1945, 1952), and George Huntston Williams, *The Radical Reformation* (Philadelphia, 1962). Stanislas Kot, 'Le mouvement antitrinitaire au XVIe et au XVIIe siècle', Humanisme et Renaissance 4 (1937), 16–58 and 109–156, although only an introductory survey, pays particular attention to France.

(Gabriel Du Préau), the *Elenchus haereticorum* of 1569.[23] In a chronological listing of the dates at which heresies first appeared, the date of the 'deistae seu trinitarii' is given as 1564, the year of Viret's book. In the article devoted to them (Liber IIII, p. 139), Du Préau says that they originated in the Polish Reformation. As for 'trinitarii', it was a term used, confusingly, by Catholic polemicists to denote those now usually called anti-trinitarians.[24] The 'execrable heresy' spread to Lyon, according to Du Préau, in 1566. Despite the slight discrepancy in date, which suggests that he was not relying on the *Instruction chrétienne*, he must be referring to the same group as Viret. Apart from the term 'deiste' itself, his main source for the article in the *Elenchus* is a work by another Catholic writer, Wigandus (Jean Wigand) attacking the Polish Arians. Wigand does not mention deists; his remarks on the heresies in Poland, especially Arianism, were simply copied by Du Préau, who however applied them to the 'deistae' as well as to the 'novi Ariani'.[25] The leader of the heretics is said to be Gregorius Paulus (Gregory Paul, Grzegor Paweł), a minister of the Polish Reformed Church at Craców.[26]

If Du Préau is to be believed, 'deistae' was far from being the name for free-thinkers who denied every Christian belief, as Viret had maintained, but was simply another of the numerous terms coined to denote the anti-trinitarian opinions which were just beginning to be propagated in Poland, after having been advanced by Servetus and Italians such as Gentile in France and Switzerland. Du Préau's summary of the 'deists'' main principles suggests how the term came into existence: in order to convey the view that there is only one true God, God the Father, not a trinity of gods.[27] The work of Gregorius Paulus to which Wigand and Du Préau refer, in tones of abhorrence, is presumably his *Tabula de trinitate*, of November 1562, which is no longer extant.[28] It was a contribution to the controversy within the

---

[23]   That is: *De vitis, sectis et dogmatibus omnium haereticorum qui ab orbe condita ad nostra usque tempora (. . .) proditi sunt, elenchus alphabeticus* (Cologne, 1569).

[24]   Wilbur, *Socinianism*, p. 340; Williams, *Radical Reformation*, p. 694.

[25]   Johannis Wigandus, *De Deo, contra novos Arianos nuper in Polonia exortos, liber secundus*, pp. 76–77. This is one of the pieces published by Théodore de Bèze in a volume denouncing Gentile: *Valentini Gentilis teterrimi haeretici impietatum ac triplicis perfidiae et periuriae, brevis explicatio* (Geneva, 1567). Bèze's preface, giving a history of Arian heresies, is reprinted in his *Correspondance*, Vol. VIII (1567) (Geneva, 1976), pp. 234f.; see p. 254, n. 55, for the contents of the volume (giving a different title for the treatise by Wigandus).

[26]   On Gregorius Paulus see Williams, *Radical Reformation*, Ch. 25, 3, and Wilbur, *Socinianism*, Ch. XXII.

[27]   Wigandus and Du Préau summarize three 'hypotheses', of which the third is: 'Unum esse DEUM, sed tantum Patrem dici unicum et verum DEUM: filium vero et spiritum sanctum non dici unicum illum DEUM'. The first two hypotheses reject the conceptions of persons and essence used in trinitarian doctrine. At the end of his article Du Préau refers for further information to his articles 'Trinitarii' and 'Valentinistae'.

[28]   Williams, *Radical Reformation*, p. 664. A letter from Paulus to the authorities at Zürich conveys his attitude (see Theodor Wotschke, *Der Briefwechsel der Schweizer mit den Polen* (Leipzig, 1908), pp. 197–202, No. 297, Gregorius Pauli an die Züricher); in it he denies the charge of Arianism, but does not mention deism.

Polish reformed Church between the orthodox Calvinists and the radicals, who were later to establish the Minor Reformed Church in Poland. Paulus himself apparently did not use the word 'deistae', which indicates that (like so many other names for unorthodox opinions) it was a pejorative term devised by antagonists.

Later references in French to the deists at Lyon (apart from what Viret said in his *Intérim*, repeating his previous points) reiterate the connection with heresy. Pierre de Saint-Julien, the fervently Catholic historian of Burgundy, says in his *Mélanges historiques*, of 1588: 'L'édit premier de pacification ne fut plutôt publié en France que soudain s'éclovit à Lyon une secte d'Ariens, couvée dès longtemps audit Lyon par un Allemand et un Italien (. . .) Aussi étaient prêts à se faire paraître les Postelliens, les Trinitaires ou Servetistes et autres jusqu'aux Achristes et Déistes, qui tous prétendaient pouvoir jouir du bénéfice de l'édit'.[29] Saint-Julien is engaged in showing the dire consequences of toleration; the edict, known also as the 'édit de Janvier', of 1562, granted the Reformers a limited freedom of worship.[30] He seems to regard deists as being one degree worse than 'trinitaires', but little can be deduced from this, for he appears vague about the differences between the sects he mentions. Elsewhere he refers to 'un Alamanni', not 'un Allemand', as the leader of the Arian group; he must have been thinking of Lodoico Alamanni, who was expelled from Lyon in 1566 for heresy. In his case, however, the trouble was caused by his views on the Eucharist, not the Trinity.[31]

[29] *Mélanges historiques et recueil de diverses matières pour la plupart paradoxales* (Lyon, 1588), p. 202. Saint-Julien also says that Viret joined forces with the Catholic authorities 'pour éteindre ce feu croissant' (the Arian sect). The reference to 'Postelliens' recalls that Guillaume Postel, the eccentric Orientalist, was said in the *Histoire ecclésiastique des église réformées au royaume de France* (Geneva, 1580; traditionally attributed to Bèze) to have 'baillé commencement à une secte de ceux qui par moquerie de Dieu s'appellent *Deites*' (sic) (see the edition by G. Baum, E. Cunitz and E. Reuss, 3 vols. (Paris, 1883–1889), Vol. I, p. 108). The writer is referring to the year 1552, and does not explain the reason for his statement. The theme of the passage is Postel's changeable and extraordinary religious views, which allegedly included Jewish and Turkish ideas. Arians were often said insultingly to be the same as Jews and Turks (i.e. in denying the divinity of Christ); perhaps Postel is being accused of Arianism. On various accusations of heresy made against him, see Busson, *Rationalisme*, p. 537, n. 5, and François Secret, 'Notes sur Guillaume Postel', BHR 21 (1959), 459–461 (Lindanus and Postel), and 23 (1961), 128–130 (Bèze and Postel).

[30] J.-H. Mariéjol, *La Réforme et al Ligue: L'Edit de Nantes* (Vol. VI, Pt. I, of Ernest Lavisse, *Histoire de France depuis les origines jusqu'à la Révolution*, 9 vols. (Paris, 1900–1911)), p. 53. The same explanation for the appearance of unbelief is given by Viret in his dedicatory epistle, discussing the 'deists': 'parmi ces différends qui sont aujourd'hui en la matière de religion, plusieurs abusent grandement de la liberté qui leur est donnée de suivre, des deux religions qui sont en différend, ou l'une ou l'autre. Car il y en a plusieurs qui se dispensent de toutes les deux et qui vivent du tout sans aucune religion' (*Instruction chrétienne*, Vol. II, unnumbered page 9).

[31] See Delio Cantimori, *Eretici italiani del cinquecento, ricerche storiche* (Florence, 1939) (cited henceforth as *Eretici italiani*), pp. 270f., and Henri Meylan, 'Bèze et les Italiens de Lyon (1566)', BHR 14 (1952), 235–249, especially pp. 242f. One of Saint-Julien's phrases, 'un Aleman et un Italien', might be a garbled reference to the Italian, Alamanni, or to Alamanni and another Italian (Cappone, to whom Meylan refers).

A more reliable historian than Saint-Julien, the diplomat Castelnau, confirms the persistence of the link between 'deism' and anti-trinitarianism in a passage from his *Mémoires*: 'il y eut à Lyon une nouvelle secte de déistes et de trinitistes, qui est une sorte d'hérésie laquelle a été en Allemagne, Pologne, et autres lieux'.[32] But the most informative of the later references to deism comes from Florimond de Raemond, in 1605, in a work directed against the Reformation, his *Histoire de l'hérésie de ce siècle*. The section on the deists says much the same as Du Préau: 'On vit d'autre côté les nouveaux Ebionites renaître en la Lithuanie, et les Déistes, et les Trithéites en la Pologne, qui établissent trois Dieux en divers degrés: Dieu le Père, le vrai Dieu et l'unique Dieu; le Fils Dieu, non unique, moindre que le Père; le S. Esprit Dieu, moindre que le Fils. Ils font Grégoire Paul qui était prédicant à Cracovie auteur de leur secte'.[33]

These references to deism reinforce each other, but are later than Viret's; his report, which has the advantage of priority, is the only one to treat deism as anti-Christian free-thought. The discrepancy is not irreconcilable, if we suppose that Viret was attacking heresy, but portraying it as irreligion. Such exaggeration was commonplace, indeed almost normal, in sixteenth-century polemics. There can be no doubt that he was aware of the threat presented by anti-trinitarianism and of its main tendencies. The movement covered a wide range of doctrines, characterized not only by the rejection of the traditional dogma of the Trinity, usually on the grounds that it is not scriptural, but also a related tendency to deny divinity, in at least some aspects, to Jesus Christ. Hence the other common appellation, Arians or neo-Arians, for the heretics. They were of course in dispute not only with the Catholic Church but also with the Reformers in Switzerland and Germany, notably Calvin. But they certainly regarded themselves as Christian; the most obvious example is Michael Servetus, whose major work is about the restoration of Christianity, *Christianismi restitutio*, but who was tried and burnt in Geneva in 1553. Among the Italians who, sympathizing with the Reformation, left their country and dispersed in Switzerland and elsewhere, anti-trinitarianism found many influential supporters.[34] It caused disruption among the congregation of the Italian church in Geneva when, in 1558, the church authorities sought to impose a declaration of belief in the

---

[32]   *Les Mémoires de Messire Michel de Castelnau* (Paris, 1621), p. 303. The reference to this, as well as to Saint-Julien, comes from Bayle's article 'Viret' (see n. 21 above).

[33]   *L'Histoire de la naissance, progrez et decadence de l'heresie de ce siecle* (Paris, 1605), Second Livre, Ch. XV, section 5, 'Des Mennonites et Ebionites' (p. 155 verso). Florimond de Raemond says that 'ces détestables Déistes' support their opinion with arguments from works by the Reformers, including Calvin. He defends Postel against the accusation of deism (see n. 29 above). In section 6 he says that among leaders of the deists were Petrus Gonesius (Peter Giezek of Goniądz; see Wilbur, *Socinianism*, pp. 285f.) and 'Farnosius' (presumably Stanislas Farnowski; see ibid., pp. 345–348).

[34]   On the Italians the basic work is still Cantimori, *Eretici italiani*. See also Antonio Rotondò,—'Calvino e gli antitrinitari italiani', *Rivista storica italiana* 80 (1968), 759–784.

orthodox doctrine of the Trinity. Some leading members of the congregation refused to sign the declaration, and one, Valentino Gentile, was put on trial for heresy. He avoided the death sentence only by retracting and submitting to public humiliation.[35]

These events were near in time and place to Lyon in 1563, and if Viret recognized anti-trinitarian views among the 'déistes' there, as seems likely, the source of his anxiety must have been closer than Poland, despite Du Préau's reference to Gregorius Paulus as the leader of the deists.[36] Lyon had a large Italian population, favourable to radical religious ideas. In order to curb their doctrinal unruliness, Viret wanted Girolamo Zanchi to come from Heidelberg as pastor;[37] Zanchi had refuted one of the earliest Polish anti-trinitarians, Gonesius, who had been influenced by Servetus.[38] Among the Italians who lived in Lyon for longer or shorter periods was the young Fausto Sozzini, who was to be, much later, the organizer of the religious movement which bears his name.[39] He was there from 1561 to 1563 and wrote his first work there, a commentary on the first chapter of St John's Gospel, perhaps the most important text for the discussion of the Trinity.[40] A letter from him has been preserved, dated 1563, which states his belief in the natural mortality of man. This or a related belief – held by many other heretics besides Sozzini – could well have been the origin of Viret's remark that some of the deists do not believe in the immortality of the soul.[41]

A more significant presence in Lyon, at the time, was that of Gentile. Between leaving Geneva after his trial and going to Poland in 1562, he was there twice, the first time publishing a work entitled *Antidota*, which

---

[35]   See Wilbur, *Socinianism*, Ch. XVI.

[36]   At the time when Du Préau was writing, 1566 (the date mentioned in his article on the deists), anti-trinitarianism was more prominent in Poland than in Switzerland, where it had been suppressed by the efforts of the Reformers.

[37]   See the letter from Bèze to Bullinger, 22 April 1564 (*Correspondance de Théodore de Bèze*, Vol. V (1564) (Geneva, 1968), p. 53).

[38]   Wilbur, *Socinianism*, pp. 286–287, 292, and Stanislas Kot, 'L'Influence de Servet sur le mouvement anti-trinitaire en Pologne et en Transylvanie', in *Autour de Michel Servet et de Sébastien Castellion*, Recueil publié sous la direction de B. Becker (Harlem, 1953), pp. 72–115.

[39]   It developed out of the Minor Reformed Church in Poland. The term 'Socinianism' is not appropriate until after about 1580 (Wilbur, *Socinianism*, Chs. XXIX, XXX; Williams, *Radical Reformation*, Ch. 29, 8, 'The Beginnings of Organized Socinianism').

[40]   The work is his *Explicatio primae partis primi capitis Evangelistae Johannis*. It was known to Zanchi and Bèze before 1567, though they attributed it to Fausto's uncle Lelio (Wilbur, *Socinianism*, p. 389 and n. 21).

[41]   See Williams (*Radical Reformation*, pp. 750f.), who says (p. 752) that the later work, *De Jesu Christo Servatore*, 'grew out of Socinus' Paduan view of the death of the soul with the body (thnetopsychism), which he had formulated several times before'. In his remarks in the *Instruction chrestienne* Viret says that, with some, 'il est question (...) s'ils croient aucune résurrection des corps ou immortalité des âmes', and later, after mentioning the deists, that 'Entre ceux-ci il y en a les uns qui ont quelque opinion de l'immortalité des âmes, les autres en jugent comme les Epicuriens' (Vol. II, unnumbered pages 7, 8).

14

contains an attack on Calvin's doctrine of the Trinity,[42] the second time publishing a kind of confession of faith in the form of a letter to a Bernese official, which was to lead to his trial and execution in Berne.[43] In 1561, he was imprisoned in Lyon for fifty days. Other well-known anti-trinitarians such as Gribaldi and Biandrata were in the area at the same period, between 1558 and 1562.[44]

In view of all these circumstances, it would be surprising if Viret had not felt obliged to denounce anti-trinitarianism. Although much of the *Institution chrétienne* concerns the divinity of Christ, he does not attack critics of the Trinity explicitly, so that it is impossible to be certain that his 'déistes' were in reality the holders of heretical opinions described by Du Préau and the later writers on the subject. In Viret's remarks there is, however, some evasiveness concerning the deists' attitude to Christianity which implies that, in their own eyes at least, they were not enemies of all religion, as Viret would have it, but Christians. He first portrays them as theists only: 'ils croient bien qu'il y a quelque Dieu (. . .) mais de Jésus-Christ ils ne savent que c'est'; later, they 'se moquent de toute religion' but nonetheless live as if they were Christians; and later again, Viret is horrified to think that 'entre ceux qui portent le nom de Chrétien, il y a de tels monstres'. The statement that 'ils ne savent que c'est' has a fine polemic ring, but if taken literally means that the deists do not perceive the true nature of Christ; Viret is probably exaggerating the anti-trinitarian view that Christ is not divine by nature. He has previously said that as regards Christ, 'et tout ce que la doctrine des évangélistes et apôtres en témoigne, ils tiennent tout cela pour fables et rêveries'; if this refers to the 'déistes', which is not clear, it would mean that they deny that Trinitarian dogma about Christ can be justified from the New Testament. The statement that the deists believe in God alone, 'comme les Turcs', and are enemies of all religion is probably an alarmist way of saying that the denial of the divinity of Christ threatens a basic dogma in Viret's theology.

Given that the execution of Servetus and Calvin's own writings against anti-trinitarianism in Poland had failed to prevent the movement spreading,[45] it is understandable that Viret should seek to blacken the reputation of

[42] Cantimori, *Eretici italiani*, p. 229; Tommaso R. Castiglione, 'La "Impietas Valentini Gentilis" e il corruccio di Calvino', in *Ginevra e l'Italia*, edited by Delio Cantimori (and four others) (Florence, 1959), pp. 149–176.

[43] Castiglione, ibid., p. 169; Wilbur, *Socinianism*, p. 234.

[44] Wilbur, ibid., Ch. XV, especially as regards Gribaldi's estate at Farges, in the County of Gex, a place of refuge for himself and other anti-trinitarians.

[45] In response to requests for help against the Polish anti-trinitarians, Calvin wrote a *Brevis admonitio (. . .) ad fratres Polonos* and an *Epistola (. . .) quae fidem Admonitionis (. . .) confirmat*, both in 1563. But in a letter to Bèze, 17 September 1563, Christoph Thretius asked for further assistance, against the followers of Blandrata and Gentile (*Correspondance de Théodore de Bèze*, Vol. IV (1562–1563) (Geneva, 1965), pp. 204–205 and 207, n. 13).

heretical 'deists', while not explaining at all clearly in what their opinions consisted, in case the information helped the heretical cause to spread further. Viret himself, with Calvin and Farel, had once been accused of unsoundness on the doctrine of the Trinity, which might have made him sensitive on the point,[46] and in general it was all too easy for the Catholics to claim that the radical heretics founded their arguments on the same principles as the Reformers, faithfulness to Holy Writ and early Christianity.[47]

In sum, the view that Viret's deists professed opinions essentially similar to those of the Enlightenment desists, a view which seems to have prevailed since Busson's work on Renaissance rationalism was first published in 1922, is very difficult to sustain in the light of the evidence that the group at Lyon were anti-trinitarians.[48] It is possible that Viret was referring to sceptical humanists like Dolet or Aneau, and somewhat more likley that he was conflating unorthodoxies from more than one source. But it is very doubtful whether the depths of unbelief portrayed by Viret existed at all, apart from a few isolated cases.[49] The ambiguities of his account, the testimony of later (and more detached) writers who regard deism as the name of anti-trinitarian heresy, and the impossibility of identifying any figures, for many decades, who professed anything resembling the 'deism' described by Viret, all suggest that the deists of Lyon were heretical Christians denying the divinity of Christ, and not anti-Christian free-thinkers. This was the view taken in 1754 by the Abbé Mallet, in the article 'Déistes' in Diderot's and d'Alembert's *Encyclopédie*, where he comments initially on the word: 'Nom qu'on a d'abord donné aux Anti-trinitaires ou nouveaux Ariens hérétiques du seizième siècle, qui n'admettaient d'autre Dieu que Dieu le père, regardant J.C. comme un pur homme, et le S. Esprit comme un simple attribut de la divinité'. He adds that the current name for them is Socinians or Unitarians.

NATURAL RELIGION AND TOLERANCE IN BODIN'S
COLLOQUIUM HEPTAPLOMERES

For a very long period the word 'déistes' continued to be used only occasionally, and without any settled meaning. Each occurrence may need separate

---

[46]   Barnaud, *Pierre Viret*, pp. 158–159. The accusation was made in 1537 by Pierre Caroli. See Williams, *Radical Reformation*, pp. 587–589, on the importance of the accusation as regards Calvin, Servetus, and the Reformed Church in Poland.

[47]   See Wilbur, *Socinianism*, pp. 15–18, on the vulnerability of the Reformers to Catholic attacks concerning Trinity doctrine. Barnaud notes that in his *L'Intérim* Viret is not tolerant towards Servetus, although the work is in favour of the toleration of religious opinions (*Pierre Viret*, pp. 618–619).

[48]   Busson's views were put forward at a time when the extent and importance of the 'radical Reformation' were still unrecognized; see n. 22 above.

[49]   For a good example, that of Pierre Strozzi, a relative of the Medicis who pursued his military career in France, see Busson, *Rationalisme*, pp. 519–520.

interpretation. Three instances close together, not long after the word's first appearance, will illustrate the situation. In 1576, in a case cited by Busson, heretical sectarians 'se nommant déistes' are reported in the diocese of Castres.[50] In 1579 Georges Pacard, another Protestant apologist, refers to deists in much the same way as Viret, treating them as unbelievers: 'nous voyons la terre et notamment ce royaume couvert de déistes, Epicuriens, athéistes et autres tels monstres'.[51] Here the meaning appears to be that typical of the Enlightenment, deistic enemies of religion. The third case is better known; it is the description by Philippe Duplessis-Mornay of an attitude which we whould now term deism, which he included in the preface to his apologia, *De la vérité de la religion chrétienne* (1581). Among the types of unbelief found in an introductory survey (a standard element of prefaces to apologias), he describes the Epicureans, who deny divine justice and providence, and follows them with a category of people who believe in God and the immortality of the soul, but reject established religions because they all claim to be the true one: 'Comme en un carrefour rencontrant tant de chemins, au lieu de choisir le droit par le jugement de la raison, ils s'arrêtent et s'étonnent, et concluent en cet étourdissement, que tout revient à un'.[52] The multiplicity of rival religions was to be a staple argument of later deists, but Mornay either did not know the word 'déistes' or considered it inappropriate, for he did not give this category of unbeliever a name. Thus within a few years we have one report which, to the modern reader, appears to be a good description of a kind of deism, but which is not so named by the author, while in other reports the word 'déistes' occurs, but seems to mean either heretics or anti-religious theists. This epitomizes the confusion which surrounded the word and the concept for the next hundred years or more.

Notwithstanding all these reservations, there is at least one work[53] which was written before the end of the sixteenth century and expresses a form of

[50]   Ibid., pp. 534–535. There is no information about the nature of the heresy involved.

[51]   Pacard, *Théologie naturelle* (1579), Dedication (dated 1574), cited by Busson, *Rationalisme*, p. 568, who refers to the second edition, 1611, p. 3. D. P. Walker believes that Pacard is a source of Mornay (see next note), and gives the date of publication as 1574 ('The *Prisca Theologia* in France', *Journal of the Warburg and Courtauld Institutes* 17 (1954), 204–259 (p. 206)).

[52]   *De la verité de la religion chrestienne* (Antwerp, 1581), Preface, unnumbered page 2. Busson seems to imply (*Rationalisme*, p. 563) that the unbelievers in this passage are atheists, but Mornay says that they believe 'qu'il y a un Dieu, et que l'homme a de lui une âme immortelle; que Dieu gouverne tout, et que l'homme le doit servir'. G. T. Buckley affirms that Mornay was describing deism (*Atheism in the English Renaissance*, 1965 edition, p. 102).

[53]   Another, perhaps, is the anonymous and clandestine *Origo et fundamenta religionis Christianae*, a work published in 1836 at Leipzig by August Gfrörer (*Zeitschrift für die historische Theologie* VI, Pt. 2, pp. 180–259); see L. I. Bredvold, 'Deism before Lord Herbert', *Papers of the Michigan Academy of Sciences, Arts, and Letters* 4 (1924), 431–442 (pp. 440–442). Bredvold and Gfrörer accept that a note on the title-page, stating that the manuscript was found in 1587, is reliable. The writer of the note adds that the work is blasphemous, atheistic, and Socinian (Gfrörer, p. 191). Since it was found in Halle, it would appear to be of German origin.

deism, or, what is closely related, a form of natural religion. This is the *Colloquium heptaplomeres*, by Jean Bodin (1529/30–1596), perhaps better known for his works on political theory. Natural religion is a concept which appears constantly in the history of deism, often as a synonym for it (which is an over-simplification).[54] The significance of 'natural' lies in the implicit opposition, or contrast, to 'supernatural': natural religion is that form of religious belief and behaviour to which man can attain unaided, in other words without the benefit of a divine revelation which would teach him the content of faith and the right form of worship. Hence natural reason, the faculties of man in the 'state of nature', is supposed to be the means by which natural religion may be acquired. Its content was of course variable, but the belief in the existence of God was an essential minimum. Other elements, so to speak optional, but usual, are the need for worship, the practice of morality (normally equated with the 'natural law'), and belief in the afterlife. The variations tended to correspond to whatever notion of reason was prevalent, especially in its relationship with the complementary notion, that of faith.

The first important appearance of the concept seems to have been in the great apologetic work of Thomas Aquinas, the *Summa contra Gentiles*, in which he puts the case for Christianity against the pagans. Aquinas stated that some religious truths, such as that of the 'pure and simple existence' of God, belong to natural religion, while God's unity and trinity transcend reason.[55] A similar approach, beginning with universal and fundamental truths before arguing for the truths of revelation, was to become standard among later apologists. In the *Summa theologica*, Aquinas says that the truths of natural religion are not articles of Christian faith, but are the 'preambles to faith'.[56] The formulation of Protestant theology by Calvin, in the *Institutes*, was rather more restrictive on the point. Calvin admits that 'il y a en l'esprit humain, d'une inclination naturelle, quelque sentiment de divinité', but immediately emphasizes the risks of impiety and error if divine revelation is neglected. No sooner do we have some idea of divinity than we distort it: 'nous ne sommes pas suffisamment instruits quant à nous par le témoignage simple et nu que rendent les créatures à la grandeur de Dieu'.[57] This is why, according to Calvin, God gives us revelation.

---

[54]   Mario M. Rossi's definition is valuable: 'Intenderò per "religione naturale" la dottrina che attribuisce la nostra conoscenza di Dio a ragioni naturali e non soprannaturali, pur senza escludere la *possibilità* della Rivelazione e di una "religione positiva" come aggiunta e complemento alla religione naturale' (*Lord Herbert di Chirbury*, Vol. I, p. 493, n. 1).

[55]   *Summa contra Gentiles*, edited and translated by Anton C. Pegis and others, 5 vols. (London, 1975), Vol. I, Bk. I, Ch. 3, 2; see Pegis' General Introduction, Vol. I, pp. 26f., especially p. 32, on the basic two-part plan of the work, first on the truths of faith which are investigable by reason, then on the truths which are above reason.

[56]   *Summa theologica*, Pars prima, Qu. II, art. 2.

[57]   Jean Calvin, *Institution de la religion chrétienne*, edited by Jean-Daniel Benoît, 5 vols. (Geneva, 1957–1963), Vol. I, pp. 59–60, 85.

18

Calvin's distrust was echoed in a very different quarter: by Montaigne. His famous essay on religion and the powers of the mind, the *Apologie de Raymond Sebond*, is ostensibly a defence of a late medieval work, Sebond's *Theologia naturalis*, a full exposition of the grounds of natural religion, which Montaigne had translated.[58] The defence of Sebond turns into a repudiation, because Montaigne decides that religion is a matter of faith, not of reason. Religious truth surpasses human understanding; 'C'est la foi seule qui embrasse vivement et certainement les hauts mystères de notre religion'.[59]

Despite such warnings, apologists from this time onward were inclined to treat natural religion as the basis of Christianity. Duplessis-Mornay, although of the same confession as Calvin, begins his *Vérité de la religion chrétienne* by affirming the value of natural reason, through which all men, Jews, Gentiles or Christians, know that God exists, that he is good and wise and the creator of the universe, and that we should serve him.[60] The Catholic Pierre Charron, who is commonly regarded as a slavish imitator of Montaigne and whose *Trois vérités* contains remarks about the inability of reason to understand God, nonetheless devotes three chapters to the natural theology which brings us to the knowledge of God.[61] The fact that an exposition of natural religion is found in a particular work does not therefore mean that its author is a deist, although by the eighteenth century deism often incorporated natural religion, for instance in Rousseau.[62] With Bodin, the question is difficult to decide.

The *Colloquium heptaplomeres* is one of the masterpieces of religious free-thought. It is a lengthy dialogue, written secretly in Latin towards the end of Bodin's life, and not published until the nineteenth century. The original and French translations circulated clandestinely.[63] The speakers are

---

[58] The *Theologia naturalis, sive liber creaturarum Magistri Raimundi de Sebonde* was published in 1487; Montaigne's translation in 1569.

[59] *Les Essais de Michel de Montaigne*, edited by Pierre Villey, 3 vols. (Paris, 1922), Vol. II, p. 149.

[60] *De la verité de la religion chrestienne*, p. 4. However, D. P. Walker remarks on the limitations placed by Mornay on the scope of natural reason ('The *Prisca Theologia* in France', pp. 211–212).

[61] *Les Trois Veritez, contre les athées, idolatres, Juifs, Mahumetans, Heretiques et Schismatiques* (Brussels, 1595), L. I, pp. 1–12.

[62] The religious philosophy of the first part of the *Profession de foi du vicaire savoyard* is said to be 'à peu de chose près le théisme ou la religion naturelle' in the fictional Rousseau's response to the Vicaire (Rousseau, *Œuvres complètes*, edited by Bernard Gagnebin and Marcel Raymond, Collection de la Pléiade (Paris, 1959–), Vol. IV (1969), p. 606); but the second part is a critique of Christianity. For a treatment of deism and natural religion together, see Jean Ehrard, *L'Idée de nature en France dans la première moitié du XVIIIe siècle*, 2 vols. (Paris, 1963), Vol. I, Pt. II, Ch. vii (cited henceforth as *Idée de nature*).

[63] I quote from the seventeenth-century French translation published in part by Roger Chauviré: *Colloque de Jean Bodin des secrets cachez des choses sublimes* (Paris, 1914). The Latin original, *Colloquium heptaplomeres de abditis rerum sublimium arcanis*, was published by L. Noack (Schwerin, 1857); see Chauviré (p. 10) on the reasons why this text is unsatisfactory. There is now a complete American translation: *Colloquium of the Seven about Secrets of the Sublime by Jean Bodin*, translation by Marion Leathers Daniels Kuntz (Princeton, 1975), to which I also give references.

seven men of differing religious loyalties: three Christians, a Jew, a Muslim, and the two whose views are of interest here, Senamus and Toralba. The former professes a kind of eclectic paganism, while in the latter natural religion is combined with scientific rationalism.

The figure of Senamus is probably to be interpreted as a humanist and 'politique', the name for one who, at the end of the sixteenth century, believed that putting an end to the Wars of Religion was more important than deciding which of the two religions was the true one. Standing aloof from the claims made by the other speakers in favour of their different religions, Senamus advocates tolerance on the Roman model. For a considerable part of Book IV, his views dominate the discussion; he maintains that, for the sake of civil concord, it is better to have many religions than to try to decide between them, since on this question there will be no agreement. He believes that God will look favourably on the sincere worshipper, whatever his religion may be. Senamus is an indifferentist, therefore, but within the variety of worship which he recommends there seems to be a common factor of monotheism.[64] He does not, despite the evils which religion causes, repudiate it altogether. His attitude bears a distinct resemblance to that described by Duplessis-Mornay in 1581.

The other free-thinker, Toralba, disagrees with the scepticism displayed by Senamus, since he believes that we should make the attempt to find out which is the true religion. Later in Book IV, it is his natural religion which is the centre of discussion. He claims that it is the oldest religion, that of Adam, who was created perfect by God, and comprises two precepts: 'd'adorer un Dieu seul éternel et de lui faire sacrifice de prières, de fruits et d'animaux'.[65] This form of religion will suffice for salvation, he says, in a reference to the context in which the concept of natural religion developed, the question of which beliefs and practices were necessary in order to achieve salvation. His monotheism is closely connected with the knowledge of nature. He refers to 'les savants qui possèdent la connaissance des choses naturelles par laquelle ils peuvent comprendre qu'il n'y a qu'un seul Dieu tout bon et tout puissant ainsi que Saint Paul même le dit manifestement',[66] which is almost a définition of natural theology. As he implies here, he is not an enemy of revealed religion (which deists are often said to be). For him, the truth of sacred texts can correspond to scientific truths, and he identifies the natural law, innate in all men, with the Decalogue.[67] He is even prepared to suggest a scientific argument in favour of the doctrine of the

---

[64] Chauviré edition, pp. 142–143; Daniels Kuntz translation, p. 251.
[65] Chauviré, p. 87; Daniels Kuntz, p. 185.
[66] Chauviré, p. 131 n. A; Daniels Kuntz, p. 243. The reference is to I Corinthians 8.6.
[67] Chauviré, p. 95; Daniels Kuntz, p. 192.

Virgin Birth,[68] and although he criticizes the dogma of the Trinity, he believes that in some sense Christ was divine.[69]

The *Colloquium heptaplomeres* ends without agreement except on the subject of religious tolerance. There is no obvious clue to Bodin's own views, which have been identified with one or other of the speakers, usually the more unorthodox among them.[70] For the history of deism, the interest of Toralba does not lie in the possibility that he may have been the vehicle for the opinions of his creator, but that, among the range of religious attitudes which Bodin considered worthy of attention in the 1590s, he should have included a form of natural religion, which clearly anticipates the fully developed systems of deism, or natural religion, of the eighteenth century. In Senamus is portrayed a preoccupation which is often said to have led to deism, the reaction against religious strife; but, fearing doctrinal loyalties, Senamus has no positive doctrine of his own. Toralba's belief in reason, morality and natural religion shows that an attitude intrinsically resembling deism could be imagined, and worked out in some detail, before the end of the sixteenth century. But the isoated creation of Toralba is not evidence that a deistic movement existed at that time.

---

[68] Chauviré, pp. 145–146; Daniels Kuntz, p. 283.

[69] Chauviré, p. 157; Daniels Kuntz, pp. 304–305.

[70] See for instance Chauviré, who quotes (p. 24) Guy Patin's remark, in a letter of 1643, that Bodin died 'Juif et non chrétien', but takes the view that all seven speakers represent aspects of Bodin's thought; Busson, *Rationalisme*, p. 540 (Bodin is 'achriste', by which Busson means 'Arian' rather than 'un-Christian'); Pierre Mesnard, 'La pensée religieuse de Jean Bodin', *Revue du seizième siècle* 16 (1929), 77–121 (p. 120: Bodin is 'achriste, théiste, et homme d'église', and is represented by Toralba); Georg Roellenbleck, *Offenbarung, Natur und jüdische Überlieferung bei Jean Bodin* (Gütersloh, 1964) (Salomon the Jew's and Toralba's opinions are the most significant, being paralleled in Bodin's other works).

CHAPTER 2

THE 1620s: MERSENNE AND THE 'POÈME DES DÉISTES'

In the early years of the seventeenth century the term 'déistes' seems to appear only in reports of the heretical group at Lyon.[1] Given the connection with anti-trinitarianism, the formulation of the Socinian creed, with its rejection of Trinity doctrine, in the catechism of Raków in 1605 is a significant event, but the common phrase 'socinien ou déiste' belongs to a rather later period of the history.[2] As for France, an important work published in 1601, Charron's *De la sagesse*, has been held to be deistic, but with little foundation.[3] It deserves attention here for almost the opposite reason, that it expresses an attitude which the earliest deistic writers were unanimous in repudiating. This is fideism, so called from its ascription of the dominant role, in the formation of personal religious belief, to faith rather than reason. Charron's version of it, taken largely from Montaigne, is characteristic of the seventeenth century. It consists in the willing acceptance, on faith, of the beliefs imposed by the ecclesiastical authorities: 'Il faut estre simple, obéissant et débonnaire pour être propre à recevoir religion, croire et se maintenir sous ses lois par révérence et obéissance, assujettir son jugement et se laisser mener et conduire à l'autorité publique, *captivantes intellectum ad obsequium fidei*'.[4]

---

[1]   See Chapter 1. Florimond's book was published in 1605 and 1611; Castelnau's in 1621. Pacard's *Theologie naturelle* was republished in 1611. I have been unable to trace the reference to deism which, so Busson implies (*Charron à Pascal*, p. 36), is in the preface to L. Lessius, *De providentia numinis et animi immortalitate libri duo* (Antwerp, 1613).

[2]   'Catechism of the assembly of those people who (...) affirm and confess, that no other than the Father of our Lord Jesus Christ is the only God of Israel; and the man Jesus of Nazareth, who was born of a virgin, and no other beside him, is the only-begotten Son of God' (following Wilbur, *Socinianism*, p. 408, n. 1). This shows incidentally how Arianism ('the man Jesus') overlapped with anti-trinitarianism.

[3]   See J.-B. Sabrié, *De l'humanisme au rationalisme: Pierre Charron* (Paris, 1913), Ch. XV (pp. 365–379), 'Le déisme et la religion du sage', e.g. p. 376: 'la religion du sage contient un germe de déisme (...) elle est en voie vers le déisme'. Sabrié follows Fortunat Strowski, *Pascal et son temps*, 3 vols. (Paris, 1907–1908), Vol. I, *De Montaigne à Pascal*, pp. 184–207. The same judgment is found in Julien-Eymard d'Angers, *Pascal et ses précurseurs* (Paris, 1954), p. 19.

[4]   Quoted from *De la Sagesse, Trois livres, par Pierre Charron*, edited by Amaury Duval, 3 vols. (Paris, 1824), Vol. II, p. 128. This contains the text of the revised posthumous edition of 1604 (Charron had difficulty in obtaining approval for his work from the Sorbonne), with the original text in notes. The quotation from the Vulgate translation of St Paul (II Corinthians 10. 5) is the favourite fideist text.

Pierre Charron (1541–1603) was an ecclesiastic and a humanist, considerably influenced by Stoicism, and he is sometimes led into phraseology (for example in describing the nature of God) which can be viewed as broadly theistic rather than specifically Christian. He also emphasizes the importance of incorporating morality into religion and the dangers of pious intolerance, a clear reaction against the barbarities of the Wars of Religion. These elements in his writings, to which may be added the scepticism concerning the powers of reason which is of the essence of fideism, have made the genuineness of his Christian faith suspect. However, to consider him as a deist makes little sense psychologically and none historically; at most he can be said to have taken Christianity (in a work intended for the laity) in the direction of humanist theism and morality.[5]

Apart from this false trail, the first twenty years of the seventeenth century have nothing to offer for the history of deism. To consider, for instance, the Italian Vanini as a deist, instead of a late representative of Italian pantheistic naturalism, stretches the meaning of terms too far.[6] From about 1620, however, it is a different story. The 'crisis of 1619 to 1625',[7] which begins with the execution of Vanini at Toulouse and ends with the imprisonment of Théophile de Viau (from which he too died, in 1626), was an episode of the Counter-Reformation in France during which the Church sought to reassert its authority in a vigorous campaign against blasphemy and *libertinage*. Among the allegations of unorthodoxy bandied about were some concerning deism. They were made by Marin Mersenne, the Minim friar who was a keen propagator of modern science and a friend of Descartes, and he was able to support his assertions by publishing a summary and extracts from the first self-confessed deist work in French, the poem now known as the 'Quatrains du déiste'.

A prelude to Mersenne's important publications was provided by the Jesuit polemicist François Garasse, in his *La doctrine curieuse des beaux-esprits de ce temps*, 1623. He denounces eight types of 'bel-esprit'. One

---

[5]   See for instance, on God, the first of the *Discours chrestiens*, of 1600, *De la cognoissance de Dieu* (*De la Sagesse*, Amaury Duval edition, Vol. III, pp. 321–348); the other themes are clearly expressed in the famous fifth chapter, 'Estudier à la vraye pieté', of Livre II of the *Sagesse* (ibid., Vol. II, pp. 117–158).

[6]   John M. Robertson, *A Short History of Freethought Ancient and Modern*, 3rd edition revised and expanded, 2 vols. (London, 1915), Vol. II, p. 55; Busson, *Charron à Pascal*, p. 39. Possibly both were influenced by Voltaire's article 'Athée, athéisme' (*Dictionnaire philosophique*, Naves edition, pp. 37, 38), in which he claims, while avoding the appellation 'déiste' or 'théiste', that Vanini was the opposite of an atheist when he spoke of 'la nécessité d'un être suprême'. On Vanini, see for instance F. T. Perrens, *Les libertins en France au XVIIIe siècle* (Paris, 1896), pp. 62–68; J. S. Spink, *French Free-Thought from Gassendi to Voltaire* (London, 1960) (cited henceforth as *French Free-Thought*), pp. 27–42.

[7]   The phrase is from Spink, *French Free-Thought*, p. 6. There is general agreement that these were years of crisis; cf. Busson, *Charron à Pascal*, p. 41 ('cette croisade contre les libertins'); Kristeller, 'Le mythe de l'athéisme', p. 343, commenting that the campaign was directed against Protestantism as well as *libertinage*.

category affirms that being obliged to accept religious doctrines (Garasse must be referring to the fideist approach) is an infringement of their freedom. They wish to keep their faith to the minimum, the belief in God, and not bother their heads with recondite questions, 'de petite conséquence', says Garasse ironically, such as the Incarnation, the Eucharist, the resurrection of the dead, and so on. Their argument derives from the debate over the salvation of pagans.[8] They say that if Socrates, for instance, can be allowed to achieve Christian salvation, then 'il suffit pour être Chrétien de croire un Dieu seulement et simplement, sans s'informer plus outre'.[9] These views are not unlike those which Mersenne was to expose as deistic.

Mersenne's *Quaestiones celeberrimae in Genesim* also appeared in 1623. It is another apologia, directed largely against Italian naturalism.[10] The first and longest 'question' is whether the existence of God can be proved rationally, and to it Mersenne appended a brief Colophon in which he mentions some 'who profess themselves deists'.[11] As usual with occurrences of the word during the seventeenth century, Mersenne feels himself constrained to define it: the deists believe in God, but deny divine providence (the definition which apologists commonly used for Epicureans). The matter is made no clearer when Mersenne goes on to say that the deists differ among themselves, some denying the justice of God, others providence, others the doctrine of the Trinity.[12] What troubled Mersenne most was the deists' claim to have reason on their side, since as a rationalist himself he believed that reason proved the truth of his own religion.

From a passage in his preface, it appears that just before the preface was written Mersenne had come into possession of the poem he called 'le poème du déiste', the content of which he made public in the next year, 1624. (It is uncertain whether he had actually read the poem at the time of writing the Colophon.) Its original title was *L'Anti-bigot ou le faux dévotieux*; it is

---

[8]   See Louis Capéran, *Le problème du salut des infidèles: essai historique* (Paris, 1912) (cited henceforth as *Salut des infidèles*), Ch. VII, on the immediate background.

[9]   *Doctrine curieuse*, p. 244: 'la preuve est prise des exemples des païens qui ont vécu moralement bien, et pour cela sont censés par les Pères de l'Eglise comme ayant été Chrétiens par leurs moeurs'.

[10]   D. P. Walker, *The Ancient Theology* (London, 1972), pp. 171, 189–192.

[11]   'Qui se deistas esse profitentur' (col. 669). Mersenne made several changes in the Colophon; see Robert Lenoble, *Mersenne ou la naissance du mécanisme* (Paris, 1943) (cited henceforth as *Mersenne*), p. XIII. The first version is supposed to have contained a notorious statement that there were fifty thousand atheists in Paris; but see Strowski, *Pascal et son temps*, Vol. I, pp. 138–139.

[12]   'Itaque hoc imprimis Deistae fateri videntur, unicum esse Deum, cui tamen denegant nostrarum rerum providentiam: ac si Deus in supremo coelo constitutus omnia quidem cerneret, imo et condidisset, verum cuncta deinceps naturae permitteret, adeout nullo numinis auxilio indigeret. Sed neque istiusmodi homines inter se conveniunt, quandoquidem negat unus, quod alter concesserit, unius omnipotentiam; alter vero providentiam, iustitiam unius, alter unicam in tribus personis renuit' (ibid.). This might come from Du Préau, who says that the ideas of the deists are obscure and complicated (*Haereticorum elenchus*, p. 139). Du Préau was writing about neo-Arianism ('novi Ariani'), however, and the denial of providence is more characteristic of the Epicurean variety of free-thought.

known by another name given by Mersenne, 'Les quatrains du déiste', because it culminates in an account of the religious attitude of 'le vrai déiste', who opposes the bigot. Mersenne refuted it at length, verse by verse, in the two volumes of his *L'Impiété des déistes combattue*. He included some dialogues with the deist, who eventually admits defeat and announces that he will join the Catholic Church. He appears less amenable in the poem itself, which Mersenne did not quote, but paraphrased, except for a few verses.[13]

The subject-matter of the *Anti-bigot* is limited. Its hundred and six quatrains, in clumsy verse, are almost entirely devoted to attacking the doctrine of eternal damnation. The 'bigot' is one who superstitiously believes in hell. Not until the final passage do we meet the deist:

> . . . seul observateur de la religion
> Il adore l'auteur de la terre et de l'onde (verse 103).

For him, virtue is its own reward, in contrast to the bigot who believes that the fear of hell is necessary to ensure morality.

Most of the poem is cast in an ostentatiously logical mould, the poet presenting the bigot with a dilemma: either God knows our actions in advance, or they are pre-ordained, and in neither case can the belief in hell be justified (verses 29–30). The argumentation which follows is often very obscure, but it is founded on a simple idea, that if God is good he will not punish men by inflicting everlasting torment on them. Other ideas which emerge are: that God cannot be vengeful, and to portray him as such (no doubt the Old Testament is meant) is to attribute human emotions to him; that in view of men's propensity to do wrong, revealed religion may be regarded as an 'utile invention pour brider les esprits' (verses 51–52), but is no more than that; hell is

> . . . un masque et supposé tourment
> Dont les religions maintiennent leur empire
> (verse 72).

A passage which has been little noticed by scholars makes the complementary suggestion, that all men will go to Heaven:

> . . . nous parviendrons tous au repos limité
> Par son divin amour pour notre meilleur être
> (verse 75).

[13] The poem was known only in Mersenne's paraphrase until Frédéric Lachèvre discovered a manuscript copy and published it, with the paraphrase, in his *Voltaire mourant* (Paris, 1908), pp. 110–136 (also in his *Le procès du poète Théophile de Viau*, Paris, 1909). There is a better text in Antoine Adam, *Les Libertins au XVIIe siècle* (Paris, 1964) (cited henceforth as *Libertins*), pp. 90–108, from which I quote. See also Lenoble, *Mersenne*, pp. 182–187; Busson, *Charron à Pascal*, pp. 102–109. The date at which the poem was written is unknown. The deist in Mersenne's dialogues (*Impiété des déistes*, Vol. I, p. 240) says that he has been a deist for nine or ten years.

The *Anti-bigot* is a good example of *libertin* protest, one of the few to have survived. It must have expressed the kind of indignation and rebelliousness which contemporary apologists stigmatized as the mark of immoral Epicureans who denied the justice of God. A loose kind of Epicureanism can even be found in the poem, when near the end the poet says that we should enjoy God's gifts and not, like ascetic penitents, reject them (verses 95–96). But the writer owes more to Stoic thought. There is some emphasis on a commonplace of Stoic ethics, the idea that virtue is its own reward (verses 101–102).[14] The idea that religion is an imposture, much used in all kinds of free-thought, also dates from antiquity; apologists tended to blame Machiavelli for it. Mersenne claimed that the poet had read Cardano and Charron. In his dialogues with the 'déiste' he explains his objections to these writers at some length. He naturally disliked Charron's fideism, among other things,[15] while as regards Cardano he criticizes the view that religion does not favour moral behaviour.[16] These criticisms are largely independent of Mersenne's remarks about the *Anti-bigot*, and give little reason to suppose that Charron had anything to do with the genesis of the poem, despite what has been held by Strowski and others.[17]

In the history of deism, the *Anti-bigot* has an important position, analogous to that of Viret's report about the 'déistes' at Lyon: it is the first text in which the writer uses the word as a name for his own version of secular free-thought. It is not an impressive poem, though the sincerity of the protest can still be felt, but it anticipates some of the ideas typical of the deistic movement during the Enlightenment. In a rudimentary way it accomplishes the same as later deists, by sketching out a religious attitude based on a concept of God, and on this basis rejecting current Christian doctrine. Apart from this, its importance as a document in the history of deism is somewhat limited. Mersenne's refusal to quote it at all fully seems to have been a successful device, since it probably had no influence on the development of deism. The only later work which resembles it significantly is a poem by the Abbé Chaulieu written in about 1708.[18] Nor can we

---

[14]   'Le déiste en repos agit tant seulement Pour l'amour du bien même' (verse 101); in verse 102, the deity to which virtue leads seems to be a Stoic one ('Vertu qui nous instruit que souverainement Nous devons adorer une Cause première').

[15]   In *L'Impiété des déistes*, Vol. I, p. 205, Mersenne lists statements in Charron which are disturbing to Catholic belief. Mersenne considers that the immortality of the soul is proved (p. 206); he cites his own *Quaestiones* in support.

[16]   *Impiété des déistes*, Vol. I, Ch. X. Again, Mersenne's rationalism is in conflict with fideism, notably on the subject of miracles.

[17]   'Le libre penseur devient *déiste*. Et ici même Charron est son maître. Charron lui apprend de distinguer Dieu et la religion' (Strowski, *Pascal et son temps*, Vol. I, p. 199. Cf. n. 3 above). Perhaps out of concern with the question of secular morality, Strowski seems to accept Mersenne's statements uncritically. There are some similarities between the *Anti-bigot* and the *Sagesse*, but they are almost certainly due to a common background of humanism. See Lenoble, *Mersenne*, pp. 185–187.

[18]   See Chapter 11 on Chaulieu's 'Trois façons de penser sur la mort'. Chaulieu's poems are in the same *libertin* tradition as the *Anti-bigot*, preoccupied with the afterlife and refusing to believe in a cruel God, but any direct influence is unlikely.

conclude from it that in about 1620 there were deists in France in any great numbers.[19] If there were *libertins* who felt in the same way as the poet about hellfire, which seems likely, they almost certainly did not regard themselves as 'déistes'. The poet's description of the deist in the final ten verses, who acts only from the love of goodness and learns from virtue that 'Nous devons adorer une cause première', has a markedly humanist air. As the Renaissance gave way to the Counter-Reformation, there were certainly some who preferred an eclectic, predominantly neo-Stoic, religious stance to the increasingly rigid Catholic orthodoxy which was spreading.[20] But the poet of the *Anti-bigot* appears to have chosen and defined the term 'déiste' for himself alone. His phrase, 'le vrai déiste', is his way of referring to his religious ideal, the sincere believer in God, and should probably be translated as 'the true theist'. No doubt he chose it precisely because it had no settled meaning and could be adapted to his own purposes.[21] He gives no indication of knowing the anti-trinitarian sense in which it had been used by Du Préau or Florimond de Raemond, and changes its connotations in such a way that the term comes to suggest secular free-thought rather than heresy. This process must have been considerably aided when Mersenne publicized the poem. Mersenne himself often referred to deists later, although he tended to confuse them with atheists.[22] The anonymous correspondent of Descartes, 'Hyperaspistes', was presumably referring to the *Anti-bigot* when he wrote in 1641 that, to the deist, it seems contradictory that a good God can consign men to eternal punishment.[23] To the modern reader, and perhaps even at the time, such a remark appears to refer to a deist having a complete religious philosophy (like the deists of the Enlightenment); the vagueness of 'déiste' allows a wide range of meanings and misunderstandings. But in spite of its adaptability, it was to remain uncommon for some time.

By a coincidence, Mersenne's book about 'le poème du déiste' was published in the same year and place, 1624 and Paris, as Lord Herbert of Cherbury's *De veritate*. The coincidence is remarkable because, since John

[19]   With reference to the *Anti-bigot*, Antoine Adam surmises that deists 'devaient être nombreux' (*Libertins*, p. 11), in view of humanist culture and the experience of the Wars of Religion, but does not explain what he understands by deism. Busson's chapter on deists (*Charron à Pascal*, Ch. II, pp. 89–114) is written on the assumption that deistic sentiments of the eighteenth-century kind were widespread before about 1670.

[20]   See Jean Jehasse, *La Renaissance de la critique: l'essor de l'humanisme érudit de 1560 à 1614* (Saint-Étienne, 1976), especially Ch. IV, on neo-Stoicism. As regards Lipsius this book supersedes Léontine Zanta, *La Renaissance du stoicisme au XVIe siècle* (Paris, 1914).

[21]   Mersenne's explanation, in the words he gives to his deist interlocutor, is as follows: 'les maîtres que j'ai eus m'ont entretenu en ces pensées, que c'était assez de croire un Dieu, mais que tout le reste avait été inventé par les hommes, et pour ce sujet veulent que nous portions le nom de Déistes' (*Impiété des déistes*, Vol. I, p. 171). This resembles the definitions current at the end of the century.

[22]   For instance in *La verité des sciences* (1625), L. I, Ch. V.

[23]   See *Œuvres de Descartes*, edited by Charles Adam and Paul Tannery, 11 vols. (Paris, 1897–1909), Vol. III, p. 402: 'Aeque clarum Deistae implicare ut summa Dei bonitas ullum poenis aeternis cruciandum tradat'.

Leland in 1754, it has been customary to refer to Herbert as 'the father of English deism'; Leland was writing after writers such as Toland, Collins, Tindal and many others had published deist works presenting religion in a form resembling the famous 'five articles' in the *De veritate*. In these, Herbert encapsulated what seemed to him the bases of all religion: the belief in God, in worship, in virtuous behaviour as a means of pleasing God, in repentance, and in the life after death.[24] However, although it seemed clear in retrospect to Leland (and later historians of the movement) that deism was first formulated in the five articles, this is not how it appeared in 1624, nor for many years afterwards. Despite some quite serious reservations, those who are known to have read Herbert during his lifetime did not consider his views to be dangerous to orthodoxy;[25] for the majority, the reverse was true. Herbert's ideas were seen as being potentially a part of a rational defence of Christianity, perhaps with eirenic value.[26] His posthumous *De religione gentilium* (1645) is anticlerical and more suspect,[27] but the abstract reasoning of *De veritate* (which is above all a treatise on epistemology) found favour with Mersenne, who as the leading expert on 'deism' as then understood must be regarded as having authority. Indeed, it was very probably Mersenne who later translated the work into French.[28] It was certainly he who saw to the publication of the French version in 1639, partly, no doubt, with eirenic intentions – Herbert considered the five articles as 'Catholic' in the sense of 'universal' – and partly because Herbert's rationalism was in harmony with his own.

The evident sympathy between the two religious rationalists, one traditionally regarded as the first of the English deists, the other the denouncer of the earliest 'deist' poem in French, may seem paradoxical but is easily explained. The rationalist movement in religion, which can be seen at an early stage in both Herbert and Mersenne, was to reach its peak in the later seventeenth century. It provided a basis for anti-Catholic systems of deism at the beginning of the eighteenth. But in the 1620s Mersenne considered deism to be the views of the author of the *Anti-bigot*, not the religious

---

[24] On the five 'catholic truths' or 'common notions' and their variants, see Rossi, *Lord Herbert*, Vol. I, pp. 531–564. Herbert probably allowed only a few copies of the 1624 edition to be distributed, but circulated the 1633 edition widely (ibid., Vol. II, pp. 399–400, 465, 518ff.).

[25] Ibid., Vol. I, pp. 589ff., on the objections made by an anonymous critic, probably a Thomist. Rossi concludes: 'Ma nell' insieme, sembra che nessuno dei critici contemporanei, per quanto avverso, vedesse chiaramente dove portava la religione naturale di Herbert. Nessuno prevedeva che sarebbe venuto un tiempo in cui Herbert sarebbe stato salutato come precursore del deismo – o dell'ateismo settecentesco' (p. 591).

[26] See D. P. Walker, *The Ancient Theology*, pp. 164ff., citing Mario M. Rossi, *Alle fonti del deismo e del materialismo moderno* (Florence, 1942), pp. 18–21. Walker (p. 165) notes the tendency to deism inherent in eirenism.

[27] Walker, ibid., pp. 175ff.; Rossi, *Lord Herbert*, Vol. III, pp. 116ff.

[28] Rossi, ibid., Vol. II, p. 531 ('È molto probabile che fosse Mersenne stesso a tradurre'); Lenoble, *Mersenne*, p. 562.

philosophy of Herbert. Even towards the end of the century the works of rationalist Catholic writers do not appear to have been regarded as deistic.[29]

That 'deism' was not a term applied to opinions which now seem to call for it is indirectly confirmed by another contemporaneous report of unbelief, more plausible than Garasse's. In 1627, Jean Silhon, who had published an apologetic work, *Les deux vérités*, in the preceding year, wrote a letter to the Bishop of Nantes in which he described his plans for a continuation.[30] He included an account of the opinions he wished to combat. There are few men, he says, who do not believe in God and the immortality of the soul (the two truths for which he had argued previously); the most widespread error is that of 'quelques déliés' who, limiting themselves to these beliefs and the belief in providence, 'croient que la vraie religion n'est autre que vivre selon la raison, et que la plus agréable sacrifice qu'on puisse faire à Dieu, est la pratique des vertus morales'. They condemn pagan polytheism because it is mere imposture ('tant de dieux que l'ambition des grands et l'artifice des législateurs avaient introduits'), but accept that the rituals of worship act as a curb on the unruliness of the populace. God, however, 'veut être servi seulement en esprit et en vérité', according to them. Christianity is the best religion, because of its moral message, and Christ is to be admired for having attacked idolatry and vice, but his nature is not divine. 'La divinité qu'il s'est attribuée' is a fiction, as are other dogmas such as the Trinity. They were invented in order to impress the ignorant masses and facilitate evangelism. Silhon seems to approve of this method: 'la difficulté d'établir une si sainte doctrine la rendait nécessaire'.

It would be interesting to know to whom Silhon was referring, if indeed he had personal knowledge of a specific group and was not relying on other apologists. He gives few clues. Some elements in his description recall Herbert, some the anti-trinitarianism represented, in 1627, chiefly by the Socinians.[31] A reference to a remark by the pagan philosopher Themistius suggests that Silhon might have been reading Garasse, who mentions it

---

[29]   See Chapter 6 on the difficulty of identifying those who were said at the time to be deists.

[30]   The letter was included in Faret's *Recueil de lettres nouvelles dédiées à Monseigneur le Cardinal Duc de Richelieu*, 2 vols. (Paris, 1627). I quote from the 1634 edition, pp. 33ff. See Busson, *Charron à Pascal*, pp. 92–94, 541–544.

[31]   In France, however, Socinianism made little impression at this time. See René Pintard, *Le libertinage érudit dans la premièe moitié du XVIIe siècle*, 2 vols. (Paris, 1943) (cited henceforth as *Libertinage érudit*), Vol. I, pp. 50–51, and Vol. II, pp. 585–586, n. 4; Wilbur, *Socinianism*, Ch. XL, especially pp. 527–528. The presence in Paris of Grotius, as Swedish Ambassador, from 1621 to 1644 with one interval, encouraged the spread of Arminian and related ideas. A few Socinians visited France, notably Martin Ruar, but Ruar's correspondence with Mersenne (another instance of the latter's interest in unorthodox thought) did not begin until 1640. On this, see Lenoble, *Mersenne*, pp. 536–576.

also.[32] The elements of positive belief are commonplaces of later Stoic religious thought, but the critical attitude to polytheism, and the qualified approval of Christianity, seem closer to what was regarded as the Machiavellian approach to religion — the cynically utilitarian idea that religion is advantageous to the ruler, even if he has no religious beliefs of his own.[33] Silhon mentions Machiavelli, but denies any moral value to his attitude: 'sa secte faisant servir la religion à l'Etat semble ne reconnaître point de Divinité, ni un autre état pour les hommes que le présent'. Perhaps the description as a whole is an unfavourable, though not harsh, summary of the famous chapters on religion in Charron's *Sagesse*.[34] In any case, Silhon does not mention deists, writing instead of 'erreurs', or occasionally of 'impies' and 'libertins'. If we can accept his report without much supporting evidence, there was an unidentified body of opinion resembling Enlightenment deism in the 1620s, but it was not then called deism. Conversely, the author of the *Anti-bigot*, who does call himself a deist, professes views which seem typical of early seventeenth-century free-thought, but are not much like the deism of the Enlightenment.

A final contribution to the problem of deistic free-thought in the 1620s comes from a *Traité des religions* by the Protestant theologian Moïse Amyraut. He was known for his broad-minded and eirenic approach, like Mersenne, but he was accused of Arminianism by his own party.[35] He published his treatise on religions, 'contre ceux qui les estiment toutes indifférentes', in 1631. By 'indifference' Amyraut means an attitude which, he says, has developed since the division between Catholics and Protestants occurred. In order to avoid strife, some prefer to keep to the religion which is 'reçue par la coutume ou autorisée par le Magistrat chacun en son pays'. Privately, they confine themselves to the internal worship of God and the

---

[32] Themistius 'représentait à l'empereur Valens que, tout ainsi que Dieu avait répandu la diversité dans la nature, et que la beauté de l'univers consistait en la proportion de plusieurs choses différentes, il se plaisait de même en cette grande variété de religions et de cultes qu'on lui rendait'. For Garasse's version see *La doctrine curieuse*, pp. 244–245. He says that Machiavelli and all the *libertins* agree with this idea.

[33] For an earlier hostile interpretation of Machiavelli's attitude, see Innocent Gentillet, *Anti-Machiavel* (1576), edited by C. Edward Rathé (Geneva, 1968), Pt. II, e.g. p. 203: the prince should maintain religious impostures if they are of benefit. Gentillet regularly describes Machiavelli as an atheist. Mersenne (*Quaestiones in Genesim*, Quaestio prima, col. 379) attributes to Machiavelli the principle 'expedit in religione civitates falli', which he says can be inferred from his works. This is the principle said by St Augustine to have been held by the chief pontiff Scaevola (*City of God*, Bk. IV, Ch. 27).

[34] The Stoic tag 'vivre selon la nature', found in Silhon's description, is the subject of a passage in Charron's *Sagesse* (L. II, Ch. 3) beginning 'Voilà pourquoi la doctrine de tous les sages porte que bien vivre c'est vivre selon nature', in which Charron quotes Cicero and (several times) Seneca (Amaury Duval edition, Vol. II, pp. 86ff., and cf. elsewhere, e.g. p. 44).

[35] See Brian G. Armstrong, *Calvinism and the Amyraut Heresy* (Milwaukee and London, 1969), especially Ch. 2, 'A Brief Biography of Amyraut'.

practice of morality.[36] Amyraut's arguments against these indifferents
(who again resemble Charron) seem to be intended to oblige them to profess
their allegiance openly – in other words, he is concerned with Huguenots
who feel it advisable, in the political circumstances of the times, to behave as
if they were Catholics.[37] Presumably Amyraut could not be very explicit
about this. His description of 'indifference' is psychologically convincing,
but, since he does not identify those whom he has in mind, it is of little
value as evidence of deistic ideas. In another chapter he gives a definition of
free-thought regarding the divinity of Christ which appears to be a direct
imitation of Silhon's in his letter to the Bishop of Nantes.[38] Amyraut is
vague about the identity of these opponents also, asking if 'ceux contre qui
je dispute' believe in the truth of Scripture or not.[39]

It is a curious situation that results from the comparison of the accounts
of free-thought in Garasse, Mersenne, Silhon and Amyraut: the accounts are
plausible in themselves, but (except of course for Mersenne's book) cannot
be correlated with the only text claiming to put the views of a 'déiste'.
The so-called deism of Silhon's 'impies', for instance, like that of Charron,
has been discovered by modern scholars, since deism as a category of free-
thought was apparently unknown to Silhon himself.[40] It is curious, too, how
often the kinds of free-thought attacked by apologists are the unorthodox
counterpart, as it were, of their own convictions. Thus Mersenne, believing
(as he says in the *Quaestiones in Genesim*) that Christianity can be proved

---

[36]   *Traité des religions*, Preface (unnumbered pages 3–4). Amyraut later describes the three kinds
of indifferentism to which the three parts of his book are devoted: 'la religion d'Epicure', which denies
providence; the 'philosophes' (Stoics?) who admit providence but deny that we have any revelation
concerning the service of God; and those who agree that, in addition to providence, 'Dieu a révélé
particulièrement quelque chose de soi, et de la manière du service qu'il lui faut rendre, mais n'estiment
pas que cela oblige à suivre une forme de religion certaine et déterminée; secte de gens inconnue des
anciens et née de nos temps' (ibid., pp. 7–8).

[37]   Ibid., Pt. III, Ch. 1, especially pp. 237ff. Indifference here involves 'la communion aux
extérieures cérémonies'; Amyraut denounces those who observe the ceremonies of a religion but do
not believe its doctrines, and criticizes the argument that externals are indifferent in themselves,
neither good nor bad.

[38]   Ibid., Pt. III, Ch. 10, 'Que ceux qui disent que Christ a pris le nom de Dieu seulement pour
rendre sa doctrine plus authentique (. . .) se montrent destitués de toute raison'; see pp. 437–438 on
true religion consisting in 'la piété intérieure' and virtue and on Christ's taking the name of Son of
God; pp. 445–446 on the admiration felt by 'ces gens' for Christ's moral message and for the Christian
abolition of idolatry and polytheism.

[39]   Ibid., p. 447. Pintard (*Libertinage érudit*, Vol. I, pp. 13–14) mentions, in connection with
Amyraut's indifferentists, the views of Eméric Crucé: 'il estime que, si des guerres éclatent entre des
confessions rivales, la cause en est la "diversité des cérémonies", non la diversité "de religion": car
"le principal point d'icelle gist en l'adoration de Dieu, qui demande plutost le coeur des hommes, que
le culte extérieur et les sacrifices, dont on fait tant de parade"'. The reference is to Crucé's *Nouveau
Cynée* (1623), Preface and pp. 50–60.

[40]   See especially Busson, *Charron à Pascal*, pp. 92–94, 541–544, but also for instance Jacques
Maurens, *La tragédie sans tragique: le néo-stoïcisme dans l'œuvre de Pierre Corneille* (Paris, 1966),
p. 167 (the attitude described by Silhon is a 'déisme d'argumentation stoïcienne, dont il est assez
remarquable que l'"orthodoxe" Jean Silhon ne conteste pas les postulats').

by reason, considers the chief danger of the 'deistae' to lie in the fact that they rely on reason. Silhon, having proved as an apologist the 'deux vérités' of God and the immortal soul, is concerned about unbelievers who limit themselves to these two truths. Amyraut's anxieties about an attitude of indifference towards confessional divisions seems to reflect his own eirenic tendencies.[41] This is not to imply that the apologists were inventing imaginary heresies which were projections of their personal doubts about orthodoxy; but they may well have been especially sensitive to any trends of contemporary free-thought which (from their point of view) perverted their own attitudes. Given, in addition, that much of their material is taken from ancient sources such as Cicero's *De natura deorum* — the recurrent accusations of 'Epicurean' disbelief in providence, for instance — the suspicion arises that some kinds of unbelief were fully formulated only in the pages of apologetic works, and not in reality. Garasse's lively anecdotes, which report disparate and miscellaneous unorthodox opinions, may well be truer to life than the more elaborate summaries in Silhon or Amyraut.

However that may be, the decade from about 1620 to 1630 stands out as a distinct stage in the prehistory of deism mainly because of the existence of the *Anti-bigot*. This apart, the picture is vague and confused, and it seems advisable to differentiate between the nomenclature and the substance of the current forms of free-thought. Where nomenclature is concerned, it is noticeable that the previous heretical sense of 'déiste', with specific reference to anti-trinitarianism, has fallen out of use, except in the re-editions of works about heresy. It is supplanted, or supplemented, by Mersenne's usage (although in his *Quaestiones in Genesim* the heretical sense is referred to) and attached firmly to the idea of *libertinage* — secular rather than religious free-thought, consciously opposed to Christianity. This development is due to the poet of the *Anti-bigot*, defining the 'déiste' as an opponent of superstition and the fear of hell. Nonetheless, the word remains rare and uncertain in meaning, since even Mersenne couples it with 'athéiste'; in this context, it seems to refer to the Epicurean concept of gods who have no concern for the world of men.

As for the substance of 'deism', leaving the *Anti-bigot* on one side, there are reports of a type of free-thought which appears to the modern reader, who knows of Voltaire and Rousseau, to be deistic, together with the publication in France of a work which is now considered to be the earliest expression of English deism, Herbert's *De veritate*. Yet the term 'deism' was not applied at the time, nor for many years to come, either to Herbert or to the free-thought reported on by Silhon and others. Insofar as there is any connection between the various manifestations of free-thought which

---

[41]   See Armstrong, *Calvinism and the Amyraut Heresy*, pp. 72–73, citing R. H. Stauffer, *Moïse Amyraut: un précurseur français de l'œcuménisme* (Paris, 1962).

resemble eighteenth-century deism, it is a diffuse neo-Stoicism.[42] This movement, Christianized in the work of Justus Lipsius, Guillaume Du Vair, and
Charron, was a powerful influence on Herbert of Cherbury and is clearly
perceptible in the moral ideas of the *Anti-bigot*. The 'libertins' described
by Silhon also profess typically Stoic ideas, of a very rudimentary kind,
although they are more critical of Christianity than the Stoics were wont to
be towards established religion. A tentative reconstruction of this neo-Stoic
attitude, on the assumption (also tentative) that it did in fact exist, might
include the belief in God, in the immortality of the soul, and in the primacy
of the moral aspect of religion. Revealed religion is viewed with scepticism,
though not necessarily with disfavour; both the *Anti-bigot* and the free-
thinkers described by Silhon concede that it may have social advantages.

The evidence is not sufficient to suppose that such an attitude was at all
widespread. However, we can conclude that a moralizing theism of a Stoic
turn was one of the strands of free thought in the 1620s. As such it intrinsically resembles the deism of the succeeding century, although, as we shall
see, there seem to be no direct links between them.

---

[42] Strowski affirms that Descartes, Balzac and Corneille are 'remplis de l'esprit stoïcien' (*Pascal et son temps*, Vol. I, p. 123). As regards Herbert, Rossi discusses the Stoic background of deism and concludes that in view of Herbert's humanist education and tendencies to Stoicism 'dobbiamo attribuire il suo deismo in gran parte a suggerimenti classici e umanistici, e sopratutto al *De natura deorum* di Cicerone' (*Lord Herbert*, Vol. I, p. 499).

CHAPTER 3

THE ABSENCE OF DEISTIC IDEAS FROM 1630 TO 1670

Before the middle of the seventeenth century, the concepts which were to be central to Enlightenment deism already existed; the word 'déiste' was in circulation; and there had been some evidence of deistic free-thought, clandestinely expressed, before 1630. If movements of thought proceeded at a steady rate, we might expect that during the next few decades French deism would emerge into prominence. Yet what occurs is the opposite. The search for deism, between about 1630 and 1670, produces extremely meagre results. Even Busson's researches have failed to turn up anything of real significance.[1] There is, it is true, one phenomenon which is of fundamental importance in the history of deism, as in the history of thought generally; it is the growth of metaphysical and religious rationalism. This is seen not only in the philosophy of Descartes and his followers, but also in the many works of rational apologetics which were published.[2] But the potential of metaphysical rationalism as a weapon of free-thought was not yet apparent, despite the opposition to Descartes,[3] and in the mid-century free-thought of any kind is rare, more so than for many years before and after.

---

[1] The relevant passages of the chapter on deists (Ch. II, pp. 89–114; cf. also pp. 453–455) in Busson's *La pensée religieuse française de Charron à Pascal* almost amount to an admission that deism cannot be found. After the *Anti-bigot* and the other evidence in the 1620s, Busson mentions only scanty and inconclusive reports, of which the most substantial is the piece by d'Assoucy (see Chapter 6), which was not published until 1676, and rumours about a *Traité des trois imposteurs*, a work supposedly denouncing the impostures of Moses, Jesus and Mohammed. (On this long-standing mystery, see also the edition of a manuscript which adopted the title, *Traité des trois imposteurs, manuscrit clandestin du début du XVIIIe siècle*, edited by Pierre Rétat (Saint-Etienne, 1973); and J. J. Denonain, 'Le *Liber de tribus impostoribus du XVIe siècle*', in *Aspects du libertinisme*, pp. 215–226.) But the *Traité* is a 'livre fantôme', in Busson's phrase (p. 94), and in any case the idea of imposture suggests atheism rather than deism. The same applies to the manuscript *De tribus impostoribus* published by Gustave Brunet ('Philomneste Junior'; Paris, 1861), allegedly dating from 1598, which Busson summarizes (pp. 97–98).

[2] Descartes's *Méditations métaphysiques*, besides being the classic statement of philosophical rationalism, should also be regarded as a work of apologetics. The original title was *Méditations sur la philosophie première, dans laquelle est démontrée l'existence de Dieu et l'immortalité de l'âme*. Cf. Henri Gouhier, *La pensée religieuse de Descartes*, 2nd edition (Paris, 1972), p. 104 (the *Méditations* 'sont un traité apologétique destiné à confondre les athées et les libertins en *démontrant*, avec une rigueur mathématique, l'existence de Dieu et la spiritualité de l'âme'); Busson, *Charron à Pascal*, pp. 442ff.

[3] Francisque Bouillier, *Histoire de la philosophie cartésienne*, 3rd edition, 2 vols. (Paris, 1868), Vol. I, Chs. X–XIII. Accusations of atheism and so on (e.g. in Holland; ibid., pp. 282–286) seem not to have been serious interpretations but attempts to discredit Descartes.

Among those who were not rationalists by principle, the situation is different, but the result is much the same. The leading representatives of intellectual *libertinage*, the 'libertins érudits', have become well known in modern scholarship thanks to the work of René Pintard, but the main characteristic of figures such as La Mothe le Vayer (1583–1672) is fideistic conformism, concealing – perhaps – some kind of unorthodoxy.[4] In one of La Mothe's early dialogues, for example, *De la divinité*, where we might look for indications of his positive beliefs, we are faced with an exercise in scepticism designed to show that any discussion of God and gods will be vain and should not be undertaken; this sceptical approach is said to be the best complement to Christian faith.[5] The noble *libertins*, by contrast, commemorated in anecdotal history by Tallemant des Réaux and others, are more notorious for their scandalous or blasphemous remarks and behaviour than for their ideas.[6] As for the unclassifiable Cyrano de Bergerac, his extraordinary narratives may well have a concealed message, but the fantasies are magical and pantheistic, having nothing to do with deism.[7]

Since deism is often regarded first and foremost as a movement opposed to Christianity, it is commonly thought to have proceeded from the negations of *libertinage*, but there are few direct affiliations.[8] On the constructive side, however, the natural religion which we have met in Bodin's character Toralba continued to be an element of religious thought during the seventeenth century. It became more and more important in apologetics, and it can also be seen in the religion of the sun invented by Tommaso Campanella (1568–1639) in his *Civitas solis*. He spent the last few years of his life in Paris, republishing there in 1637 his plan for a Utopian theocracy of sun-worshippers, as well as other works intended to further his aim of a reformed, universal Catholicism.[9]

[4] See Pintard, *Libertinage érudit*, on the extent of free-thinking among intellectuals. On deism, Pintard (Vol. I, pp. 48–49, 61–65) adds nothing to Busson . On the most interesting figure apart from La Mothe le Vayer, Gabriel Naudé, see pp. 156ff.; Pintard portrays him as nothing more radical than a Catholic of independent mind. The status of scepticism or Pyrrhonism is still a controversial subject; for a different approach from Pintard's, see R. H. Popkin, *The History of Scepticism from Erasmus to Descartes*, revised edition (Assen, 1964); for arguments from opposed viewpoints, Kristeller, 'Le mythe de l'athéisme'; Pintard, 'Problèmes de l'histoire du libertinage, notes et réflexions', *XVIIe siècle* 127 (1980), 131–162.

[5] 'Aussi n'y a-t-il point de façon de philosopher qui s'accommode avec notre foi, et qui donne tant de repos à une âme chrétienne, que fait notre chère Sceptique' (François de La Mothe le Vayer, *Deux dialogues faits à l'imitation des anciens*, edited by Ernest Tisserand (Paris, 1922), pp. 73–74). *De la divinité* was first published in the nine *Dialogues faits à l'imitation des anciens par Orasius Tubero*, 2 vols. (Paris, 1630–1631, falsely dated 1506).

[6] Perrens, *Libertins*, provides a large selection of the anecdotes.

[7] See for instance Luciano Erba, *Magia e invenzione, note e ricerche su Cyrano de Bergerac e su altri autori* (Milan, 1967), Ch. II, 'L'incidenza della magia nell'opera di Cyrano de Bergerac'.

[8] This interpretation is perhaps most commonly found in Catholic scholarship, e.g. Julien-Eymard d'Angers, *Pascal et ses précurseurs*, p. 21.

[9] See Frances Yates, *Giordano Bruno and the Hermetic Tradition* (London, 1964), Ch. XX, 'Giordano Bruno and Tommaso Campanella', pp. 386ff.; 'the faith which Campanella wanted to promulgate throughout the whole world was, of course, the Catholicised natural religion' (p. 388, citing Louis Blanchet, *Campanella* (Paris, 1920), p. 53).

Campanella's imaginary religion has some significance in the history of deism as a forerunner of another religion of sun-worship, that of Denis Veiras, but in the 1620s natural religion was important in quite a different context of discussion, the debate over the salvation of pagans. Toralba had referred to this, as had one of Garasse's 'beaux-esprits' who wished to reduce his Christian beliefs to theism. The debate had become enmeshed with another, that concerning grace, and the problem was especially pressing in relation to to two categories of unbeliever, who seemed to have been denied any normal possibility of grace: the pagans of classical antiquity, who had lived before the Christian faith was known (and who were of particular concern to Renaissance humanists); and the 'savages' of lands where Christianity was unknown until it was brought by missionaries.[10] If pagans and savages, lacking faith, were to have any hope of salvation, the concept of natural religion provided an obvious foundation on which to argue it. The division between reason and revelation which was inherent in this concept exactly paralleled the distinction in moral theology between the state of pure nature and the state of grace, which was elaborated in the later sixteenth and early seventeenth centuries. According to Bernard Tocanne, the concept of pure nature, typical of Jesuit thought, could lead (even within the strictly theological domain) to conclusions favourable to natural religion.[11] A similar development was to take place, much more clearly, in stories of imaginary travels about the end of the seventeenth century, when authors invented countries with natural religions which are the first forms of deism.[12]

The pagans of antiquity did not offer the same scope for imaginative treatment; they were a problem for theologians. By the end of the sixteenth-century the Catholics were inclined to favour their chances of salvation. The seventeenth century saw a reaction, Jansenist teaching on grace leading to a firm denial of the possibility. In the *Augustinus* of 1640 Jansen stated, renewing the views of another Augustinian, Baïus of Louvain, that since infidels lacked knowledge of Christ and the true God they could not observe the natural law without sinning.[13] A little earlier, the Arminian Huguenot Moyse Amyraut had faced censure from his more orthodox and stricter colleagues for suggesting that divine grace might reach even those who were ignorant of Christ.[14] Considering the vogue for Austral deism later, it is

[10] Capéran, *Salut des infidèles*, especially Chs. VII and VIII, on which I rely for much of what follows.

[11] Tocanne, *L'Idée de nature en France*, p. 252: 'A l'intérieur d'une démarche théologique qui veut sauver les droits absolus de la liberté divine, la théorie de la pure nature dessine dans un cadre d'ailleurs surtout aristotélicien une anthropologie métaphysique en droit autonome, et elle esquisse une sorte de religion naturelle, qui se résume dans la connaissance et dans l'amour de Dieu comme auteur de la nature, et où l'on peut voir comme le noyau d'un déisme rationnel'. Tocanne refers particularly to Suárez.

[12] See Chapters 5 (Foigny and Veiras), 8 (Gilbert) and 12 (Tyssot de Patot).

[13] Capéran, *Salut des infidèles*, Ch. VIII, Article 2 (pp. 311ff.).

[14] Ibid., p. 305, on the *Brief traité de la prédestination*, 1634.

interesting that one of Amyraut's arguments concerned a pagan living in the Austral Land.[15]

The debate on the salvation of pagans provided one of the very few occasions on which ideas related clearly, if rather distantly, to deism were put forward by one of the *libertins érudits*, namely La Mothe le Vayer. In a work which is not typical of him except in appearing suspect, he employs a concept of natural religion, or 'religion des philosophes', which amounts to a rudimentary form of constructive deism. The work is *De la vertu des païens*, of 1641, a treatise dedicated to Richelieu. It is an answer to Jansen's *Augustinus*, at least as regards its own subject, and may have been meant as a contribution to the measures taken by Richelieu against the Jansenist movement.[16] La Mothe's material was taken largely from a work of 1622–1623 by Collius, though he did not share Collius' view.[17] The theological argument he used depends on the idea of 'implicit faith': pagans of virtuous lives, who were not idolatrous but believed in God (who, in other words, followed natural religion and the natural law), may be supposed to have had an implicit knowledge of Christ's role as redeemer. In this way the division between reason and revelation can be surmounted, and La Mothe discusses the likelihood that a special grace might have brought salvation to a distinguished array of virtuous pagans. These are mainly the philosophical heroes of antiquity, but also include Confucius. At times, for instance with Epicurus or Julian the Apostate, La Mothe seems deliberately provocative. He also evokes the case of a pre-Columbian American and invents an eloquent prayer for an Austral deist.[18] Apart from the matter of implicit faith, La Mothe's contention is simple: that the belief in God and the practice of morality will suffice for a religion. In making a case for Plato, for example, while admitting some difficulties over the second point, La Mothe states that he taught 'l'éternité d'un seul Dieu, créateur de toutes choses' and the immortality of the soul, which involves rewards and punishments after death.[19]

It is perhaps superfluous to say that La Mothe does not mention deism. However, there is some evidence, which is unreliable, that Antoine Arnauld saw deism in La Mothe's treatise.[20] Arnauld's *De la nécessité de la foi en*

[15] Ibid., p. 308.

[16] See Tisserand, Introduction, p. 23, to the edition of two of La Mothe's dialogues cited in n. 5 above. On the date, 1641, of the *Vertu des païens*, Busson, *Charron à Pascal*, pp. 405 and 406 n. 2, is certainly correct, although the year 1642 is often given. See also Florence Wickelgren, *La Mothe le Vayer, sa vie et son œuvre* (Paris, 1934), p. 183.

[17] Franciscus Collius, *De animabus paganorum libri V*; see Capéran, *Salut des infidèles*, pp. 286ff. and p. 317.

[18] La Mothe le Vayer, *Œuvres*, 14 vols. (Dresden, 1756–1759), T. V, Pt. I, pp. 86–89 (and reprint, 2 vols., Geneva, 1970, Vol. I, p. 141).

[19] Ibid., pp. 135–136 (reprint p. 153).

[20] Cf. Busson, *Charron à Pascal*, p. 410. Busson appears to be accepting the Jansenist view when he says (p. 406) that deism is 'le dessous de la thèse' put forward by La Mothe le Vayer.

Jésus-Christ pour être sauvé was written as an immediate reply to *De la vertu des païens*, but not published in Arnauld's lifetime. In 1701 Ellies Du Pin published it as a contribution to the controversy then in progress over Jesuit missionary activity in China, the 'querelle des rites chinois'. The text of 1701 contains several references to deism, especially in the final chapters and the foreword, according to which Arnauld was 'alarmé d'une proposition si scandaleuse, qui tendait au déisme, et à la destruction entière de la religion chrétienne'.[21] So sensational a view of deism is more likely to come from after 1654, when (as we shall see) the idea that deism was subversive first gained credence. Du Pin appears to have changed Arnauld's text considerably.[22] Thus it is very doubtful that in about 1641 Arnauld saw any connection between La Mothe's ideas and deism as it was then understood, although the connection had been made by the end of the century.

Whether the idea that virtuous theists might achieve Christian salvation reflected La Mothe's own position is a separate question.[23] *De la vertu des païens* is not obviously a vehicle for self-expression, although as a humanist La Mothe no doubt wanted to defend the memory of some great men of antiquity. He seems most deeply involved personally on the subject of Pyrrho and the Pyrrhonians, and if this impression is correct his attitude would correspond to what is now called agnosticism.[24]

Still within the fideist tradition, a slightly later work by another layman, Philippe Fortin de la Hoguette's *Testament, ou conseils d'un bon père à ses enfants*, will serve as a measure of the distance which divides fideism from deism, even when the two attitudes seem close. Published in 1648, the *Testament* went into three editions.[25] Fortin de la Hoguette extols faith and belittles reason, like La Mothe, but with him the fideism is certainly sincere; he is a Catholic conformist, encouraging obedience to the established mode of worship. In one respect he can be said to be deistic: his worship is theocentric, directed towards God rather than Christ. The same tendency is found in Saint-Evremond, who comes much nearer to deism. Not even Saint-Evremond, however, and much less Fortin, makes the typical deist claim to decide his religious creed for himself, as an individual. There seems to be an

---

[21]   Arnauld, *Œuvres complètes*, 38 vols. (Paris and Lausanne, 1775–1783), Vol. X (1777), p. 328.

[22]   Ibid., Vol. X, Préface historique et critique, pp. VIII–XI; Du Pin admitted that he had added to Arnauld's text.

[23]   See for instance Busson, *Charron à Pascal*, pp. 210–214; Boase, *Fortunes of Montaigne*, p. 260 and n. 2 (arguing that in his later life La Mothe's fideistic statements were sincere); Pintard, *Libertinage érudit*, pp. 140–147 and p. 303 (on the works after 1640: 'dans lesquels un théologien ne saurait, sans de longues recherches, trouver ni une proposition condamnable ni une page vraiment rassurante').

[24]   *Œuvres*, 1756–1759, T. V, Pt. I, pp. 285ff., especially pp. 305–310 (reprint, Vol. II, pp. 190ff.).

[25]   On the *Testament*, see Boase, *Fortunes of Montaigne*, pp. 279–285. Spink, *French Free-Thought*, p. 26, holds that the work is deistic; see especially *Testament*, Pt. I, Ch. 2.

impassable barrier between the fideist's recourse to faith and the deist's reliance on the 'natural light' of reason.

What remains to be said of deism in the mid-century does not concern tenuous evidence from texts which might possibly reveal deistic tendencies, but the resounding polemical use of the word 'déisme' in connection with the Jansenist controversy. A dramatic accusation, that the Jansenists had plotted to install deism on the ruins of Christianity, spread the idea that deism was dangerous. The accusation was made in a book by Jean Filleau, a lawyer from Poitiers; the study of his discovery of the plot can be most conveniently followed in Arnauld's *Seconde lettre à un duc et pair*, written at the height of the dispute over the 'five propositions'.[26] In 1654, inspired by the recent publication of Jansen's letters, Filleau launched an attack on Jansenism, *Relation juridique de ce qui s'est passé à Poitiers touchant la nouvelle doctrine des Jansénistes*, which included wild allegations about the so-called 'assemblée de Bourgfontaine'. Seven conspirators, six of whom Filleau designates by the initials of leading Jansenists, had met near Paris in 1621, and had plotted to overthrow religion. They were to begin 'par la destruction des mystères (dont la créance est illusoire et inutile) et particulièrement de celui de l'Incarnation, qui était comme la base et la fondement de tous'. The seventh conspirator, now repentant, is the alleged source of the story; Filleau had met him passing through Poitiers, and had been told that the purpose of Jansenism was to 'ruiner l'Evangile, et à supprimer la créance que l'on avoit de la rédemption des hommes par le moyen de la passion de Jésus-Christ, qui était parmi eux une histoire apocryphe'. Hence, according to Filleau, the Jansenists should really be called deists, since deists believe only in God and regard the 'mysteries' as illusory.[27]

This cock-and-bull story was to re-echo through the controversies surrounding Jansenism for at least half a century.[28] Its origins can only be guessed at; there seems to be some garbled memories of the early heretical meaning of 'déiste', perhaps coupled with equally vague memories of the Rosicrucian scare of the 1620s, when it was believed in Paris that the Rosicrucians were meeting there with obscure but probably devilish

---

[26]   For a brief account of the circumstances of the *Seconde lettre*, see Pascal, *Lettres provinciales*, edited by Louis Cognet, Classiques Garnier (Paris, 1965) (cited henceforth as 'Cognet edition'), Introduction, pp. xix–xxiv; also Arnauld, *Œuvres complètes*, Vol. XIX (1778), Préface historique et critique, pp. XXXVIIff.

[27]   J. Filleau, *Relation juridique de ce qui s'est passé à Poitiers touchant la nouvelle doctrine des jansénistes* (Poitiers, 1654), Ch. 2. I quote from Arnauld's *Seconde lettre à un duc et pair, Œuvres complètes*, Vol. XIX, pp. 431–432, the notes to which give the quotations from Filleau.

[28]   See Chapter 6 for Jurieu's use of the story; but it was still in circulation much later (Pascal, *Lettres provinciales*, Cognet edition, p. 319, n. 2).

intentions.[29] The outcome was yet another meaning for 'deism', now combining theism, disbelief in basic Christian doctrines, and subversion. Arnauld was indignant, not suprisingly; his initials has been among those of Filleau's conspirators. (He pointed out that he could not have been more than nine years old at the time.)[30] Besides giving prominence to the accusation in the *Seconde lettre,* which was eagerly read, he returned to it, with details, in several later works.[31] It had meanwhile been repeated by a Jesuit polemicist, Bernard Meynier, and Pascal had taken it up in the sixteenth of the *Lettres provinciales,* which ensured even wider and more lasting publicity.

Deism thus acquired a disturbing reputation, as in Pascal's quotation from Meynier, according to which the Jansenists had formed a conspiracy 'pour ruiner le mystère de l'Incarnation, faire passer l'Evangile pour une histoire apocryphe, exterminer la religion chrétienne, et élever le déisme sur les ruines du Christianisme'.[32] Both sides, Jesuit and Jansenist, could agree on the sinister nature of deism, the Jesuits in order to calumniate Port-Royal, and Pascal and Arnauld in order to illustrate the shamelessness and absurdity of the allegations. Yet, it need hardly be said, no one makes any attempt to identify the deists whose wickedness they casually assume. The anonymous author of the *Quatrains du déiste* seem unlikely to have had the revolutionary ideas which 'deism' comes to denote when used in religious polemics; the word seems to exist independently of any known doctrine which would give it a meaning.

By the time he wrote the *Pensées,* a few years after the *Provinciales,* Pascal had come to take a cooler view, but the definition which he produced was no less influential than the former rebuttal of Filleau's accusation. In a passage on the enemies of Christianity, he wrote: 'Et sur ce fondement ils prennent lieu de blasphémer la religion chrétienne, parce qu'ils la connaissent mal. Ils s'imaginent qu'elle consiste en l'adoration d'un Dieu considéré comme grand, puissant et éternel: ce qui est proprement le déisme, presque aussi éloigné de la religion chrétienne que l'athéisme, qui y est tout à fait

---

[29]   On the sources of the conspiracy idea, see Jean Orcibal, *Jean Duvergier de Hauranne, Abbé de Saint-Cyran, et son temps (1581–1638), Appendices, bibliographie et tables* (Les origines du Jansénisme, III) (Paris, 1948), pp. 84–86 n.5. Jansenius and Saint-Cyran had studied the Augustinian doctrine of grace together in summer of 1621 and had agreed on code-words to enable them to communicate safely by letter on the subject. The use of the code in letters, and perhaps knowledge of later meetings between the two and other friends, seem to have aroused the suspicions of Pinthereau and Filleau, and to have provided grounds for a scare-story. On the Rosicrucian scare see Frances Yates, *The Rosicrucian Enlightenment* (London, 1972), Ch.VIII, pp. 103ff.

[30]   Arnauld, *Seconde lettre, Œuvres complètes,* Vol. XIX, p. 433.

[31]   For example *Œuvres complètes,* Vol. II, p. 14; Vol. XXX, pp. 520 ff.

[32]   *Lettres provinciales,* Cognet edition, p. 320. The references is to Meynier's *Port-Royal et Genève d'intelligence contre le Très-Saint Sacrement de l'Autel* (Poitiers, 1656), p. 14. Meynier found heresy in a work of piety by Mère Agnès (Jeanne-Catherine Arnauld) and claimed that it supported Filleau's idea of a consipracy.

contraire'.[33] In the passing remark about deism and the distinction between it and Christianity Pascal is pursuing a favourite theme, the difference between a religion of reason and the religion of Jesus Christ.[34] Although he is severe towards deism, it seems clear that he understands it as meaning simple theism, with no subversive connotations. As for the source of his definition, it was probably the obvious etymology of the word. Pascal knew Mersenne, but there is no reason to suppose that he needed to have read *L'Impiété des déistes combattue* in order to have formed an idea of the word's meaning.[35] His definition is frequently quoted in modern dictionaries, and seems to have been the basis of that given in Richelet's *Dictionnaire français* of 1680: 'Déisme. Créance de ceux qui pour toute religion ne croient qu'un Dieu'.[36] By another of the paradoxes which abound in the early history of deism, one of its most formidable enemies seems to have been responsible for the generally accepted modern meaning of the word.

Looking back, it would seem that after Mersenne in 1624 nobody was very sure what the word meant. Every one who uses it seems to think that it requires defining. The uncertainty may perhaps have been due to the fact that two different, almost contradictory, definitions were available, Mersenne's quotations from the *Anti-bigot* being hard to reconcile with the information about anti-trinitarians given by Florimond de Raemond. The flurry of denunications of free-thought in the 1620s, which had thrown up reports suggesting the existence of some kind of deistic doctrine, dies away after 1630, and nothing comparable follows until after 1670. A hundred years after Viret's first reference to 'déistes' there is still nothing remotely resembling a deist movement, in the sense of a recognized body of doctrine to which individuals could subscribe. The assumption that such a movement must have existed, found in much scholarly work, is untenable; at most, we can speculate that some individuals may privately have restricted their

---

[33]   I quote from Pascal, *Pensées*, edited by Philippe Sellier, Les Classiques du Mercure (Paris, 1976), p. 376 (No. 690; Brunschvicg No. 556). The Port-Royal edition of the *Pensées*, in 1670, replaced 'ils' by 'les impies' at the beginning of the passage.

[34]   See in the same fragment the famous passage begining 'Et c'est pourquoi je n'entreprendrai pas ici de prouver par des raisons naturelles ou l'existence de Dieu, ou la Trinité, ou l'immortalité de l'âme' (Sellier edition, p. 377). Another relevant passage occurs a little later: 'Tous ceux qui cherchent Dieu hors de Jésus-Christ et qui s'arrêtent dans la nature, ou ils ne trouvent aucune lumière qui les satisfasse, ou ils arrivent à se former un moyen de conaître Dieu et de le servir sans médiateur. Et par là, ils tombent ou dans l'athéisme ou dans le déisme, qui sont deux choses que la religion chrétienne abhorre presque également'. Here too the meaning is basically the mere belief in God, but there is a hint of the early heretical sense, according to which deism involved above all denying the divinity of Christ, in the phase 'le servir sans médiateur'.

[35]   Julien-Eymard d'Angers (*Pascal et ses précurseurs*, p. 44) is doubtful whether Pascal had read Mersenne's apologetic works.

[36]   In Richelet's list of authorities Jansenist works are well represented. They include the *Pensées*. Mersenne also appears, but only as a writer on music. For *Déiste*, Richelet's definition is: 'Qui croit seulement en Dieu'.

positive beliefs to the belief in God. But deism as a doctrinal system had not yet come into existence. The nearest approach to it is the sketchy 'natural religion' utilized by La Mothe in his argument about the salvation of pagans. A complete doctrine which did exist, Socinianism, seems not to have been associated with deism in people's minds at this time; the currency of the phrase 'Socinien ou déiste' and its like is a feature of the end of the century.

It is possible, of course, as Busson says, that evidence of deism has been lost and will be recovered, but the chances seem poor.[37] The meticulous researches of Pintard into 'libertinage érudit' reveal, among a small minority, scepticism, Epicureanism, immorality and the refusal to conform; Pascal's priest, Pierre Beurrier, records a meeting in about 1660 with one Basin, who fits into the Epicurean category because he believed, apparently, in a God who does not concern himself with human affairs; there are rumours that a treatise developing the idea that Moses, Christ and Mohammed were impostors (also believed by Basin) circulated throughout the century.[38] However, none of this, nor the other kinds of free-thought studied by J.S. Spink or Antoine Adam, gives grounds for thinking that deism existed as a distinct category of free-thought.

The reason for this state of affairs, in general terms, is that the religious atmosphere of the mid-century (in contrast to the turbulent politics of the time) was one of piety, a tribute to the success of the Counter-Reformation in France. This is the time of the 'humanisme dévot' portrayed by the Abbé Bremond.[39] Even the intensity of the Jansenist dispute testifies to the dominant position of the Catholic Church in intellectual life. Reason and faith, potentially in conflict, were then at one, since rationalism was still at the service of religion. By the end of the century, Cartesian rationalism was to compete with and triumph over fideism, and became the preferred philosophical system of the first French deists. Until then, however,

---

[37]   Busson, *Charron à Pascal,* p. 99; on the possibility of unknown manuscripts resembling the *Traité des trois imposteurs.*

[38]   The relevant extracts are published in Adam's anthology *Les libertins au XVIIe siècle,* pp. 113–117. Adam's view is that 'la religion de ce Basin est nettement celle des *Quatrains du déiste*' (p. 111), but the resemblance is not at all obvious. The most interesting passage in Beurrier's anecdote contains Basin's criticisms of Trinity doctrine (p. 116). The phrase used by Beurrier to denote his attitude is 'ce libertinage de croyance et cette irréligion' (p. 114); Basin himself is supposed to have said that 'je n'ai point d'autre religion que d'être philosophe' (p. 115). On the 'three impostors' see n.1 above. Walker (*Ancient Theology,* p. 209) implies that Beurrier's portrayal of Basin might have been contrived to demonstrate the effectiveness of Beurrier's methods of conversion.

[39]   Henri Bremond, *Histoire littéraire du sentiment religieux en France,* 11 vols. (Paris, 1915–1933), Vol. I, *L'humanisme dévot (1580–1660).* Yves de Paris (c. 1590–1679), whom Bremond describes as 'l'humanisme dévot fait homme' (p. 507), is a good example of a writer whose belief, much influenced by Platonic thought, is markedly theocentric, but who cannot possibly be considered as having leanings to deism, in any sense. See especially Bremond, ibid., pp. 487–496, on his *La théologie naturelle,* 4 vols. (Paris, 1633–1636).

manifestations of 'deism', in any sense, are scattered and uncertain. It is only after 1670 that the beginnings of a coherent movement can be traced, in writers for whom the conflict of religious reason and religious faith is serious. They can justifiably be said to tend towards deism, either because of the weakening of faith or because of the new-found strength of 'natural reason', and it is they whose works are the main feature in the early history of deism proper, after the many decades of contradictory and confusing reports, descriptions and accusations. As we shall see, such secondary evidence continues to appear, and indeed increases in quantity, while still remaining largely unconnected with the quasi-deistic works of Saint-Evremond, Foigny and Veiras.

Part II

The later seventeenth century: precursors and definitions, from Saint-Evremond to Bayle

CHAPTER 4

SAINT-EVREMOND AND THE DECLINE OF FIDEISM

The transition from *libertinage,* which may be described as free-thought in the fideist tradition, to early deism, which is free-thought of the rationalist variety, is too complex a development to be studied in the work of any one writer. It took some time to complete, and individuals seem to have remained true either to reason or to faith. But the first part of the process, a gradual detachment from faith, is exemplified in the writings, over many years, of the exiled moralist Charles de Saint-Denis de Saint-Evremond. He was, according to the standard evaluation, the most elegant of the *libertin* writers, a link between Montaigne and Voltaire. His life (1614–1703)[1] would have been conventional for a cultured French nobleman – a soldiering youth, the Fronde (more or less on the Court side), and an old age spent in literary dilettantism and *salon* intrigue – except that his satirical habits kept· getting him into trouble. He was in the Bastille in the 1650s for imper- tinences at the expense of Mazarin. After the disgrace of Fouquet, in 1661, he had to leave France because his *Lettre sur la paix des Pyrénées,* full of ironic and trenchant criticisms of Mazarin's conduct of the peace negotiations in 1659, was found among Fouquet's papers. From then on Saint-Evremond lived in exile, three years in England, five in Holland, and the remainder again in England, in the society of the Court and Hortense Mancini, the Duchesse Mazarin. Meanwhile his books were being brought out in Paris by Barbin, the leading French publisher. To the knowledge of Protestant thought which Saint-Evremond gained during his exile is due the substance of some of his most significant reflections[2].

The writings on religious topics (he wrote much also on literature, history, and moral matters) date from the 1640s to the 1690s, and the attitudes expressed in them are far from constant. Saint-Evremond wrote in both verse and prose, in letters intended for circulation among friends and acquaint- ances, and in closely argued discourse. The preferred form is a short prose piece, something between a letter and an essay, in which Saint-Evremond

---

[1]   For the date of birth, 1614 and not 1616 or 1613 as is sometimes stated, see Ternois's edition of the *Oeuvres en prose* (details in n. 3), Vol. I, p. XXIII, n. 1.

[2]   In what follows I owe much to D.C. Potts, 'Saint-Evremond and Seventeenth Century *libertinage*', unpublished D. Phil. thesis (Oxford, 1962), cited henceforth as *Saint-Evremond.*

often has the air of a layman giving spiritual advice. There are also fictional or dialogue pieces, predominantly satirical in tone, like Voltaire's 'facéties', and of these the *Conversation de M. le Maréchal d'Hoquincourt avec le P. Canaye* is the best example. Three main periods can be distinguished. The first lasts from about 1647 until the middle or late 1650s, and contains pieces in the tradition of Montaigne, written from the point of view of the 'honnête homme', the Catholic courtier and man of action. The middle period is that of Saint-Evremond's stay in Holland. Among the very diverse pieces which he wrote there, the most important, at least as regards the advent of deism, dates from about 1670. It is the *Considération sur la religion,* on the differences between Catholicism and Calvinism. After what appears to be a pause of a few years, the later period begins in about 1675, when Saint-Evremond wrote more rarely, mainly in the didactic letter form. Detachment borders on disillusion in these works of old age, which have contributed more than his earlier works to building up the image of Saint-Evremond as a disbeliever in all things except bodily comforts.

EARLY FIDEISM

Saint-Evremond began his writings on religion with an essay or letter entitled *Que l'homme qui veut connaître toutes choses ne se connaît pas lui-même* (Ternois edition, Vol. II, pp. 107ff.)[3]. This is a classic exposition of sceptical fideism. Its subject is the archetypal insoluble problem in the sceptic's philosophy of religion, the soul and its survival.[4] The argument adumbrated in the title is that we cannot reach certainty on the subject, and that the attempt to do so (Saint-Evremond is ostensibly writing to a friend who has retired to the country to meditate) reveals ignorance of the capacity of the mind. Only faith can make us certain that the soul survives the body, and we must therefore stop looking for enlightenment and submit to the teachings of religion, that is, the Catholic Church. Fideism in *L'homme qui veut connaître* is aggressively anti-rationalist. The ancient philosophers, who represent reason, are said to be charlatans. Socrates, 'un railleur', tears his hair out from intellectual frustration, Aristotle 'parle presque toujours de mauvaise foi (...) il veut étourdir le monde et s'étourdir lui-même de son caquet'. The model to be preferred is Solomon; his wisdom

---

[3]   Saint-Evremond, *Oeuvres en prose,* edited by René Ternois, 4 vols. (Paris, 1962–1969). On the date of *L'homme qui veut connaître*, see Vol. II, pp. 107–108. Ternois has also edited the *Lettres,* 2 vols. (Paris, 1967–1968). For Saint-Evremond's dramatic and poetic works it is still necessary to refer to other editions; I have used Saint-Evremond, *Oeuvres mêlées,* edited by Luigi de Nardis (Rome, 1966).

[4]   For a full view of the arguments which were current, see Busson, *Rationalisme*, Chs. II, VII, VIII; on the normal seventeenth-century attitude of fideism concerning the soul his *Charron à Pascal,* pp. 139 ff., and pp. 160 ff. on Saint-Evremond.

lay in placing providence and 'la seule sagesse éternelle' above his own reason. The tirade concludes with remarks such as: 'je fais plus d'état de la foi du plus stupide paysan, que de toutes les leçons de Socrate'. The later Saint-Evremond was to be less enthusiatic about the faith of the stupid.

L'homme qui veut connaître is an immature piece of writing, with rather crude imitations of Montaigne's or Charron's bluntness as well as their arguments. It has had doubt cast on its sincerity,[5] but if the fideism is not genuine, if the contention that we must accept revelation in order to escape from the uncertainties of reason is regarded as a pretence, then the whole piece becomes meaningless. Such doubts are better justified with the second version, from which much of the violent anti-rationalism was removed, and where the sophisticated style of the later Saint-Evremond seems to be full of suspicious implications.[6]

One aspect of fideism which may make it easier to understand is conveyed in the vocabulary which Saint-Evremond employs to express the idea of 'submitting' to Christian faith. The phraseology comes from the sphere of politics: 'se soumettre aux ordres de la Providence'; 'sitôt qu'elle' (la raison) 'veut se connaître, elle entreprend sur les droits de son Créateur'; 'à moins que la Foi n'assujettisse notre raison, nous passons la vie à croire, et à ne croire point'. The implicit assimilation of religious to political conformity, which is almost universal in fideist writing, is very clear in such passages. By implication, the individual who relies on his own resources in religion is a rebel who suffers himself from the disturbance he causes.

Further advice for the conformist is given in the brief *Jugement sur les sciences où peut s'appliquer un honnête homme* (Vol. II, p.6), which was probably written in the late 1650s, shortly before Saint-Evremond had to go into exile. Its rejection of theology, philosophy and mathematics in favour of 'morale', politics and literature reads like a reply to the first part of Descartes's *Discours de la méthode.* By contrast, Saint-Evremond praises Gassendi, 'le plus éclairé des philosophes et le moins présomptueux'. Pursuing the theme that theological speculation encourages indocility and even conflict, Saint-Evremond blames the subtleties of Aristotle for the doctrinal strife between Protestants and Catholics. The suggestion is the same as in Charron, that acceptance of religious authority is a means of avoiding conflict.

Little else, in Saint-Evremond's writings before 1660, is of religious significance. A persistent impression of Epicurean hedonism, together with some mockery of pagan religion, is conveyed by such essays as *Sur Pétrone* (Vol. I, p. 169, and Vol. II, p. 174) and the anecdote translated from Petronius, *La matrone d'Ephèse* (Vol. I, p. 187). In this, worldly values

---

[5]   Ternois's edition, Vol. II, p. 111.

[6]   For instance on Descartes's 'démonstration prétendue d'une substance purement spirituelle' and the perfunctory fideism of the conclusion (Vol. II, pp. 134 ff.).

triumph over spiritual when the entombed widow abandons mourning in order to enjoy life with the young soldier. Saint-Evremond's views about the right way to live are also implied in his comments on famous writers in the *Jugement sur Sénèque, Plutarque et Pétrone* (Vol. I, p. 147). The Stoic is castigated and Petronius praised again, for expertise in the *art de vivre*, partly because − a theme dear to Saint-Evremond − he did not allow the pursuit of pleasure to interfere with 'les affaires', the political career of the courtier.

A rather different attitude to Epicureanism is found in the essay *Sur les plaisirs* (Vol. IV, p. 5), which may also belong to the early period.[7] It begins with a defence of 'divertissement', the conscious use of worldly activities in order to distract us from reflections on the human condition, which lead inevitably, it seems, to doubt and even despair. The answer propounded by Saint-Evremond is to pursue 'la gloire, les fortunes, les amours, les voluptés bien entendues et bien ménagées'. This entirely secular response to doubt is precisely the kind scornfully rejected by Pascal, in the *liasse* on the subject.[8] Saint-Evremond does mention the religious response, to take refuge in faith, but it is relegated to a few lines at the end, about true Christians. For them 'divertissement' is unnecessary, since they believe in the survival of the soul and live in innocence. These lines may be ironic. At the very least, Saint-Evremond is detaching himself from fideism, which he had strenuously advocated before 1650.

SATIRE, EIRENISM AND CHRISTIAN MORALITY IN HOLLAND

The Holland period, after a lapse of some years, sees a number of changes. The influence of Montaigne fades away, for a time, to be replaced by a more individual moral attitude, and there is also some very accomplished mockery of religion in three 'facéties' or anecdotal dialogues. The first and most straightforward of these is *Le prophète irlandais* (Vol. IV, p. 56), about an Irish faith-healer. A married couple complain that they are plagued by demons, who disturb their sex-life. Two sessions with the faith-healer bring no improvement, and finally the couple expose him as an impostor. Saint-Evremond and his friend d'Aubigny witness the scene. They represent the

---

[7]   Vol. IV, pp. 5−23. Desmaizeaux, the editor of Saint-Evremond's works in 1705, associated the essay with a duel which, he thought, had taken place in 1657; Ternois gives the date at 1647. The evidence of date is not entirely convincing, and the bibliographical problems considerable. The lines at the end might be a late addition. See Vol. III, p. XI, for references concerning the Godolphin manuscript, a factor in the problem (on this manuscript, see D.C. Potts, 'Desmaizeaux and Saint-Evremond's Text', *French Studies* 19 (1965), 239−252).

[8]   *Pensées*, Sellier edition, Nos. 165 ff., especially No. 168 (Brunschvicg No. 139), in *liasse* IX. On the connection with Pascal see H. Barnwell, *Les idées morales et critiques de Saint-Evremond* (Paris, 1957), pp. 62−63.

'gens éclairés', who do not share the credulity of the ignorant multitude, but do not dare to reveal their scepticism until after the Irishman's discomfiture.

This light-hearted tale should not be given too much significance, but it is noticeable that the authoritarian vocabulary of fideism is now applied to superstition, from which Saint-Evremond clearly distances himself: 'ces prodiges étaient appuyés d'une si grande autorité, que la multitude étonnée les recevait avec soumission (...) La connaissance timide et assujettie respectait l'erreur impérieuse et autorisée'. Still, even though faith may have been demoted to the level of gullibility, it remains unclear whether the watching aristocrat is himself an enlightened kind of fideist, or something more radical.

The other two 'facéties' are a comic masterpiece, the *Conversation de M. le Maréchal d'Hocquincourt avec le P. Canaye* (Vol. III, p. 167) and its sequel, the *Conversation de M. d'Aubigny avec M. de Saint-Evremond* (Vol. IV, p. 33). They can be attributed only with some hesitation to the Holland period, but if topicality is any guide, as it often is with Saint-Evremond, both the *Conversations* should belong to the years around 1668, the date when the 'paix de l'Eglise' put a provisional end to the Jansenist controversy.

The early part of the first *Conversation* describes how the fiery Maréchal gives the Jesuit his opinions on free-thinkers, love and religion, brandishing a knife to demonstrate his devotion to Mme de Montbason, and lending the gentle cleric a horse, which, like its master, is too spirited for him. At the end we hear the views of Père Canaye about Jesuit policy against the Jansenists. The essence of the satire is a technique perfected by Voltaire: religious acts are performed for reasons which have nothing to do with religion. The Maréchal turns to Jansenism because 'un bougre de Jésuite' prevents him from shooting one of his free-thinking soldier friends, an action which (in the circumstances) was intended to preserve his friend's honour; later, he turns away from it because, he alleges, 'un certain abbé de Rancé, un petit janséniste' was paying unwelcome attentions to Maréchal's mistress. Similarly with the Jansenist dispute generally: theology is not involved, according to Père Canaye; instead, 'la jalousie de gouverner les consciences a tout fait. Les Jansénistes nous ont trouvés en possession du gouvernement, et ils ont voulu nous en tirer'.

The dialogue eventually becomes a burlesque parody of fideism. The Maréchal had been so confused about the Fall of Man, because of a philosopher, that he was about to lose his faith. Now, however, although he cannot say how the change occurred, 'je me ferais crucifier pour la religion; ce n'est pas que j'y voie plus de raison; au contraire, moins que jamais'. For Père Canaye, the Maréchal's faith is the work of grace: 'C'est la vraie religion cela. Point de raison!'

This is mockery of a silly form of fideism, and so resembles *Le prophète irlandais*, but it is not a complete repudiation. Compared with the attack on faith by the Militaire philosophe thirty or forty years later, it is positively affectionate. (Père Canaye is commonly supposed to have been Saint-Evremond's teacher.) The way is still open for more serious reflections on religion, which we find in the companion piece, the *Conversation de d'Aubigny*. In this, after an initial exposure of Jansenist policy, the ideas expressed about morality, and the opposition between religious and social life, are more typical of Saint-Evremond's writings after 1670, especially in a passage about sectarianism. We also find what might be called an Aristotelian principle of ethical moderation, when extremes are rejected in favour of a middle-way compromise. This pattern was a fertile method of composition for Saint-Evremond, and is almost a *leitmotif* of his later work.[9]

In the *Conversation* with d'Aubigny, the pattern appears in the central section, about religion and nature. D'Aubigny says that he disapproves both of too much austerity, or harshness, and of too much indulgence. He is referring specifically to the moral element in religion. The final compromise is: 'Je veux, en un mot, une morale chrétienne, ni austère, ni relâchée', which in most versions is the conclusion. In other words, Saint-Evremond regards both Jansenist and Jesuit moral teachings as extremes to be avoided. There is a further implication, that he rejects all the divisions of Catholicism and is primarily concerned with morality, but there is no satire, and no indication of insincerity over 'une morale chrétienne'.

A final section of the *Conversation*, which is found in only one version (Vol. IV, pp. 54–55), deals with the competing demands made by religion and society. Sectarian religion, the reference here being to Protestants and Catholics, is socially divisive, says Saint-Evremond; similarly, the contemplative's withdrawal from 'le monde' for religious motives runs counter to the needs of society. We should try to improve social life, not ignore it, since 'la justice et la charité ne se pratiquent point hors du monde'. This may have the appearance of recommending a purely social morality, but the intention seems rather to be that of reconciling religion with worldly society.

Beginning as it does with reminiscences of the *Conversation du Maréchal d'Hocquincourt* and ending with hints of an undenominational Christian morality, the *Conversation de d'Aubigny* is perhaps the best expression of Saint-Evremond's ideas on religion during the middle period. Fideism is now almost absent. There is only a passing reference to 'submission', with the usual political overtones: 'C'est à Dieu de faire des catholiques ou des protestants; c'est à nous de vivre paisiblement en sujets fidèles'.

Although these pieces were probably written during Saint-Evremond's

---

[9]   A good example from about the same period is the triple essay entitled 'L'intérêt dans les personnes tout à fait corrompues. La vertu trop rigide. Les sentiments d'un honnête et habile courtisan sur cette vertu rigide et ce sale intérêt', which dates from 1667 (Vol. III, p. 2). The courtier 'fait le tempérament' between excessive moral rigidity and excessive selfishness.

stay in Holland, there is nothing in them to suggest any great concern for that country or its religion. The first indication of an interest in Protestantism comes in the *Lettre écrite de La Haye* (Vol. II, p. 21), in which he seems content to repeat standard opinions about Dutch tolerance.[10] But in the *Considération sur la religion* (Vol. IV, p. 140), the most important essay of the Dutch period (and for the history of deism the most important generally), there is an extended discussion of the differences between Catholic and Calvinist Christianity. The *Considération* is attached by editors to a long and rambling piece, the nearest Saint-Evremond ever approached to a *summa*, *A M. le Maréchal de Créqui, qui m'avait demandé (...) ce que je pensais sur toutes choses* (Vol. IV, p. 97). The last section of the essay for Créqui is about justice as a moral ideal. Saint-Evremond discursively praises the Natural Law school of jurists, especially Grotius, recommends justice to princes, and, in a lengthy disquisition on the personal qualities involved in giving and receiving, advises the regulation of spontaneous impulses by 'un ordre constant de la raison' – a rare admission that reason can have value.

The *Considération* itself begins on metaphysics, doubting the immortality of the soul; goes on to 'l'examen des religions', preferring Catholicism but asking for tolerance and the rights of conscience; and then discusses in detail the two branches of European Christianity, with the declared intention of finding a basis for unity. Following the middle-way pattern, Saint-Evremond contrasts the two religions in terms of excess and deficiency. In doing good works, Catholics are too enterprising, because of the doctrinal emphasis on the value of works, while Protestants are not active enough, being influenced by the doctrine of predestination. In worship, the Protestant is apt to be too austere, the Catholic too elaborate. 'Que nos catholiques fixent ce zèle qui les fait un peu trop agir d'eux-mêmes; que les huguenots sortent de leur régularité paresseuse'. Saint-Evremond also argues in favour of a practical, not an intellectual approach to the problem of reunion: 'Le moyen de nous réunir n'est pas de disputer toujours sur la doctrine (...) Faisons tant que de bien agir ensemble, et nous ne serons pas longtemps à croire séparément'. This hostility to polemical debate extends to an attack on religious speculation generally, which is often, says Saint-Evremond, the effect of curiosity and presumption. The remedy is to abandon speculation for action.

The anti-rationalist strain in Saint-Evremond leads here to a moralizing conclusion, not the fideism of this earlier works: 'Soyons justes, charitables, patients, par le principe de notre religion: nous confesserons Dieu et lui obéirons tout ensemble'. Some final reflections on Christianity in general end similarly, but with greater emphasis on the emotional appeal of religion.

---

[10] See Gustave Cohen, 'Le séjour de Saint-Evremond en Hollande (1665–1670)', I, RLC 5 (1925), 431–454, especially p. 440.

God's intention seems to have been to base religion on 'les mouvements de notre coeur', not on 'les lumiéres de notre esprit'. (This corresponds to a remark earlier in the piece, that Christ ordained charity, but did not teach any dogma.) Christianity, because it canalizes spontaneous feelings of 'tendresse', has a moral force superior to that of philosophy, other religions and rational morality or justice. 'La seule religion chrétienne apaise ce qu'il y a chez nous d'agité, elle adoucit ce qu'il y a de féroce, elle emploie ce que nous avons de tendre en nos mouvements, non seulement avec nos amis, et avec nos proches, mais avec les indifférents et en faveur même de nos ennemis'. In all this passage love, 'tendresse', the impulse of the heart, is seen as the basis of religious action: 'il y a je ne sais quoi au fond de notre âme qui s'émeut secrètement pour un Dieu que nous ne pouvons connaître'.

The *Considération,* obviously, contains much that is new in Saint-Evremond's work, and incidentally is totally at variance with his usual reputation of hedonistic *libertinage.* The change is due to new influences: those of the eirenic movement in the years about 1670, and of Spinoza's *Tractatus theologico-politicus,* published in the same year.[11] Saint-Evremond was interested in the controversies and negotiations between Catholics and Protestants, and kept himself informed about current developments.[12] In the *Considération,* his approach is specifically that of Isaac d'Huisseau, one of the leading Protestant advocates for union (but not well viewed by his own side). His short *La réunion de Christianisme,* of 1669, sought to achieve union by simplifying Christianity to its essentials, on which all could agree. This was the method used by Bossuet also, in his *Exposition de la foi catholique,* but whereas Bossuet tried to reduce the number of controverted points of doctrine, d'Huisseau was more radical. He excludes the discussion of doctrine entirely, apart from giving a list of the points on which there is agreement, and prefers to seek unity in the sphere of behaviour, practising Christian charity and piety.[13] Saint-Evremond, by rejecting speculation in favour of obedience to Christian morality, is close to d'Huisseau's position. He is not far, also, from the Spinoza of the *Tractatus,* who claimed that the Christian Gospel taught not doctrine, but submission or obedience to God: 'God has required nothing from men but knowledge of his divine justice and charity', according to the end of Chapter 13. In Chapter 14, the essence of faith is not belief, but action (the precept to love one's neighbour). A

---

[11] On Saint-Evremond and Spinoza, see G. Cohen, 'Le séjour de Saint-Evremond en Hollande', II, RLC 6 (1926), 28–78, section XI; Potts, *Saint-Evremond,* pp. 331 ff.; René Ternois, 'Saint-Evremond et Spinoza', RHLF 65 (1965), 1–14. There is nothing relevant in Paul Vernière, *Spinoza en France,* 2 vols. (Paris, 1954), Vol. I, pp. 15–18, on Saint-Evremond.

[12] See Saint-Evremond's letters to a young Protestant friend, Anne Hervart, in *Lettres,* Ternois edition, Vol. I, Ls. 36–49, especially L. 40, pp. 197–198, and L. 47, pp. 213–214. These show that the polemics he thought vain were those between Arnauld and Claude.

[13] See Potts, *Saint-Evremond,* Ch. 3; *Oeuvres en prose,* Vol. IV, p. 141. Saint-Evremond's comment on d'Huisseau's book was 'fort bien pensé et fort mal traité' (*Lettres,* Vol. I, p. 214).

more detailed borrowing from the *Tractatus* is found in remarks in the *Considération* about the difference in emphasis placed by St Paul and St James on faith and works.[14]

Saint-Evremond was ready to accept what he read in d'Huisseau or Spinoza partly, no doubt, because it fell in with his own previously expressed opinions. The desire to exclude doctrinal speculation from religion was bound to appeal to him; the *Considération* opens with a recapitulation of his agnosticism about the soul and his attacks on 'une vaine curiosité de tout connaître'. In earlier works, however, he had gone on to recommend submission to Church authority. Now the consequence changes; the ensuing recommendation is to practise charity. In its immediate context, this is a method of reuniting the two branches of Christianity. Against the background of Saint-Evremond's former development, however, it acquires a different look; it appears as the replacement of fideistic 'submission' by a morally based, undenominational Christianity of a pragmatic and tolerant kind.

Another new element is the importance allotted to religious love. Passages such as the following give an impression of sincerity, in strong contrast to the satire found in other pieces: 'Nous regardons ce premier Etre comme un objet souverainement aimable, qui doit être aimé, et les âmes tendres sont touchées des douces et agréables impressions qu'il fait sur elles (...) si cet amour a une pureté véritable, rien au monde ne fait goûter une plus véritable douceur'. This must be the foundation of the remarks about the value of Christianity at the end of the *Considération,* and provides the elements of a positive religious attitude, hitherto absent from Saint-Evremond's writings except in the form of recommendations to accept Catholic faith. If we could be sure that he was expressing his personal views, and not merely advancing arguments to support the Catholic side in the eirenic negotiations, we might conclude that he had arrived at a new and individual form of religion. Intrinsically, because of its moral emphasis and freedom from dogmatic or sectarian limitations, this attitude resembles deism. If the concept of Catholic deism did not seem contradictory, it might take this form. Yet Saint-Evremond does not appear to conceive of religion practised outside one of the established churches, and despite the eirenism he still favours Catholicism, rather than a completely undenominational Christianity.

DETACHED WORLDLINESS IN THE LATE WORKS

In the early 1670s Saint-Evremond seems to have written little. The works of

---

[14]   The quotation is from the translation by R.H. M. Elwes, *The Chief Works of Benedict de Spinoza* (London, 1883). On St Paul and St James, Saint-Evremond in the *Considération* (Vol. IV, pp. 157–158) attributes the differences to the fact that they were addressing different audiences, as does Spinoza (*Tractatus theologico-politicus,* end of Ch. 11).

1675 and later, the last period of his literary career, tend to be less formal than before, and more obviously adapted to particular circumstances. The division between Protestants and Catholics and the persecution of the Huguenots prior to 1685 are the background for a piece in which the approach is somewhat similar to the *Considération sur la religion,* but which casts doubt on the impartiality of the earlier essay. This is the *Lettre à M. Justel,* of 1683 (Vol. IV, p. 252). Writing to a prominent Huguenot recently arrived in England, Saint-Evremond advises him to return to France, despite the restrictions he will face in the observance of his religion. The letter defends the Catholic use of images in worship, proposes that each side should keep to its own beliefs about the Eucharist (with a strong implication that the doctrine is inexplicable), and expresses the hope that Justel can accept the 'Catholicité purgée' of Bossuet, together with Gallican independence of Rome. If Justel cannot do this, and at this point Saint-Evremond's attitude hardens, then he cannot complain about the measures taken against his Church: Huguenot criticisms of Catholicism are wilful opposition to the King, virtually inviting persecution.

After the unifying appeal of the *Considération,* the change in style is remarkable, and Saint-Evremond runs the risk of seeming inhumane. He refers to the measures against the Huguenots as 'de petites rigueurs' and fails to show any understanding of religious conviction. Despite his reputation as a free-thinker and his professions of tolerance, both in the *Considération* and the *Lettre à Justel* itself, Saint-Evremond in the *Lettre* is quite unyielding in his arguments for the Catholic position.

The advocacy of French government policy is modified to some extent by the worldliness of the 'honnête homme'. Advice to submit to the national religion takes the form of concentration on external 'cérémonies' at the expense of personal belief: 'Que chacun demeure attaché à sa doctrine comme il lui plaira, mais accordons-nous dans l'usage du Sacrement'. After the history of embittered controversy about the Eucharist it is hard to see how Justel could accept such advice, but that does not prevent Saint-Evremond from playing down the denominational differences. His arguments and tone imply that civilized people should ignore them: 'Est-il possible que les différences si peu considérables ou si mal fondées troublent le repos des nations et soient cause des plus grands malheurs qui arrivent aux hommes?' The principle to which he refers is the right of the secular power to regulate public religious behaviour: 'Les princes ont autant de droit sur l'extérieur de la religion qu'en ont les sujets sur le fond de leur conscience'; it is the principle of a state religion, and we shall meet it again in Veiras' imaginary theocracy. Applying it to France, Saint-Evremond says that Catholicism there is 'réglée avec autant de sagesse que de piété par nos lois et maintenue avec fermeté par nos parlements'. He had written similarly about the Dutch government's policy of toleration in the *Lettre écrite de La Haye.*

At the end of his letter Saint-Evremond admits that his attitude may appear unreligious, but again resorts to worldly advice: 'Soyez sage, soyez prudent, quand les emportés devraient vous appeller tiède'. Looked at in political terms, his advice is logical, and is in harmony with the acceptance of authority which he had proclaimed since before 1650; however, now it is not faith that should be accepted – by definition, Catholic faith must differ from Justel's – but only the rituals of Catholicism. Such advice seems likely to have encouraged the indifference and undenominational Christian belief which is only a step away from deism.

In other works of the later period, there are important discussions of faith in the *Réflexions sur la religion* of about 1675 (Vol. III, p. 360), and a letter to Mme Mazarin, of 1677 (*Lettres,* Vol. I, p. 331). The two are similar in plan, both beginning on the difficulty of faith and ending with statements that, while true faith comes from God alone, men can at least carry out the moral duties of religion. According to the *Réflexions,* a rather despondent little essay, we desire the happiness promised by religion, but most of us cannot manage true belief. For those who can, even misfortunes and deprivation can be satisfying; others return periodically to worldly pleasures. The difficulties of faith contrast with the ease of virtue: 'Il n'y a jamais à se méprendre aux actions de justice et de charité'.

In a middle section, Saint-Evremond illustrates his remarks with the example of the Cardinal de Retz. This corresponds to a different example in the *Lettre à Mme Mazarin,* that of Baron Wurtz, who, it seems, professed the religion of whatever country he was in. Wurtz appears to be a Christian deist (the term is not in Saint-Evremond), believing that there is a generalized Christianity, common to all the different sects, 'aussi simple dans sa doctrine que pure dans sa morale'.

At first sight, this might seem the same as the religion of obedience to God's commands recommended at the end of the *Lettre,* which in turn is similar to that of the *Considération sur la religion*. However, Saint-Evremond expresses firm disapproval of Wurtz, saying that a Christian should hold to his own church (unless divine grace intervenes); independence of a church is not Christianity. He adds: 'quand vous ne serez plus chrétien, vous deviendrez philosophe; ou vous serez sans religion, ou vous vous en ferez une qui ne vaudra pas celle que vous avez quittée.' This is a plain rejection of deism and religious individualism. Saint-Evremond's recognition that faith may be difficult does not, then, lead to what might seem a natural result, the creation of a private mode of belief. This seems to have been too great a step for him to take. Even when showing disillusion with fideism, he preserves the concept of religion as something imposed by authority on the individual.

Many of Saint-Evremond's later works on religious topics, such as devoutness, contain interesting comments on the psychology of religion (for some women, he says in letter, without obvious irony, 'Dieu est un nouvel amant, qui les console de celui qu'elles ont perdu'),[15] but do not concern the history of deism. There is an unexpected excursion into natural theology when Saint-Evremond offers counsel of piety for a woman who lives in 'le monde' (Mme Mazarin): 'La vue du soleil vous fera comprendre la grandeur et la magnificence de celui qui l'a formé; cet ordre si merveilleux et si juste, cet ordre qui lie et entretient toutes choses, vous donnera la connaissance de sa sagesse' (*Lettres*, Vol. I, p. 338). This could be deistic, rather than Christian, but it is followed by flattery which detracts from its seriousness; in Mme Mazarin's case, says Saint-Evremond, the worship of God ought to consist in diplaying her beauty to mankind.

Perhaps the clearest indication of his later attitude is given by the essay *De la retraite* (Vol. IV, p. 282), a counterpart for men of the secular cases of conscience which he was in the habit of deciding for women.[16] Retirement, or in the words of the verses at the end 'un doux et saint repos', is the proper course in old age; and having criticized the austerity and discipline of monastic retreat, on the grounds that there is nothing wrong with comfort and that good acts done by order are of no merit, Saint-Evremond imagines a new kind of institution, to which 'les honnêtes gens' could retire: 'ils pourraient goûter la joie d'une retraite pieuse, et le plaisir innocent d'une honnête et agréable conversation; mais dans ce lieu de repos je ne voudrais d'autres régles que celles du Christianisme qui sont reçues généralement partout'. This last clause means that there would be no obedience to a monastic rule; the rules in question might well be the precepts of justice and charity, so often singled out in previous works. In Saint-Evremond's monastery, 'l'on ne regarderait pas Dieu comme un Dieu chagrin, qui défend les choses agréables parce qu'elles plaisent; mais (. . .) rien ne plairait à des esprits bien faits, que ce qui est juste ou tout-à-fait innocent'.

In these last works religion takes on an Epicurean air, with reminiscences of the later Montaigne as well as of Rabelais's Abbaye de Thélème. In both piety and morality, pleasure and spontaneous impulse play a large part, and much less is said of submission, either to revelation or to moral precept. The outlook seems to be essentially human, although the religious framework is preserved.[17]

Towards the end of his life, Saint-Evremond wrote a self-portrait (Vol. IV, p. 305). It concludes with a few lines of verse about his religion:

---

[15]   *Lettre à une dame galante qui voulait devenir dévote* (*Oeuvres en prose*, Vol. IV, p. 212).
[16]   The date of the essay is about 1686 (*Oeuvres en prose*, Vol. IV, pp. 283–285).
[17]   Potts, *Saint-Evremond*, pp. 399–401, believes that he tends towards deism in his last writings, but describes his attitude as 'ethical humánism'. For a statement of the traditional view, see Antoine Adam, *Histoire de la littérature française au XVIIe siècle*, 5 vols. (Paris, 1949–1956), Vol. V, pp. 204–205 ('épicurien (. . .) sans doute incapable de s'attacher à aucune foi').

De justice et de charité
Beaucoup plus que de pénitence
Il compose sa piété:
Mettant en Dieu sa confiance,
Espérant tout de sa bonté,
Dans le sein de la Providence[18]
Il trouve son repos et sa félicité.

Taken in isolation, this variation on the theme of faith, hope and charity is certainly deistic. Its only positive elements are moral values and belief in a beneficent providence. It is far from being an accurate summary of Saint-Evremond's writings on religion before the 1680s, but it might be taken to justify the view that, in his last years, he drew near to the deist position. Yet it seems preferable to regard it as worldly Christianity rather than deism; there is no hint of the critical side of the deistic position. His attitude had always been that of a 'mondain', one who accepted that Catholicism was part of the established social order, and was prepared to argue for it on that basis; and who also recognized the emotional rewards of piety. The judgement of Mgr Calvet on Cléante, in *Tartuffe,* could be applied to Saint-Evremond: 'Les mondains ne sont pas libertins, Cléante est chrétien. Mais il comprend le christianisme comme Molière et Montaigne: c'est un rite traditionnel, un décorum social, une hygiène personnelle. Nous pouvons le pratiquer pour nous et chez nous, à notre gré.'[19]

The distinction between worldly Catholicism and deism is slight; the Marquis de Lassay, whose deistic writings date from the 1720s, shared much of Saint-Evremond's outlook. In Saint-Evremond's essays many typical elements of deism are present, among them the secular point of view, the emphasis on morality, and the indifference to doctrine. If we look for professed beliefs, there is little except the belief in God. But then the advocate of submissive faith does not need, in the nature of things, to define his position, which is decided by the authority of the Church. This was Saint-Evremond's standpoint throughout. However, in his later works, the fideism comes to seem empty. It is undermined, perhaps as a result of the years spent in exile, until it tends towards the political prudence urged on the Huguenot Justel in 1683, or becomes merely the habit, in other late works, of excepting cases of true faith from the usual worldly indifference. It is possible to doubt Saint-Evremond's sincerity in many of his writings, but it is impossible to imagine him elaborating any serious criticism of the religion of his country, unlike the deists of the period immediately after

---

[18]   I quote the Desmaizeaux text; the text published by Barbin in 1692 has 'les soins de la Providence' (*Oeuvres en prose,* Vol. IV, p. 308).
[19]   Jean Calvet, *La littérature religieuse de François de Sales à Fénelon* (Paris, 1956), p. 431.

1700. Since the critical side is so important in the deist movement as a whole, Saint-Evremond should be treated as one of the last representatives, with Bayle, of the tradition of Christian faith. The rationalism which was to lay the foundation for early deism held no attractions for him.

CHAPTER 5

THE UTOPIAN RELIGIONS OF FOIGNY AND VEIRAS

Between the *Considération sur la religion* of Saint-Evremond in about 1670 and his *Lettre à Justel* in 1683, and against the same background of tension between Catholics and Protestants, two works appeared which are always linked in the history of French religious ideas: Gabriel Foigny's *La Terre australe connue* and Denis Veiras' *Histoire des Sévarambes*.[1] They came out almost simultaneously, Foigny's book in 1676, in Geneva, and Veiras' in 1677–1679 in Paris, having been published partially in England in 1675;[2] both are Utopian travel-stories narrating voyages to the 'Austral Land', the name for a huge land-mass known to exist but as yet unexplored. Both too, in different ways, illustrate further themes already found in Saint-Evremond. Foigny's curious hero, Sadeur, is more tempted than Saint-Evremond by rational religion (the portrayal of which makes his story of great interest for the history of deism), but finally prefers Catholic faith. Veiras, the more able and influential writer, develops in considerable detail an idea which is close to the surface in the *Lettre à Justel*, that doctrinal freedom can be accommodated within a state religion based on community rituals.

FOIGNY'S *LA TERRE AUSTRALE CONNUE*: FAITH AGAINST REASON

Gabriel Foigny was a Franciscan monk until 1666, when he turned Calvinist.[3] Information about his life before then has to be gleaned from a document found by Frédéric Lachèvre in the archives of the Consistoire of Geneva: 'Jeudi 8 mars 1666. Gabriel de Foigny, du lieu de Foigny en Champagne,

---

[1] On both writers see Lanson, *Origines de l'esprit philosophique*, pp. 67–81; Gilbert Chinard, *L'Amérique et le rêve exotique dans la littérature française au XVIIe et au XVIIIe siècle* (Paris, 1913), cited henceforth as *Rêve exotique;* and Geoffroy Atkinson, *The Extraordinary Voyage in French Literature before 1700* (New York, 1920), cited as *Extraordinary Voyage before 1700*. Pierre Bayle's article 'Sadeur' in his *Dictionnaire* remains fundamental on Foigny. On Veiras, see also Georges Ascoli, *Quelques notes biographiques sur Denis Veiras d'Alais*, in *Mélanges offerts à Gustave Lanson* (Paris, 1922), pp. 165–177, and an excellent monograph, Emanuel Von der Mühll, *Denis Veiras et son Histoire des Sévarambes 1677–1679* (Paris, 1938), which contains a good bibliography.

[2] See Atkinson, *Extraordinary Voyage before 1700*, Appendix. The volumes which appeared in English in 1675 and 1678/79 were apparently not by Veiras except for the first one.

[3] For biographical and bibliographical information see Frédéric Lachèvre, *Les successeurs de Cyrano de Bergerac* (Paris, 1922). This gives the text, from which I quote, of the only surviving copy of the first edition, 1676, of *La Terre australe connue*.

s'est présenté avec déclaration qu'ayant croupi l'espace de trente-six ans en l'église romaine, où il a été cordelier de l'observance et prédicateur, Dieu l'ayant daigné illuminer, il a pris résolution de venir se ranger à la vraie Eglise et religion réformée'. He married, became a teacher, and wrote books of various kinds, including an almanac and Latin primers. He was in trouble with the religious authorities more than once. They took proceedings against *La Terre australe connue,* but Foigny was protected by the secular power, the Petit Conseil. In 1684 he caused another scandal by fathering an illegitimate child. Eventually he returned to Catholicism, and died, in a monastery in Savoie, in 1692. In the same year an expurgated edition of his novel was published in France, probably by the Abbé Raguenet.[4]

For his hero, Nicolas[5] Sadeur, Foigny picked on the idea of a hermaphrodite (although his conduct reveals that he is predominantly masculine). After an early life which is crowded with adventure, he is shipwrecked in the southern seas. He faces perils from giant birds but finds sanctuary in the Austral Land. By a fortunate chance, the Australians are also hermaphrodite, and they welcome him as one of themselves. The fantasy continues with the description of their country, where all the hills have been flattened and summer is perpetual. The inhabitants can create animals, manufacture interesting gadgets, and make themselves invisible. The population numbers almost a hundred million and lives in fifteen thousand townships, geometrically divided into quarters, houses, and compartments. Each has a combined temple and senate, the Hab, and four schools. The Australians are all virtuous. They have no government, but take decisions together in assembly. Sadeur describes their science, moral and religious beliefs, daily life and social organization. But in this Utopia not everything is perfect. The Australians have belligerent neighbours called Fondins, with whom there are savage battles. Moreover, in the end Sadeur quarrels with his hosts, and escapes to Madagascar.

Foigny's Austral Land suggests a monkish dream of idealized institutionalism on a vast scale.[6] He refers to the Australians as 'les frères'; their occupations, called 'exercices' in the title of Chapter 8, are chiefly learned debate, private mediation (carried out, however, by four hundred of them at a time, in the Hab), and gardening. Their hermaphroditism, which Bayle regarded as being taken from the ideas of Antoinette Bourignon, an eccentric

---

[4]   This is the traditional attribution. Lachèvre, ibid., p. 62, states without any evidence that Foigny assisted with the revision. M. E. Storer, 'The Abbé Raguenet, Deist, Historian, Music and Art Critic', *Romanic Review* 36 (1945), 283–296, expresses some doubts about the attribution but seems to accept that Raguenet was the editor (p. 285). The 1692 edition was entitled *Les Avantures de Jaques Sadeur dans la découverte et le voiage de la Terre Australe.*

[5]   This is his correct name (Lachèvre edition, p. 69), but the relevant passage was omitted from the 1692 edition and Sadeur acquired the name of his father, Jaques (Atkinson, *Extraordinary Voyage before 1700,* p. 36, n.2).

[6]   Chinard makes the same point (*Rêve exotique,* p. 105).

mystic,[7] seems to be an attempt to reconcile the necessity of reproduction with monastic celibacy. They are shocked by the elements of 'European' sexuality in Sadeur's behaviour; their own children are produced by an unexplained process which does not involve intercourse.

As regards Foigny's religious ideas, the most important passage of his novel is a lengthy conversation between Sadeur and an elderly Australian called Suains, who befriends him. Like his fellows, Suains believes only in natural religion; Sadeur is a Christian. In discussion they agree about the existence of a creator God, but differ over divine providence and part company completely on the question of the soul. Suains virtually denies its existence, while Sadeur adheres by an act of faith to the Christian doctrine. From their discussion it is not immediately clear which side Foigny himself supported, although the usual assumption is that it shows him to be a deist.

Sadeur begins by asserting the existence of God: 'La nature nous enseigne un Etre Souverain, l'auteur et le conservateur de toutes choses' (Lachèvre edition, p. 109); he goes on to prove it by a rudimentary First Cause argument. Then he joins forces with Suains in order to denounce and refute the theory of creation from atoms, the standard atheistic theory, derived from Epicurus and Democritus. The Australian partly explains atheism by observing that 'la grande abstraction de cet Etre des Etres, qui ne se découvre non plus que s'il n'était pas' makes it difficult to believe in a divine creator of the universe: 'il est trop au-dessus de nous pour se manifester à nous autrement que par ses effets' (p. 110).

Sadeur thinks that God is not so detached from us as this would imply. In the narrative sections of the book he often prays and affirms his submission to divine providence;[8] he describes himself as 'un homme nonobstant tant de peines, d'un esprit fort rassis, soumis à la volonté de Dieu et résigné parfaitement à ses ordres' (p. 84). But Suains does not believe in prayer. For him it is a blasphemy against divine providence, an attempt to make God change his plans: 'nous concevons cet Etre Souverain comme incapable de changement et come voulant toujours ce qui est plus parfait'. However, he accepts the decisions of his immutable deity with as good a grace as Sadeur (pp. 115–116). The difference between them is that Suains believes in a general providence, more or less equivalent to the laws of nature, whereas for Sadeur there is a particular providence which can meet the needs of individuals.

Discussing the worship of God, both agree that men should express their gratitude and veneration. To talk of God, says Sadeur, should be our most cherished activity, with the aim of arousing gratitude (p. 111). However, he

[7]   See Bayle's article 'Sadeur' (and cf. 'Bourignon'). He based his comment on a passage from Foigny concerning hermaphrodite reproduction and the perfect unity of God.
[8]   The first paragraph of the book, omitted in 1692, says that the story exemplifies 'la divine conduite sur ses créatures'. Rather puzzlingly, a reference to providence in another passage (Lachèvre edition, p. 87) was changed in 1692 to a remark about 'la fatalité inévitable des choses humaines'. There are several other apparently sincere references to providence: pp. 75, 82, 85, 153, 155, 156.

is forced by Suains to admit that, in Europe, debate about God can lead to dissension. This danger is the reason why in the Austral Land 'leur grande religion est de ne point parler de religion' (p. 108). The Australians gather at the Hab 'pour le reconnaître et l'adorer', but do not have any formal, organized worship. Their name for the deity, 'le Haab', denotes incomprehensibility, a concept found frequently in fideist writers, for instance Charron. In him and perhaps also in Foigny, there is an obvious political motive for the rejection of theology, namely the desire to avoid sectarian conflict. Foigny's change of religion may have made him more sensitive than most to the danger. Suains' view is that, since God's being is incomprehensible, 'nous sommes toujours unis et toujours en respect' when any of the Australians speaks his name, 'ce qui serait impossible si nous voulions nous donner la liberté d'en discourir' (p. 111).

The passage including this last remark, which draws a significant contrast between the unity of religion in the Austral Land and the conflicts in Europe, was left out of the 1692 edition of the book, together with most of the chapter in which it occurs. It provides the context for a critique by Suains of Christianity, or more precisely of the intolerant claims to exclusive truth which the Christian churches make, and which deepen the divisions between them. Suains' argument is that God cannot have 'spoken', or provided a special relevation, to one particular group of men (the Christians), and he denies that miracles can confirm the truth of a special revelation, except for the gullible, 'ceux qui se laissent plus facilement persuader' (p. 113). Sadeur's reply is that the differences between the Christian churches result from varying interpretations of the same original revelation. Foigny's changes of religion might indicate that he held the same ecumenical view. In any case, the criticisms of the value of miracles as proof of revelation seem to be part of the argument about religious divisions, not a *libertin* attack on the whole Christian religion. Foigny was not hostile to the idea of miracles generally, if we are to judge from the extraordinary events and beings which he invented in profusion in the pages of his novel. At the end, for instance, the inhabitants of Madagascar capture an Australian, who commits suicide. His body and those of his servants are put into the sea, whereupon they all float away in the direction of the Austral Land (pp. 162–163).[9]

Despite Suains' criticisms, the debate between him and Sadeur is far from being decided at this point. He goes on to draw further conclusions from his conception of a supreme God who is above particularism. All creatures are 'également siennes' but he has no special concern for men, being too much superior to them. The espousal of this view by Suains puts him into a very un-Christian category, that of the Epicureans. If his arguments were to defeat Sadeur here, *La Terre australe connue* would probably seem opposed

---

[9] For many other examples of miraculous events, see Atkinson's summary of the novel (*Extraordinary Voyage before 1700*, pp. 40–51).

generally to Christianity, but they do not. The discussion continues in another chapter, on the subject of the soul. About this Suains is agnostic. He rejects the Christian belief, adding that those Australians who do believe in the survival of the soul are unable to explain themselves clearly. He has his own conception, which Sadeur in turn finds difficult to understand: 'un génie universel qui se communique par partie à chaque particulier (...) ce génie s'éteint dans la mort sans cependant être détruit' (p. 117).[10]

Left alone after this long debate, Sadeur reflects on the unhappiness of the Australians, who are deprived of revelation, that is, of 'la foi que nous avons d'un Dieu mort et ressuscité pour notre salut' (pp. 113–114). This is not a perfunctory remark, as it might be in Tyssot de Patot forty years later. Sadeur's general view of the Australian nation is also fideistic: 'la raison qui est sa guide (...) la ferait incomparable si Dieu voulait l'éclairer, mais cette même raison qui l'élève tant sur les autres, au regard des connaissances naturelles, l'abaisse au-dessous de toutes en ce qu'elle ne connaît pas son salut' (p. 114). However, he decides not to try to convert the Australians, for fear of being ridiculed. Later he is shown to be right, when Suains makes innumerable objections to the Christian doctrine of the afterlife (pp. 116–117).

In sum, the uncompromising deistic rationalism of the Australian confronts 'European' fideism in Sadeur, whose position is less fully expounded. This could be because Foigny's readers would have been familiar with it. But if it is regarded as insincere, the novel must be interpreted as a vehicle for expressing the anti-Christian sentiments of Suains. The next chapter, however, Chapter 7, contains a fictional portrayal of the life without faith in which the Australians' situation appears less enviable than we might have thought. There are no more descriptions of technological wizardry or perfect rational organization; the theme is now the unhappiness of life. Although the Australians are free from European defects such as illness, childbirth, eating (they eat very little and are ashamed of having to do it at all), excretion and sexual reproduction, they are all agreed that 'cette vie n'est qu'une agitation, qu'un trouble et qu'un tourment' (p. 120). The cause of their anguish is the necessity of dying, combined with their beliefs about the nature of God: 'nous nous considérons les victimes nécessaires d'une cause supérieure qui se plaît de nous détruire (...) nous sommes soumis à la liberté d'un Souverain qui ne nous a faits que pour nous changer quand et comme il veut, et qui fait consister sa toute-puissance à nous détruire autant qu'à nous faire exceller' (pp. 122–123). Such is the result of believing in the Epicurean God and not in divine providence. The Australians believe that human nature, despite its

---

[10] Bayle, who is sympathetic to some fideist themes in Foigny, thought this 'un galimatias aussi absurde que l'âme du monde de quelques anciens philosophes' ('Sadeur', Note C). Lanson, *Origines de l'esprit philosophique,* p. 70, commented that it recalls the Stoics and Spinoza; he mentions other possible sources later (pp. 74–75).

excellence and nobility, is degraded by mortality and its dependence on inferior thing (such as food, presumably); it would be better not to exist than to exist as they do. More tangible reasons for their despair are given in Chapter 12, in accounts of battles with the Fondins and the monstrous birds, called Urgs, which carry many of them off for food.

Although pessimists, the Australians are morally admirable. In Chapter 5, which indicates that their situation represents the state of nature, we are told that innocence, purity, equality and fraternity reign. Sadeur has to explain what 'ambition' and 'avarice' mean. Australian perfections include nudity (clothes are unnatural) and hermaphroditism (not the 'ardeurs animales' of Europe). In a bizarre reflection on 'la production de la seconde personne de la sainte Trinité' (p. 100), Sadeur claims that hermaphroditism is nearer to divinity than sexual reproduction. But in general, 'cette attache si étroite à la raison qui les unit tous, et les porte à tout ce qui est bon et nécessaire, sont des fruits de personnes consommées en tout ce que nous pouvons concevoir naturellement de parfait'. The continuation makes it clear that Foigny is here referring to reason in a theological sense, reason destitute of revelation: 'et si Dieu daignait encore les éclairer de sa grâce, ce serait un peuple qui ferait un paradis en ce monde' (p. 107).[11] Since they are not so enlightened, the most their reasoning can achieve is agnosticism about the afterlife, which with their disbelief in providence causes their gloom about life and death.

All this gives greater force to Sadeur's fideism than it might possess otherwise. Statements such as 'j'adorai la divine providence de m'avoir donné d'autres lumières plus claires et plus assurées, et de m'avoir fait comprendre qu'étant mon Sauveur comme il avait été mon Créateur, il m'avait doué d'une âme immortelle qui devait jouir de sa gloire' (p. 114) appear to be a genuine expression of the comfort afforded by Christian belief when contrasted with the barrenness of pure reason. In spite of their gifts, as individuals the Australians want only to die, and when they have produced a child and reached the age of a hundred years they commit suicide (in a rather agreeable manner, by the use of a euphoric drug). Foigny's Austral Land is not, therefore, a conventional Utopia, in which every feature represents an ideal. It is the ultimate achievement of reason, but does not provide for the religious needs which are satisfied by Sadeur's faith in Christianity. Nor does life there turn out happily for him. Various rather ludicrous incidents lead to his being formally arraigned as a criminal. He is accused of making love to a woman of the Fondin nation, asking awkward questions about hermaphrodite generation, and failing to show enough enthusiasm for the massacre of Fondins (pp. 96, 152). He is consequently expected to commit suicide. The Australians have become enemies, and Sadeur finds a way of escaping.

[11]   For other statements that the Australians are naturally perfect but deprived of grace, see pp. 105, 136. Foigny does not use the term 'natural religion', although it would seem appropriate; nor does he refer to deism.

In this context, the criticisms of Christianity made by Suains cannot be taken as the most important element in Foigny's book, representing his personal opinions. Suains' criticisms of revelation, potentially far-reaching, are limited in scope because they are aimed only at the claims of the separate Christian churches; they leave the basis of Sadeur's faith untouched. There are passages which can be seen as satire of the Book of Genesis, but are more likely to be fictional imitations of the exotic myths reported by travellers and missionaries; in Chapter 9 the Australians are said to believe that they are descended from God ('le Haab'), 'qui en souffla trois en même temps' (p. 132). Europeans originated from the union of a hermaphrodite and a giant snake, whose offspring were malicious and brutal; this could be a semi-rationalizing version of the myths of Original Sin.[12]

In modern studies of Foigny it is normal to treat him as a *libertin* whose aim was to attack Christianity. The fideism of Sadeur is dismissed, and the objections of Suains classed with those of the eighteenth-century *philosophes*.[13] It is certainly true that these objections were to reappear many times and were destructive of Christian belief. It also seems true that Foigny was a *libertin* in morality. However, his criticisms of the religious conflicts of the seventeenth century can scarcely be regarded as audacious, and to put him with figures like Voltaire or d'Holbach is anachronistic. In any case his personal opinions matter less than the fact that in portraying the opposition between natural religion and Christianity, in the form of an encounter with Australians, he had hit on a method which had great potential. Utopian deism or the related deism of the 'noble savage' (as in Lahontan) could serve a number of purposes, and that of attacking Christianity was to be one of the most important. In *La terre australe connue,* it seems to have rather a different function, that of allowing the writer to conduct a kind of fictional experiment with the religion of reason, which in the event turns out unfavourably. Foigny appears to have been prepared to try deism in imagination, but not to have been convinced by it. His Austral deism began a tradition which can be traced through to Tyssot de Patot, for whom deism was clearly more attractive than Christian faith. But a more immediate sequel to Foigny's book was its republication in 1692,

[12]   Bayle suggested that Foigny's main unorthodoxy lay in the idea that the Australians were not descended from Adam. This is a less severe judgement than in modern works on Foigny, but Bayle had not read the original edition of his novel.

[13]   Chinard, *Rêve exotique*, p. 202 ('il a exposé avec trop d'enthousiasme la philosophie des Australiens pour que nous en soyons dupes (...) c'est bien à la religion chrétienne qu'il en a'); Atkinson, *Extraordinary Voyage before 1700*, p. 67 ('the attack is conscious, carefully thought out, and therefore more dangerous' than the (presumed) subversiveness of travellers' reports on Incas and Tartars). Lachèvre (*Successeurs de Cyrano*) treats Foigny as a *libertin de moeurs* above all, but from his account (pp. 35–51) of the proceedings in Geneva against Foigny's book it seems that a less serious view was taken at the time. The pastors thought it indecorous, impious and foolish, but failed to convince the Conseil de Genève that Foigny should be expelled. In a recent work, Bernard Tocanne (*L'Idée de nature en France*, p. 274) asserts that Foigny 'développe un déisme anti-chrétien'.

in a form which seems to have a kind of apologetic purpose; the removal of some of the criticisms made by Suains permits Sadeur's Christian faith to triumph more definitely.

The value of Utopian fiction as a means of portraying deistic natural religion was partly, as Bayle pointed out with reference to Foigny, that in this way the censorship might be circumvented; in addition, every aspect of religion, theological, personal and political, could be portrayed. In the debate between Sadeur and Suains, the subjects discussed include the nature of God, providence, the nature and survival of the soul, forms of worship, prayer, revelation, miracles and the sources of religious conflict. Whether or not Foigny subscribed to the rather harsh type of natural religion which he defined, his adaptation of the travel novel to accommodate so complete a definition was a most important step in the early development of deistic ideas.

VEIRAS' *HISTOIRE DES SÉVARAMBES:* RITUAL AND TOLERANCE

Denis Veiras d'Allais came from the south of France and was almost certainly of Huguenot descent. He spent the twenty years of his life that are known to us, from about 1665 to 1685, mainly in France and England, teaching both languages, acquainted with some eminent men, including Pepys, Locke and Bayle, closely linked with Buckingham, and no doubt involved in political intrigue. *L'Histoire des Sévarambes* was published in Paris in 1677–1679. Its publication in England in 1675 had been interrupted after one volume by Veiras' sudden departure for France, probably because he was implicated in the disgrace of Buckingham. He also wrote language manuals and theorized about language. After about 1685 he disappears, somewhere in Holland, presumably because of the Revocation of the Edict of Nantes.[14]

With its adroit combination of plausibility, romantic and moralizing tales, and moderate idealism, the *Histoire des Sévarambes* remained well known for many years; it was an influence on Swift. The story is of a sea-captain, Siden, who discovers in the Austral Land a sun-worshipping Utopian nation, founded by a Persian religious leader called Sévarias.[15] The early history of religious strife there, Sévarias' experiences as a Parsee in his native country, the views of his Venetian tutor Giovanni, the prayers and religious ritual of Sévarambe (the name of the country as well as its inhabitants), and the speech by a philosopher called Scromenas, all contribute to the description of religion. But there are other centres of interest in the book, especially in

[14] Von der Mühll, *Denis Veiras*, pp. 5–27.
[15] An anagram of another spelling, Vairasse, of the author's name; compare Siden, from Denis. On the question of orthography, see Von der Mühll, p. 9.

the political and social domains. At a time when projects of colonization were topical, Veiras' ideas are probably to be seen as advanced rather than Utopian.[16] The political context is important because Veiras writes of religion as a human phenomen. Politico-religious subjects such as tolerance, theocracy and the social value of religion are very prominent.

The distinctive feature of the Sévarambe religion is that it combines belief in God with worship of the sun, and of the two elements the latter is dominant. Veiras used Garcilaso's account of the Incas as a source, but according to the imaginary history of Sévarambe its sun-worship derives partly from the early religion there, which existed before Sévarias' arrival in the early fifteenth century, and partly from Persia.[17] Sévarias had originally been a high priest of the minority Parsee religion, tolerated but persecuted by the Muslim rulers of Persia. He decides to take some of his people in search of the Austral Land because he hears from a sailor about its religion.

Once there, Sévarias is responsible for certain religious reforms, such as the inclusion of theism in the Austral form of worship; this is because his tutor Giovanni, an eclectic Christian, proves to him that the sun cannot be the supreme deity. The proof is achieved by natural reasoning, after arguments from Scripture have failed. Giovanni argues that the sun is only one of a number of stars, and that 'cette multiplicité de soleils dans le monde et leur égalité sont choses incompatibles avec la Divinité suprême, qui doit être une, et qui ne souffre point d'égal' (1734 edition, II, p. 89).[18] Sévarias thenceforward believes that the sun is 'du moins un Dieu subordiné, ou l'un des grands ministres de Dieu dans la nature' (p. 90), using the vocabulary of kingship which is habitual in Veiras. A prayer to the Great God reveals another source of the Sévarambe belief in God, a rudimentary piece of natural theology: 'Toutes choses ici-bas nous parlent journellement de vous (...) ces astres innombrables (...) nous témoignent assez par leur mouvement juste et réglé que c'est votre main toute-puissante qui les guide et les soutient' (pp. 187–189). The reference to the movements of the stars relates this closely to Giovanni's argument.

Besides the belief in God, the only other important belief in Sévarias' religion is the doctrine of the soul. The official doctrine is that it is immortal, and that there are rewards and punishments after death (p. 94), though some

[16]   See Von der Mühll, p. 15, on John Locke and Carolina, pp. 33ff. on Colbert and French colonialism.

[17]   Atkinson, *Extraordinary Voyage before 1700*, pp. 108–109, Von der Mühll, pp. 188–192. The particular sources were Garcilaso de la Vega 'el Inca' 's *Commentarios reales de los Incas* translated by Jean Baudouin (*Commentaire royal, ou l'histoire des Yncas*, 1633) and no doubt *Les six voyages de J.-B. Tavernier* (1676). Von der Mühll shows that the more general influences were Copernican astronomy and the philosophy of Giordano Bruno (pp. 191–192).

[18]   Quotations are from the two-volume edition, Amsterdam (Desbordes), 1734, which replaces the complicated divisions of the first edition by an arrangement in two parts. There is no modern edition. Lachèvre, *Successeurs de Cyrano*, reprints the history of the impostor Stroukaras or Omigas and the speech of Scromenas.

Sévarambe philosophers hold more esoteric views. Veiras devotes much less space to dogma than to worship and ritual. Indeed, even dogma is presented in the context of worship, through the symbolism found in Sévarambe temples. God is shown by a black curtain, denoting incomprehensibility, and the sun by a luminous globe. A trinity is formed by the addition of a statue of a many-breasted woman, presumably a version of the Roman Rumina,[19] giving suck to her children (I, p. 83; II, p. 93); she represents the motherland. Captain Siden learns the meaning of these symbols from the Sévarambes, who tell him of the three indispensable religious duties – veneration for God, gratitude to the sun, and love of the native land (II, p. 93). The common factor is the sense of obligation to beings responsible for our existence, found also in Foigny's version of Austral religion, and a commonplace of natural religion.

The ceremonies in which these feelings are expressed are described with considerable care. The ceremony in honour of God takes place only once every seven years, encouraging the sense of awe and mystery appropriate to the supreme and unknowable deity (II, pp. 92, 180). The sun is worshipped more frequently, especially on its return after winter (II, p. 195). There are also services consecrating children to the sun when they reach the age of seven, communal marriage festivals, a holiday in memory of Sévarias and a harvest festival. A notable episode of a similar sort is the solemn occasion on which Sévarias is designated 'lieutenant du soleil'. For the Sévarambes, then, religion is very much a matter of 'un culte extérieur'. An explanation for this emerges from one of the ceremonial prayers, the 'Oraison du Grand Dieu'. It emphasizes the unintelligibility of God, affirming that God can only be known through his works. He has given the sun to mankind as a 'Dieu visible et glorieux' (II, pp. 179–180). The idea is that religion should consist in worship and that the sun is a more suitable object of worship than the unknowable God. Foigny, for whom religion is a more private affair, had preferred meditation.

A separate section of the *Histoire des Sévarambes* is devoted to cosmological speculation: the speech of the philosopher Scromenas. He believes, like the common people, that the universe is infinite and eternal, but also has a rather obscure general theory of the interaction in the universe between spirit and matter. Physical change is due to the 'vertu formatrice' of spirit. Whether the individual soul survives the death of the body remains unclear. Scromenas says 'que dans la dissolution des corps il n'y avait que leur forme qui pérît pour en prendre une nouvelle, sans qu'il se perdît rien de leur matière, que l'esprit qui l'abandonnait ne périssait point non plus, mais qu'il allait opérer dans d'autres sujets' (II, pp. 182–183). At all events, Scromenas' ideas tend strongly to animism. His theme is the conjunction of spirit and

[19] Atkinson, *Extraordinary Voyage before 1700*, p. 108, mentions a Tartar idol of the same kind, reported in Pierre Bergeron's *Relation des voyages en Tartarie* (1634).

matter, not the distinction between them, an attitude which must be due to Brunonian influence.[20] In a later passage, facing the problem of evil in a defence against atheism, he refers directly to God and providence, without explicitly identifying God and spirit.

There is yet another form of belief in tolerant Sévarambe: the heterodox Christianity of the Giovannites, a sect founded by Sévarias' Venetian tutor. Veiras based them on a sect recently discovered in Persia, the Mandaeans or Christians of St John.[21] The Giovannites have an Arian theology. For them, Christ was divine not in nature, but 'par assomption ou association à la Divinité'. He had been originally an angel, and was adopted by God as a son. In their views about the Eucharist the Giovannites, we are told, resemble the Calvinists. They treat Communion as a ceremony held in memory of the Crucifixion. But they celebrate Mass as the Catholics do, and believe in purgatory, the value of works, and the intercession of the saints. They honour the Pope, but deny that all Christians are obliged to obey him, an attitude which might be Gallican or eirenic. It was Giovanni who converted Sévarias to theism, and as theists the Giovannites participate with the other inhabitants of Sévarambe in the worship of God (II, pp. 96–98).

As with these somewhat idiosyncratic Christians, so too the Catholic Captain Siden and his men are met with tolerance. The Sévarambe principle is 'de n'inquiéter personne pour ses opinions particulières, pourvu qu'il obéisse extérieurement aux lois, et se conforme à la coutume du pays, dans les choses qui regardent le bien de la société' (II, pp. 84–85); this recalls the policy which we have met in Saint-Evremond.[22] Anyone living in Sévarambe is expected to observe all the ceremonies, but in them only the most universal religious beliefs are embodied. Scromenas' speech, the content of which is not officially approved doctrine but which he is free to pronounce in public, includes the statement that in a well-ordered society everyone should live in natural liberty. For him, intolerance is reckless zealotry which violates all the laws of justice and humanity (II, pp. 190–191). Doctrinal differences have often caused wars and massacres, attempts to convert should be made only in reasoned argument, otherwise any conversion will be false. Scromenas' subsequent remarks are strongly Protestant in tone, although they refer ostensibly to the situation in Sévarambe: 'qu'on pouvait par la force de la raison vaincre les préjugés de l'éducation, et descendre de certaines religions superstitieuses à d'autres plus épurées, mais qu'il était impossible de monter,

---

[20] Von der Mühll, pp. 224–225. Spink, *French Free-Thought*, p. 248 and n.1, suggests that Scromenas might represent the distorted version of Spinoza found in Jean-Baptiste Stouppe's *La religion des Hollandais*, 1673.

[21] See Von der Mühll, pp. 218–219; the sect was apparently Gnostic rather than Christian. Von der Mühll considers (p. 217) that, through the Giovannites, Veiras was attacking irrational elements in Christian theology. This may be so, especially as regards the Trinity, but the eclecticism of the Giovannities may also have ecumenical implications.

[22] See Chapter 4, on the *Considération sur la religion*, from Saint-Evremond's Holland period.

et d'embrasser sincèrement des croyances contraires à la raison et au témoignage des sens' (II, p. 192). These considerations have some success with Siden's men, who embrace the Sévarambe religion. Siden himself remains staunchly Catholic, but in this role his remarks seem insincere, more like those of Jacques Massé in Tyssot de Patot than Foigny's Sadeur.[23]

The clear implication of Scromenas' arguments is that religious opinion is a matter of indifference, since is cannot be socially harmful if the outward forms of religion, the 'cérémonies', are observed. Social values thus take precedence over religious, which is typical of Veiras. In his ideal state, the viceroy has both political and religious authority, and priests are eligible for secular office. Thus, it appears, they will no longer wish to advance themselves by fomenting destructive fanaticism. Veiras is probably referring covertly to the French clergy in the years before 1685. The viceroy's aim is that of 'tous les sages politiques' (II, p. 84), to preserve civil peace.[24] The fundamental reason why the Sévarambe religion is so markedly ritualistic, then, is that in this way the risk of doctrinal dispute will be avoided. Foigny's Suains argues similarly about excluding debate about God from religion.

The dangers of religion, for those who might be unaware of them, are illustrated in the history of Sévarambe before the arrival of Sévarias. The country had then been under the rule of the wicked impostor Stroukaras (also called Omigas).[25] He had corrupted the original religion of the sun and driven away the Prestarambes, who had remained faithful to it. With their assistance, Sévarias conquers the Stroukarambes. Stroukaras, who is portrayed without nuances as a villain, had resorted to trickery in order to prove that he was of divine descent. He had blamed his opponents for a drought and then had them burnt to death (II, pp. 110–119). He is eventually divinized. His priests seduce women under the pretence that the god is visiting them, and deal with enemies by having them sacrificed (II, pp. 122–126). A successor to Stroukaras finds out how to walk through fire; when another man finds out also, the priests have to outwit him by faking a miracle (II, p. 131–139). A piece of romantic fiction included at this point, the story of Dionistar and Ahinomé, tells how two lovers have to flee to the mountains because Ahinomé is the object of the lustful desire of a Stroukarambe priest. The lovers finally commit suicide in full view of watching crowds, Dionistar having made a speech against the Stroukarambe religion in the name of nature and right reason (II, pp. 165–169).

[23] For instance, after explaining Sévarambe views about the worship of God, Siden comments 'C'est ainsi qui raisonnent ces pauvres aveugles qui préfèrent les faibles lueurs de leur esprit ténébreux aux lumières éclatantes de la révélation et au témoignage de la Sainte Eglise de Dieu' (II, p. 94).

[24] See Von der Mühll, ppl 118 ff., on Veiras' political ideas and the influences they reveal.

[25] In view of Veiras' fondness for anagrams, there may be something in the idea that Omi- and Strouk- are based on the names Moïse and Christ. Another impostor, Sug-Nimas, recalls Simon Magus.

Stroukaras is a fine example of a contemporary stereotype, the religious impostor-cum-legislator. Sévarias exposes all the deceptions of his religion. Nonetheless, Sévarias too does not wholly eschew deceit while establishing his rule. He claims to be acting on the orders of the sun (I, pp. 197–199), but is plainly lying, and his artifice in praying to the sun, to ask if he should be ruler, attracts a favourable comment from Siden (I, p. 217). The effect is reminiscent of Jean de Silhon's apparent approval of the 'Machiavellian' idea that Christ employed imposture.[26] What differentiates the religion of Sévarias from that of Stroukaras is not that one is true, in rationalist terms, and the other false, but that one is a means to social cohesion and happiness, the other oppressive and vicious. In both cases, religion is seen in an exclusively human perspective. As Von der Mühll comments: 'Sévarias se sert de la religion pour le bien public, (...) alors que Stroukaras n'exploite le besoin de croire qu'à son profit personnel et pour celui de ses disciples'.[27]

The philosopher Scromenas sees religion in terms of stages in human development. He asserts boldly that men originally had no more religion than animals. Religion began with 'les méditations de quelques personnages contemplatifs, qui par la considération de l'ordre de la providence s'étaient peu à peu élevés à la pensée d'un être suprême et indépendant'. This means that Veiras does not share the ordinary view that natural religion is innate and based on reason. According to Scromenas, the first religious impulse was reverence and gratitude towards the sun. Later worship became more elaborate, and was corrupted by amibtious and greedy priests; later still, came impious doctrines designed to 'captiver les esprits' (a phrase typical of Catholic fideism). Scromenas denounces them in the name of reason. He also criticizes the Islamic religion, for being sensual and tyrannical, and the Greek myths, for disfiguring men's ideas about the true God (II, pp. 101–102).

In other passages, it is the Christian supernatural which seems to be the object of criticism. The Sévarambes say that Christian miracles must have been unusual but natural phenomena. They make a comparison with the extraordinary apparition in the sky over Sévarambe of three ships; this seeming miracle was due to a trick of light. In the Stroukaras episode, some incidents might be innuendoes directed against the Bible. Stroukaras claims that he is the son of his god, the sun; he suborns men into saying that they are infirm, and then cures them; he talks with the sun at the top of a mountain (II, pp. 110–111). His successor Sug-nimas dries up fig-trees, like Christ (II, p. 129), and competes to do greater miracles than others, like Moses and the magicians of Pharaoh; he strikes water from what seems to be dry land (II, p. 140–141). The parallels are so many and so close that Veiras must have meant to imply that the Biblical miracles were not supernatural. Yet Sévarias respects Moses and Christ as founders of religions and

---

[26] See Chapter 2, p. 28.
[27] Von der Mühll, p. 203.

believers in the true God, he also says that Christian morality is admirable and seems to contain some element of the divine. It would seem that the insinuation that Christian miracles are done by human agency need not mean, in Veiras' opinion, that Christianity is any the worse; Sévarias uses similar methods in establishing this religion. The association of biblical miracles by innuendo with the wicked impostor Stroukaras, however, has more hostile overtones.[28]

Like Foigny's Australians, the Sévarambes reject the Christian concept of revelation. With them, the impact of their criticism is not diminished by anything corresponding to Foigny's reflections on the depressing effect of life without faith. Sévarambe religion derives rather from 'la philosophie et du raisonnement, que de la révélation et de la foi' (II, p. 88), and they mock at any doctrines which are contrary to reason. The 'mysteries', the fideist's dogmas which transcend reason, are in their eyes ridiculous; Veiras prudently gives no examples (II, pp. 99–100). Possibly the Giovannite interpretation of the Trinity, which is rationalist – Christ is divine by association with God, the Holy Ghost is the agreement between God and the Son (II, pp. 98–97) – indicates how doctrines might have to be modified in order to suit the Sévarambes. Veiras may have been imitating the anti-trinitarianism of the Socinians. A passage in the Stroukaras episode, by contrast, may be a Reformed criticism of a Catholic doctrine, that of the Real Presence; the Stroukarambe belief that the divine Stroukaras can be present in different places simultaneously (when giving oracles) is shown to be absurd (II, p. 127).

These criticism, more or less veiled, of miracles, the priesthood and revelation, parallel the negative elements in the typical deist work. On the positive side, the theism of the Sévarambes obviously resembles the basic belief of the deist, but Veiras' main intention seems to have been to design ritual observances into which religious feeling may be channelled without risk to society. The worship of the supreme unknowable God plays a small part in comparison with the worship of the sun, and does not seem to be the foundation for the criticisms; they derive from the idea that religion should benefit the state and its inhabitants. Some, too, must come from Veiras' Protestant loyalties. However, his book was published in France, and also contains ostensibly Catholic elements and pleas for tolerance. For these reasons it seems likely that the theocratic leader Sévarias was meant as a model to be imitated by a Catholic king. In the reign of 'le Roi-Soleil' it cannot be mere concidence that Veiras should have devised a religion of

---

[28] Von der Mühll seems to want to defend Veiras against the accusation that he attacks Moses (p. 204). He quotes (p. 212) Plutarch approving of religious imposture for political purposes and Gabriel Naudé's favourable judgement of Moses. However, the implications of Veiras' treatment of religion do seem damaging to belief in the Old Testament, although it is possible that Veiras did not mean them to be so.

sun-worship on the basis that men of all beliefs can join in observing its rites. The resemblance to Campanella's *Civitas solis* is suggestive.[29]

THE TWO UTOPIAS COMPARED

Foigny and Veiras wrote books so similar that the comparison is inevitable, but there are considerable divergences as regards their main themes and intellectual background. Foigny's sources in travel literature are known from the studies by Chinard and Atkinson; apart from these, it is plain that the relevant traditions are those of fideism and natural religion. The conversations between the Australian, Suains, and Sadeur are a sort of meditation in dialogue on the differences between natural and revealed religion. The Australian's most powerful argument is that the Christian revelation is not simple and unique, but controverted, since the European churches are divided about it. In the hesitant response made by Sadeur we can perceive the effect on a religious man of these dissensions. Foigny had moved from a Franciscan monastery to Calvinist Geneva, and was to move back again; unless sexuality was the overriding factor, we may presume that he sought religious assurance. If the rational deism of the Australians provided a certain proof of the afterlife, or if Christian faith were not open to the charge of sectarianism, perhaps either form of religion might have been satisfactory.

In Veiras, the conflict between reason and faith is much less important. It is necessarily implied in the confrontation between the Europeans and the Sévarambes, but Veiras does not dwell on it. Although Siden introduces the Sévarambe religion as 'la plus conforme à la raison humaine' (I, p. 88), he himself is only a luke-warm fideist, and reason in Sévarambe is practical, almost utilitarian; it is not the basis of a rational deistic theology, such as we find in Foigny and the other inventors of Utopian deism, Gilbert and Tyssot. Even the belief in God, according to Scromenas, is due to the reflection of contemplatives, and not natural to the generality of mankind. Veiras should be placed in a different tradition from Foigny, that of the 'politiques' of the Wars of Religion, Campanella, and perhaps the *libertins* influenced by Montaigne.[30] Of later deistic writers, he is closest to Montesquieu. Unlike Foigny, who appears to have let his imagination play with the data furnished by a variety of travel-books, Veiras largely confined himself to a single model, the religion of the Incas of Peru, as reported by Garcilaso de la Vega 'el Inca'.[31]

[29] See F.A. Yates, *Giordano Bruno and the Hermetic Tradition*, Ch. XX; on the Sun-King, Von der Mühll, pp. 240–241.
[30] Von der Mühll, *passim*, especially p. 239. He notes the importance of obvious sources such as the Old Testament and Plato.
[31] Atkinson, *Extraordinary Voyage before 1700*, p. 49; Von der Mühll, p. 138.

Both writers are commonly, but not invariably, said to have put forward deism in their books, although contemporary opinions do not seem to support this in so many words.[32] In devising the religious institutions of Sévarambe, Veiras created a system in which the political and social problems caused by religion might be overcome. In the genesis of the *Histoire des Sévarambes* the conflict between Catholic and Protestant churches seems to have been as important as with Foigny. The passages concerning tolerence, such as the remarks about enforced conversion made not only by Scromenas but also by Siden, show that the Huguenot question often underlay the discussion. Sévarambe religious organization allows dissenting minorities, the Giovannites and Catholics like Siden, to remain in a country where the head of state holds both the secular and the religious power. Both writers, then, are concerned with the divisions within Christianity, and resort to Utopia for possible answers. While Veiras sees the problem in political terms, the preservation of civil peace being the first aim of 'les sages politiques', for Foigny it is personal. Sadeur is not a legislator like Sévarias, but his complementary counterpart, the private individual or subject, faced with choosing between two societies and their religions, which he himself cannot influence. This is the situation in which many protagonists of deist works find themselves, and it tends to evoke expressions of religious individualism. Hence Foigny is the more significant of the two writers as a precursor of deism, while he and Veiras together gave considerable impetus to the typically deistic *genre* of the Utopian travel-story.

[32]   For contemporary reactions, see Von der Mühll, pp. 22, 251–253, 255 ff.; Atkinson, ibid., p. 88 and n. 6, quoting Daniel Georg Morhof, on Veiras apparently being one of the tribe of atheists or naturalists ('Pertinere et ad hanc Atheorum et Naturalistarum tribum videtur'; *Polyhistor*, 1714 edition, Ch. VIII); Bayle, article 'Sadeur'. Prosper Marchand, in the article 'Allais' of his *Dictionnaire historique*, 1758–1759, seems to have been the first to say that Veiras was a deist. In modern scholarship this view seems to be due above all to Lanson, *Origines de l'esprit philosophique*, pp. 67, 79. See n. 13 above, and also Busson, *La religion des classiques (1660–1685)* (Paris, 1948), p. 395; Atkinson, ibid., pp. 131, 138; Von der Mühll, pp. 194, 219; Tocanne, *L'Idée de nature en France*, p. 274.

CHAPTER 6

DEFINITIONS AND ACCUSATIONS, 1670–1700:
'DEISM' AS A TERM OF OPPROBRIUM

The novels of Foigny and Veiras, and some of Saint-Evremond's writings, already show which general factors are of significance for the origins of French deism: the idea of natural religion, distinct from revelation; knowledge of foreign countries and their religions, gained from experience or books of travel; and the divisions between the Christian churches. Only as regards Foigny are all three factors operative. Veiras does not employ a concept of natural religion, still less does Saint-Evremond. All three have personal knowledge of the antagonism between Protestantism, in Switzerland, Holland or England, and Catholicism in France. Foigny and Veiras depend on travel books for much of the background detail in their works. However, in none of the three do we find deism pure and simple, since sooner or later they fall back on the religion of the nation-state, as exemplified by Genevan Calvinism, French Catholicism, Anglicanism or, in fiction, the religion of Sévarambe.

Natural religion, travel and religious conflict
The concept of natural religion and the influences of travel literature and religious dissension were all reinforced during the last thirty years of the century; indeed, they reinforce each other, as can be seen from the interplay of factors in Foigny. Knowledge of foreign societies seems to have determined the forms and setting of deistic literature rather than its content. Information came in abundance; travel books by traders, missionaries or explorers were generally popular. The most famous are probably those by Rycaut on Turkey, Tavernier and Chardin on Persia and Bernier on India – some of the sources of Montesquieu's *Lettres persanes.* But there were very many others, from virtually all parts of the world except the interior of Africa and the 'Austral Land'.[1] The 'relations' of the missions to China and the Far East have a special place in the literature of travel because of the 'querelle des rites chinois', the controversy occasioned by the manner

---

[1]   Atkinson, *Extraordinary Voyage before 1700*; Chinard, *Rêve exotique*; Pierre Martino, *L'Orient dans la littérature française au XVII e et au XVIII e siècle* (Paris, 1906); Guy Turbet-Delof, *L'Afrique barbaresque dans la littérature française aux XVI e et XVII e siècles* (Lille, 1973). More generally, Hazard, *Crise,* Pt. 1, Ch. 1.

in which the Jesuits presented Christianity to the Chinese and made concessions to Chinese religious observance.[2] After 1700 the most interesting case is Lahontan's memoirs of Canada, which through various chances became one of the earliest expressions of deism.

The second influence, that of religious conflict, works in more than one way; the tendency it produces towards undenominational Christianity is prominent before 1685. The eirenic phase in Saint-Evremond is the leading example hitherto. Outside France, Spinoza, who himself influenced Saint-Evremond, defined a seven-point universal faith intended to eliminate sectarian dissension.[3] It can be taken as being Christian theism, although Spinoza probably meant it to be universal in the full sense. Saint-Evremond's other source, Isaac d'Huisseau's *Réunion du Christianisme* (1669), is much less radical. D'Huisseau's idea is to distinguish between essential and unessential Christian doctrines,[4] but he has to face the objection that to list the points on which all Christians can agree will lead to indifference and even irreligion. Against this interpretation, he protests: 'Quoi donc, serait-ce être sans religion, que d'être pleinement persuadé qu'il y a un Dieu, qui a créé le Ciel et la terre, qui a formé le genre humain, qui punit les méchants, et chérit les gens de bien? Est-ce être sans religion que de croire fermement que nous n'avons autre moyen de sortir de la misère où le péché nous a jetés, sinon en embrassant les promesses que Dieu nous fait en son Fils Jésus-Christ?'.[5] A Jansenist would have given an affirmative answer to the first question, since it is an excellent definition of natural religion, but there can be no doubt of the sincerity of d'Huisseau's Christian faith. An analogous case is Leibniz's universalist version of the Lord's Prayer, which Antoine Arnauld refused to accept because it did not mention Jesus Christ.[6]

After the Revocation of the Edict of Nantes in 1685, eirenism became pointless. When it reappears in deistic writings, the dissensions to be settled occur in oriental fictions such as the *Lettres persanes*.[7] However, the spirit of the 'république des lettres' continued, on the whole, to be cosmopolitan; Bayle's works, after his furious attack on intolerance in *Ce que c'est que la France toute catholique* (1686), either directly propagate tolerance, or imply

[2] Virgile Pinot, *La Chine et la formation de l'esprit philosophique en France (1649–1740)* (Paris, 1932); Basil Guy, *The French Image of China before and after Voltaire*, SVEC 21 (1963).

[3] *Tractatus theologico-politicus*, Ch. XIV. Interpreted as 'un déisme neuf' by Paul Vernière, *Spinoza et la pensée française avant la Révolution*, 2 vols. (Paris, 1954), Vol. I, p. 212, a remark which makes the assumption that some other kinds of deism existed previously; cf. Albert Monod, *De Pascal à Chateaubriand: les défenseurs français de Christianisme de 1670 à 1802* (Paris, 1916), p. 30: 'Le déisme est conteau dans le Traité théologico-politique'.

[4] *Réunion du Christianisme*, p. 154.

[5] Ibid., pp. 184–185.

[6] Jean Baruzi, *Leibniz et l'organisation religieuse de la terre* (Paris, 1907), pp. 86–87. The prayer is quoted in Hazard, *Crise*, Pt. II, Ch. V.

[7] Lettre 46; see Chapter 13. A later example, no doubt in part an imitation of Montesquieu, is the chapter *Le Souper* in Voltaire's *Zadig*.

it, by adopting an attitude of philosophical detachment from dogmatism.[8] The journalists and scholars of the time communicate privately, regardless of differences of religion; they write for a European and Christian public, not nationalist and sectarian, even though sectarian polemics are carried on in such works as Bossuet's *Histoire des variations* (1668) and Jurieu's *Lettres pastorales* in reply.[9]

The most important of the causative factors in the advent of deism is the refinement of the notion of the part played by reason in religion. This came about in two interconnected ways: the spread of Cartesianism and the continued development of rational apologetics. The example of Malebranche, both as religious philosopher and as apologist, seems to have been paramount.[10] Descartes' approach and ideas become an intrinsic part of a comprehensive Christian system of thought, instead of being a separate philosophical adjunct or preliminary to faith. In the apologias, although reason is ostensibly at the service of revealed truth, reason has pride of place, the universal rational truths being 'proved' first, and with greater confidence, than the particularities of the Christian revelation. The early deists, after 1700, accept the basic rational truths, but reject the elaborate apparatus of proofs constructed in order to bring the Bible and Church traditions into harmony with reason. Catholic faith and the facts of the history of Christ both become liable to critical examination. The development of reason in religion means that the idea of natural religion develops simultaneously, one of the tenets of rationalism being that reason is 'la lumière naturelle'.

For some years, however, the threat presented by Cartesian philosophy to the Church, presciently described in 1679 by Bossuet, did not materialize.[11] Like the eirenic writers, rationalist Christians approach very near to deism but do not reach it. At the end of the century, the resemblance between rational Christianity and the constructive side of deism is so great that Bernard Tocanne, in a recent study, has found it necessary to deny that a number of writers, including Fénelon and the two Lamys, Bernard and

[8]   See Jean Delvolvé, *Religion, critique et philosophie positive chez Pierre Bayle* (Paris, 1906), Pt. I, section ii, Chs. 6–7; iii, Ch. 5; etc.; Elisabeth Labrousse, *Pierre Bayle, Hétérodoxie et rigorisme* (The Hague, 1964), Chs. 18, 19.
[9]   See Alfred Rébelliau, *Bossuet historien du protestantisme* (second edition, Paris, 1892). (On Jurieu: pp. 312–314, etc.)
[10]   This is most clearly observable in Gilbert, the 'Militaire philosophe' and the *Examen de la religion;* see chapters 8, 10 and 11, and also Busson, *Religion des classiques*, Ch. XVI.
[11]   In a letter to the Marquis d'Allemans, a follower of Malebranche, Bossuet attacked Malebranche forcefully and gave a warning about rational individualism: 'je vois (...) un grand combat se préparer contre l'Eglise sous le nom de la philosophie cartésienne (...) sous prétexte qu'il ne faut admettre que ce qu'on entend clairement, ce qui, réduit à certaines bornes, est très véritable, chacun se donne la liberté de dire: J'entends ceci, et je n'entends pas cela; et sur ce seul fondement, on approuve et on rejette tout ce qu'on veut' (*Correspondance de Bossuet,* edited by Ch. Urbain and E. Levesque, 15 vols. (Paris, 1909–1925), Vol. III (1910), pp. 372–373).

François, are deists;[12] but despite the common ground, enlightened Christianity is not the same as deism; the deist and the apologist remain opposed.

The same can be seen in the work of a writer who, as a layman, might perhaps be expected to have a less strong attachment to his faith than apologists from the ranks of the Church. Pierre-Sylvain Régis published his *Cours entier de philosophie* in 1690.[13] Its section on metaphysics is natural theology carried out in an elaborately Cartesian manner. Anyone, we are told, can establish the existence of the Perfect Being for himself, by the natural light of reason; he will discover that God is (among other things) one, simple, immutable, eternal, immense and all-powerful.[14] On the soul, Régis defends innate ideas and a form of occasionalism.[15] It is difficult now to see how Christian faith can accompany so firm a system of natural religions; Régis may have felt this himself, for he later wrote a separate work to prove the compatibility of reason and faith.[16] In the *Cours*, he distinguishes the truths of reason, which are necessary, from those which are contingent. The latter are the truths of revelation; based on the authority of God, they are more certain than knowledge from experience or the senses. Consequently, we must believe that Christ is God and man and that he will bring the dead to life, even if we cannot understand these things.[17]

For the transition to deism to be made, the Cartesian theology has to be isolated from the incomprehensible mysteries of faith, and reason turned against them, a process carried out by writers like Gilbert ten or fifteen years later; but in Régis himself the barriers against it still seem firm.

D'Assoucy

At or near the end of the century, then, the conditions for deism appear to be present, yet it remains latent or exceptional. The shape of things to come begins to be discernable from about 1690, with the publication in full of Marana's *Espion turc* in 1692–1694 and the remarks on deism in Bayle's *Dictionnaire* (1697). From about 1670 until the 1690's the paradoxical situation of the 1630s is repeated: deism is much discussed, as we shall see, but its written manifestations are sparse and uncertain. This applies to

---

[12]   Tocanne, *L'Idée de nature en France dans la seconde moitié du XVII e siècle* (Paris, 1978) (cited henceforth as *Idée de nature*), p. 260 (Fénelon), p. 263 (Dom F. Lamy), pp. 263–264 (Bernard Lamy, the Oratorian). Cf. p. 267, on Huet's comparatism, a scholarly attitude which can also be interpreted as tending to deism.

[13]   *Cours entier de philosophie, ou Systéme général selon les principes de M. Descartes.* I quote from the edition in three volumes, Amsterdam, 1691.

[14]   *Métaphysique,* Livre I, Pt. i, Chs. 5–7.

[15]   Ibid., I, ii, 8. The section concerning the soul is revealingly short.

[16]   *L'Usage de la raison et de la foy, ou L'Accord de la raison et de la foy* (Paris, 1704).

[17]   *Réflexions métaphysiques,* following *Métaphysique* I, ii, 9 (pp. 137 ff.).

Marana also. No doubt the censorship is an inhibiting factor.[18] The history was somewhat similar in England; Herbert, regarded now as the first English deist, had not been so regarded when publishing his works in the 1620s and 1630s. True deism appears in clandstine writings of the 1670s and is refuted by various writers including Dryden, in his *Religio laici* (1681), but remains hidden until the publications of Charles Blount and John Toland in the 1690s.[19]

At this time the number of those who took the step from Christianity to deism must have been very small. One such, at least for a time, may have been the musician and writer of 'burlesque', Charles Coypeau d'Assoucy, who in 1676, the year of Foigny's *La terre australe connue,* published a description of deism in his *Pensées dans le Saint-Office de Rome.*[20] In the course of a wandering life, the subject of entertaining books of autobiography, he found himself imprisoned in Rome, apparently for making anticlerical remarks. His reflections there are recorded in the *Pensées,* a short work of piety dedicated to Marie-Thérèse, the devout queen. It concerns the graces he has received from the Divinity and the proofs of the immortality of the soul; there are also arguments for the existence of God. Thus the *Pensées* is a work of natural theology. A long introductory passage describes three types of opponent: sectarians (Protestant or radical), deists, and atheists (very few, according to d'Assoucy; he knew Cyrano de Bergerac). Deists are in error, he says, in refusing to take any cognizance of religion, by which Catholicism must be meant. They practise the observances of established religion only for form's sake. D'Assoucy mentions the imposture theory, but for his deists it is not simple destructive criticism to call religions 'des inventions humaines'; all religions 'ont pour objet la Divinité', and have social value. 'C'est pourquoi ils les approuvent toutes, mais ils n'en suivent pas une, parce que, comme ils sont venus à la connaissance de Dieu par eux-mêmes, ils se font encore eux-mêmes une religion, et lui dressent un culte à leur fantaisie. La plupart vivent moralement bien, ne prient que mentalement, et avec des larmes.'[21]

The most likely hypothesis concerning the deists' identity is that d'Assoucy was referring to his own attitude. He disapproves strongly of the 'sectaires' and atheists, but only very mildly of the 'déistes', whom he portrays with touches of sentimentality: 'Les Sectaires sont obstinés et opiniâtres comme des diables: les Déistes, au contraire, sont simples et traitables comme des colombes, cherchant de toute leur puissance la vérité'.

[18]   See H. -J. Martin, *Livre, pouvoirs et société à Paris au XVII e siécle (1598–1701)*, 2 vols. (Geneva, 1969), Pt. III, sections ii, iii.
[19]   Phillip Harth, *Contexts of Dryden's Thought* (Chicago, 1968), pp. 62–94.
[20]   See Busson, *Charron à Pascal* (many references in index). I quote from Emile Colombey's edition, *Aventures burlesques de Dassoucy* (Paris, 1858), pp. 339 ff.
[21]   Ibid., p. 353.

In them, 'la lumière naturelle est trop puissante pour laisser aucune entrée à la surnaturelle'; they confine themselves to natural religion, then, the two basic truths of which are maintained later in the *Pensées*.[22] The cause of the deists' blindness and ignorance is travel, we are told; it makes them forget what they have been taught.[23] D'Assoucy thus picks out two of the factors generally conducive to deism, but says nothing about religious conflict. The background of his adventures is always Catholic.

It is possible that others with *libertin* tendencies evolved in the manner described by d'Assoucy, but few cases are documented,[24] and d'Assoucy does not regard the attitude he portrays as common. He ends by claiming that 'déistes' are found in all religions, but are 'bien difficiles à connaître, et ne s'entreconnaissent pas eux-mêmes'. Both parts of the comment seem amply justified.[25]

Jurieu's usage

Quite a different picture is gained if we turn to the references to deism made in the course of religious polemic. They are numerous and unfavourable. If we are to believe the majority, deism is a particularly abhorrent form of free-thought, probably stemming in some way from the Socinians or their allies the Arminians, who for both Protestant and Catholic writers were cast in the role of villains. The polemical references usually suggest a religious belief limited to theism, but not d'Assoucy's gentle variety; it is seen as subversive and dangerous, threatening to overthrow Christianity. To read some descriptions one might imagine that Voltaire was already publishing, or that Pierre Viret's warnings in 1564 still needed to be repeated.

In the development of this image the first important figure is Pierre Jurieu, the exiled Huguenot minister, enemy of Bayle and many others, proponent

[22] Ibid., pp. 361 ff., on God, proved musically; pp. 378 ff., on ths soul. D'Assoucy relates, as evidence of the supernatural, the mysterious omens and prophetic dreams in his own experience.

[23] 'Ceux-ci font tout au rebours des autres hommes; car au lieu qu'à force de voyager, de courir la terre et les mers, fréquenter les nations différentes, les autres apprennent quelque chose, ceux-ci au contraire, à force de voyager, oublient si bien ce qu'ils ont appris, que l'aveuglement et l'ignorance est le résultat de leurs voyages' (pp. 352–353).

[24] Busson mentions two outstanding figures of the Court aristocracy (*Religion des classiques*, p. 397): the great Condé, well-known as a free-thinker (Busson suggests, but without documentation, that he had deist opinions); and Anne de Gonzague, Princess Palatine, who confessed to Rancé that she believed in God but not in the mysteries. Both returned to piety, in celebrated 'conversions'. Lanson (*Origines de l'esprit philosophique*, p. 82) makes a similar suggestion, apparently following Prosper Marchand's *Dictionnaire historique* (1758–1759), about the Abbé de Saint-Réal, who had lived in London in the society of Saint-Evremond. Vernière (*Spinoza et la pensée française*, Vol. I, p. 212) quotes a letter from Lambert de Velthuysen in 1671, saying that there are many deists in France, but this seems to be based on Mersenne's *De l'impiété des déistes* of 1624, which Velthuysen had read.

[25] D'Assoucy concludes on deists by saying that Charron and Montaigne might be among their numbers; perhaps he knew of Charron's reputation from his *libertin* friends. He also mentions Aristotle, for no clear reason.

of revolutionary politics and ardent propagandist for the Reformed cause.[26] The story begins, however, with another formidable personality living in Holland, Spinoza. Biblical criticism in the *Tractatus theologico-politicus* (1670), in which he denied the ordinary assumption that Moses was the author of the Pentateuch and interpreted Christianity as obedience to the moral precepts of Christ, aroused a storm of indignant refutations.[27] Among the defenders of Moses was Pierre-Daniel Huet, the scholar and Bishop of Avranches, in the fourth 'Proposition' of his *Demonstratio evangelica* of 1679. He introduced his rebuttal by the accusation that Spinoza sought to destroy the foundations of Christianity, adding that he 'obviously tends to maintain the fatally destructive heresy of the deists, as they are called, which is only too widespread nowadays'.[28] Huet had been in Holland, and must have known of the Socinian scriptural criticism which had been published there in the *Bibliotheca fratrum polonorum* in 1665–1668;[29] he is probably referring to Socinians when he mentions the deist heresy. But he did not make the identification, with the result that deism became assoicated with Spinoza.[30]

Huet thus prepared the way for the misunderstandings to which, deliberately or not, Jurieu added. In the general introduction to the *Demonstratio,* Huet had written of the continuous increase in impiety, but without saying anything of deism. His remarks were picked up by Jurieu in *La politique du clergé de France* (1681), the principal target of which was the conversion policy of the French clergy, and in particular Bossuet's *Exposition de la foi catholique.* Jurieu asserted, implausibly, that works like the *Exposition* could increase a 'party' in the Catholic Church consisting of bad Catholics, and went on: 'Le monde, la Cour et les armées sont pleins de Déistes, des gens qui croyent que toutes les religions sont des inventions de l'esprit humain'. They doubt everything, and (a reference to Spinoza, but probably also to Richard Simon, since Spinoza was not in France) 'ils sont

---

[26]   On him see Elisabeth Labrousse, *Pierre Bayle,* Vol. I, *Du pays de Foix à la cité d'Erasme* (The Hague, 1963), Chs. 6, 8, 9, and her 'Note sur Jurieu', *Revue d'histoire et de philosophie religieuse* 58 (1978), 277–297.

[27]   For the effect in the French-speaking world, see Monod, *De Pascal à Chateaubriand,* Ch. II; Vernière, *Spinoza et la pensée française,* Ch. IV.

[28]   *Demonstratio evangelica,* Propositio IV, C. XIV, i: 'Prodiit vero nuper e tenebris in lucem Tractatus, qui prae se fert, Theologico-Politicus (...) planeque eo inclinat, ut exitialem ac pestiferam et nimis haec aetate contagiosam Deistarum, ut vocant, haeresim tueatur' (p. 140). See Vernière, *Spinoza et la pensée française,* Vol. I, pp. 126 ff.

[29]   Wilbur, *Socinianism.* pp. 569–570. The *Bibiotheca* was edited by Andrew Wiszowaty and includes the works of Fausto Sozzini, but devotes more space to those by Johannes Krell, Jonas Schlichting and Johann Ludwig von Wolzogen.

[30]   Pierre Poiret, in one of the earliest refutations of the Ethics, regarded the *Tractatus* as deistic; Spinoza, he said, went from Judaism to Christianity, then to deism and finally to atheism (Vernière, *Spinoza et la pensée française,* Vol. I, p. 51, on Poiret's *Cogitationes rationales de Deo, anima et malo,* 1685 edition).

armés de méchantes difficultés contre les livres du V. et du N. Testament, pour n'être pas obligés de croire que ces livres soient véritablement des auteurs dont ils portent le nom'.[31]

In this passage, Jurieu avoids saying that his remarks about deists came from Huet's *Demonstratio,* although he refers insultingly to the book immediately afterwards,[32] and matters might have rested there if he had not also launched an attack on what he called a 'tiers parti' in the Catholic Church. His phraseology pointed to the Jansenists. He accused them of being Socinians and doubting the doctrines of the Trinity and the Incarnation.[33] He did not elaborate, but Antoine Arnauld almost at once responded angrily in the second part of his *Apologie pour les Catholiques* (1681). Arnauld devoted one chapter to Jurieu's allegations about deists, Socinians and other *libertins,* and another to the 'horrible calomnie, que le livre de M. de Meaux favorise les Déistes, que doutent de la divinité des livres de l'Ecriture'.[34] Deists were still, therefore, followers of Spinoza. Arnauld's defence of Bossuet is even more involved than Jurieu's accusations had been; he is more interesting when he turns the accusation of Socinianism (which he does not connect with deism) against Jurieu, since he can argue with conviction that Socinianism has similar principles to those of the Reformation.[35]

Predictably, Jurieu renewed his attack, in a particularly bitter fashion, in the *Esprit de M. Arnauld,* in 1684. He reiterated his statement that there were 'un grand nombre de Déistes et de Sociniens' in the Catholic Church, and claimed that the assertion about deism in France made in the *Politique du clergé* (which he pretended not to have written) was supported by Huet's *Demonstratio.*[36] However, Jurieu seems to have forgotten the correct reference. He quotes at length from Huet's introduction, instead of the section on Spinoza. The quotation describes the threat of impiety but does not mention deism, with the result that Jurieu's alleged deists become, in the quotation from Huet, insolent free-thinkers who treat Christianity as an invention, but are not Spinozist critics of Scripture. Confusing the issue still further, Jurieu continues by recalling the thirty-year-old allegation made by

---

[31] *Politique du clergé,* Premier entretien, pp. 73–74 (third edition, 1682).

[32] Ibid., p. 74: 'si quelque pédant fait une rhapsodie de rabbinage et de critique sur les livres du V. et du N. Testament, ou sur quelques textes particuliers, il appelle cela, Démonstration évangélique (...) et la plupart de ces recueils sont plus propes à confirmer ces Déistes dans leur incrédulité qu'à les en faire revenir' (because of the weakness of the apologists' arguments).

[33] Ibid., p. 78: 'quelques sociétés graves, sages, et qui font une grande parade de la pureté de leurs moeurs et de leur attachment pour la foi catholique'.

[34] *Apologie pour les Catholiques,* Pt. II, Chs. 2, 3 (Arnauld, *Oeuvres,* Vol. XIV (1778), pp. 597, 599 ff.).

[35] Ibid., p. 600. Simon also defended Bossuet against the charge of favouring deism (see Paul Auvray, *Richard Simon (1683–1712), étude bio-bibliographique* (Paris, 1974), pp. 75–76).

[36] *L'Esprit de M. Arnauld,* Sixième observation (p. 194).

Jean Filleau, that Jansenism was a deistic conspiracy.[37] Deism now reassumes its ancient meaning, the denial that Christ is divine, as Jurieu bolsters up his unlikely charges with Pascalian passages from Arnauld's *Perpétuité de la foi de l'Eucharistie;* Arnauld had said that the truths of faith are not so clear that the impious may not be deceived. Jurieu's marginal note drives home his meaning: 'Les Jansénistes dans leurs principes ne peuvent être assurés de la Divinité de Notre Seigneur Jésus-Christ', later he maintains that Arnauld accepts Socinian principles in the interpretation of Scripture.[38]

Jurieu's books were widely read, but Arnauld did not deign to reply to his arguments, which are only slightly less incredible than the accusations against Jansenism made by Filleau and Meynier in the 1650s. The allegations about deism had become looser and wilder with every repetition. There had been some justification in Huet's original statement that Spinoza's scriptural criticism helped to spread the deistic heresy, if by 'deists' he meant the Socinians. But apart from the utter confusion over the meaning of deism which Jurieu perpetrated, the most significant point to emerge from the exchange with Arnauld is his inability, in 1684, to name or otherwise identify any French deists. When Arnauld denied his statement about the prevalence of deism in France, Hurieu could not produce any supporting evidence except a muddled reference to Huet and a rehash of Filleau's discredited accusation. If, when challenged, the best that Jurieu could do was to claim that Arnauld, of all people, was a deist, we may conclude that even after 1680 (and consequently after the publications of Foigny, Veiras and d'Assoucy) there was no French deistic writing recognized as such by contemporaries. At this time the accusation of deism is simply a weapon of polemic, its effectiveness being due to fears about the radical religious ideas which circulated in Holland.[39]

Abbadie and Le Clerc

A sober contrast to Jurieu, in the same year as the *Esprit de M. Arnauld,* is provided by a description of deism in the *Traité de la vérité de la religion chrétienne,* the best French Protestant apologia of its period, by Jacques

---

[37] See Chapter 3. Jurieu's words were: 'Nous ne voudrions pas pronouncer d'une manière aussi positive qu'ont fait Filleau et le Jésuite Meynier, que "ceux qu'on appelle Jansénisties sont de véritables Déistes, ennemis des mystè res de la Religion Chrétienne". Mais il est vrai qu'il leur est échappé de dire des choses contre la Divinité de Jésus-Christ, qui donnent lieu de soupçonner qu'ils cachent dans le coeur de terribles monstres' (*Esprit de M. Arnauld,* p. 196).

[38] Ibid., pp. 199–200, 209. Jurieu's allegations are quoted at length in Bayle's article 'Socin', Note M, in the *Dictionnaire historique et critique.*

[39] Besides Spinoza, Le Clerc and the Socinians, another source of such ideas was the Jewish-Christian Uriel Acosta or da Costa, who died in 1647 in Holland and whose biography, relating his religious doubts and deistic opinions, was published in 1687 by Philipp van Limborch, under the title *Exemplar humanae vitae,* in his *De veritate religionis Christianae: Amica collatio cum erudito Judaeo.* See Lanson, *Orignes de l'esprit philosophique,* pp. 217–218.

Abbadie.[40] The second section of Part I 'établit la vérité et la nécessité de la religion contre ceux qu'on nomme Déistes'.[41] Like Huet before him, Abbadie is vague about who exactly are called deists, and it seems probable that the word is his own term for different false opinions, all including some kind of belief in God. There are four of them: those who 'se font une idée bizarre de la divinité', by whom Abbadie seems to mean Stoic pantheists and believers in the world-soul; those who think that God takes no cognizance of earthly doings, the long-familar category of the Epicureans; those who imagine that God is pleased by superstition and 'égarements', apparently pagans who (like the Greeks) have myths in which gods behave immorally; and finally the proponents of natural religion, whom Abbadie defines as 'ceux qui reconnaissent que Dieu a donné aux hommes une religion (...) qui en réduisent tous les principes aux sentiments naturels de l'homme, et qui prennent tout le reste pour fiction'.

Abbadie's definition was authoritative enough to be quoted in full in the principles in rebuttal of the four types of deism (or, better, theism).[42] God is a personal deity, he argues; feelings of gratitude and worship should be expressed in organized worship (here the second category of deists seems to resemble Foigny's Australians, who deny that God takes notice of worship). Against the superstitious pagans, Abbadie contends that natural religion is superior,[43] but he avoids the trap of implying that it is sufficient — the view of the fourth category — by a restatement of Calvin's argument, that natural religion becomes corrupt in practice, and has to be protected and restored by the Christian revelation.

Abbadie's definition was authoritative enough to be quoted in full in the Abbé Mallet's article 'Déistes' in the Encyclopédie of Diderot and d'Alembert. The fact that the first three kinds of deist are types taken from classical antiquity shows, like Bayle's Dictionnaire, that their attitudes were

---

[40]   See Monod, De Pascal à Chateaubriand, Ch. IV. The first edition of the Traité, from which I quote, was published in Rotterdam and London, 1684. A fuller edition appeared in 1688. It continued to be published down into the nineteenth century.

[41]   Title of section II (Vol. I, p. 152); it is not clear whether the 'on' means Abbadie himself.

[42]   The chapters developing the four anti-deistic principles do not correspond exactly to the four deist catogories, which renders Abbadie's definitions a little hazy. In Chapter III, the 'idées bizarres' seem to be materialistic conceptions of God and of the soul of the world ('une grande âme qui anime le monde', p. 161). Chapter II, on the necessity and uniqueness of God, is presumably against such ideas. The argument against the second category is found mainly in Chapters III and IV, and against the third, apparently, in Chapter VII (especially pp. 192–194, on polytheism). This also contains the Calvinistic argument on the need for a revelation.

[43]   For Abbadie's description of natural religion, see section II, Ch. V, 'Où l'on établit la vérité de la religion naturelle', and Ch. VI, 'Qu'il y a en nous des principes d'une religion véritablement naturelle', especially p. 178: 'la religion naturelle, qui consiste dans la connaissance que la nature nous donne de Dieu, dans le sentiment des obligations que nous lui avons, dans ces principes d'équité et de justice, que nous appelons communément loi naturelle, et en ce que nous ne saurions violer quelqu'un de ces principes, sans sentir naître les remords dans notre coeur, à moins qu'un obstacle étranger ne nous en empêche'.

still significant, presumably because of the prevalence of a classical education. The fourth category of deist, however, is certainly modern. Abbadie's treatment of them equates deism with natural religion more firmly than d'Assoucy had done. It thus added another to the welter of definitions and implications thrown out during the dispute between Jurieu and Arnauld, but Abbadie was not an alarmist and the equation of deism with natural religion was more lastingly influential than any other definition.

From Jean Le Clerc, the Biblical scholar and journalist, came an Arminian contribution to the history of the idea of deism. He was another Huguenot refugee, but from Calvinist intolerance rather than Catholic.[44] He had turned to the Arminians, under the patronage of their leader Philipp van Limborch, in 1683. The *Sentiments de quelques théologiens de Hollande,* of 1685, was the last of several early works showing him to be radical, on the fringe of free-thought.[45] The book is however an attempt to protect the Bible against Spinozist criticism. Its more impressive Catholic competitor in this respect was Richard Simon's *Histoire critique de Vieux Testament* (which had so scandalized Bossuet on its appearance in 1678 that he had it suppressed immediately).[46] Le Clerc rejected Simon's Catholic argument, that the assistance of Church tradition was required for the correct understanding of Scripture; he put forward his own defence against Spinoza in the form of opinions allegedly held by a friend, 'M. N.', who had written an 'écrit sur l'inspiration'. According to this, the text of the Bible was not literally due to divine inspiration; it was inspired only as regards the sense in the prophetic books, and in the historical books only as far as was necessary to convey the basic Christian truths.[47]

This principle allows Le Clerc to concede that there are contradictions in minor matters, thus depriving Spinoza's objections of their force. But as his argument develops it turns into a reinterpretation of Christianity. The writers of the historical books, he says, had a moral purpose, to teach the doctrine of a providence which rewards the 'gens de bien' and punishes the wicked; they supported this example of piety and vertue.[48] Scripture was

---

[44]   See Annie Barnes, *Jean Le Clerc et la république des lettres* (Paris, 1938), pp. 90 ff. The Arminians were notably particularly for their rejection of the Calvinist doctrine of Original Sin. They were the only sect to permit the Socinians to worship with them when the Socinians were expelled from Poland in 1658–1660.

[45]   Especially his *Liberii de Sancto-Amore Epistolae theologicae,* which attacks 'Scholastic' errors (Saumur, 1681), and a work written in collaboration with Charles Le Cène, *Entretiens sur diverses matières de théologie* (Amsterdam, 1685). See Barnes, ibid., pp. 59, 102–103.

[46]   The incident, which occurred in Easter Week, has often been recounted; see for instance Jean Steinmann, *Richard Simon et les origines de l'exégèse biblique* (Paris, 1960), Pt. II, Ch. 7. Simon's work was published in Holland in 1679.

[47]   *Sentiments de quelques théologiens de Hollands sur l'Histoire critique de Vieux Testament, composée par le P. Richard Simon, de l'Oratoire* (Amsterdam, 1685). The 'écrit de M. N.' is in Lettres XI and XII (pp. 219–287).

[48]   Ibid., p. 231.

preserved by Providence so that it should lead us to salvation, which we can obtain if we observe the commandments of Christ, since Christ alone was constantly inspired by God.[49] 'M. N.''s conclusion is that the adoption of his views would end sectarian dispute and answer the *libertins*.[50]

Simon's reaction was less favourable, which was not surprising, for Le Clerc had suggested that the *Histoire critique du Vieux Testament* could as well have been written by a protestant, a Christianised Jew or a Spinozist, as by a Catholic.[51] But Le Clerc too was vulnerable, since his approach restricted the Christian message to certain fundamental points. Simon observed that these points could be found in Judaism or deism as well as in Christianity. Replying, Le Clerc counterattacks: 'Croyez-vous, Monsieur, qu'un homme qui croit en Jésus-Christ puisse dire, en parlant de sang-froid, que l'on trouve dans le judaïsme, dans le mahométisme et même dans le déisme la connaissance de bonheur éternal où nous aspirons naturellement, et les moyens d'y parvenir?', going on to insinuate that Simon's faith was 'extrêmement suspecte' and that the deistic, Muslim or Jewish tendencies were his, not Le Clerc's.[52] But Simon's remarks had their effect. In the *Sentiments,* Le Clerc had suggested that 'M. N.''s ideas were deistic, but had not seemed to regard this as a serious matter; in the *Défense des Sentiments,* he takes more care to distinguish his ideas from those of the deists. Here he seems to mean Spinozists. Readers of Spinoza, he says, have fallen into deism and atheism;[53] in a subsequent 'éclaircissement' about M. N., he denies that his principles are the same as 'ceux des Déistes, qui rejettent toute sorte d'inspiration, et qui regardent l'Ecriture Sainte comme un ouvrage plein de mensonges, et où il n'y a rien du tout que de purement humain'.[54] In this passage Spinoza is not mentioned, but the definition of deism is probably a tendentious description of the *Tractatus theologico-politicus,* especially its Chapter 14, which contains the seven articles of the universal faith and treats of divine inspiration. The obscurity is increased by Le Clerc's lack of frankness over the identity of M. N.[55] The letters ascribed

---

[49]   Ibid., p. 260: 'Comme il a été le seul de tous les hommes incapable de pécher, il a été aussi le seul que Dieu ait élevé à une infaillibilité absolue'.

[50]   Ibid., p. 286: if Christians were required to believe only 'ce qui est le plus essentiel' in Jewish and New Testament history and 'la divinité de la doctrine de Jésus-Christ, où l'on ne trouve rien qui ne soit parfaitement conforme au bon sens', then the *libertins* would be obliged to admit that the Christian religion was of divine origin.

[51]   *Sentiments,* pp. 93–94; see Steinmann, *Richard Simon,* p. 199 (and Pt. II, Chs. 6, 7, 11 on the Simon – Le Clerc dispute generally).

[52]   *Défense des Sentiments de quelques théologiens de Hollande* (1686), p. 60. This answered Simon's *Résponse aux Sentiments de quelques théologiens* (1686), which he published under the pseudonym of 'Le Prieur de Bolleville'.

[53]   *Défense,* pp. 220–221. On p. 217, deism is 'cette abominable opinion'. The remark about atheism must refer to the *Ethics.*

[54]   Ibid., p. 228.

to him put forward other heterodox ideas, for instance that Christ was human rather than divine, which could also be the basis of an accusation of deism.[56]

All these considerations make the appellation 'deist' more credible when applied to Le Clerc than to any other figure in the 1680s, except Spinoza (in the *Tractatus*) and the Socinians, for both of whom it is justified, at least etymologically speaking, by their restriction of religion to the worship of God. It must however be remembered that the Socinians, like Le Clerc and even Spinoza, wrote from a Christian standpoint; the assumption that deists were enemies of Christianity was made by those who used the term pejoratively. But any hostile critic reading a piece by Johannes Krell (Crellius), for instance, a treatise on God published in the *Bibliotheca fratrum polonorum,* would have regarded it as a deist work.[57] It states that religion entirely consists in the highest worship and obedience to God.[58]

Simon and Bossuet
Soon after his controversy with Le Clerc, Simon confronted an adversary from his own side, the Oratorian Michel Le Vassor.[59] His *Traité de la véritable religion* (1688) was directed against the scriptural criticism of Simon, Le Clerc and Spinoza, and includes a description of deism which could be based on Spinoza's universalist articles of religion. It might also be taken from Abbadie's classification of deists, since Le Vassor seems not to know to whom he is referring, calling them 'certains déistes du temps'. They accept the principles of natural religion and morality; 'mais ces principes, ajoutent-ils, suffisent, et nous n'avons besoin ni de Révélation ni de loi écrite pour nous marquer nos besoins à l'égard de Dieu et du prochain.'[60]

[55] That 'M. N.' is a pseudonym for Le Clerc is clear enough, but similarities of ideas would confirm it if necessary. For instance, 'M. N.' on Job in Lettre XII expresses the same view as Le Clerc writing in his own person in Lettre IX; *Sentiments,* pp. 179, 271. Simon, however, chose to assume that M. N. was Noël Aubert de Versé (an assumption shared by Steinmann, *Richard Simon*), who was discredited at the time for his work on Spinoza, *L'Impie convaincu,* 1684; see Vernière, *Spinoza et la pensée française,* Vol. I, pp. 81–89.

[56] See notes 49 and 50 above. In the *Défense,* Le Clerc says that divinity has always been 'très étroitement unie' to Christ, an ambiguous and no doubt heretical phrase. The *Sentiments* includes statements (e.g. p. 280) that the religion of Christ consists in the observance of his commandements, which is close to Spinoza's interpretation.

[57] *Liber de Deo eiusque attributis,* in the edition of Crellius in the *Bibliotheca, Operum exegeticorum tomus tertius.* Crellius died in 1633. See Wilbur, *Socinianism,* pp. 571–572, on Andrew Wiszowaty's views; his *Religio rationalis* was published in Holland in 1685.

[58] *Liber de Deo,* p. 2: 'Supremo enim domino et rectori suo summum etiam cultum atque obsequium debent homines, in quo religio tota consistit'.

[59] On Le Vassor, who later became an Anglian, see Vernière, *Spinoza et la pensée française,* Vol. I, pp. 155–159.

[60] Pt. I, Ch. 2; quoted from Hazard, *Crise,* Pt. III, Ch. 2.

In response, Simon showed that Le Vassor took all his material from the writers he attacks; Le Vassor is accused of plagiarism and Le Clerc of heresy. The Oratorians, says Simon, were once reputed to include men of ability (Simon had been forced to leave the Oratoire after the uproar over his *Histoire critique du Vieux Testament*), but they are now 'réduits à copier les livres des Protestants modernes, des Sociniens et des Déistes'.

Previously, keeping up the constant round of controversies, Simon has turned the tables on Jurieu, whose most eccentric production, *L'Accomplissement des prophéties,* of 1686, contained yet another attack on the *Histoire critique.* It was intended to further the struggle against Catholicism, and prophesied the end of the rule of Antichrist, that is the Pope, in 1710 or 1715. Some of Jurieu's expressions implied that the Messiah had not yet come, and Simon took the opportunity thus offered. He composed a false letter to Jurieu from two rabbis of Amsterdam, who congratulated him on his un-Christian sentiments. They found that his arguments exactly resembled those of Jewish theologians, who say that Jesus is not the Messiah promised in the Old Testament.[61] A sequel came in 1706, when Louis Bastide published an apologia, *L'Incrédulité des déistes confondue,* which attacks both Simon and Jurieu. Now it is Simon who is said to be a deist; in Bastide's eyes, the *Lettre des rabbins d'Amsterdam* puts the views of deists and Jews combined, 'que Jésus-Christ n'est ni Dieu ni le Messie, et que le Christianisme n'est qu'une illusion'.[62] The Arian connotations of 'deist' still survived; Bastide's book is mainly about the divinity of Christ.

The numerous allegations and counter-allegations which occurred in the middle years of the 1680s must, in part, be a side-effect of the sectarian polemics aroused by Louis XIV's policy towards the Huguenots; it also seems that the elements of eirenism found in both Le Clerc and Spinoza, when they put forward versions of Christian belief reduced to basics, might have given rise to the accusation of deism. But in both, as in Simon, the presumed implications of scriptural criticism (for instance, that the Bible is full of lies, in a remark of Le Clerc's) were associated with deism; this may be because the works of the Socinians, made known to Western Europe since 1665, were mainly Biblical exegesis. Abbadie's usage, treating 'déiste' as the equivalent simply of 'theist', seems to be personal to him, but his *Traité* went on being read for much longer than the polemical works. Whatever

[61] *Lettre* (or *Réponse) des rabbins d'Amsterdam,* in Simon's *Lettre choisies,* 1730 edition, Vol. I, pp. 319–338 (first edition 1700). See Steinmann, *Richard Simon,* Pt. III, Ch. x.

[62] Louis Bastide, *L'Incrédulité des déistes confondue par Jésus-Christ,* 2 vols. (Paris, 1706), Préface. In the dedication to the Pope, Bastide writes: 'les Rabbins d'Amsterdam et les Déistes ont conclu, dans un écrit blasphématoire, qu'ils ont répandu partout, que Jésus-Christ n'est pas le Messie, et que selon les principes de M. Jurieu la religion chrétienne n'est qu'une illusion'.

meaning is attached to the word, its polemical uses preserves it as a term of opprobrium.

After 1690, the situation becomes less heated, at least as regards sectarian debate. In controversy Bossuet writes of deism, but only occasionally, and seemingly with reluctance, mentioning it in connection with Protestantism, Simon's critical works and Quietism. In passages which suggest that he is thinking of deism, he often warns instead of the risks of impiety or religious indifference.[63] His argument against Protestantism in the *Histoire des variations* (1688), that it necessarily produces a succession of new sects, reveals his particular concern with Socinianism, but he does not refer to 'Socinians or deists'.[64] In the *Défense de l'Histoire des variations,* against Jacques Basnage de Beauval, the word does appear. Bossuet observes that Basnage's tolerant principles would permit any kind of heterodoxy to be immune from punishment, and the position he allots to deism in his list of undesirable opinions indicates his contempt: 'il n'y qu'à être browniste, anabaptiste, Socinien, indépendant, tout ce qu'on voudra; mahométan, si l'on veut; idolâtre, déiste même ou athée'.[65] In the sixth *Avertissement aux Protestants,* the sequel to the *Défense,* he quotes the incorrigible Jurieu in his *Tableau du Socinianisme,* making the same accusations as before, that there are deists at the French court and Socinians in the Church. Bossuet makes no comment on the first, confining himself to the remark that 'les Sociniens font peu de bruit dans le monde'. From what he says against another opponent, William Chillingworth, it is possible to deduce that he means, by 'déiste', a believer in God but not Christ; the Muslim and the deist could claim, like the Jew and the Christian, to have an implicit faith formulated in the words 'Je crois tout ce que Dieu sait'.[66] Bossuet makes almost exactly the same criticism, but of Quietist contemplation, in 1695.

[63]   For instance, in the *Oraison funèbre* for Henriette de France (1669), he says, commenting on the multiplicity of sects after the Reformation, that some men grew tired of disputes and sought 'un repos funeste, et une entière indépendance, dans l'indifférence des religions, ou dans l'athéisme'; and on religious innovations after Luther mentions Socinians, 'les sectes infinies des Anabaptistes', Independents, Quakers and Seekers, but not deists (*Oeuvres complètes de Bossuet,* edited by F. Lachat, 31 vols. (Paris, 1862–1866), Vol. XII (1863), pp. 452, 453). Deism is not included in the 'Dénombrement de quelques hérésies' appended to the *Etat présent des controverses de la religion protestante* (Ibid., Vol. XVI (1864), p. 242).

[64]   Indices to Bossuet contain numerous references to Socinianism. His view of them is concisely given in the *Premier avertissement aux Protestants,* section 19: 'Ils nous ont fait un christianisme tout nouveau, où Dieu n'est plus qu'un corps, où il ne crée rien, ne prévoit rien que par conjectures comme nous; où il change dans ses résolutions et dans ses pensées; où il n'agit pas véritablement par sa grâce dans notre intérieur; où Jésus-Christ n'est qu'un homme; où le Saint-Esprit n'est plus rien de subsistant; où pour la grande consolation des libertins l'âme meurt avec le corps, et l'éternité des peines n'est qu'un songe plein de cruauté' (*Oeuvres,* Lachat edition, Vol. XV (1863), pp. 203–204).

[65]   Ibid., p. 493. The *Défense* precedes the sixth and last *Avertissement aux Protestants,* the whole series of which appeared from 1689 to 1691.

[66]   *Sixième avertissement,* section 16 (*Oeuvres,* Lachat edition, Vol. XVI, p. 128) and section 109 (ibid., p. 128).

First he condemns Mme Guyon's description of the mystic's union with God alone on the grounds that it tends to destroy the concept of the Trinity; then he says about Malaval, a predecessor of Mme Guyon, that his conception of God is too general, since it does not allow for the 'distinction de personnes'. As a consequence: 'point de Jésus-Christ; et ainsi (...) un vrai adorateur de Dieu devrait suivre les notions les plus approchantes de celles des mahométans ou des Juifs, ou si l'on veut des déistes; autrement il serait dégradé de la haute contemplation, et il retomberait dans ce qu'on appelle *multiplicité*'.[67]

Bossuet's anxieties about the Socinians, a constant theme of his works concerning Protestantism, and his references to 'Jewish' and 'Muslim' ideas, reflect the assumption that Trinitarian doctrine was under threat. To say that he conceived of deism simply as anti-trinitarianism would be too cut-and-dried, but the equation is approximately correct.

In all the definitions and pejorative references of the time, the meaning of 'déisme' varies with the context. The general presupposition is that, following the etymology, it must mean belief in God alone; but this implies that belief in some other thing is rejected. Depending on the context, the thing rejected can be belief in the Trinity, in the divinity of Christ, in the Christian religion or in any organized religion. Such concepts needed words to signify them, but from the existence of the words and the concepts it does not follow that a body of deistic doctrine also existed. The evidence points the other way, despite the assumptions apparently made by modern historians of thought on the basis of seventeenth-century descriptions.[68] It is untrue that before 1700 there was a diffuse form of deistic free-thought already in existence, which contemporaries knew, to which they referred in apologias and polemics, and which was merely waiting to be better expressed by Voltaire. Deism as the modern historian understands it did not exist until it was created by writers like the Militaire philosophe and Montesquieu after 1700. Its elements existed previously; they were principally natural religion and *libertin* or radical criticism of orthodox faith. But the combination does not appear to have been what contemporaries meant by deism, except possibly as regards Spinoza. Broadly speaking, the word 'déistes' (much commoner than 'déisme') is used in one of two ways. Either it refers to attitudes easily distinguishable from what we now call deism, such as anti-trinitarianism or Epicureanism; or else it is brought in as a term appropriate for a concept

---

[67] *Instruction sur les états d'oraison, Oeuvres,* Lachat edition, Vol. XVIII (1864), p. 411. On Malaval see Chapter 7, note 16, below.

[68] To cite only two of the most authoritative: Gustave Lanson refers to Abbadie's four categories of deism and says that the second and third are forms of 'déisme philosophique'; he adds: 'cela prouve que le courant que nous retrouverons au XVIII e siècle existait déjà au moment où l'auteur écrit' (*Origines de l'esprit philosophique,* p. 98); and Paul Hazard, when quoting Le Vassor in 1688, seems to assume that deism was already an established doctrine (*Crise,* Pt. III, Ch. 2).

which its user wishes to define, such as the theism of the *Quatrains du déiste* or Abbadie's four categories of deism sixty years later. Where we might expect the term to appear, as with Foigny's 'Australian' religion in 1676, it is neglected.

Fontenelle and Bayle

In histories of 'philosophe' thought, the last quarter of the seventeenth century is usually presented as the age of Bayle and Fontenelle, seen as precursors of the Enlightenment, especially of its criticism of religion. This view is undoubtedly correct, although it has been demonstrated more convincingly with regard to Bayle.[69] The influence of Fontenelle must have been weaker.[70] For example, the implications in the *Histoire des oracles* (1686), that religion is imposture, are much less clear, and more obviously compatible with enlightened Christian belief, than the same implications (with veiled reference to Moses) in Veiras' *Histoire des Séverambes,* also a popular book, a decade earlier. The idea of religious imposture was current and the 'philosophes' did not need to read Fontenelle in order to learn it.

As for deism, both writers kept at some distance from it, Bayle by professing distaste for it and Fontenelle by extreme circumspection.[71] Fontenelle's writings, particularly the *Entretiens sur la pluralité des mondes* (1686), suggest, if anything, scientific materialism, theoretically compatible with deism, but intrinsically tending to atheism.[72] Only in 1724 did he publish a piece, of uncertain date, which implies a deistic attitude, a proof of

[69]   See Pierre Rétat, *Le Dictionnaire de Bayle et la lutte philosophique au XVIII e siècle* (Lyon, 1971), and on the most important single example of Bayle's influence H. T. Mason, *Pierre Bayle and Voltaire* (Oxford, 1963).

[70]   For one definite example, in copies of the *Examen de la religion,* see Chapter 11, pp. 162–163. The treatment of the subject in Louis Maigron, *Fontenelle, l'homme, l'oeuvre, l'influence* (Paris, 1906), Pt. V, is disappointing; see especially pp. 404–421. See also Werner Krauss, *Fontenelle und die Aufklärung* (Munich, 1969), pp. 60–68; Alain Niderst, *Fontenelle à la recherche de lui-même* (Paris, 1972), pp. 599–601.

[71]   He went beyond the usual limit in sending a famous little satire to Bayle for inclusion in the *Nouvelles de la république des lettres* early in 1686. The *Relation de l'île de Bornéo (Oeuvres de Fontenelle,* edited by G. Depping, 3 vols. (Paris, 1818), Vol. II, pp. 603–604) is a parody of sectarian conflict in Europe, written just after the Revocation of the Edict of Nantes, but little can be deduced from it as regards Fontenelle's personal religious viewpoint.

[72]   See Lanson, *Orignes de l'esprit philosophique,* pp. 199–201, on the godless universe of the *Entretiens,* an interpretation which is widely followed. J. -R. Carré remarks that Fontenelle proves the existence of God 'grâce à la nécessité établie selon lui d'une préordination du mécanisme', but is doubtful whether such a deity 'ait gardé assez de substance pour être le Dieu des déistes' (*La philosophie de Fontenelle ou le sourire de la raison* (Paris, 1932), pp. 402–403; cf. pp. 408, 471). Niderst agrees that Fontenelle's system of the universe required the concept of a creator God, who however leaves the universe to operate according to pre-ordained physical laws (*Fontenelle à la recherche de lui-même,* pp. 528 ff.). Niderst also quotes (pp. 537–538) an undated manuscript description of a class of deists who deny the existence of the soul, the afterlife and moral distinctions, and regards Fontenelle as a representative of this class.

the existence of God which may be merely a *jeu d'esprit* or, just possibly, a sign of his personal beliefs.[73] By 1724, however, any such confession no longer had any great significance. There is little else in Fontenelle's published writings, except conformist expressions of piety, to denote religious affiliations of any kind. During the eighteenth century his name was attached to various clandestine works of free-thought, but few of the attributions are plausible.[74]

With Bayle the picture is more complicated. Despite his early admiration for Malebranche and his expert handling of critical reason, Bayle is the principal defender of fideism and enemy of metaphysical rationalism at the end of the century, and such a position rules out from the start any move towards deism.[75] Bayle believes strongly in the natural law of morality, but not at all in natural religion, as is shown by his polemic against the rationalists, Le Clerc, Jaquelot and others.[76] Nonetheless, the *Dictionnaire's*

---

[73]   The piece *De l'existence de Dieu* (*Oeuvres de Fontenelle*, Depping edition, Vol. II, pp. 373–377) is a criticism, based on the fact of animal generation, of the Lucretian or Epicurean theory of creation by chance, 'la rencontre fortuite des atomes'. Fontenelle does not accept that, given the fixity of species, the first two of any species could have been created fortuitously; 'il a fallu que ces ouvrages soient partis de la main d'un Etre intelligent, c'est-à-dire de Dieu même' (p. 377). Niderst (*Fontenelle à la recherche de lui-même*, pp. 523–528) shows that the argument was taken from one of the Huguenot rationalist theologians, Isaac Jaquelot, in his *Dissertations sur l'existence de Dieu*, published in 1697, which suggests that Fontenelle's piece was written soon after that date.

[74]   The weightiest of these works is *La République des philosophes ou Histoire des Ajaoiens*, published in 1768 under the imprint of Geneva; see Werner Krauss, 'Fontenelle und die "Republik der Philosophen"', *Romanische Forschungen* 75 (1963), 11–21, accepting as true a statement in the *Journal encyclopédique* of 1771 that it is an early work of Fontenelle's. the attibution is hesitantly accepted by Niderst, *Fontenelle à la recherche de lui-même*, pp. 22–23 and 528 ff. The Ajaoiens have a religion of nature, pantheistic rather than theistic; see 1768 edition, Ch. III, reprinted in *Fontenelle: Textes choisis (1683–1702)*, edited by Maurice Roelens (Paris, 1966), pp. 68–75. Three other pieces are published in *Oeuvres de Fontenelle*, Depping edition, Vol. II: *De la resurrection des corps* (pp. 634–636), *Traité de la liberté de l'âme* (pp. 605–617), and *Réflexions sur l'argument de M. Pascal et de M. Locke, concernant la possibilité d'une autre vie à venir* (pp. 617–634). The first, which is hardly more than a pleasantry, is in all probability by Fontenelle. The other two were first published in a volume entitled *Nouvelles libertés de penser* (Amsterdam, 1743); the *Traité*, on freewill and the prescience of God, is thought by Carré (*Philosophie de Fontenelle*, pp. 523–524) and Niderst (op. cit., p. 23) to be correctly attributed. Carré (pp. 459–460), but not Niderst (p. 21), also accepts the attribution to Fontenelle of the *Réflexions*.

[75]   See E. Labrousse, *Pierre Bayle*, Vol. II, *De l'hétérodoxie au rigorisme*, Ch. X, on his fideism.

[76]   See P. Delvolvé, *Religion, critique et philosophie positive chez Pierre Bayle* (Paris, 1906), Pt. II, Ch. 10. In the *Réponse par Mr. Bayle à Mr. Le Clerc* dated April 1706 (*Oeuvres diverses*, 4 vols. (The Hague, 1727–1731), Vol. III (1727), pp. 989 ff.) there is a 'Précis de la doctrine de Mr. Bayle' in section III, concerning the concept of God: 'I. La lumière naturelle et la Révélation nous apprennent clairement qu'il n'y a qu'un Principe de toutes choses, et que ce principe est infiniment parfait. II. La manière d'accorder le mal moral et le mal physique de l'homme avec tous les attributs de ce seul Principe de toutes choses infiniment parfait, surpasse les lumières philosophiques, de sorte que les objections des Manichéens laissent des difficultés que la raison humaine ne peut résoudre. III. Nonobstant cela il faut croire fermement ce que la lumière naturelle et la Révélation nous apprennent de l'unite et de l'infinie perfection de Dieu, comme nous croyons par la foi et par notre soumission à l'autorité divine le mystère de la Trinité, celui de l'Incarnation, etc.' (pp. 992–993).

intricate discussions of the chief problems in the philosophy of religion contributed, perhaps more than any other factor, to creating an atmosphere of theocentrism which is conducive to the appearance of deistic thought. Bayle may conclude, on the problem of evil, by resorting to the Bible as the only answer, but the conclusion is routine, whereas the discussion is full of interest, and in it the only religious concept employed is that of God. So too on the problem of creation or the concept of God itself.[77] Although the philosophizing is compatible with Christian belief, especially since most of it concerns pre-Christian thinkers, its assumptions are theistic only. Quite apart from what Bayle himself believed, therefore, and despite his anti-rationalism, the *Dictionnaire* encouraged a critical, philosophical attitude to religion barely distinguishable from that found in the rational deists.

Bayle's importance in the history of deism was not restricted to encouraging theocentric, or perhaps theistic presuppositions. Among other things, the *Dictionnaire* is a huge repertoire of unorthodoxy, and although Bayle wrote nothing exclusively about deism his articles contributed powerfully to the formation of the image of deism prevalent when the first fully deistic doctrines were being developed. His usual attitude, of deep disapproval, is conveyed in a well-known remark about Arminians, in a letter of 1685 which found its way to Le Clerc and caused lasting discord between the two men.[78] On the subject of Le Clerc's *Sentiments de quelques théologiens,* Bayle wrote that the book would strengthen suspicions that the Arminians favoured Socinian, or perhaps even worse opinions: he added that Arminianism was 'l'égout de tous les athées, déistes et Sociniens de l'Europe'.[79] In the *Dictionnaire* his disapproval is expressed just as clearly, though less brutally. He sees the autobiography of the Jew Uriel Acosta as a lesson on the deistic or atheistic tendencies fostered by the use of reason in religion, and draws attention to the dangerous doctrines circulating in England.[80] He knew of Charles Blount's publication, the *Oracles of Reason* (1693), which included anonymous deistic tracts developing Herbert of Cherbury's ideas, and gave a slightly mocking warning about it in a note to the article 'Apollonius (de Tyane)'. Blount's work 'a furieusement scandalisé les bonnes âmes': Herbert was 'un grand déiste, s'il en faut croire bien des gens'; and the many notes of the publication 'sont remplies de venin: elles

---

[77]   See mainly the articles 'Manichéens', 'Marcionites' and 'Pauliciens' on the problem of evil, and on God and creation 'Anaxagoras', 'Simonide de Ceos' and 'Spinoza' among others.

[78]   Barnes, *Jean Le Clerc,* pp. 230 ff.

[79]   *Oeuvres diverses,* Vol. IV, p. 623 (letter to Jacques Lenfant, 6 July 1685).

[80]   'Voilà un exemple, qui favorise ceux qui condamnent la liberté de philosopher sur les matières de religion; car ils s'appuient beaucoup sur ce que cette méthode conduit peu à peu à l'athéisme ou au déisme' (article 'Acosta', main text). In Note G Bayle makes the connection between deism and rationalism.

ne tendent qu'à ruiner la religion révélée, et à rendre méprisable l'Ecriture Sainte'.[81]

The article on Fausto Sozzini ('Socin') and the Socinians is more important. Bayle makes the same point as in the letter of 1685: 'L'objection la plus générale que l'on propose contre eux, est qu'en refusant de croire ce qui leur paraît opposé aux lumières philosophiques, et de soumettre leur foi aux mystères inconcevables de la religion chrétienne, ils frayent le chemin au pyrrhonisme, au déisme, à l'athéisme'. Bayle supports this objection. Socinian biblical exegesis implies, he says, that New Testament phraseology about Christ is mere panegyric, and not the result of divine inspiration – a more sober criticism that the common charge against the Socinians, that for them the Bible was mere untruth. However, in the notes to 'Socin' Bayle added a selection of the wilder imputations made by Jurieu, who had accused the Jansensists both of Socinianism and of deism. Filleau's and Meynier's violent accusations are not forgotten.[82] In pursuing his feud with Jurieu (he reveals Jurieu's intemperateness and lack of candour), Bayle thus kept alive the alarmist view of deism and its association with the Socinians.

The article 'Socin' was on a subject which was of the greatest contemporary interest, and there can be no doubt that the ideas it contained about deism, supported by Bayle's immense authority, reached a very large public, over a period of many years. Nor was this all. Readers wishing to find out, from the *Dictionnaire's* somewhat inadequate index, what Bayle had said about deism were directed to the article on Pierre Viret, where they found long quotations from his *Instruction chrétienne* of 1564, presenting deists as hypocritical enemies of the Christian religion.[83] This was confirmation, or so it must have seemed, that deism had had an underground existence for well over a century, as subversive during the Reformation as in the Jansenist 'conspiracy of Bourgfontaine' invented by Filleau in 1654. Few single words can have been so influential as the entry in Bayle's index in determining intellectual presuppositions; Bayle's and Viret's attitude to deism have affected the historiography of the subject down to recent times.[84] Taken together, the articles 'Socin' and 'Viret' finally established the image of deism as a dangerous and radical type of free-thought, somewhere between Socinianism and atheism.

Bayle's writings after the *Dictionnaire* are of lesser interest for the history of deism. An instance which deserves notice occurs when he is arguing against Jacques Bernard in the *Réponse aux questions d'un provincial.*

[81] Article 'Apollonius (de Tyane)', text and Note I.
[82] Article 'Socin', text and Note M.
[83] Article 'Viret', Note D.
[84] The passage from Viret's *Instruction chrétienne* is the main evidence cited by Busson (and before him by Robertson, *Short History of Freethought,* Vol. I, p. 466) for the existence of deism in the sixteenth century; see the discussion in Chapter 1 above.

Bayle contends that 'universal consent' to the belief in God cannot be established beyond doubt. It is Bernard's use of 'déisme' that is the more significant here. For him it means theism, in the context of comparative religion – the ordinary modern sense. He was probably following Cudworth and adapting the term 'theism', which Cudworth introduced in 1678.[85] Bayle is plainly not at ease with this usage, which was quite at variance with his own, and emphasizes that he refers to 'déisme' only in Bernard's sense, 'la doctrine de l'existence de Dieu'.[86]

Two end-of-century examples

The period during which the bad image of deism was created is contemporaneous with the dates of publication of Marana's *Espion turc,* from 1684 to 1696, which convincingly portrays free-thought with deistic tendencies; it is the subject of the next chapter. Two contrasting views about deism will provide a postscript to this one. The first, a retrogressive view, is that of Ellies Du Pin in his edition (1701) of Arnauld's critique of La Mothe le Vayer, *De la nécessité de la foi en Jésus-Christ pour être sauvé.*[87] At the height of the controversy over the 'rites chinois', Du Pin is returning to Arnauld's arguments against the salvation of pagans, in order to counter Jesuit conversion policy in the Far East. La Mothe had defended Socrates as a monotheist who conformed to the polytheistic Greek religion only to avoid dissension;[88] Du Pin stigmatizes this as 'la plus claire leçon de déisme et de libertinage qui fut jamais'. He defines the main principle of deism, 'cette secte diabolique', as consisting in 'ne reconnaître qu'un seul Dieu dans la loi de nature, et pour le reste de la religion, à ne point violer les lois de l'Etat où l'on se trouve' (not a usual definition, but appropriate for his purposes), inferring from the principle that one may be a pagan in China, a Muslim in Turkey, a Lutheran in Saxony, and so on – abominations which are now threatening.[89]

Jansenist claims that the Jesuits encouraged deism are slightly more plausible than the counter-claim made by Jesuits, a point which emerges

---

[85] Ralph Cudworth's *True Intellectual System of the Universe* (1678) had been summarized by Le Clerc in the *Bibliothèque choisie* in 1704. Bayle attacked Cudworth, Le Clerc defended him. See Barnes, *Jean Le Clerc,* pp. 232–233.

[86] *Réponse aux questions d'un provincial,* Ch. 99, notes (c) and (d), and Ch. 103, note (a) (*Oeuvres diverses,* Vol. III, pp. 698–699, 707).

[87] See Chapter 3, p. 37. For the reasons given there I regard Du Pin as the author of the passages concerning deism in his edition of Arnauld's manuscript.

[88] La Mothe le Vayer, *De la vertu des païens,* Pt. II (*Oeuvres,* 1756–1759, T. V, Pt. I, p. 124; reprint Vol. II, p. 150).

[89] *De la nécessité de la foi en Jésus-Christ,* Pt. IV, Ch. XVI (*Oeuvres d'Antoine Arnauld,* Vol. VIII, pp. 328–329).

from René Pomeau's study of Voltaire's schooling; but it was saom time before even so free-thinking a pupil of the Jesuits as was the young Arouet brought upon himself the accusation of deism in'his turn.[90] In 1701, Du Pin was simply taking an opportunity to denigrate his enemies. By contrast, in 1696, there was already at least one Catholic layman, of distinguished birth, who was prepared to consider deism impartially in spite of its disrepute.[91] In a letter to Jesuit about the apologias he has read (they include those of Grotius, Pascal and Abbadie), the anonymous nobleman explains his opinion: the 'honnête homme' should be Christian, because of the strong arguments that Christianity is the one true religion; but it is better to be 'simplement déiste' than a member of a Christian sect. What he means by a sect is doubtful, but for him Christianity should be believed 'conformément à l'Evangile'. He thinks that established religions disfigure natural religion, 'n'étant selon moi qu'un produit de plusieurs vues humaines qui ne font qu'avilir ce que nous devons à Dieu et à nous-mêmes'.[92] He is aware that deism can be at odds with Christianity, since he mentions the autobiography of Uriel Acosta, 'qui est mort déiste, et qui a fait un traité sous le nom d'*Exemplar humanae vitae* où il prétend détruire toutes les religions',[93] but his tone is detached and not unfavourable. If the date and the attribution, given by Jean-Frédéric Bernard in 1740, can be trusted, the letter is a unique example of a balanced and knowledgeable expression of French opinion about deism before 1700.

[90] René Pomeau, *La Religion de Voltaire* (Paris, 1956), Pt. I, Ch. 2, especially pp. 54–60 on the 'rites chinois'; Ch. 3, pp. 80–81, on an anonymous informant who accused Voltaire of preaching deism, probably in about 1715.

[91] Jean-Frédéric Bernard, who published the letter in the first of two volumes entitled *Dissertations mêlées sur divers sujets importants et curieux* (The Hague, 1740), says in the 'Avis' in Volume I that the writer is more to be esteemed because of his rank than through any reputation which is to be gained as an author. The letter is headed 'A Lyon, ce 22 juillet 1696'; a passage about Pascal (p. 160) indicates that the addressee is a Jesuit.

[92] Ibid., pp. 151–152. On p. 161, deists are said to refuse to be Christian only out of *libertinage*.

[93] Ibid., p. 163. On Acosta, see notes 39 and 80 above.

CHAPTER 7

THE TURKISH SPY

THE QUESTION OF MARANA'S AUTHORSHIP

With Marana's *Espion turc*, deistic ideas come nearer to the centre of the European stage than in the tales by Foigny and Veiras, but the new mode of expression, involving a foreign commentator on European ideas, was to be equally important for the propagation of deistic attitudes. Giovanni Paolo, or Jean Paul, Marana (1642–?1693) was of Genoese extraction and lived in France from about 1682 to 1689.[1] In 1684 and 1686 he published two small volumes of letters, the first volume both in Italian and in French translation, under the title *L'Espion du Grand Seigneur.* The Ottoman Emperor's spy, by the name of Mahmut, is supposed to have lived in Paris, in disguise, from 1637 to 1682. He sends reports to Constantinople on politics and current events in France, but corresponds privately on other subjects including religion, and adds stories and acecdotes for diversion.

The 102 letters of the first volumes are certainly by Marana; the manuscript of the first sixty-eight has survived and official documents virtually confirm his authorship of the others.[2] There is some doubt over the many further letters which compose the work as we now have it. The original French publication was interrupted, but an English version ('Letters writ by a Turkish spy') began to appear in 1687, and continued with new letters until a total of eight volumes and 644 leters had been reached by the end of 1692. Then the whole series was retranslated into French, in 1696, under the title *L'Espion dans les cours des princes chrétiens,* and bearing one of the

---

[1] For biographical information, see (in addition to the article by Almansi cited in note 2) William H. McBurney, 'The Authorship of "The Turkish Spy"', PMLA 72 (1957), 915–935.

[2] See Guido Almansi, '"L'Esploratore turco" e la genesi del romanzo epistolare pseudo-orientale', *Studi secenteschi* 7 (1966), 35–65, cited henceforth as 'L'Esploratore turco', an article of fundamental importance. On the extremely difficult bibliographical problem, it supersedes previous work, notably the article by McBurney cited in note 1, and that by Joseph E. Tucker, 'On the Author-ship of the *Turkish Spy:* an Etat Présent', *Papers of the Bibliographical Society of America* 52 (1958), 34–57. For the details of early French editions, i.e. before 1690, see Almansi, pp. 48–50, and for the documentary evidence pp. 50–51. A briefer account is in G. Almansi and D.A. Warren, 'Roman épistolaire et analyse historique: l' "Espion turc" de G.P. Marana', *XVIIe Siècle* 110 (1976), 57–73. The manuscripts of the first 63 letters are in the Bibliothèque nationale (Fonds italien, 1006, 1007) and have been published by Almansi and Warren under the title *"L'Esploratore turco" di Giovanni Paolo Marana* in consecutive issues of *Studi secenteschi* from 1968 to 1973, with full annotation; the bibliography is ibid., 18 (1977), 245–261.

commoner false imprints of the time, 'Cologne, chez Erasme Kinkius'.[3] Editions in both languages, and in others, continued to appear for many years, as did various continuations, one of which, in 1718, was attributed to Daniel Defoe.[4] The title by which the work is now known in French, 'L'-Espion turc', comes from one of the later editions.

The assumption that Marana is the author of the whole series, which is difficult to rebut in the light of the arguments advanced by Guido Almansi, is based on similarities between the letters and other works by Marana, on the internal coherence of the whole series (which is noticeable in the letters concerning religion, as will become apparent), and on external evidence such as Marana's own statements.[5] There is little plausibility in the other suggestions made regarding authorship, among them Charles Cotolendi, the editor of the *Saint-Evremoniana,* and a bewildering variety of minor English writers, who, had they written so successful a work, would certainly have made their claims public.[6]

In literary history *L'Espion turc* is best known as the model for the *Lettres persanes,*[7] but its importance is greater than that would imply, even as regards the question of literary influence. If the *Lettres persanes* had never been written the invention of the foreign letter-series, a device to satirize European life, would probably still have been one of the favourite forms of literary expression in the eighteenth century. Marana's variation of subject-matter and boldness in speculation (on subjects other than politics) showed the potential of the *genre,* which he exploited to advantage in the area of religion. The subject occupies more than forty letters in whole or in part and innumerable passages elsewhere.

Marana's views should properly, no doubt, be classified as part of the European movement towards deism, rather than the French movement, since apart from his nationality his work belongs to the 'république des lettres' in its totality. However, the work was written about France and presumably in

---

[3]   Almansi, 'L'Esploratore turco', pp. 52–54.

[4]   *Continuation of the Letters writ by a Turkish Spy at Paris,* 1718.

[5]   Marana's unpublished works *Le più nobili azioni della vita e del regno di Luiggi il Grande* and *Il trionfo di Parigi* (BN, Fonds italien 867–868, 862), and his *Les événemens les plus considerables du règne de Louis le Grand* (Paris, 1690), are also panegyrics of the French king. See Almansi, 'L'Esploratore turco', pp. 36, 45. In the present context, they are noteworthy because they share with the *Espion turc* an attitude of severe disapproval for the Huguenots; see for instance *Evénemens,* pp. 45 ff. Almansi also points out that the unfavourable attitude shown by the Turkish Spy towards Spain is consistent with Marana's hostility, known from other sources, to the pro-Spanish policy of the Genoese government (ibid., p. 64).

[6]   The attribution to Cotolendi is found in the *Menagiana,* but without supporting evidence (Almansi, 'L'Esploratore turco', p. 56); the English hypothesis was renewed by Tucker, 'On the Authorship of the Turkish Spy'.

[7]   Pietro Toldo, 'Dell' *Espion* di Giovanni Paolo Marana e delle sue attinenze con le *Lettres persanes* del Montesquieu', *Giornale storico della letteratura italiana* 29 (1897), 46–79; for examples of Marana's influence on Montesquieu additional to those mentioned by Toldo, see modern critical editions of the *Lettres,* especially the edition by Paul Vernière, Classiques Garnier (Paris, 1961).

France; no doubt Marana had greater opportunities to publish there than in Italy. Even so his attitude in religious matters seems to have caused him some trouble from the start, since the Comte Pidou de Saint-Olon, the French ambassador to Genoa and Marana's patron in Paris, expressed reservations about the earliest letters on religion, while in 1686 passages from later letters had to be removed in order to satisfy the censor.[8]

Apart from the obvious freedom of the Spy's religious opinions, deciding on their nature is not easy; he is eclectic to the point of obsession. Christianity, materialism, deism and agnosticism can all be reliably discerned in his pages. The work's main significance for present purposes lies in three letters about halfway through the series, which concern fundamental religious questions and are certainly deistic. Thus *L'Espion turc* helps to fill a chronological gap in the history of deism, between the Utopias of the 1670s and the first deistic treatises of the eighteenth century.

MAHMUT'S PIOUS DOUBTS

Its fictional framework gives *L'Espion turc* a degree of unity, at least as regards religious matters. A rudimentary narrative emerges, as the Spy becomes gradually disenchanted with strict Muslim orthodoxy, experiments with other possibilities, including deism, and takes an increasingly radical approach to his problems. He returns time and again to the same questions, never finding a completely satisfactory answer.

The first stage in his development is faithful allegiance to Islam and its authorities. Since he is devout, he has scruples over pretending to be a Christian, even for the service of the 'Grand Seigneur'. He has to participate in the rituals of Easter, in order to maintain his disguise; but will this not put his salvation at risk? Marana's fictional Mufti, to whom the spy appeals for guidance (Volume I, L. 12),[9] takes the strict view and gives an unhelpful response; not only does he refuse the anxious Mahmut permission to neglect his Muslim duties, but sentences him to the Muslim equivalent of excommunication (I, L. 41). (Throughout the work, different aspects of Christianity are transposed bodily into a Muslim setting.)

[8]   Writing to Marana, Pidou de Saint-Olon commented that, even allowing for the Turkish *persona*, the use of the fictional letter form 'vous donne même une occasion peu nécessaire de parler irrespectueusement des mystères de votre religion' (quoted after Almansi, 'L'Esploratore turco', p. 45). In an ambiguous reply, Marana took refuge behind the approval of his work by the king and his confessor, Père La Chaise. Permission to publish later instalments of the letters was refused until Marana had deleted four passages, which in Almansi's opinion probably concerned religion (ibid., pp. 45–46, 50).

[9]   I quote from the 1715–1716 edition, in six volumes, said by the publishers to be the fourteenth: *L'Espion dans les cours des princes chrétiens, ou lettres et memoires d'un envoyé secret de la Porte dans les cours de l'Europe*. The imprint, 'Cologne, chez Erasme Kinkius', probably denotes Amsterdam.

In the course of explaining his quandary, the Spy has already taken an important step towards one kind of deism, that which results from comparing religions with a view to finding the common ground between them. Islam and Christianity, he says, have the same God, 'le Dieu des Chrétiens est celui-là même que nous adorons', but their modes of worship are quite different. The distinction between belief and ritual, prominent in Veiras and Saint-Evremond, is no less so in *L'Espion turc*. The Spy explains to the Mufti some of the oddities of Catholic worship: 'ils mangent d'un certain pain qu'ils appellent le Sacrement de l'Eucharistie, où ils s'imaginent que leur Messie est réellement présent, aussitôt que leurs Prêtres ont prononcé certaines paroles'. Simply by the use of a foreign *persona,* which is a necessary part of Marana's chosen *genre,* he gives the impression that religions are divided only by superficialities.

In some later editions, this impression was made very much more pointed, probably not by Marana's agency. After Mahmut's reference to the Catholic doctrine of the Real Presence, an interpolation occurs, in editions after 1700, which is aggressively anti-Catholic: 'As-tu jamais rien vu de si fou?'. Evidently the interpolated question was a Protestant jibe inserted as a 'Muslim' remark.[10] The consequences were curious, since the anti-Catholic comment seems to have been the source of Rica's famous comments on the Eucharist in L. 24 of the *Lettres persanes*. Montesquieu had presumably read one of the French (or rather Dutch) editions in which the interpolation occurs, and was emboldened to imitate 'the Spy's example. If legend is correct, it was the audacity of L. 24 which prevented him from being elected to the *Academie française.*[11]

The Spy's doubts occupy several other letters in the early volumes. He has a tendency to give long lists of the Muslim practices which he faithfully observes (I, L. 41; III, L. 58). He worries when he is offered wine to drink, by suspicious Frenchmen who know that Muslims are forbidden to do so (III, L. 73). He finds the Koran obscure. While not doubting the truth of Islam, his soul has no rest; he is 'un voyageur perdu dans un désert de doutes et d'incertitudes'; he might have incurred the Prophet's wrath and be sent to hell (III, L. 58). The letter which expresses this anguish ends in anti-climax when Mahmut asks whether to abstain from meat (animals might have immortal souls, he says). However, he returns to the question in other letters, as if he took it seriously, and it typifies a frequent source of doubt, whether even the most punctilious observance of ritual is sufficient to ensure salvation.

---

[10] For the original text, see *"L'Esploratore turco" di Giovanni Paolo Marana,* edited by Almansi and Warren, *Studi secenteschi* 9 (1968), p. 216 (L. 12): 'si cibano poi di certo pane sopra il quale è effigiato il loro Christo, dicono essi, morto sopra la Croce, che chiamano sagramento dell' Eucaristia, nel quale vogliono che Christo sia esistente in corpo reale Hispostatico divino, e umano'. There is nothing which corresponds to the clause about the words spoken by priests.

[11] Robert Shackleton, *Montesquieu: A Critical Biography* (Oxford, 1961), pp. 87–88.

Mahmut's anxieties derive partly from Christian intolerance, as he observes in an early letter. The Christians claim that there is only one truth, 'de sorte que nous sommes perdus si nous ne sommes pas chrétiens, ou ils sont damnés s'ils ne sont pas musulmans' (I, L. 13).[12] Some years after this was first published, but while the *Espion turc* was still much read, the writers of clandestine anti-religious works such as the *Examen de la religion* were to use the same consideration disingenuously, as a reason for critically 'examining' Christianity in order to disprove its claims. The Spy, however, is not of a critical disposition, and confines himself to wondering whether virtuous conduct might not be the key to salvation. 'Ne crois-tu pas, toi qui es Dervis, et le plus éclairé de tous, que de quelque religion qu'on soit, pourvu qu'on soit honnête homme, l'on peut être heureux après la mort?' In the second volume, the idea is put forward with greater assurance. Discussing the 'virtuous pagan', La Mothe le Vayer's subject, Mahmut rejects the view that anyone can suffer damnation for being in a state of involuntary ignorance of the Christian revelation, provided that he has followed 'les préceptes de la nature et de la raison', which, he says, are true marks of virtue and religion (II, L 57). Another letter attributes a similar view to the Mufti, who, in a rather startling change from his former rigorousness, has turned indifferentist. He now believes, so Mahmut says, that 'tous ceux qui vivent en gens de bien seront heureux au dernier jour, puisque l'objet de leur adoration est le même' (II, L. 77). The Mufti has become an advocate of natural religion defined in the same way as by La Mothe, the belief in God and virtuous conduct. He even illustrates his view by the common indifferentist image, used for instance by Voltaire in the *Lettres philosophiques:*[13] the various religion are 'autant de routes qui condüisent un homme au même lieu de repos'.

For Mahmut, it might be said that there are several ways by which to approach deism. We have now seen two of them, the comparaison between religions which have differing forms of worship but the same God, and the argument that virtuous conduct will ensure the salvation of a believer in any religion. The second makes the suggestion that morality is more important than belief, but Mahmut is as yet far from abandoning his Muslim faith (which may be regarded as the equivalent of Catholic fideism). For him, the world is still divided between mutually exclusive religions, and even if doubts intrude it is normal to belong to one of them, not to devise a religious viewpoint of one's own. Thus in the many reflections on religion which, in the first three volumes, are not connected with the persistent problem of salvation, his tone may be detached or even sceptical, but never destructive.

---

[12] For the original text, see the edition by Almansi and Warren cited in note 10, p. 228–229 (L. 13): 'Una cosa m'inquieta l'anima, che non vi è che una sola verità. O' noi siamo perduti, se non siamo Christiani, ò sono perduti questi, se non sono con noi circoncisi'.

[13] 'Un Anglais comme homme libre, va au ciel par le chemin qui lui plaît' (Cinquième lettre, *Sur la religion anglicane*).

The tendency is to see similarities or common factors in the three related monotheistic religions, Judaism, Christianity and Islam.

The theme in these scattered reflections is the same as before, that despite their antagonism the three religions worship the same God. The Spy can thus hope to convert a Jewish friend to Islam (II, L. 103). Both Mohammed and Christ, and no doubt Moses also, were sent by God; Mahmut writes with reverence of all founders of religions. He is, however, dissatisfied with the divisions within the great religions (he knows rather more about those within Christianity than the others) and is sceptical when points of faith become controversial: 'Je ne me détermine qu'en ceci seul, c'est que je crois en un Dieu éternel, et que j'ai de la vénération pour ses saints ambassadeurs et prophètes' (II, L. 11). At times he is conciliatory or eirenic, as when he writes to the Mufti about the Incarnation of Christ — 'il s'ensuit nécessaire- ment que Dieu a pris un corps humain, puisque notre saint Prophète appelle la Parole de Dieu celui que les Chrétiens adorent comme un Dieu incarné' (II, L. 9) — but elsewhere, speaking perhaps as his readers might expect in a Muslim, he is doubtful about the divinity of Christ. Christ was only a man; 'en l'appelant homme je ne fais que suivre son exemple, puisque dans tout l'Evangile il ne s'est jamais appelé Dieu, ou le Fils de Dieu, comme les Chrétiens le qualifient' (III, L. 98). Perhaps Marana had been reading Socinian books. However, in order to make this statement he would have needed only to have heard of the anti-trinitarians' commonest argument, or to have read in polemicists the description of their views as a 'Turkish' objection.[14]

Among other critical comments, some of the most frequent concern the Bible, or rather the Koran; in either case, the principle of a particular divine revelation is at issue. According to Mahmut, the Christians will consider the Koran to be 'une fausseté et une imposture' if they can find a single error in it (II, L. 9).[15] The Koran says that the markings on the moon were caused when the archangel Gabriel brushed against it with one of his wings. Mahmut (as we learn later) has read Descartes, and knows how big the moon is; how

[14]   'Turkish' was a common term of opprobrium for those of Arian views; Viret had written in 1563 about the 'déistes' of Lyon that they believed in God 'comme les Turcs' but did not known what Christ was (see Chapter 1, p. 9). See Chapter 6, p. 89, for a remark by Bossuet linking deists and Muslims; it was preceded in the *Défense de l'Histoire des Variations* (*Œuvres*, Lachat edition, Vol. XV, pp. 489ff.; section 3) by a passage in which Bossuet says that in Protestant countries, because of the doctrinal laxity of the Reformers, 'on peut blasphémer sans craindre, à l'exemple de Servet; nier la divinité de Jésus-Christ avec la simplicité et la pureté infinie de l'Etre divin, et préférer la doctrine des mahométans à celle des chrétiens'. In 1707 Mathurin Veyssière de Lacroze argued at length that the positions of Socinianism and Islam were the same (*Dissertations historiques sur divers suject* (Rotter- dam, 1707), especially pp. 47ff.).

[15]   Busson quotes Père Vincent Contenson arguing similarly, in 1681, about textual criticism of the Bible: 'si minimus error obreperet, posset de totius libri volumine dubitari, sicque tota scriptarum labefactaretur authoritas, subindeque, totius Christianismi fundamentum convelleretur' (*Religion des classiques*, p. 411, n. 3, quoting Contenson's *Theologia mentis*, III, p. 13).

big, then, must Gabriel's wing have been? Again, the Christians mock at passages in the Koran which imply that the sun rises at a particular spot on earth; they call it 'un amas confus et mal digéré des romans orientaux et des fables superstitieuses' (II, L. 13). Turning the tables, like a loyal Muslim, Mahmut applies exactly similar arguments to the Bible. It is hard to know how much weight to give them, despite the references to imposture, since they concern points of only minor importance, such as the use of holy water (described in a 'Muslim' style, II, L. 1), or two cases of allegedly miraculous resurrections (II, L. 17 and L. 41). Since the prevalent mood is respect, which is very noticeable in the early volumes of the letters, it would seem that the Spy's objections to Christianity are not intended to do more than give verisimilitude to the fiction that a Muslim is the author. Nonetheless, he is a Muslim of independent mind, and in the later volumes his deistic tendencies become more pronounced. At the same time, he pursues other avenues of religious speculation. The change is marked by the three letters mentioned already, which are found at the end of Volume III and the beginning of Volume IV.

THREE DEISTIC LETTERS

The first and perhaps the fullest expression of the Spy's new attitude is contained in a letter, philosopical in tone, to the 'Président du Collège de Sciences à Fez' (III, L. 78). After a reference to the Cartesian *cogito,* there is a passage of philosophical introspection, another (more pessimistic) on human weakness and helplessness, and some thoughts concerning death. As usual the Spy is sceptical in the presence of conflicting opinions, in this case about the afterlife. 'J'entends parler les philosophes de l'immortalité, les poètes des Champs Elysées, les ecclésiastiques chrétiens du ciel, de l'enfer, et du purgatoire, les brachmanes indiens de la transmigration. Mais je ne sais ce que je dois croire de tout cela'. Moreover, people worship in different ways depending on their upbringing: 'Cette diversité me donne souvent envie de croire que la Religion n'est autre chose que l'effet de l'éducation'. Even worse, perhaps 'tant de cultes différentes ont été inventés par les politiques', each one adapting his religion to the nation concerned. But the Spy rejects this idea, and also Cardano's theory that religions owe their origin to the influence of the planets.[16] In sum, he says, reason is powerless to settle all the points at issue. 'Croire tout, est au-dessus de la raison, mais ne croire rien est au-dessous. Je veux prendre un juste milieu, et diriger ma foi par ma raison'.

[16]   This seems to be a reference to the notorious fact (mentioned by Bayle, *Dictionnaire,* article 'Cardan' and Note Q) that Girolamo Cardano (1501–1576), the physician, astrologer and algebraist, had cast the horoscope of Christ.

For a fideist, a sceptical survey of the infinite diversity of religion would have been the preliminary to 'submitting' one's reason to authority, but Mahmut prefers to look for common factors uniting all religions. Asking whether he should offer his gratitude and worship to anything visible, or imaginable 'sous quelque figure', to a part or to the whole of the universe, he decides that 'A cet Etre qui n'a point de ressemblance, qui n'est ni divisé, ni borné; dont le centre est partout, et la circonférence nulle part: Au seul Tout-Puissant, d'où émanent toutes les autres choses, et auquel elles retournent: A cet Etre, dis-je, je suis redevable de tout ce que j'ai; et je veux lui rendre ce que je puis'. In this there seem to be tendencies both to pantheism and to a deity with personal attributes; but however we describe the attitude, the Spy has decided not to seek truth by choosing one or other of the rival religions which he has considered, but to determine his own religious beliefs. The contemporary phrase, 'la religion d'un philosophe', might be the best name, especially since there are echoes of Stoic pantheism which are found also in the next important letter.

The Spy takes a slightly different route to a similar conclusion in this letter, which is to his friend Dinet Golou (III, L. 111). It too begins gloomily, with doubts concerning life and death and regrets about the lack of guidance. Mahmut admits now to virtual disbelief regarding the life after death, but denies that he is an atheist, 'mon esprit vole d'abord à la cause première: et c'est là où je me fais mille questions'. The questions relate to chronology, matter, and creation. Mahmut finds that he cannot accept what was still the standard Christian chronology, that the world is five or six thousand years old, but refuses to settle for any other theory of creation, 'de peur de profaner la gloire de l'Etre souverainement bon, qui est le souffle de nos narines'.[17] He admits to hesitation (which after all provides material for much correspondence), 'je suis chancelant sur tout', except for Muslim theism: 'qu'il y a un esprit éternel, qui est partout, la base et l'origine de toutes choses visibles et invisibles, et que nous appelons *Alla,* le soutien d'une infinité de siècles, le roc et l'appui de l'univers'. Having resolved his doubts by recourse to the concept of 'spirit', endowed with a Muslim name, the Spy can now turn to practical matters. The duty of a believer in an eternal spirit is to 'adorer cette essence des essences avec une dévotion profonde et véritable (...) Pour le reste, vivons selon la nature et selon la raison, en tant qu'hommes: et soyons persuadés que nous plairons au bon Père de toutes choses si nous vivons conformément à cette règle, sans prétendre à la perfection des anges'.

It may not be accidental that this passage, from the last letter of Volume III, marks the halfway-point of *L'Espion turc.* In substance, its conclusions resemble those of the previous letters about what is necessary for salvation,

---

[17]   For a survey of the chronological problem and its implications, see Hazard, *Crise,* Pt. I, Ch. 2.

when Mahmut had taken the view that belief in God and a virtuous life were sufficient. He seldom indicates the sources of his ideas, the reference to Cardano being a rare example, but the formula 'live according to nature and reason', like the apparent use of the world-spirit concept and the ambiguity over pantheism and theism, are signs of Stoic thinking, decked out in Oriental garb.[18]

The most interesting indication of sources is tantalizingly vague. In L. 35 of Volume IV, the Spy writes of 'une sorte de gens qu'on appelle Déistes', with whose views, he says, he is in agreement − the first statement since the 'déiste' of the *Anti-bigot*.[19] Mahmut has been discussing Epicurean theories of creation and the problem of evil, and defines the deists as 'faisant profession de croire un Dieu, mais sceptiques en toute autre chose', which corresponds to his own attitude in many earlier letters. In addition, and this corresponds to the criticisms of the Koran and the Bible which are especially frequent in Volume II, 'ils n'ont point une foi implicite pour la religion historique; ils croient au contraire que le devoir des gens raisonnables est de douter des écrits des mortels aussi bien qu'eux, quoiqu'ils aient passé pour de très grands prophètes'. Sacred texts should therefore be subjected to critical scrutiny, so as to 'choisir tout ce qui est conforme à la raison, et de rejeter le reste comme fabuleux et inséré par la fraude des hommes, ou par l'artifice du diable'.

This may very well be an imprecise and not very favourable description of Socinian methods with scripture; it was known that Socinian anti-trinitarianism was based on rational criticism of the New Testament, on the assumption that the text was not divinely inspired. The currency of the phrase 'Socinien ou déiste' would explain Mahmut's reference to deists. Another possibility, since Huet and others had connected Spinoza with deism, is that Marana was referring to the *Tractatus theologico-politicus*.[20] The rather clumsy 'douter des écrits des mortels aussi bien qu'eux' must refer either to the notorious question raised in the *Tractatus,* the Mosaicity of the Pentateuch, or to the radical sects' assumption of purely human authorship of the Bible. (As a Muslim, of course, Mahmut is also thinking of the 'Prophet' and so uses the term when referring to Moses and the authors of the New Testament.)

Whether Marana knew anything definite about the deists is not clarified by what he says about them as a group; he praises their good sense and virtue, but states that they keep themselves to themselves ('ce qu'ils font ils le font sans bruit'). But he says considerably more about a similar group

---

[18] Almansi and Warren, in their edition of the Italian text of the early letters, note Marana's predilection for Seneca (e.g. *Studi secenteschi* 10 (1969), p. 250, n. 3, to L. 20; 11 (1970), p. 120, n. 12, to L. 36).

[19] See Chapter 2, p. 25.

[20] See Chapter 6, pp. 81 ff.

which, so he tells us, existed in Turkish history. They held that the Muslim religion was corrupt, 'qu'elle avait dégénéré de sa première institution, qu'il s'y était fourré plusieurs erreurs, et que le seul moyen de la rétablir dans son ancienne pureté était d'y joindre la philosophie des anciens'. Apart from the reference to ancient philosophy, this is the phraseology which in Marana usually denotes sixteenth-century reformers. But what he then says about their meetings and their efforts to achieve moral perfection suggests the clandestinity and private idealism of the early radical groups in the sixteenth century, Anabaptist or anti-trinitarian.[21] The reformers held frequent meetings, 'où ils pussent parler de tout avec liberté, afin qu'étant unis par une amitié inviolable, ils pussent se perfectionner les uns les autres dans la science et dans la vertu, sans avoir égard ni aux légendes ni aux harangues des Mollahs' (the preaching of the clergy).

Perhaps Marana had come across a garbled but persistent tale, first recorded in 1676, about the so-called 'collegia Vicentina', northern Italian groups based on Vicenza, in about 1545, which were supposed to have been the first beginnings of the anti-trinitarian movement.[22] Forty refugees were said to have escaped to Turkey when the groups were found out and persecuted by the authorities. Mahmut himself does not wholeheartedly approve of the reformers in question, confining himself to the safe comment 'qu'il y a des bigots parmi les sectateurs du Prophète, et que ces bigots méritent correction'. Projects of reform are not for him, although he would like to see less of the intolerant devoutness of the 'bigots'. As he describes it, 'deism' seems to signify moderate reform of the established religion, not anything more revolutionary.

THE LATER VOLUMES

Marana's tone gradually becomes more confident; the change may be gauged by comparing letters from the beginning of Volume IV with what he had said previously on the same subject. On salvation, the Spy had asked tentatively whether it might suffice, for a man to be saved, for him to be virtuous; in L. 3 of Volume IV he is less concerned with being a faithful Muslim, and more with virtue in itself. He ends with a story about the oracle of Delphi, with the moral that 'le très haut' takes no pleasure in rich sacrifices, but only in the 'pures flammes' of the devout heart. In L. 23, while protesting his loyalty to the Koran, Mahmut is more critical than before about the idea of bodily resurrection. He gives several arguments

---

[21]   Marana's account recalls the description of the conditions under which these groups met and spread their ideas given in Kot, 'Le mouvement anti-trinitaire', *Humanisme et Renaissance* 4 (1937), 16–58 (pp. 26–29).

[22]   Wilbur, *Socinianism*, pp. 80ff.

against it, even saying that the doctrine was invented, although for good motives, in order to persuade people that 'les bonnes et les mauvaises actions étaient récompensées et punies après cette vie'. Perhaps Marana did not regard the imputation of imposture as a serious criticism, since he makes a similar point elsewhere without indicating that what he says is particularly audacious.

In a number of letters dispersed throughout the later volumes, a mood of indifferentism prevails as regards both doctrine and the observance of ritual. Writing to Dinet Golou, the Spy finds it absurd that 'les Musulmans se querellent sur de pures bagatelles en matière de Religion' (IV, L. 56). The example given, whether the Koran was eternal or created, seems to be merely a disguise for issues like the Jansenist 'five propositions' or doctrines of the Eucharist. The Spy thinks that the only topics which should be sacred and above debate are the existence of God and the mission of Mohammed, and that we should obey 'la loi pure' instead of speculating. As for the rituals of public worship, Mahmut is much franker than before when he asks, again in the context of fruitless speculation: 'Qu'importe que nous croyions à la loi écrite ou à l'Alcoran; que nous soyons disciples de Moïse, de Jésus, ou de Mahomet? Qu'importe que nous priions ou ne priions pas? Que nous nous mettions à genoux devant des images, ou dans une mosquée toute nue? Ce sera la même chose pour l'action' (V, L. 42).

Later in the same volume, Mahmut looks back on what his opinions had once been, and notes the change: 'J'ai cru quelquefois que l'extérieur de la vertu purifierait mon âme'; now he has decided that 'les ailes qui m'avaient soutenu si longtemps n'étaient que des plumes empruntées' (V, L. 101). He goes further than this in Volume VI, denouncing as 'une vaine mômerie' the type of worship about which, in the past, he had been so reverent and scrupulous. He rounds off his criticisms with the clichés of the imposture theory, talking of 'les prêtres et les conducteurs fourbes et artificieux' and 'les peuples superstitieux'. 'Tout cela ne se faisait que pour faire donner la populace rustique et ignorante dans le piège tendu par les prêtres artificieux, pour la tenir dans la crainte (...) afin qu'après l'avoir rendue plus docile, ils pussent la tourner come ils voudraient' (VI, L. 38). We have entered the world of Veiras' villainous priest Stroukaras, or even of d'Holbach's denunciations of religion. All Marana's examples are taken from classical antiquity, but the relevance for Christianity is obvious, since it is Friday fasting and the sign of the cross which had introduced the letter.

Such attacks do not mean that Marana thinks of the whole of religion in terms of imposture. He has a way of making small matters – in this case, the hypocrisy of rich Christians who eat oysters on Fridays – the basis of sweeping generalizations. However, his reservations about ritual observances do seem to have turned into total rejection, following the appearance of a new factor in this thought. This is his approval for Quietist doctrines of inward piety. In the letter recalling his previous scruples (V, L. 101), Mahmut continues in the style of Mme Guyon, writing of 'un canal des cieux, qui de la source pure du Paradis vient répandre dans nos âmes les torrents de ses eaux salutaires'.[23] He defines his new-found piety in the advice to abandon public worship and await the bidding of Heaven: 'Retranchons-nous plutôt au-dedans de nous-mêmes, jusques à ce que le Ciel nous ouvre volontairement ses portes, et fasse une sortie pleine de tendresse pour nous inviter d'y entrer et pour nous y introduire'.

Later letters confirm the Spy's interest in Quietist doctrine. A letter in Volume V, the heading of which tells us that he 'paraît avoir pour elle des sentiments bien favorables', begins by reporting on the success of Malaval's *Pratique facile,* of 1664, a chief source of Mme Guyon's ideas (V, L. 108).[24] Mahmut's account of Quietism contains a long list of religious leaders and philosophers who taught it (they include Mohammed, Orpheus, and the rabbis); the doctrine is found in all religions, despite their other differences, and it is therefore 'la voix et la volonté de Dieu, et non un effet de l'invention humaine'. The first letter of Volume VI contains a theory of prayer which resembles some of the Quietist ideas which Mahmut has already reported. He dismisses various 'formalités indifférentes' of prayer, implying that they were instituted for political reasons, and maintains that 'l'intelligence et sagesse supérieure regarde principalement à l'intention et à la ferveur de notre esprit'. The letter as a whole is presented as an attack on casuistry.

Mahmut's conversion to Quietism, whether or not it was planned by Marana from the start of *L'Espion turc,* provides an effective ending to the series of letters about the place of ritual observance in religion. It also testifies to an important element of contemporary religious thought generally, the disillusion with ritual, considered as only an empty mark of difference between religions. A similar attitude is found not only in works which are recognizably part of the Quietist movement, such as Fénelon's *Lettre à Louis XIV* castigating the superficialities of official religion,[25] but in less likely places such as the dialogue between the Frenchman and the Quaker at the beginning of Voltaire's *Lettres philosophiques.* The semi-mystical piety involving only the individual worshipper and God is another aspect of Marana's theism, which suggests a natural affinity between Quietism and the deistic movement. Another example is that of Andrew Michael Ramsay, Fénelon's Scottish convert.[26]

---

[23]   Cf. Mme Guyon's book, *Les Torrents spirituels,* written in 1682. But although it circulated in manuscript it was published only 1704 (L. Cognet, *Crépuscule des mystiques* (Paris, 1958), p. 71), and perhaps Marana knew Mme Guyon's *Moyen court pour l'oraison,* 1685, or Malaval (see next note).

[24]   *Pratque facile pour élever l'âme à la contemplation,* 1664 and 1670, by François Malaval (1627–1719), the blind mystic of Marseilles. The book was condemned by the Vatican in 1688.

[25]   'Votre religion ne consiste qu'en superstitions, en petites pratiques superficielles', and the whole passage (*Lettre à Louis XIV,* edited by Henri Guillemin (Neuchâtel, 1961), p. 69).

[26]   See Chapter 14, pp. 235–237.

As a man of philosophical inclinations, the Spy returns often to meta-physical problems, especially the relation between matter and spirit. Discussing this or the destiny of the soul, Marana works his way through a profusion of more or less fanciful theories, and displays a remarkable willingness to exchange one for another. The letters which treat of the soul and its survival form the sequel to the earlier letters asking about Mahmut's prospects in the afterlife. He continues to affirm that virtue will be rewarded, and in Volume IV he is still moderately sure that the soul is immortal. In Volume V, however, there is greater diversity. Writing to a 'santon' (a holy man), Mahmut experiments with the atomist doctrine of the Epicureans, which writers (including Mahmut himself, previously) usually attacked as atheistic. He now thinks that even if we are created 'par le concours fortuit des atomes', we can still be immortal, since the atoms themselves are; but later he says that only God knows what becomes of us after death (V, L. 42). In L. 62, to a doctor, he puts a string of questions, seeming to think that the soul will be absorbed (it is apparently a material entity) either into the fires of Hell or the air of Heaven. Mahmut is afraid that his soul will be 'précipitée par l'éternelle Némésis dans les fatales cavernes de Mont Etna, Stromboli, ou Vésuve, pour y être incorporée avec les rivières ardentes et les lacs de soufre, et autres minéraux'.[27] Another letter to the doctor contains a long passage in even more poetic vein: 'un être est successivement ou la seringue ou l'éponge d'un autre. Les élements s'enivrent tour à tour, ce n'est partout qu'Epicurisme et ivrognerie' (V, L. 109); and in the only important letter of Volume VI on the subject, L. 59, the atmosphere borders on the bizarre. Mahmut rejects 'les contes que les ecclésiastiques débitent', particularly the resurrection of the body, and reviews, as possibilities only, such concepts as metempsychosis and the oblivion referred to in the classical poets. These are followed by what the letter's heading calls 'plaisanteries assez singulières'; Mahmut says that, if he were to go to Heaven, he would like to linger on the way, to talk with various people, and then pursues a fantasy, recalling those of Cyrano, about adventures among the constellations of the Zodiac.

With the other main series of philosophical questions, those concerning God, matter and creation, Marana shows the same ability to explore materialistic ideas without foregoing his assumptions that there is a personal God and an afterlife. The atomist theory of creation is given a religious turn (IV, L. 35). Who can know, asks the Spy, whether all things are not due to chance? But even if they are, 'ce hasard même (...) mérite des honneurs suprêmes, et des sacrifices, d'avoir si bien fait le personnage de la sagesse et de la prévoyance infinie, en formant et en conservant l'univers'. Elsewhere, he takes the view (which, he says, is more reasonable than the Old Testament

---

[27] Similar reflections are found in V, L, 109; Mahmut is uncertain, as usual, but believes in some kind of immortality, if only because 'nous ne pouvons jamais être exclus de la liste éternelle des atomes',

account of creation) that matter is eternal, but he avoids materialism by recourse to the concept of enamation; 'la matière émane aussi naturellement de l'essence divine que la lumière émane du soleil' (IV, L. 45).[28]

This compromise between theism and materialism is still not Marana's last word on the eternity of matter, since in Volume VI, describing the transformations undergone by natural bodies, including humans, he develops the theme that the world has declined from its previous state, but will one day be changed into 'une forme plus brillante qu'il n'a jamais eue' (VI, L. 31). We have had immortality interpreted as the perpetual existence of atoms, and it now seems that Paradise is a 'brilliant' state of matter in general.

What then has become of the concept of God, the only article in Mahmut's creed to have survived the scepticism of the early volumes? In Volume IV, the Spy objects to authropomorphism about God; 'j'entends dire que Dieu a un corps comme la nôtre, des yeux, des oreilles, un nez, des mains, une langue' (IV, L. 56). Mahmut is prepared, notwithstanding, to adopt the supposition that God has a body; if so, 'il est aussi étendu que le Ciel, et également partout (...). Ce corps infini se communique à tout le monde, et comme ce que nous appelons esprit, il est tout-à-fait indivisible'. The pantheistic or Stoic outlook is somewhat modified when Mahmut says that the human mind is not adequate to express the nature of God (a remark he often makes). Materialistic phraseology recurs in Volume VI, L. 29, in a lyrical glorification of God and his attributes.

TITE DE MOLDAVIE AND CHRISTIANITY

The later letters make it difficult to classify *L'Espion turc* simply as a deistic work, because Mahmut has apparently transcended pseudo-Muslim theism and moved on to materialistic pantheism. To complicate things further, there is a sequence of letters putting forward a kind of liberal Christianity, but this too is contradicted elsewhere by distinctly intolerant views on the Huguenots.

From the beginning of the book, one of Mahmut's correspondents had been an Austrian monk with the curious name of Guillaume Vopsel. To Vopsel, the Spy writes under the name he assumes in Paris, that of Tite de Moldavie, who is of course supposed to be a Christian.[29] This enables Marana to give views about the politics of Christianity which would be inappropriate coming from a Muslim; for example, Tite de Moldavie suggests that the Catholic Church should include the Greek Orthodox and other churches, and criticizes papal power from a royalist Gallican standpoint (V, L. 58).

[28]   In V, L. 41, 'l'univers n'est pas Dieu, mais la production de Dieu, production qui ne subsiste que par lui, et qui ne sera jamais séparée de l'essence éternelle'.
[29]   Jan Lavicka, ' "L'Espion turc', le monde slave et le hussitisme', *XVIIe Siècle* 110 (1976), 75–92, puts forward the unlikely theory that a real 'Tite de Moldavie', not Marana, is the author of the letters.

The Austrian monk, we gather, gradually becomes suspicious of his friend's orthodoxy. In Volume II, Tite is obliged to point out that to be a Christian it is not necessary to be a monk. But he makes some criticisms of papal infallibility, relics, and newly-canonized saints, and Vopsel eventually summons him to declare his faith. Tite responds (VI, L. 54) by stating first what he does not believe; he is not intolerant, in the sense of restricting all hope of salvation to Christians, nor is he a hypocrite, one who devoutly observes the rituals which, by now, he has denounced in other letters; nor a worshipper of relics and images. Being non of these, 'Je me trouve ici dans l'embarras pour me donner un nom, à moins que je ne prenne celui de Chrétien'. But the name does not involve joining a church; for Tite, it means one who 'honore Jésus comme notre souverain et maître, tâchant paisiblement d'obéir à ses lois comme doit faire un fidèle sujet'. His Christianity, then, is largely a matter of ethics. He cites Christ's precept 'do unto others . . .' and lists some more principles: 'de craindre Dieu, de servir mon roi, d'honorer mes parents et de leur obéir, d'aimer mes amis, et rendre justice à tout le monde, sans m'embarrasser de vaines formalités et d'inutiles cérémonies, ou sans me mettre en peine dans quelle nation, dans quel climat, ou dans quelle société de chrétiens je suis'. This undenominational, moralizing Christianity, lacking any reference to the divinity of Christ, is hardly to be distinguished from the deism of the letters at the end of Volume III, and as in the letter on the 'déistes' there are hints that Marana has been influenced by Socinian ideas.[30] Since the last letter to Vopsel is also the last important letter on religion except for one on the soul, it might seem that Mahmut the Turkish Spy is supposed finally to be converted to Christianity.

Such an interpretation is given some support by a letter in Volume V to Dinet Golou. Mahmut recalls having disapproved of certain aspects of Christianity, including image-worship, but now considers that the Incarnation can be reconciled with the Koran.[31] He debates with himself whether he can become Christian: 'si j'étais convaincu que Jésus fût le fils de Dieu, et qu'il a souffert la mort pour l'amour des hommes, j'embrasserais volontiers et sans scrupule la plupart des autres dogmes des chrétiens' (V, L. 67). But, hesitant to the end, he would not be able to decide which of the Christian churches to join. He therefore will not overtly profess himself a Christian, but 'je veux avoir des idées avantageuses de Jésus, aussi bien que de Marie sa mère (...) je veux en général demander l'intercession de tous ceux qui sont auprès de Dieu (...) Pour le reste je tâcherai de ne faire en tout que ce que je voudrais qu'on me fît, et de garder ma conscience pure, afin de pouvoir vivre en paix par ce moyen'. After Mahmut's disclaimers of any denominational attachments, it

---

[30] The main point of resemblance here, which could easily be mere coincidence, is Tite's desire to be called simply Christian. Cf. Kot, 'Le mouvement antitrinitaire', article cited in n. 21, p. 49.
[31] Similar reflections are found much earlier, in II, L. 9.

seems odd that his references to the Virgin and the intercession of the saints should align him with Catholicism. The explanation is probably that Mahmut's attitude is supposed to be what a fictional Turk might be expected to have in a work intended for a French Catholic public; an ending in which he is formally converted would be too obvious, but he can sympathize with Catholicism without forfeiting all plausibility. A similar development in attitude, as regards French society and women rather than religion, can be observed in Montesquieu's Persians.

As for the Spy's hostility to the Protestants, it relates to a slightly different aspect of Marana's work, his role as a disguised advocate for the religious policies of Louis XIV. The Gallicanism of certain letters is an illustration of this;[32] the quarrel with Innocent XI over the 'droit de régale' was at its peak in the years when Marana's first volumes of letters were published, the early 1680s.[33] Many other passages are explicable as attacks on the Huguenots during the years of harassment before 1685. In Volume II, Mahmut curtly reproves a cousin for joining a schismatic sect of Muslims, 'qui se prétend plus pure que les autres', and rehearses anti-Calvinist arguments. Perhaps the best example of such propaganda is in Volume VI, L. 57, which denigrates the Huguenots while defending a decree of 1680 directed against them. Calvinists and the English are belittled, and the issue dividing them and the Catholics, the doctrine of the Eucharist, is described as so trivial that 'les Huguenots n'ont pour fondement de leur séparation que l'opiniâtreté reconnue de leurs conducteurs'. It is strange to find in Marana the same approach as in Saint-Evremond to the Huguenot question, and with apparently the same source, Bossuet's *Exposition de la foi catholique.*[34] The letter ends with a eulogy of Bossuet.

In another letter in Volume VI, the condemnation of the Huguenots is accompanied by a keen sense that religion has political value. Here it is part of an argument for orthodoxy: 'Il est certain que la religion rend le vulgaire plus obéissant à ses supérieurs (...) J'entends la religion autorisée par l'état: car dans les lieux où les sujets se donnent la liberté d'innover, de faire des schismes, et de former de nouvelles sectes ou factions, plus chaque parti a du zèle pour son culte, plus sont cruels et tragiques les désordres qui se commettent sur le général' (VI, L. 38). Despite Marana's boldness in religious speculation he can scarcely be regarded as a defender of tolerance. He argues that unbelievers, if virtuous, may be saved, and denounces the Inquisition

---

[32]   For instance I, L. 117 (the Pope's power over kings is 'une étrange et incompréhensible puissance', a phrase no doubt imitated by Montesquieu in L. 24 of the *Lettres persanes*); II, L. 28, L. 57; III, L. 60.
[33]   See E. Préclin and E. Jarry, *Les luttes politiques et doctrinales aux XVIIe et XVIIIe siècles*, Histoire de l'Eglise, 19, 2 vols. (Paris, 1955), Vol. I, pp. 153–164.
[34]   See Chapter 4, p. 52 ff.

and 'bigots fureux',[35] but the prevalent view is that 'la religion établie dominante' should be protected, even from criticism in conversation.[36]

Mahmut's reflections on Christianity in the person of Tite de Moldavie, his *alter ego,* lead him to an attitude which may be summed up as undenominational with Catholic overtones. But this is only one strand of his thought, since (apart from the political propaganda for a state religion) he also leans towards Quietism and pantheism. The eclecticism is partly due to his habitual approach. He surveys a number of different and mutually exclusive possibilities, and after doubts and hesitations takes whatever is common to them all. If writing as a Turk, and discussing Islam, Judaism and Christianity, he will end as a monotheist; if he adopts the *persona* of a Christian, as in his letters to Vopsel, he will confine himself to a minimal Christianity. From the variety of beliefs about the soul which he frequently lists, he extracts the basic idea that there must be some sort of immortality; when considering the intolerant claims made by each religion, he maintains that men can be virtuous in any religion, and hopes that virtue will earn salvation. He even compromises between the dualism of matter and spirit, when discussing the tricky problem of creation, by using the concept of 'essence' or 'matière subtile', which partakes of both substances.

Marana's deistic moods occur when this approach is applied to the doctrines which are disputed among different religions. His scepticism leads him to say that he is unsure about everything except God, or agrees with the deists who are 'sceptiques en toute autre chose' (III, L. 111; IV, L. 35). He is not, though, a sceptical fideist like La Mothe le Vayer, despite several points of resemblance.[37] He prefers, as he says, to 'diriger ma foi par ma raison' (III, L. 78), and the compromise solutions he reaches, usually by taking what might be called the highest common factor of all the alternatives, are rational, or at least reasonable.

The effect of the literary convention chosen by Marana is also relevant. Correspondence from a foreign observer was destined to become one of the most popular and typical eighteenth-century *genres,* and Marana's importance as an innovator can hardly be overrated. But the device also has religious implications. The Muslim secret agent, living among Christians, can scarcely avoid comparing the two religions, if he considers the subjects at all, and the comparison of religions is the essence of Mahmut's approach. It is not necessary that he should invariably end up with the compromise between them, believing only in God – in the *Lettres persanes,* Rica and Usbek

---

[35] For instance in II, L. 73; V, L. 42, L. 108.

[36] In IV, L. 56, Mahmut reminisces about the freedom of conversation in cafés, many years previously, but is not tolerant towards those who express criticism, even in this setting.

[37] Marana's suggestion that virtuous theists might be saved is like La Mothe in *De la vertu des païens,* and his fondness for surveying a long list of ideas on a particular subject is a favourite method of composition with La Mothe also, as in the dialogue *De la divinité* (see Chapter 3, n. 5), but La Mothe concludes with scepticism and recourse to faith.

continue to profess themselves Muslims – but such a conclusion is natural and understandable. There are parallels between Mahmut and his creator, the Genoese living in France who, though evidently a free-thinker, supports the official policies of his adoptive country, but since little is known of Marana himself the influence of his personal situation can only be guessed at.

Because of the fluctuations and eclecticism of Marana's religious ideas, especially his tendency to materialist pantheism when discussing God, creation and the soul, he cannot be regarded simply as an early exponent of deism. About his theism few resevations are necessary; he maintains the belief in God even in the most unpromising situations, such as when he seems to accept Epicurean atomism. If, as is likely, 'déisme' in the 1680s and 1690s could mean theism without any obvious implication of hostility to Christianity, several of Mahmut's letters would fit the definition. As for the letter (IV, L. 35) in which he himself expresses approval for the 'gens qu'on appelle déistes', the most likely interpretation is that he meant Socinians or a similar group, Christian, but rationalist critics of Scripture. If so, his approval for their opinion is the fictional 'Muslim' equivalent of tolerant Christian unitarianism, the views of the 'Sociniens ou déistes' attacked by Jurieu or Bossuet. To see him as a direct precursor of anti-Christian Enlightenment deism is less convincing. There are some criticisms of the Christian religion, rather obviously Muslim in tone; the more severe of them concern ritual observance, and culminate in the confession of Quietist inclinations in worship. The imposture theory of religion often obtrudes, but as with the direct criticisms of Scripture its scope is always limited by Mahmut's habitual hesitancy. The criticisms often seem little more than local colour, a necessity of the *genre.* In the *Lettres persanes,* Mahmut's descendants Rica and Usbek are also conciliatory to established religion, or only moderately critical; it was in Voltaire's hands that the letter-series became more perceptibly aggressive.

Part III

The first French deists, 1700–1715

CHAPTER 8

GILBERT'S *CALEJAVA*: RATIONAL DEISM
WITH PROTESTANT OVERTONES

The first year of the new century saw the modest inauguration of deism proper. Modest, because Gilbert's *Histoire de Calejava* is a work of small distinction, and was not distributed or sold; but its historical significance is considerable, since it contains, for the first time, a religious system which is unequivocally deistic. The 'Avaïtes' profess a complete and coherent form of natural religion, obviously Cartesian in character, which is independent of Christianity and to some extent opposed to it. Thus begins the series of works, in print or manuscript, which during the first ten or twelve years of the century are the textual expression of the first phase of French deism. With Gilbert we move out of the ambiguous area of antecedents and into comparatively open territory where there is no doubt about what we are exploring.

Claude Gilbert, who was born in 1652 and died in 1720, was a lawyer of Dijon. He was acquainted with the Abbé Philibert Papillon, the author of a *Bibliothèque des auteurs de Bourgogne* (1745), who provides some information about him. His book was privately printed in 1700, but the printer was warned that he might get into trouble because of it and handed over the entire edition to Gilbert, who had it burnt, preserving only one copy. According to Papillon, it was he who saved this surviving copy from the same fate when, after Gilbert's death, his widow wanted to destroy it.[1]

The work is divided into twelve 'livres', of which the seventh and eighth were suppressed by the printer on his own account. Papillon describes them as 'quelques endroits dangereux concernant le christianisme et le judaïsme'. The first book describes another imaginary land, Calejava. Gilbert situates it in the far north, perhaps to make a change from the Austral Land utilized by Foigny and Veiras. Three French subjects and their Turkish guide arrive there, to find that it is an egalitarian, rationally organized republic, founded

---

[1] Papillon, *Bibliothèque des auteurs de Bourgogne*, Vol. I, p. 249. The full title of Gilbert's book, which is anonymous, is: *Histoire de Calejava ou de l'isle des hommes raisonnables: Avec le parallele de leur Morale et du Christianisme*. The only known copy is in the Bibliothèque nationale. The last two *livres* (including the 'Parallele') were reprinted by Lachèvre in his *Les successeurs de Cyrano*, together with Papillon's *Notice*.

eight or nine hundred years before, by a doctor who discovered an elixir of life.

Of the four travellers, Alatre takes the leading part; 'Alatre était bon philosophe, bon mathématicien, et bon jurisconsulte (...) Quoiqu'il n'eût pas beaucoup de religion, il avait beaucoup d'honneur et de probité; il jugeait de tout sainement et sans prévention' (pp. 15–16). With his wife Eudoxe, whose name indicates equally sound judgement, and his father-in-law Abraham Christofile, he had left France because of the persecution of Protestants in the 1680s. Christofile is a Huguenot, but we are not told whether Alatre is also of Huguenot descent.[2] Gilbert is not a sophisticated author, and it seems very likely that his heroes directly reflect his own background. Their guide, however, is presumably pure invention. He 'se nommait Samieski, il était Turc d'origine fort entêté du mahométisme, il ne manquait pas pourtant d'esprit et de savoir' (p. 23).

After some strange adventures, the party is rescued from the wastes of Lithuania by some Avaites, the inhabitants of Calejava.[3] Once installed in Calejava, the four travellers are subjected to a lecture, from one of their Avaite rescuers, about the artificial and excessively luxurious life of Europe. The Avaites try to avoid contact with European countries, but Alatre, and apparently Eudoxe also, is invited to remain — presumably because he lacks enthusiasm for the Catholic religion.

The proposal made to the other two Europeans is the starting-point for the long discussions which make up the bulk of the *Histoire de Calejava*. They too may remain, says the Avaite, on certain conditions: 'Pourvu (...) qu'ils soient persuadés de l'existence d'un Dieu, de l'immortalité de l'âme, et des peines et des récompenses de l'autre vie, nous nous pourrons accommoder d'eux, et même de Samieski; mais il faut qu'ils soient convaincus de ces vérités par des raisons solides et naturelles, et non par l'autorité' (p. 32). In other words, natural religion, originating in reason, is to replace faith. It is noticeable that Alatre, unlike other visitors to deist Utopias, already professes the views of his hosts, and he joins the Avaite in order to instruct the others in rational religion. The discussions begin by establishing the method to be followed, proceed to consider the concept of God and the human soul, and work round (after the missing books, no doubt largely critical, on Judaism and Christianity) to ethical matters. This is the pattern of several later treatises of rational deism.

---

[2]   In his brief study of the *Histoire de Calejava*, Lanson observes that the name means 'no worship' (*Origines de l'esprit philosophique*, p. 222). This corresponds to Furetière's definition of a deist, in 1690: 'qui reconnaît seulment un Dieu, sans lui rendre aucun culte extérieur'. The significance of 'Abraham Christofile' is no doubt that he is attached to both the Old and New Testaments.

[3]   Did Gilbert know that in far-off Lithuania there had existed a rational religion, that of the early anti-trinitarians and the Minor Reformed Church of Poland, later the Socinians? It had been suppressed in 1660.

Rationalism reigns supreme in the first set of educative dialogues; the principles of Christofile, who is a fideist, are swept aside. The atmosphere is overwhelmingly Cartesian. Alatre will accept as truthful only such principles as 'je pense donc je suis' or (an axiom which he claims is his own) 'ce qui est si clair qu'on n'en peut douter est vrai'. There is only one class of genuine truths, those which 'ne dépendent que des principes immuables et établis par l'Auteur de la nature' (pp. 34–35). The incompatibility of reason with faith is illustrated with great clarity when, basing himself on these principles, Alatre attacks one of the central concepts in fideism, that of authority. Beliefs imposed by authority, by which he means the religions of different nations, are not immutable; varying from country to country, they must be false – such is the implication. Authority itself is no more than the reputation of a small number of learned men.[4] Nor does the Bible, or so it seems, have the power to decide belief; words are ambiguous (only ideas can be clear and distinct). The example is 'Ceci est mon corps' (p. 46), the scriptural authority for doctrines of the Eucharist which are sadly at variance with each other. The ambiguities of words also allow it to be claimed that prophecies (in the Old Testament) have been fulfilled.

The repudiation of biblical authority is tempered somewhat in the second dialogue, in which it is conceded that the Bible may contain a degree of historical truth. Following Descartes and perhaps Bayle, Eudoxe is doubtful whether historical truth can be established; the discussion skirts New Testament history, but does not conclude that both religious and secular history is equally unreliable. We are told instead, vaguely, that 'pour le bien de la société civile' it is advisable that men should accept as true things that often are not, 'plutôt que de laisser tout indécis' (p. 56). This seems to mean that the authority of Scripture must be accepted because the religion founded on it has social value. When Cartesian scepticism about factual history is too radically destructive, Gilbert draws back.

The final dialogue of the second book rounds off the system of rationalism by extending it, in the manner of Malebranche, but with echoes of Cicero, into the sphere of ethics. Reason is 'cette heureuse guide qui nous conduit toujours au bien'; it raises men to the level of gods (p. 57). The Avaite, who is the spokesman at this point, concludes that rational beings are capable of making errors, but denies that the weakness lies in reason itself; it is due to men who make a bad use of their free will. This theory of error

---

[4] The overt reference in Gilbert is to Seneca, *De vita beata,* but almost certainly Gilbert was influenced by Bayle's destructive analysis of the concept of tradition in the *Pensées diverses sur la comète,* section VII. In the first three books of *Calejava* there are points of detail and general arguments concerning atheism and the unreliability of history which seem to come from the *Pensées diverses;* cf. n. 23 below.

presumably comes from the *Méditations métaphysiques,* perhaps by way of Malebranche.[5]

All that has been said hitherto has revealed harmonious conformity between the views of Alatre and Eudoxe on one side and the Avaite on the other. It is only when Alatre reports their conclusions to the others that he meets opposition, for Christofile responds with fideism in its purest form: the Christian should believe before he has any reason, except obedience, for doing so. The illustration is the apostle Peter, walking on the waves at Christ's behest.

When we reach the central subject in any deistic treatise, the concept of God, in the *Livre troisième,* the Avaite curiously adopts a *précieux* style in order to attack atheism: 'il faut s'étourdir furieusement pour donner dans l'athéisme' (p. 73). After a Baylian analysis of the motivation of atheists (they cannot accept the degraded ideas about God which superstition spreads), a remedy is proposed, which is to remodel on Cartesian lines the prevailing conception of God: 'un Etre infiniment parfait qui existe de tout temps par lui-même et nécessairement' (p. 77). However, there is some criticism of Descartes's own proofs of the existence of God; Eudoxe finds them too metaphysical, and Samieski prefers arguments from design and final causes – the architectural quality of the universe and the structure of the human body. Among the list of phenomena which, for him, lead to the knowledge of God is breast-feeding (p. 80; God has arranged that mothers would be uncomfortable if they did not feed their offspring themselves).

Despite all this, there are rebellious spirits, we are told, atheists again, who believe the universe to be uncreated and eternal. This ancient idea even turns into Bayle's version of Spinozism in the *Dictionnaire* when Christofile asks: 'Ne peut-il tomber dans l'esprit d'un homme que l'univers est incréé, qu'il est Dieu?' Gilbert's characters closely follow Bayle's arguments on the subject (pp. 81–83).[6] The risks of materialism are also perceptible in the discussion about the nature and existence of the soul. Alatre and Eudoxe agree that it must be an immaterial substance. If she is thirsty, says Eudoxe, but decides that it would be harmful for her to have a drink (perhaps she is thinking of dropsy), her soul is in conflict with itself, which would be impossible if it were a material entity (pp. 89–90). Her husband in turn parades a series of standard Cartesian arguments (doubting cannot be square,

---

[5]   The original source must be the fourth of the *Méditations métaphysiques,* but the direct influence seems more likely to be Malebranche (e.g. *Recherche de la vérité,* Livre I, Ch. 2) in view of other signs of his thought in Gilbert.

[6]   For instance, in saying that it is absurd that one part of the universe-god can be unhappy because of another part. Cf. Bayle's article 'Spinoza', Notes N and O. Bernard Tocanne, 'Aspects de la pensée libertine à la fin du XVII e siècle: Le cas de Claude Gilbert', *XVII e Siècle* 127 (1980), 213–224 (p. 216), suggests another possible source, Malebranche's *Entretiens sur la métaphysique,* IX, 2.

and so on) designed to demonstrate the irreducible division between things extended and things intellectual. Eventually he states flatly that 'il est clair et évident par la seule considération de l'idée de la substance qui pense qu'elle n'est point étendue' (p. 94).[7]

These arguments are the foundation of the further demonstration that the soul is immortal. However, Gilbert now shows signs of a decline in confidence. He starts by claiming that the soul, not possessing extension, does not perish with the body, but at the end of a series of replies and objections, in the second dialogue of the fourth book, he admits that the immortality of the soul may be problematical. Later, we are offered a list of the advantages of believing that the soul is immortal; we should not fear death, for instance. The *Livre quartrième* ends with a promise from the Avaite that the theologians of his country will supply proofs that there are rewards and punishments in the afterlife, a truth believed universally, but 'plutôt par instinct que par raison' (p. 114). Some fifty pages later, the argument is developed (pp. 163–166): men do not always obey the laws of society, and those who disobey are not always found out and punished; hence there must be a life after death, in which retribution will be meted out to wrongdoers (among whom 'faux dévots' are prominent). A note at the end of this section informs us that 'Ce discours suppose et prouve l'immortalité de l'âme'. Gilbert may be guilty of naïve or wishful thinking, but it is a sign of the times that, when his rational demonstrations are inadequate, he resists what had been a common tendency, to resort to faith.[8] He prefers the argument from social utility, which was to be no less common in the eighteenth century.

With the *Livre sixième,* the dialogue form hitherto adopted gives way to a series of 'Leçons' on Avaite moral and theological ideas. In this book the arguments also appear to be less derivative; this suggests that the opinions ascribed specifically to the Avaites are more Gilbert's own than the conventional rationalism of the earlier books. The influence of Malebranche is still noticeable, however.

Gilbert's views are a form of providentialism. God is good, and his providence is extended to all men; it is 'à volontés générales' (p. 154). Since he does not will the good of any man or group of men, the Jews are not the chosen race, favoured above other nations (p. 154).[9] God wishes all men to

---

[7]   Gilbert remarks (p. 91), no doubt with irony, that these arguments are customarily said to be due to St Augustine. See Busson, *Religion des classiques,* p. 325 and n. 1, referring in this connection to Arnauld and De La Forge.

[8]   See Busson, ibid., pp. 324 ff., on the confidence of earlier Cartesians over the spirituality of the soul and their hesitations over its immortality.

[9]   In another comment Gilbert shows his legal interests, when he says that since God does not favour individuals, the medieval custom of relying on the divine judgement in trials by duel was wrong (p. 140).

be happy; and with this, Gilbert's providentialism takes on a secular look. Providence, it seems, applies to the life on earth, not the life to come (despite the arguments about retribution for crime). The Avaites have followed God's will, and constructed a society intended to ensure the happiness of all its members. In order to do the same as individuals, 'nous devons prendre pour manière d'agir celle qui contribue le plus à rendre les hommes heureux, sans avoir égard sur qui le bien doit tomber' (p. 161). The impression is that the well-being of mankind is a matter for mankind itself, with God playing only a subordinate role. As for what happiness consists in, the answer is downright: 'Dieu ne veut que notre bien physique', according to a remark at the end of the book (p. 318).[10]

God does not intervene directly in human affairs, and we are told at one point that his 'indépendance' (p. 133) puts him beyond any need for gratitude or worship. In Foigny, very similar considerations of an Epicurean type had been the basis for Australian pessimism about life.[11] Gilbert, however, believes that God is benevolent and has given men both the will and the means to be happy. Self-help is advised; if we want to fill our granaries, we should not just pray, but carry the corn there ourselves (pp. 154–155). Furthermore, men can attain happiness naturally, through the enjoyment of pleasures (p. 227).

Gilbert's utilitarian, or even materialistic, tendencies are obvious here; in the first year of the eighteenth century, he seems to have advanced disproportionately far beyond his immediate predecessor in the history of deism, Marana, who had only with difficulty freed himself from fears of eternal damnation. The reason seems to be reflection on Nicole's concept of 'amour-propre éclairé', found more than once in the *Histoire de Calejava,* and on Malebranche's arguments that pleasure can make men naturally happy.[12]

At the end of the *Livre sixième,* a note informs the reader that the seventh and eighth, which concern the Jewish and Christian faiths, have been suppressed because their content 'ne serait peut-être pas de notre goût'. These are the passages which Gilbert's friend Papillon called 'dangereux'. It is possible that the criticisms were not particularly damaging. Those made of Islam in the ninth book are mild, although the target was a safe one. Several might apply to Christianity also. Debating whether miracles demonstrate the truth of a religion, Alatre asserts that a miracle ascribed to Mohammed was

---

[10] A dialogue in the tenth book amplifies this; Eudoxe explains that some activities are utilitarian but provide natural pleasure also (p. 222).

[11] See Chapter 5, p. 62.

[12] Gilbert's reference here is to the ideas of 'un habile homme' (p. 326), which was elucidated by Lanson (*Origines de l'esprit philosophique,* p. 224): the ideas are those in Pierre Nicole's treatise *De la charité et de l'amour-propre,* published in 1675. Malebranche stated the principle that pleasure is a good in the *Recherche de la vérité,* Livre IV, Ch. X.

due only to natural causes (p. 187); the Avaite adds a remark critical of the credulity of those who were converted to Christianity by the miraculous incident of Jesus and the woman of Samaria (pp. 191–192).[13] Again, Pascal's wager argument is mentioned when the speakers are discussing the Koran, the Avaite saying that any religion could employ the same argument (p. 185).[14] The fourth dialogue of this book also relates to Christianity, when Alatre makes objections to the Quietist concept of 'le pur amour', which he regards as an illusion (pp. 201–204).

There are critical passages elsewhere, scattered among the later books. At the end of the tenth book, in an argument with Christofile, Alatre refutes – or reinterprets – the doctrine of Original Sin: it is not scriptural, he says, and Adam's sin consisted in making laws (p. 232).[15] Alatre defends human nature and the passions, in arguments which, as Roger Mercier has shown, are typical of the early eighteenth century.[16] The force of the criticisms is limited by the fact that Alatre relies on the authority of the Bible, despite his rationalism.[17] The same is true of the criticisms in the *Livre onzième*. Here, Eudoxe cites the Bible systematically in order to demonstrate to her father that Avaite beliefs and practices are compatible with his Huguenot convictions; she wishes to persuade him that he can continue to live in Calejava. Whatever the suppressed criticisms of Christianity may have been, the purpose at the end of the *Histoire de Calejava* seems to be conciliatory.[18]

From Christofile's point of view, the attempt at reconciling Christianity and Avaite deism fails. He believes in tolerance (providing that the non-conformist 'ne trouble pas le repos de l'état', pp. 255–256), and is prepared to extend Christian love to the heretical Avaites, but is not persuaded by Hobbes's argument, that Christian salvation depends only on believing that Jesus the son of Mary was the Messiah, a principle which would have allowed

---

[13] John 4. 7 ff.

[14] This is described by Busson (*Religion des classiques*, p. 345, n. 2) as the first attack on the 'pari', but from his preceding account of contemporary reactions to Pascal it does not appear that such a criticism as the Avaite's would have seemed unduly bold.

[15] Alatre supports this from St Paul, citing Romans 5. 20.

[16] Roger Mercier, *La réhabilitation de la nature humaine (1700–1750)* (Villemonble, 1960), Pt. I, ii: *La critique morale*.

[17] A note at the end of the *Livre dixième* (p. 250) advises the reader to consult with care the scriptural passages cited, even to the extent of reading the Greek text.

[18] The conciliatory nature of Eudoxe's 'parallele' between Christian and Avaite religion is the main reason for disagreeing with Tocanne's hypothesis, in his article cited in n. 6 above (p. 215), that in the lost books of *Calejava* Gilbert put forward a version of the 'three imposters' theory (Moses, Jesus, Mohammed) as an attack on Christianity. It seems more likely that any criticisms were anti-Catholic rather than anti-Christian, and that if Gilbert used the imposture theory he would also have recognized the value of religion, like Veiras of Boulainviller (see Chapters 5 and 11). The fact that Samieski defends Mohammed against the charge of imposture (pp. 193–194) bears no implications for Christianity, since the charge was a normal Christian view of Islam.

him to be saved while remaining in Calejava.[19] His view is that since the Avaites are heretics, he cannot live among them; Eudoxe, however, regards reason as a Christian principle. At one point an exchange occurs which expresses neatly the difference between her and her father. He says that 'la raison (...) ne peut nous enseigner que la loi naturelle. Et la loi naturelle, répondit Eudoxe, en quoi diffère-t-elle de l'Evangile?' (p. 257).

For Christofile, or course, the difference consists in the requirement, over and above the beliefs due to reason alone, for Christian revelation. The argument resembles that between Foigny's Sadeur and the Australian Suains, but in Foigny the division had been deeper — between European and Australian, rather than between two generations of the same family. Even so, Christofile remains unpersuaded that scriptural belief is compatible with such things as the communal ownership of property, the abolition of baptism, and the dissolution of marriage.[20]

Christofile's reluctance no doubt reflects the reaction which Gilbert expected from conventional opinion, but he made a sustained effort to show that the religion of Calejava was not inimical to Christianity, or at least not to a version of Christianity which could be derived from the New Testament alone. For instance, Eudoxe defends the lack of external or ritual forms of worship in Calejava by referring to St John's Gospel (p. 291),[21] even though she can be critical of the Scriptures on other subjects, such as St Paul's doctrine of marriage (p. 271). In the end, Christofile refuses to listen any longer to the flood of biblical quotations and heretical opinions. Alatre, on the other hand, regards his wife's 'parallèle' as the true meaning of Scripture, which has been abandoned by those he calls 'les Pharisiens du Christianisme' (p. 304). He seems to be referring to Catholics.[22]

The whole discussion raises the question whether Gilbert's imaginary religion is really separate from Christianity — in other words, whether it should be classified with the anti-Christian deism of the Enlightenment, or with the heresies which Christofile frequently mentions. There is something to be said for the view that the religion of Calejava is Gilbert's personal and idiosyncratic version of Christianity, devised (by a man of Huguenot descent) as a kind of imaginative compensation for being forced to live in Catholic France after 1685. Yet the basis of Avaite natural religion is reason, and it is the exposition of its rational elements which occupies all the early

---

[19] Gilbert provides the references: to Hobbe's *De cive*, Book III.

[20] *Calejava*, pp 260, 261, 273–279. Marriage is the subject of a long section of the 'parallèle', pp. 264 ff.: marriage is an obligation of the natural law, celibacy leaves numberless souls to 'croupir dans le néant' (p. 271), polygamy can be justified.

[21] John 4. 23. Here Eudoxe's argument, about the sufficiency of internal worship, has greater plausibility than many of her interpretations of Scripture.

[22] This is suggested by an ensuing attack on human traditions, the ban on usury, and monasticism (pp. 304–308).

sections of the work. The conciliatory parallel with Christianity comes at the end; biblical support appears to be desirable rather than essential. The religion of Calejava should therefore be considered as independent of Christianity, despite the many links between them. While there is little that is hostile to Christian belief in general, in the work as it has come down to us, there is a degree of implicit hostility to later seventeenth-century Catholicism.

At the end of the book the Turk and the Huguenot depart for France. Before they go, they receive more advice, apparently intended for Huguenots remaining in France after the proscription of their religion in 1685. They should obey the law, for the good of society generally, but obedience is not due to laws which, when observed, produce no material benefits (p. 317). This must refer to the legal imposition of Catholic worship. The revealing word 'superstition', perhaps the commonest anti-Catholic accusation, is a further clue.

Gilbert's 'théologie' and 'morale', which are presented as a single system, are a combination of metaphysical rationalism and social utilitarianism, with little to bind them together except the principle that God wishes men to be happy. The Avaite deity is the creator of the universe, but he is 'indépendant', having no need of worship, and plays no part in human life except for sanctioning the pursuit of happiness. Presumably he also punishes malefactors after death. The religion of Calejava is thus open to the objection often levelled at deism, that it tends to remove religion to the plane of philosophy, or subordinates it to requirements that are intrinsically secular. The sources of this implied separation of religious and social concerns may be more diffuse than the influence of any one or two writers, but it is akin to Bayle's separation of religion and morality, especially in his argument that a society without religion would survive, and to Nicole's idea of a society based only on 'amour-propre éclairé'.[23] Gilbert's Avaites are theists, whereas Bayle (and Nicole, by implication) was writing about atheism, but Avaite society, in order to function, does not appear to need the belief in God, only the desire for material happiness.

As regards metaphysics, it is clear that Gilbert owes much to Descartes and Malebranche for questions of method and the truths of the existence of God and the spirituality of the soul. Lanson said that Gilbert was 'imprégné de Malebranche', which is a little exaggerated — the secularist tendencies of Gilbert give quite a different impression from Malebranche's intensely Christian philosophy — but there are many borrowings.[24] The result is a

---

[23]   Bayle. *Pensées diverses sur la comète*, sections 133, 161ff. on an atheist society. On Nicole, see n. 12 above.

[24]   Lanson, *Origines de l'esprit philosophique*, p. 224.

cruder version of Malebranche. The theory of vision in God, for instance, becomes a cursory acknowledgement of divine power – 'c'est par lui que notre âme voit, qu'elle sent, qu'elle pense, et qu'elle veut' (p. 133) – instead of a theory which, had it been taken seriously, would have rendered the deistic utilitarianism of Calejava impossible. An element in Malebranche's thought which might have had greater significance for Gilbert is the principle that God's will is general in application. This could have given him the basic Avaite doctrine that providence is 'à volontés générales', unless he took it from Foigny's *Terre australe connue*.[25]

The presence in Calejava of obvious and overt references to particular writers should not obscure the fact that the concept of a deity possessing abstract and general attributes, the God of 'natural religion', prevailed so widely in the late seventeenth century that the investigation of possible sources is hardly necessary. Avaite religion is contemporary theocentrism taken to an extreme, so much so that it becomes destructive of the doctrines of particular religions – the faith of Christofile, and Samieski's rather less definite Muslim allegiances. Although nothing is said directly about Christ in the work as we now have it, Eudoxe appeals to the New Testament only when arguing with Christofile, not otherwise, since she condescends to recognize that Scripture has authority for him. What Gilbert might have said about the figure of Christ is a matter of guesswork, but some conclusions can be drawn from Christofile's response to Eudoxe's 'parallèle'. He retires, 'en murmurant quelque chose entre ses dents d'Arius, de Pélage, de Déisme et d'Epicurisme qu'on ne put pas entendre' (p. 302). He must mean that the Avaites are Arian in denying the divinity of Christ (which would still permit them to honour him), and Pelagian in denying Original Sin and supposing that men can be virtuous without grace. As for 'déisme', its position after the names of two heresiarchs recalls its sixteenth-century associations, which however are counterbalanced by 'Epicurisme'; this could refer either to the Epicurean gods unconcerned with human affairs (like the Avaite God who has no need of worship) or to the Avaites' defence of physical pleasures.[26] By 1700, there were at least three meanings of deism which Gilbert might have had in mind: theism pure and simple; theism specifically excluding 'external' worship; and rational Arian opinions. Gilbert's use of the word indicates, interestingly, that it was now a suitable (through hostile) term for

[25]   On Foigny, see Chapter 5, pp. 61, 62. Malebranche developed his distinction between 'volonté générale' and 'volontés particulières' in God after the *Recherche de la vérité*; it was expounded in the 'Premier discours' of the *Traité de la nature et de la grâce*, 1680, and was a basic issue in the subsequent controversy with Arnauld; the principle that 'Dieu n'agit point par des volontés particulières' is common in the *Méditations chrétiennes*, 1683. See André Robinet, *Système et existence dans l'oeuvre de Malebranche* (Paris, 1965), L. I, section III, Ch. I, especially p. 92.
[26]   The latter alternative is Tocanne's interpretation (article cited in n. 6, p. 224).

a non-Christian, rational, natural religion – assuming he meant Avaite deism and not merely Eudoxe's half-way house, her commentary on the New Testament. The 'parallèle' suggest, in broad terms, that Christ's moral teachings are valuable, but Eudoxe reinterprets them in a secular manner.[27]

Gilbert's book can hardly be said to be in the front rank of religious works, but precisely because of its lack of distinction, it is convincing evidence that rational Christian thought had developed into deism. Gilbert was an educated layman, like the other deist writers of the first decade of the eighteenth century, but (like most of them also) was an amateur both as a writer and as a religious thinker. That the transition from enlightened Christianity to deism should have been made first by him was partly due to chance, since other deist works are very close in date to his, but shows too that the conditions for the appearance of deist thought were fully present. The special reason for Gilbert's move into deism was unquestionably the Huguenot background, indicated in many passages of the *Histoire de Calejava*.[28] The motive for his invention of an undenominational religion, barely distinguishable from the natural religion defined by apologists such as Abbadie, must lie in the situation of the Huguenots who were faced with the problem of defining their religious position after 1685. In that year Gilbert was aged thirty-three, and it is a plausible guess that Christofile represents his parents' generation, while he himself corresponds to Alatre. In this perspective, the Utopian deism of Calejava appears as a form of wish-fulfilment, an ideal, universalist religion which is compatible with the New Testament, and therefore acceptable to all Christians, but more especially Protestants. Some passages seem to imply criticism of the Catholic religion, but in a relatively mild form. There is an interesting contrast with Foigny's Catholic background; his hero Sadeur rejects the natural religion of the Austral Land. The relationship between Christofile, Eudoxe and Alatre suggests that the generation which was mature in 1700 was in the process of exchanging Christian faith for a newer and more abstract religion.

[27] See especially the commentary on the Lord's Prayer, pp. 293 ff.; references to our daily bread and the forgiveness of sins mean, it seems, that God wishes us to be happy in this world.

[28] This factor has been inexplicably neglected in studies of Gilbert, who is customarily regarded as being deistic through *libertinage*.

CHAPTER 9

LAHONTAN AND GUEUDEVILLE: NATURAL RELIGION FROM CANADA

The real successors to Gilbert's rational deism are the manuscript treatises, the *Examen de la religion* and *Difficultés sur la religion,* but chronologically they are preceded by another dialogue between the religious representatives of Europe and a distant country, in this case Canada, or New France. In order to compose the *Histoire de Calejava,* Gilbert had devised a Utopian setting for an indigenous French form of natural religion, based on Cartesian rationalism. Lahontan reversed the process: he observed a real primitive religion in the New World and, apparently with some help from an ex-Benedictine named Gueudeville, transformed it into a conventional natural religion including some criticisms of French Catholicism. In the resultant work, known now as the *Dialogues curieux,* Lahontan discusses religion and other matters with a Red Indian chieftain, 'Adario', the spokesman for a simple deistic religion which is not merely a theoretical construction. Adario comes from the tribes in Canada among whom Lahontan had lived and whom the missionaries were trying to convert. His views in the *Dialogues* are a compromise between a descriptive report of Red Indian belief and the abstract idea of natural religion which had long been current in French thought.

The Baron de Lahontan was a soldier, born in 1666.[1] He was in the New World for at least eleven years, from about 1683 to 1694, during the period of rivalry between England and France over the colonization of Canada, and sent letters home about what he saw there, later incorporating them into a book. He was of a critical disposition, and at times his relations with the military and political authorities were stormy. After a quarrel with the governor of a French settlement in Newfoundland, he left the army to wander round the northern countries of Europe, avoiding France for fear of punishment. Eventually, in Holland, he turned to writing for a living, and in 1703 he published two volumes which appeared under the titles of *Nouveaux voyages* and *Mémoires de l'Amérique septentrionale* by the Baron de Lahontan. They contained the material for the volume with which we are mainly concerned, the *Dialogues curieux,* but there is some doubt whether

---

[1]   For biographical information see Gilbert Chinard's Introduction to his edition: *Baron de Lahontan, Dialogues curieux entre l'auteur et un sauvage de bon sens qui a voyagé et Mémoires de l'Amérique septentrionale,* edited by Gilbert Chinard (Baltimore, 1931), cited henceforth as Chinard, Introduction; and now (1982) the monograph by Rosenberg cited in n. 3.

the *Dialogues* were written by Lahontan himself, or by the former monk to whom they have often been attributed, Nicolas Gueudeville.

The dialogues were first published by Lahontan, still in 1703, but in England and in English. From the researches of Gilbert Chinard, it appears that they were immediately republished in Holland, in French, by the L'Honoré brothers, who had published Lahontan's first two books.[2] The title they used was: 'Supplément aux voyages du Baron de Lahontan, où l'on trouve des dialogues curieux entre l'auteur et un sauvage de bon sens qui a voyagé'. (The savage was supposed to have visited Europe.) Chinard's view is that Gueudeville was not responsible for this volume (although the contrary had been asserted by Jean Le Clerc, the Arminian writer), but that his role was confined to revising the dialogues later, for an edition which appeared in 1705; for this Gueudeville wrote a new dialogue on the subject of property. Several point remain obscure, however, so that the degree of collaboration between Lahontan and Gueudeville cannot be reliably assessed.[3] In any case, the *Dialogues curieux* were closely modelled on Lahontan's travel books and letters, which were published with them and utilized, in the dialogues, to present criticisms of the Christian religion made by the Red Indian who symbolized natural reason.

The *Mémoires* and *Nouveaux voyages* are in some respects more interesting than the celebrated but artificial *Dialogues*. They give a vivid portrayal of life in Europe and Canada, as seen by a man who presents himself as a Catholic, but not devout. He is anti-clerical, and does not believe in stories of witchcraft. His acquaintances, he says, view this in the worst possible light: 'On me prend pour un athée, (...) parce que je me tue de dire à nos prêtres et à nos gentilshommes qu'il n'appartient qu'à des cerveaux creux de donner dans le panneau de ces rêveries (...). Sachez, Monsieur, qu'il faut absolument nier la toute-puissance de Dieu, si on établit dans le monde les sorciers, les magiciens, les devins (...) et le diable visible que nous

---

[2]   Ibid., pp. 19–25. Chinard concludes that Lahontan revised the *Mémoires* 'après avoir fréquenté les libertins et les réfugiés de Hollande' (p. 29), and that 'écrits en 1703 par Lahontan, les *Nouveaux voyages* et les *Dialogues* furent révisés en 1705 par le polygraphe à la solde des libraires de La Haye' (p. 41). Some passages in the later dialogues are revolutionary in tone (ibid., pp. 42–44), and Gueudeville might well have been responsible for these.

[3]   It is not known whether Lahontan had any dealings with Gueudeville before or during the composition of the 1703 *Dialogues*. The dialogue on religion has some features which are not found in the *Mémoires* or *Nouveaux voyages*, and it seems likely to me that these are due to Gueudeville (see n. 12 below). Jean Le Clerc believed that all the dialogues were written by him (*Bibliothèque ancinne et moderne* 22 (1724), Pt. I, p. 221, cited by Chinard, Introduction, pp. 37 and 38, n. 1); he disapproved of Gueudeville, whom he called 'un libertin déclaré'. The matter has been discussed recently by Aubrey Rosenberg, *Nicolas Gueudeville and his work (1652–172?)* (The Hague, 1982), pp. 123–130, who gives good reasons for supposing that the revisions of the *Dialogues* were indeed by Gueudeville. For further reasons, see note 12 below.

mettons à la queue de toutes ces chimères' (*Mémoires,* p. 189).[4] Lahontan himself regards his attitude to magic as that of an 'esprit fort', and he defines the phrase: 'un homme qui approfondit la nature des choses; qui ne croit rien que ce que la raison a mûrement examiné' (p. 190).

The passage about God's omnipotence and the Devil is the nearest approach to deism that can be found in the *Mémoires,* which seem to be the authentic expression of opinion by a Catholic layman enlightened enough to deplore the superstitions of the French countryside in the late seventeenth century. He also tells a picturesque but unedifying anecdote about being taken for a Huguenot in the depths of Béarn,[5] and relates an argument with a Portuguese doctor about the ancestry of Red Indians; being beardless, they cannot, according to the doctor, be descended from Adam. On this point, Lahontan is fideist, a little too emphatically for his sincerity not to be questioned: 'il n'est pas permis de douter, sans être dépourvu de foi, de bon sens, et de jugement, qu'Adam est le seul père de tous les hommes' (*Nouveaux voyages,* p. 252).[6]

In what he says about Canada, Lahontan admires the Indians for their defiant independence, and is scornful of missionaries. Their only successes, he says, are the conversions of 'enfants moribonds' and decrepit old men, and he thinks that they treat the Christian mysteries cavalierly when trying to convert Iroquois Indians in haste, before they die at the stake.[7] As for the Iroquois religion, it seems from Lahontan's account to have consisted in an uncomplicated belief in nature gods called spirits. There is a 'grand esprit' or 'maître de la vie'; he appears and acts in all things visible and imagined (*Nouveaux voyages,* p. 31; *Mémoires,* p. 110–113). Not all spirits are good. The Iroquois believe that spirits are present in anything which they do not

[4]   Quotations are from: *Nouveaux voyages de Mr. le Baron de Lahontan dans l'Amérique septentrionale* (…), 2 vols. (The Hague, 1703), Vol. II being entitled: *Mémoires de l'Amérique septentrionale, ou la suite des voyages de Mr. le baron de Lahontan* (…); and for the dialogues from: *Dialogues de Monsieur le baron de Lahontan et d'un sauvage, dans l'Amérique* (…) (Amsterdam, 1704), which contains the same text as the *Suplément aux Voyages du baron de Lahontan, où l'on trouve des Dialogues curieux entre l'auteur et un sauvage de bon sens qui a voyagé* (The Hague, 1703). As regards the passage quoted here, see on superstitious beliefs about witchcraft Ehrard, *Idée de nature,* Pt. I, Ch. 1.

[5]   In order to convince his interrogators that he was a Catholic, he showed them a picture on his snuff-box, of a naked woman, whom he claimed was Mary Magdalene. He expresses regret that, for the sake of saving his life, he was obliged to be so profane (*Mémoires,* pp. 202–204).

[6]   In the Preface to the *Dialogues,* Lahontan explains that his letters were addressed to 'un vieux cagot de parent, qui ne se nourrissait que de dévotion, et qui craignait les malignes influences de la cour. Il m'exhortait incessamment à ne rien écrire qui pût choquer les gens d'église et les gens du roi, de crainte que mes lettres ne fussent interceptées'. If this is true, it would account for the fideistic comments about the origin of Red Indians, mentioned above, which occur in Lettre 24 of the *Nouveaux voyages.*

[7]   On the missionaries, see *Nouveaux voyages,* L. 14 (p. 115) and L. 23 (p. 234). On Red Indian pride, ibid., p. 31: 'Ils se regardent comme des souverains qui ne relèvent d'autre maître que de Dieu seul qu'ils nomment le Grand Esprit'.

understand, and they talk about them jokingly. No doubt thinking of himself, Lahontan compares their attitude with that of an 'esprit fort' towards sorcery.

For Lahontan, such beliefs seem to have exemplified natural religion, and in reporting them he tends to adopt them to Christian theological concepts. He credits the Iroquois with a form of design argument for the existence of God and with the argument that God's existence is inseparable from his essence. On the subject of the soul, he takes more care to distinguish Indian from Christian ideas, while seeing resemblances between them. He says that the Iroquois believe in immortality, but do not know of the argument based on the unity of the soul. According to them, if the soul were mortal, all men would be happy in this world, because God in his wisdom would not allow otherwise (*Mémoires,* p. 114). For Lahontan, this examplifies rational demonstration, and he compares it with the Christian proofs. He seems to be trying to turn what must have been a straightforward imaginative mythology into a consistent set of theological propositions.

The Iroquois, then, are rationalists. They hold reason to be the noblest faculty of man (p. 117); it should not be forced to accept the incomprehensible, that is, the mysteries of Christian dogma. Faced with Jesuit teaching, the Indians are 'incrédules', for they refuse to surrender reason and accept the articles of faith; indeed, they mock at the whole idea of faith (p. 118). Some of this may well be Lahontan's own attitude, projected upon the Red Indians whom he admired. The impression we receive is of untutored but reasonable minds, the proper perquisite of men in the state of nature.

Lahontan's account is sometimes very close to the dialogue form into which it was transformed later, and one of the most interesting passages is a conversation he had while hunting with his friend, a Huron whom in the *Mémoires* he calls Le Rat. Le Rat was in fact a chieftain by the name of Kondiaronk, and famous for his character and attainments.[8] Of his view on religion, Lahontan says: 'il était si prévenu que la foi des Chrétiens est contraire à la raison, que je n'ai pu le convaincre après avoir tâché plusieurs fois de le détacher de ses préjugés. Quand je lui mettais sous les yeux les révélations de Moïse et des autres prophètes, ce consentement presque universel de toutes les nations à reconnaître Jésus-Christ, le martyre des disciples et des premiers fidèles, la succession perpétuelle de nos sacrés oracles, la ruine entière de la république des Juifs, la destruction de Jérusalem prédite par Notre Sauveur, il me demandait si mon père ou mon aïeul avait vu tous ces évènements, et si j'étais assez crédule pour m'imaginer que nos Ecritures fussent véritables, voyant que les relations de leur pays, écrites depuis quatre jours, étaient pleines de fables' (p. 122). The 'relations'

---

[8]   Chinard, Introduction, pp. 47ff., referring to Charlevoix's *Histoire de la Nouvelle France,* 1744.

are the missionaries' accounts of their success in converting the pagan Indians. What Le Rat has rejected is a selection of the standard apologetic proofs, which we shall see rejected at greater length in the clandestine manuscript works.

When the *Dialogues curieux* were written up from the *Mémoires,* Le Rat acquired a more decorous name, Adario, and his religion became more clearly an example of the traditional idea of natural religion. Talking to Lahontan, Adario expounds a comprehensive, though rudimentary, system of religion which is, of course, independent of Christianity and opposed to it. The opposition is emphasized by the attacks he makes on European society and morals. He thus enters the same category as Foigny's Australian, Suains, or Gilbert's Avaite, the representative of deism in a remote part of the world — except that his Canada is not Utopian.

To clarify matters from the start of the dialogues, Lahontan's or Gueudeville's new version of Kondiaronk is soon given a formal credo: 'Quoi! tu nous crois sans religion après avoir demeuré tant de temps avec nous? 1. Ne sais-tu pas que nous reconnaissons un créateur de l'univers, sous le nom de Grand Esprit (...) 2. Que nous confessons l'immortalité de l'âme. 3. Que le Grand Esprit nous a pourvus d'une raison capable de discerner le bien d'avec le mal?' (p. 2). For about half of its length, the dialogue on religion stays close to the *Mémoires,* adducing various arguments to show that if God had furnished men with a revealed religion, it would have been clear and unambiguous, and not confined to a single nation among the multitude. The Book of Genesis is treated merely as legend; revealed truth, says Adario, is inevitably distorted when it is handed down by tradition (p. 6).[9] From the *Mémoires* also comes the argument that the redemption of all men by Christ is inconsistent with theories of predestination (p. 10), together with Red Indian complaints about Christians who are immoral despite the excellence of their moral code. Throughout the dialogue, there are slighting remarks about the Jesuit presentation of Christianity.

The imitation by Adario of the previous Indian arguments is not all that is to be found in the *Dialogues;* they omit much that had been in the *Mémoires,* but also make important additions. Among the omissions, apart

---

[9]   Adario makes other criticisms: God would not have created man and woman by different methods; the temptation of Eve by the serpent is more fable than truth; if writing was invented three thousand years ago and printing 'depuis quatre ou cinq siècles', there can be no certainty of the truth of the Bible. Cf. *Mémoires,* pp. 118–119: 'ils disent que les écrits des siècles passés sont faux, supposés, changés ou altérés, puisque les histoires de nos jours ont le même sort. Qu'il faut être fou pour croire qu'un Etre tout-puissant soit demeuré dans l'inaction pendant toute une éternité et qu'il ne se soit avisé de produire des créatures que depuis cinq on six mille ans, qu'il ait créé Adam pour le faire tenter par un méchant Esprit à manger d'une pomme, qui a causé tous les malheurs de sa postérité, par la transmission prétendu de son péché (...)', and so on, about the Incarnation, sectarianism and the ambiguities of the Christian revelation. It is hard not to suspect that here, before the *Dialogues,* Lahontan is using the Red Indian as a mouthpiece for some criticisms of his own.

from idiosyncrasies of phrasing which the reviser presumably thought unseemly,[10] are many detailed objections to Scripture, the argument between faith and reason, and the information about nature spirits. 'Le Grand Esprit' becomes merely a name for God. What is added, although sometimes it is a matter of emphasis rather than new material, is criticism of a number of specifically Catholic beliefs and institutions, and an intermittent discussion about salvation.

The attacks on Roman Catholicism usually appear in the context of differences between French and English Christianity (because of the English presence in Canada). The half-fictitious Lahontan is now a condescending, narrow-minded Catholic. He explains the controversy over Eucharistic doctrine ('les Français croient que le Fils de Dieu ayant dit que son corps était dans un morceau de pain, il faut croire que cela est vrai, puisqu'il ne saurait mentir', p. 9), from which Adario deduces, like Gilbert, that 'il y a de la contradiction ou de l'obscurité dans les paroles du Fils du Grand Esprit'.[11] Lahontan also refers to the English refusal to accept papal authority and the belief in Purgatory. Questions from Adario, in a tone of pretended naïvety, satirize the Pope, excommunication and the sale of indulgences (pp. 29–31). In another passage, monasticism is contrasted with the freedom of Indian customs. The Frenchman is impressed by the innocence of the Indians, but alarmed by the attitude to sex; they apparently permit free love and divorce. He says that impure desires will be punished by hellfire. Adario counters with practical reasons for free love, and attacks celibacy, listing the deplorable consequences of clerical vows of chastity (about which he knows considerably more than might be expected even from 'un sauvage de bon sens qui a voyagé'), and evoking images of luxury and lust in monastery cloisters (pp. 23–27). Lahontan admits that what Adario says about the clergy is true but states, feebly, that it is irrelevant.[12]

The subject of salvation arises because the discussion of differences in religion is carried on in the light of the Christian claim to be the unique way of salvation. Passages about Hell (pp. 4–5), punishment for Adam's sin (p. 11) and the damnation of pagans (p. 32) are all aspects of the response to the claim. The risk of hellfire seems never to be far from the minds of the interlocutors, and gives an edge to what they say about diversity in religion. When Adario argues that the very existence of more than one religion shows

[10]   For instance, 'ce que nous appelons article de foi est un breuvage que la raison ne doit pas avaler, de peur de s'enivrer et s'écarter ensuite de son chemin' (*Mémoires*, p. 117). In the *Dialogues*, there is nothing resembling this in the passages about faith.

[11]   Gilbert, *Histoire de Calejava*, p. 46; see Chapter 8, p. 119. The similarity shows how direct was the connection between the religious conflicts of the time and rejection of scriptural authority.

[12]   Such passages in the *Dialogues* of 1703 suggest that Gueudeville had a part in the production of this volume, as well as in the 1705 edition. The attack on monasticism and the concern with salvation are more plausibly attributed to the journalist in Holland who had been a Benedictine monk than to an adventurer like Lahontan.

that none is true (p. 8), or that, if God had revealed the true religion to mankind, only one religion, and not five or six hundred, would have been established (p. 16), he seems to be denying first and foremost that men are damned for not being members of a particular Christian church. Behind remarks that the 'innocence' of the Hurons will preserve them from the wrath of God (p. 22), or that the Great Spirit requires them to be virtuous (p. 33), there seems to be the complementary argument, that obedience to moral precepts, rather than belief in certain articles of faith, is sufficient for salvation.

The double preoccupation with salvation and the diversity of religions produces a distinct resemblance, in the *Dialogues curieux,* to Marana's *Espion turc,* when in the early volumes the Spy is troubled by the conflicting claims of Islam and Christianity. But Adario rejects Christian pretensions, and European civilization in general, more thoroughly than the Spy. Where literary quality is concerned, Marana's presentation of the religious situation is more effective than that of the *Dialogues curieux,* since the fictional Adario has no real reason to be affected by anxieties over salvation. He has little difficulty in shrugging them off, and the doubts expressed by the Catholic are only by implication answered by the Huron's profession of deistic belief. In *L'Espion turc,* Mahmut himself resolves his doubts, by placing his trust in virtue and a universal deity.

The *Dialogues curieux* produce a mixed impression. Adario had the distinction of being the literary ancestor of a more famous noble savage with deistic views, Volaire's *L'Ingénu,*[13] but he is a less interesting character than the real Le Rat and the other Hurons and Iroquois of Lahontan's travel books. In the *Nouveaux voyages* especially, Lahontan seems to have been sufficiently detached and honest an observer for us to be able to guess roughly what is original Red Indian belief and what has been reinterpreted to suit European mental structures. Adario has the perfunctory theism and morality, with pseudo-naïve criticisms of Christianity to match, which make of him a literary stereotype. Possibly influenced by *L'Espion turc,* the writer of the *Dialogues* saw the opportunities presented by Lahontan's Indian for expressing European, and particularly Protestant, objections to the Bible and Catholic faith. They are a considerable advance in boldness over those in the later volumes of Marana.

Contemporary reviews of Lahontan noted that his defence of Christianity was inadequate;[14] the reviewer of the Jesuit *Journal de Trévoux,* on Le Rat's

---

[13]   See Chinard, Introduction, pp. 63 ff., on echoes of Adario down to Chateaubriand's *Les Natchez;* also Maurice Roelens, 'Lahontan dans l'*Encyclopédie* et ses suites', *Recherches nouvelles sur quelques écrivains des Lumières,* edited by Jacques Proust (Geneva, 1972), pp. 163–200. Like William R. Jones, in his edition of *L'Ingénu* (Geneva, 1957), p. 36, Chinard hesitates to say that Lahontan is the direct source of Voltaire's hero, although Voltaire had the *Nouveaux voyages* in his library.

[14]   For the reviews, see Chinard, Introduction, pp. 46, 50–51. The *Journal de la République des Lettres,* reviewing the *Dialogues* in November 1703, considered it not surprising that Adario won the exchanges on religion, his opponent being a Catholic.

criticisms in the *Mémoires,* said that they were 'le précis de ce que les Déistes et les Sociniens disent de plus fort contre la soumission que nous devons à la foi et contre cette captivité de la raison sous l'empire de la révélation'. The *Histoire des ouvrages des savants* wrote that Adario's opinions were 'plus déistiques qu'orthodoxes'.[15] These comments show, more clearly than in Gilbert or Marana, that the word 'déiste' could by this time refer to the attitudes which are normally regarded as deistic by modern scholars; this contrasts with the works of Veiras and Foigny, which seem not to have been regarded as 'deistic' by reviewers.[16] The context of the Jesuit reviewer's remark about 'deists and Socinians' suggests that he had rationalist sectarians in mind, who from the Catholic standpoint would be heretics, though not necessarily anti-Christian. The religion of Adario, however, does appear to be hostile to Christianity.

Little is known of Lahontan after the publication of the *Dialogues.* Leibniz knew him in 1710, at the court of the Elector of Hanover; he is believed to have died in 1715. His personal religious attitude, that of an unsubmissive Catholic, was only one factor in the creation of a new spokesman for deism in the shape of Adario; the politico-religious situation of conflict between French Catholicism and Anglo-Dutch Protestantism was probably more important. The conflict figures largely in the *Dialogues,* and also accounts for their publication. Holland offered an obvious refuge for Frenchmen who (like the Huguenots) wanted to leave France, and the Dutch publishing trade gave equally obvious opportunities for Lahontan to profit from his knowledge of life in Canada. The resultant sequence of writings, concerned among other things with Canadian natural religion, was at first only moderately sceptical about Catholicism, but became more defintely hostile with the *Dialogues,* perhaps because of the influence of the other exile, Gueudeville, who had abandoned his monastery to work as a hack writer in Holland. An exemplary version of what we now call deism thus evolves from a combination of natural religion, beliefs of a positive sort which are 'plus déistiques qu'orthodoxes' according to one reviewer, and on the negative side criticisms directed largely against Catholicism, which are typical of 'les Déistes et les Sociniens' according to another. Although there is room for fine distinctions about the meaning of such expressions, this is the first occasion on which the modern concept of deism, based on later versions found especially in Voltaire and Rousseau, clearly corresponds to an attitude regarded at the time as deistic.

---

[15] *Histoire des ouvrages des savants,* March 1704. It supports the description with an almost direct quotation of Adario's credo.

[16] See Chapter 5, n. 32.

CHAPTER 10

THE ANTI-CHRISTIAN DEISM OF THE MILITAIRE PHILOSOPHE

Among the many clandestine writings of the early eighteenth century, not even Meslier's celebrated *Testament* is more remarkable than the treatise known by the name of its unidentified author, an army officer turned philosopher.[1] His massive and elaborate *Difficultés sur la religion proposées au Père Malebranche* is one of the most impressive achievements in the history of deism. Its defects, mainly repetitiveness, are largely due to the author's lack of literary or philosophical training. It was written in about 1710.[2] For many years its circulation must have been very limited, although abridgements were made, again anonymously. In 1767 Naigeon edited what purported to be the Militaire philosophe's work, it was in fact a small selection of his criticisms of Christianity, with an extra chapter on religion and morality, almost certainly written by d'Holbach.[3] This caricature, bereft of the whole of the Militaire philosophe's system of constructive deism, was enthusiastically welcomed by Voltaire. Not until 1912 did Lanson rediscover the original manuscript, which Roland Mortier has recently edited in its entirety.[4]

Although we cannot name the author, we know considerably more about

---

[1]   On the manuscripts in general, see Lanson's articles cited in n. 4 below and Ira O. Wade, *The Clandestine Organization and Diffusion of Philosophic Ideas in France from 1700 to 1750* (Princeton, 1938), cited henceforth as *Clandestine Organization,* the conclusions of which should be treated with caution; Pt. I, Ch. 2 on the Militaire philosophe. On the Curé Meslier and his atheist and communistic *Testament,* found after his death in 1729, see especially, among much recent work on him, Jean Meslier, *Œuvres complètes,* edited by Jean Deprun, Roland Desné and Albert Soboul, 3 vols. (Paris, 1970–1972).

[2]   The data can be established reliably, to within about two years, by numerous references in the text. See Mortier's edition, cited in n. 4, pp. 33–34.

[3]   A.-A. Barbier, *Dictionnaire des ouvrages anonymes,* gives the attribution. See Rudolf Brummer, *Studien zur französischen Aufklärung im Anschluss an J.-A. Naigeon* (Breslau, 1932), pp. 240–301. Naigeon's edition gives the impression that the Militaire philosophe was of atheist views.

[4]   G. Lanson, 'Questions diverses sur l'histoire de l'esprit philosophique en France', RHLF 19 (1912), 1–29, 293–317; *Difficultés sur la religion, proposées au Père Malebranche par Mr. ... officier militaire dans la marine,* edited by Roland Mortier (Brussels, 1970), cited henceforth as Mortier, edition or Introduction.

him than most of the early deist writers.[5] Probably he was born in the middle 1660s.[6] He was one of the many impoverished members of the aristocracy, brought up as a devout Catholic, and was given the technical training normal for intending army officers. Much of the material which might have identified him was removed by the copyist or editor who wrote an introduction for the *Difficultés,* in which he describes the original manuscript.[7] In compensation, we have the Militaire philosophe's own account of his religious development. In some preliminary pages, he presents the work to Malebranche, whom he addresses throughout as 'M.R.P.', Mon révérend père. 'Ces petits cahiers', he explains, with modesty rather than accuracy, since the work is huge, are the product of a man with little education. He has read the *Recherche de la vérité* twice, and also Malebranche's *Entretiens sur la métaphysique* and *Conversations chrétiennes,* but not 'le Spinoza', nor Lucretius, nor anything by Socinians or deists (Mortier edition, pp. 75–75).[8] He invites Malebranche to refute him, although he plainly regards his arguments as unanswerable, but warns him not to make the accusation of *libertinage;* the accusation is valueless, because of the moral defects of those who employ it, the defenders of the 'religions factices'. This term is to recur frequently, and the Militaire philosophe defines it: 'J'appelle religions factices toutes celles qui sont artificielles, qui sont établies sur des faits, et qui reconnaissent d'autres principes que ceux de la raison et d'autres lois que celles de la conscience' (p. 76).[9] In his own case, he adds, belief in such a religion did not mean being virtuous; he had been 'Catholique à brûler' and entirely debauched, 'au lieu que présentement (...) je mène une vie réglée et quasi exempte de passions'.

A detailed account of the process of his enlightenment occupies the early

[5]   Mortier, Introduction, pp. 36–37, and André Robinet, 'Boulaninviller auteur du "Militaire philosophe"? ', RHLF 73 (1973), 22–31. Robinet argues that the *Difficultés* should be attributed to the Comte de Boulainviller, whose religious opinions were certainly unorthodox; see Chapter 11. There are however problems of date, style and content which Robinet does not overcome. Mortier has investigated the more promising possibility that the author was a member of the Villeneuve family; there was a Robert de Villeneuve who lived in Canada, had the technical knowledge of the Militaire philosophe (he was an engineer) and seems to have been regarded as a *libertin,* but Mortier is not apparently prepared to accept that these resemblances amount to proof of authorship (Introduction, pp. 17–19, 38–39). On the questionable hypothesis recently advanced by F. Deloffre and M. Menemencioglu, that the author of the *Difficultés* was Robert Challe, see the Appendix.

[6]   Mortier, Introduction. p. 34. Robinet (see n. 5) argues for a date of about 1660.

[7]   Mortier edition, p. 72. The copyist apologizes for any incoherence in the arrangement of the subject-matter, explaining that the original was in disorder: 'le nombre des renvois et des interlignes est si grand dans l'original, il y a tant de petites pièces attachées avec des épingles, qu'il a été comme impossible de ne se pas tromper'.

[8]   An obscure reference on p. 77 ('votre *Métaphysique,* M.R.P.') is elucidated on p. 420 by a remark about Malebranche's *Conversations chrétiennes,* 1677, and a work which must be the *Entretiens sur la métaphysique et sur la religion,* 1688. The Millitaire philosophe does not say explicitly that he has read Descartes.

[9]   It is not certain whether the apparent confusion between the senses 'factual' and 'factitious' is deliberate.

part of his 'Premier cahier', the first of the four parts of the treatise. When not yet seven years old, he was taken on a pilgrimage to see a statue of the Virgin, the Notre-Dame des Ardilliers, near Saumur. Expecting to see the Virgin floating in the air, as in pictures, he was disappointed: 'je ne vis qu'une mauvaise petite figure de pierre noire, à laquelle on faisait toucher des chapelets au bout d'un bâton' (p. 82). At twelve, he was already cynical about preachers. In his philosophy year at school, his questions about Scholasticism were met only by appeals to the authority of the Pope and the Councils. He continued to be pious out of the fear of devils, but this disappeared when he became a soldier and had to face 'des dangers plus réels que ceux-là'. He took part in the 'dragonnades', the most violent part of the campaign against the Huguenots, in the early 1680s, and the experience seems to have affected him deeply: 'Ah! M.R.P., quelles cruautés et quelle fermeté n'ai-je pas vues! Quand il me revient que, pleins de vin, nous tirâmes un misérable vieillard, accablé de goutte, de son lit où il ne pouvait souffrir le poids de ses draps et le fîmes danser en pleine place, sans que ses cris pitoyables et les larmes de deux pauvres filles qui se traînaient à nos pieds pussent fléchir notre barbarie — quel cruel souvenir! — la plume me tombe de la main et mes yeux ne la peuvent plus guider. Mais quelle atteinte à cette religion dont on fait sonner si haut l'équité et la douceur, quelle atteinte à l'opinion de cette grâce qui soutenait les martyrs, car tout cela n'eut point d'effet; il nous fallut abandonner la maison après l'avoir ruinée' (p. 84).

In consequence he looked again at the New Testament, the works of some of the Church Fathers, and some Christian philosophers; he found them vague and unsatisfactory. Autobiography here turns into criticism. The Militaire philosophe is capable of producing a swarm of objections on almost any pretext, and provides a comprehensive introductory sample. Some are idiosyncratic: why do the Pope and the bishops not say Mass more often, since there can be no more important duty than giving glory to God?; some are contemptuously ironic: if the Pope's faith cannot fail, why does he not tell the mountains to rise up and fall on the Barbary pirates? (pp. 88–89). Others are more closely reasoned. Christians are told to love a God who is portrayed, in the doctrines of hellfire and the small number of the elect, as hateful; the notions of baptism and predestination cannot be reconciled (pp. 91–92). Anti-clericalism, often expressed violently, is a recurrent theme. The Pope is 'un malotru' and has concubines; priests are brutal and vicious, and violate people's wives and daughters; great churchmen 'ont l'impudence de prêcher la pauvreté, regorgeant de biens' (p. 80). As a convinced monarchist, the Militaire philosophe is indignant with the Pope, who dares to dispute against Christian kings, and with the clergy, since the monarch should have absolute power within the state. Another theme is intolerance. There are attacks on the cruelty of the Inquisition, the persecution of Hugenots and Jews, who are perfectly good citizens, and on the suppression of new ideas: teachers have to swear to teach only Aristotelian philosophy. Here a marginal note mentions Descartes (p. 85).

Summing up, the Militaire philosophe concludes that 'tout cela mérite bien sans doute un examen. Le joug que nous portons est assez pesant pour nous y soustraire, si nous pouvons' (p. 94). The results of giving up Christianity can only be good: 'quand je connaîtrai Dieu tel qu'il est, je l'adorerai de bon coeur, et par choix (...) au lieu que dans les sentiments des dogmes chrétiens et sous le poids des lois papistes, je ne puis que le craindre et l'avoir en horreur' (p. 95). Indeed, he has already improved morally: 'Je consulte la raison et la seule conscience qui m'instruisent à la véritable justice, au lieu que je ne consultais que la religion, qui m'étourdissait de préceptes frivoles et injustes' (p. 96).

CRITICAL DEISM: RATIONAL PRINCIPLES AND THE ATTACK ON BELIEF AND FAITH

The first step in his enormous critique is to establish twenty-one 'vérités' which constitute the second 'cahier'. They are presented in the full panoply of logical proof. In laying the philosophical foundations of his attack, the Militaire philosophe takes over basic principles from Malebranche; for instance, that the attinment of truth is possible and that the means for attaining it is reason (*Vérités* 4 and 6). It is implied throughout, most obviously in the examples he gives, that for him the truths of reason are of a mathematical nature (pp. 111–112); he is fond of contrasting the certainties of geometry to the dogmas and miracles of religion. The second *Vérité* contains the core of his rational approach to religion, which he defines as 'une chose purement spirituelle entre des êtres spirituels' (p. 107) – God and the mind. God acts directly on the soul: 'il a instruit l'âme par le moyen de la raison, de la reconnaissance de l'ordre, et de la vue des vérités réelles, nécessaires et éternelles' (p. 105).

The effects of the Cartesian way of philosophizing are clearly to be seen in the second *cahier*. The universalist claims of rationalism, well expressed in a remark from the introductory section, 'Je ne me fonde que sur la raison commune à tout le genre humain' (p. 100), lead the Militaire philosophe to reject Christianity on the grounds that it is only one religion among many; both he and Malebranche were Christians, he says, only by the chance of birth, not for rational causes. Philosophic individualism leads him to maintain that his salvation is his own concern, not that of the government or the public (*Vérité* 1). The Catholic Church took him by surprise, as a child not responsible for his actions, so that he has the right to abandon Catholicism if mature reflection tells him that its pretensions are unfounded (*Vérité* 9).

The early *Vérités* are often more interesting when the Militaire philosophe forgets about his apparatus of syllogistic 'arguments démonstratifs' and lets his talent for criticism take over. The first *Vérité* contains many powerful arguments in favour of the rights of the individual conscience and against intolerance; the second, a destructive analysis of the metaphor 'father' in definitions of the Trinity; and the fourth, a fable satirizing the Catholic clergy's claim to possess the unique revelation – 'un roi fut contraint de quitter ses états' (p. 113). He leaves behind the beautiful princess whom a 'gueux malotru' claims to be his by right. The ninth *Vérité* ends with a short denunciation of the religion in which the Militaire philosophe was born, a passage the controlled violence of which impressed Voltaire:[10] 'S'il faut examiner, voici, après mûres réflexions, le jugement que j'en porte. Je la trouve folle, extravagante, injurieuse à Dieu, pernicieuse aux hommes, facilitant et même autorisant les vols, les séductions, l'ambition et l'intérêt de ses ministres, la révélation des mystères des familles. Je la vois comme ayant été une source de meurtres et de traitements tortionnaires faits sous son nom. Elle me semble un flambeau de discorde, de haine, de vengeance, un masque propre à l'hypocrite et à tous ces malheureux vêtus de noir qui vantent cette religion ou ses effets prétendus. Enfin, j'y vois dans son tronc l'idolâtrie, la superstition et les fraudes pieuses' (p. 128).

In the later *Vérités,* from the tenth onwards, rationalism is the basis of a highly original attack on the factual elements in revealed religion, the 'religious factices' in the Militaire philosophe's phrase, which, like Christianity, are founded on documents (the Bible or Koran) giving an account of the historical events from which such religions arose. The essence of the argument is contained in the tenth to the twelfth *Vérités,* each of which is wider in scope than the last: no religion can establish its factual bases as positively as is required by the ordinary processes of proof in a law-court; the kinds of beliefs which the churches claim to be true would require constant and continuous proof by miracles if they were to be acceptable; generally, facts can never be more than probably true, and lack the certainty of mathematical demonstration. The thirteenth and fourteenth *Vérités* return to the question of revelation, pointing out that the 'religions factices' do not, and cannot, ask their adherent for anything but belief, which is inferior to knowledge; the next two *Vérités* declare that God did not use, and could not have used, 'des livres et des discours humains' to instruct mankind in the truths of religion. Such imperfect methods would be beneath God's power, wisdom and justice.

The last *Vérités* become repetitive. The long *Vérité 18* gives another comparison between truths which enforce consent and those which can be doubted (the Militaire philosophe adduces an incident in which he persuaded

---

[10] In a letter of 8 February 1768, to Damilaville (Besterman D.14738); see Mortier, Introduction, p. 40, on this and other letters from Voltaire about the Naigeon version.

his brother-officers that a circle has a shorter circumference, for a given area, than any other shape). It also shows that he regards his own religion as natural; he remarks that 'Toutes les religions factices contiennent la religion naturelle, mais elles en défigurent les principes en les couvrant de fausses conséquences. Tous les hommes professent la religion naturelle. Le mal est qu'ils ne s'en sont pas tenus là' (p. 160). The nineteenth and twenty-first *Vérités* both argue, like the ninth, that no one should retain belief in a 'religion factice', but the twenty-first goes further, asserting that to belong to such a religion is criminal (p. 165). The crime in question is that of offending God, by idolatry and insulting ideas about the deity.

The treatment of some subjects is distributed random among several *Vérités*. The sixth, thirteenth and fourteenth all contain reflections on the concept of belief. The Militaire philosophe distinguishes it from sight or knowledge with a wealth of contradicting examples, from geometrical reasoning and factual report. Geometry produces invincible certainty: 'Les plus grandes passions, les plus grandes menaces n'engageront pas un instant à chercher un point dans un carré qui soit également éloigné de toutes les extrémités' (p. 138); but belief has its degrees: 'Croire signifie ne pas contester, acquiescer jusqu'à une meilleure instruction. Ce mot emporte[11] du doute et laisse la porte ouverte à une croyance contraire' (p. 139). The strength of the Militaire philosophe's position (and no doubt also its weakness) lies in the distinction he makes between factual and rational truths. When reason is understood on the Cartesian mathematical model, it seems to have nothing to do with the history of Christ, yet even an apologist of Malebranche's calibre sought to utilize historical facts as proofs within a rationalist system. A section of the *Conversations chrétiennes* is headed 'Preuves de la religion par des faits certains'; the argument is that Bible history is unshakably true.[12]

In the course of his attack on belief, the Militaire philosophe is led to describe the present state of Catholicism. Belief, he says in the fourteenth *Vérité*, opposing himself directly to advocates of submissive faith such as Saint-Evremond, cannot be enforced by authority: 'on ne peut faire un commandement de la croyance. On peut seulement exiger qu'on agisse comme si l'on croyait' (p. 145). Because there can be no absolute conviction where the factual element in religion is concerned, French Catholicism is largely a sham: 'Les gens savants ne croient point pour la plupart, les personnes médiocrement éclairées ont des doutes, le paysan et l'homme borné dit qu'il croit et ne sait ce qu'il dit par le mot de croire'. For the majority, religion is mere conformism, 'c'est la mode'. The thirteenth *Vérité*

---

[11] In the sense of 'implies' or 'involves'.

[12] *Conversations chrétiennes*, IV, in which Aristarque takes the role of a friend of his who asserts that Moses is an impostor (*Oeuvres de Malebranche*, edited by André Robinet, 21 vols. (Paris, 1958–1970), Vol. IV (1959), pp. 136–151).

has already given a typically vivid account of the process of religious indoctrination (pp. 139–140).

At the beginning of his next *cahier*, the Militaire philosophe observes that 'Il ne me reste plus qu'un monstre à combattre' (p. 170), but the monster is faith, and the preceding reflections on belief already constitute a redoubtable onslaught on it. The polemical reasoning he employs in the 'Réfutation de la foi' resembles previous arguments. All religions require faith, it is suspect because the clergy profit from it, it cannot attain to mathematical certitude: he has developed such considerations many times, but pursues them with unflagging energy. One of his new criticisms is a destructive analysis of a definition of faith which he found in a catechism: 'un don de Dieu par lequel on croit en lui et à tout ce qu'il a révélé à son église' (p. 175). This is meaningless, says the Militaire philosophe, 'une fumée, un pur néant'. The idea of 'don' is empty, since all things are the gift of God; 'on ne croit pas Dieu, on le sait' (p. 179), so that there is no need for external assistance; and the last clause assumes what is in question, whether there was a revelation at all. Later come ironies over the idea that faith is meritorious; if this were true, the more absurd or monstrous our faith is (there is a selection of bizarre examples), the more merit it has.

In this *cahier,* more so than in others, the Militaire philosophe betrays a kind of exasperation. He cannot let his subject go. The cause of his irritation is that the attitude which he attacks is the exact negation of his own rationalism; virtually by definition, faith is irrational, so that no one rational argument will succeed against it better than any other. The Militaire philosophe continues to pour out reasonings as if he will sooner or later hit on the finally convincing proof. Eventually he concludes, as rationalists in this situation were wont to conclude, by the remark that all the 'religions factices' are false and ridiculous, and most of them abominable – an extreme formulation of the imposture theory. It follows from this that he has the right, indeed the obligation, to stick to natural religion, which is as plain as the midday sun, or as the sound of a shell-shot.

However, it immediately occurs to him that there is more to be said, and he sets off on a particularly sharp attack on the morality of religion. This is based on an analogy with faith: having distinguished faith from rational certainty, he now distinguishes religious virtues from true virtues. The former, roughly speaking, are the ritual observances prescribed in every religion, such as suttee, circumcision or baptism (p. 187). By contrast, says the Militaire philosophe (presumably making a philosophical hypothesis rather than indulging in self-congratulation), 'quand je tiens ma parole, quelque chose qu'il m'en coûte, quand je m'expose généreusement aux dangers pour conserver la liberté de mon père, de mes frères, de ma famille (...) quand je tire le dernier sol de ma bourse pour payer mes dettes, quand je vis pauvre plutôt de m'enrichir par des tromperies, par des hâbleries et par des flatteries etc., voilà de véritables vertus'. Later they are named moral virtues. Following up the distinction, the Militaire philosophe asserts that sermons always recommend piety, never probity, and do not cause any moral improvement. The Christian virtues of celibacy and 'monacalité' are not as difficult as is claimed, for it is harder to be a good father or a good husband 'que de n'être ni l'un ni l'autre'; the small number of pleasures which priests and monks forgo 'ne sont qu'une bagatelle en comparaison des embarras qu'on évite' (p. 188). People who are devout display 'religious virtues', but do not bother with sincerity and integrity. The Militaire philosophe detests 'dévotion' and reserves some of his most telling recriminations for it.

CRITICAL DEISM IN DETAIL

The third *cahier,* entitled only 'E',[13] is the fullest exposition of critical deism in the early eighteenth century, and probably the fullest until Voltaire and Rousseau. It is a rationalist's response, not to irrational faith or facts, but to the rational apologias for Christianity, and is methodical and comprehensive, dealing with all the standard proofs in turn. They are listed in an introductory passage: eleven items to which the 'preuves de la religion chrétienne prises en général' can be reduced (pp. 196–197). The Militaire philosophe's ambitious undertaking is hard to summarize. Its argument, in 'sections' some of which are divided into 'articles', roughly follows the order of a typical apologia, but, as in the *Vérités,* there is much repetition and digression. The first two sections, on the Old and New Testaments, together account for about two-thirds of the whole; later sections are more closely confined to their ostensible subjects. But the question of prophecy, for instance, is discussed under several different headings, and when he gets on to moral issues the Militaire philosophe's indignation is apt to run away with him.

He begins with a general denunciation of the Christian concept of God, the Trinity being, in his eyes, no less opposed to true theism than the Greeks' multiplicity of gods, while the notion of a deity who can punish the innocent is execrable. 'Vous criez au blasphème, j'y crie aussi M.R.P.' (p. 195). After this, if we neglect the Militaire philosophe's rather haphazard arrangement, the material can be grouped into those sections or articles which concern revelation, and which, in broad terms, are a critique of the Bible; those on the 'external' proofs, so-called, the prophecies, miracles and other phenomena, such as the success of the Christian religion, which

---

[13] Lanson and Mortier suggest that the letter stands for 'Examen'; cf. such remarks as 'mais tout cela mérite bien sans doute un examen' (p. 94), at the end of the *Premier cahier.* The content of 'E' closely resembles that of the contemporary manuscript work, the *Examen de la religion,* on which see Chapter 11.

support its claim to be divine, those concerning morality; and finally those concerning a number of Christian doctrines which, taken together, add up to the view that human nature is sinful and corrupt.

With both the Old and New Testaments, the starting-point is a question, 'si ces livres sont divins?'. The reply repeats arguments from the second *cahier:* God communicates with man by way of the spirit, not in any particular language; only metaphysical truths are divine (p. 202). Yet the Old Testament was written in Hebrew, an imperfect language, lacking vowels, in a text which is 'sans distinction de mots, sans virgules' (p. 203), and it must have been inadequately translated, because of our lack of linguistic knowledge (p. 212). It has an abundance of scientific inaccuracies, logical impossibilities and inconsistencies, the Militaire philosophe gives a generous selection. Underlying the bewildering variety of his specific objections is the theme that a revelation sent from God would be universally comprehensible, clear and stylistically above reproach.[14] One complaint about the New Testament is that the style of the Apostles recalls that of the ancient Gauls.

When he is discussing biblical narrative, such as the stories of the Creation and the Flood, or the birth of Christ, the narrow-mindedness to which Cartesian rationalism can lead is very manifest. Often the Militaire philosophe objects merely to the absurdity of the narrative, meaning that it lacks the consistency and realism of stories based on real life; more seriously he will list implausibilities. On the Flood, he says (among other things) that it was unknown in America, that God had no reason to punish the animals which were drowned, that the wood of the Ark would have rotted before the vessel was completed, and that there were not enough people aboard to man the pumps, machines which, he adds, had not been invented at the time (pp. 215–217). This last objection, he tells us, has been made many times. Such arguments may appear facile and superficial, but are seemingly put forward in all sincerity; there seems to be a refusal to accept anything in the nature of imaginative truth. The Militaire philosophe describes the Old Testament as myth ('des fables, Origène a tranché le mot', p. 197), but for him this amounts to saying that it is simply untrue. He is always looking for proof, and what he says about the Virgin Birth shows the standard of proof which he regards as desirable: if we are to admit that the belief is divine, the Virgin Birth would have had to be publicly prophesied when Mary was six years old; she would thenceforward have had to be kept away from men; and so on. Even so, for the birth of Christ to have been irrefutably miraculous, 'il eût fallu le faire naître d'un rocher ou d'un homme' (p. 237).

---

[14]   This is typical of the arguments which the *Difficultés* has in common with the *Examen de la religion;* see Chapter 11, pp. 167–168, for a discussion of the possibility (which I consider unlikely) that the two works are directly related.

In examining the 'external' proofs, miracles, prophecies, the allegedly supernatural success of Christian evangelism and the constancy of the martyrs, the Militaire philosophe's arguments are largely dictated by the apologists who had developed this aspect of the demonstration of Christianity. His most wide-ranging method of refutation is a theory of the miraculous, or rather a theory intended to exclude the miraculous. He does not deny that God could suspend the normal course of nature if he wished; but he does not do so, because 'il a prévu toutes les combinaisons possibles des mouvements qu'il a imprimés, il a donné en même temps tout l'ordre nécessaire et tous les remèdes possibles aux inconvénients qui pouvaient résulter' (p. 267) – a theory which falls neatly between the Malebranchian universe of 'ordre' and Leibniz's best possible world.

It follows that the power of pray is a delusion; an event will occur, whether or not it answers anyone's prayers. It is also a delusion, we are warned, to suppose that even a genuine miracle can testify to the truth of revelation, since a miracle would be required for each individual believer (pp. 273–273); here the Militaire philosophe anticipates the dilemma put by Hume in his famous essay on miracles.[15]

It is not that the Militaire philosophe is wholly opposed to the concept of miracle, since for him the creation of the universe was miraculous (p. 267), but he almost always explains, or explains away, any supposed miracle in natural terms. Discussing the raising of Lazarus from the dead, he casts doubt on the language used to describe it: was it not exaggerated, in oriental style, and was not Lazarus near death rather than completely dead (p. 270)? Another instance is a painting of St Geneviève, showing her intervention during the famine of 1709; nobody believes its truth, since all know that a third of the number of the Parisian poor died in the famine, but equally nobody bothers to deny it; in two hundred years, the belief will grow up that the saint performed a miracle (p. 271). In similar fashion, in the section entitled 'La manière surprenante dont le christianisme s'est établi' (p. 276), the Militaire philosophe eliminates the supernatural by evoking what he knows of the all-too-human methods of conversion in this own time, such as the tricks used by the missionaries in America and the brutalities of the 'dragonnades' in France.[16] In his opinion, the triumphant progress of Islam is more impressive than that of early Christianity. The apostles, who, he says in passing, 'ne prêchèrent que le pur déisme, auquel ils mêlèrent le nom de

---

[15] *Enquiry concerning Human Understanding*, Section X, especially paragraphs 91, 100–101. The ironic conclusion is: 'that the Christian Religion not only was at first attended with miracles, but even at this day cannot be believed by any reasonable person without one'.

[16] The reference to North America and the missionaries, like other criticisms (such as the remark on the fabulous nature of the Old Testament, p. 197), is an obvious point of contact with Lahontan (see Chapter 9, pp. 131, 133). Such parallels abound in critical deism, and it is not practicable to mention any except the most striking; they arise because the application of rationalism to the same *corpus* of religious phenomena produces the same results in different writers.

J. -C. (...) comme d'un prophète envoyé de Dieu' (p. 278) had little to contend with except a decadent paganism. By 'le pur déisme' is meant simply the belief in God; this phrase was used at the time without the critical or heretical overtones of 'déisme' alone.

The Militaire philosophe's attitude is not totally rigid. He succeeds in explaining the bravery of Christian martyrs solely in human terms (p. 280), but another apologetic proof, the destruction of the Temple in A.D. 70 and the Jewish Dispersion, finds him less confident (p. 290). He is obliged to admit that the events were strange, sufficiently so to give credence to the view that they were a punishment for the execution of Christ. He has various arguments against this view, but is not, it seems, entirely certain that nothing miraculous occurred. If he had been, he presumably would not have discussed the matter at such length.

On prophecy, as on miracles, the Militaire philosophe refutes the apologists both in general terms and with reference to particular examples. Anything which depends on human freewill, he argues, cannot be foretold (p. 222); he attacks the 'figurative' or symbolic reading of the Old Testament (the method applied in the interpretation of prophecies) and the belief that Jesus was the predicted Messiah or liberator. On two of the best-known prophecies, those of Jacob and Daniel,[17] he goes into considerable detail; apologists had devoted more ingenuity to the prophecies than to any other proof. Much of his material is unpromising, but can be enlivened by his critical verve, as when he imagines ironically what might happen if Jesus were to preach in the Spain of the Inquisition, or denounces the factiousness and unreliability of the Councils of the Church (pp. 282, 286–287).

The most deeply felt of all the different forms of protest made by the Militaire philosophe is undoubtedly in the sphere of morality. Writing of 'la doctrine incomparable de Jésus-Christ et la pureté de sa morale' (Section 2, Article 4), a subject usually treated with respect by deists even much later in the eighteenth century, he begins: 'je ne puis traiter cet endroit tranquillement: outre de la mauvaise foi, il y a de l'impudence. Pardonnez, M.R.P., je suis hors de moi quand je vois des fraudes si infâmes soutenues avec tant d'effronterie' (p. 239). The cause of his anger here is his *bête noire*, devoutness (specifically, the habit which bigots have of ascribing any virtuous act to faith rather than to moral probity), but he is no less indignant in many other passages. A diatribe against the immorality of much of the conduct described in the Old Testament culminates in an apparently unconscious allusion to Bossuet: 'j'ai lu quelque part le titre d'un livre: *Politique tirée de l'Ecriture Sainte. Ce doit être bien pis que Machiavel'* (p. 206); the section on 'Les merveilleux effets du Christianisme' (p. 292) contains a list, repeated on occasion throughout the *Difficultés*, of notable

---

[17] Genesis, 49. 10; Daniel, 9. 24–26.

crimes and misdeeds – the proceedings of the Inquisition, the 'dragonnades', the conquest of America by the Spaniards and Portuguese and the Massacre of St. Bartholomew's Day.

In this *cahier,* much is simply moral outrage eloquently expressed. But there is also a development of the theoretical distinction made in the 'Réfutation de la foi' between religious and true virtues. The Militaire philosophe is now somewhat less aggressive, saying that actions like going on pilgrimages, or paying for the celebration of Mass, are indifferent, neither good nor bad, in terms of social morality. He also surveys Christian moral doctrine, accepting that some maxims are laudable (although 'il n'y a rien dans l'Evangile que la seule lumière naturelle ne dise clairement', p. 245), but they must not be taken too far. If we were always to forgive injuries, the 'gens injustes' would be able to do as they pleased; loving our enemies is 'une parole en l'air' (p. 254); what would happen if everyone devoted himself to contemplation and the celibate life? Further, some elements in Christianity are detrimental to morality: predestination makes efforts to be virtuous seem pointless (p. 242), confession provides an easy way of atoning for sin. Mme Brinvilliers, the poisoner, believed that in order to expiate her crimes, all she had to do was confess them; and 'a-t-on jamais refusé l'absolution au bienfaiteur du couvent?' (p. 243). On the concept of grace, the Militaire philosophe remembers an incident which shows how a little theology can be used to excuse misconduct: 'je l'ai oui dire à une bigote prise en flagrant délit; elle répondit au juge d'un air de métier, Dieu m'avait abandonée' (p. 242).

Criticisms of a more conventional kind, for instance that casuists encourage immorality, that Christians do not practise what they preach, or that valuable moral precepts are found in other religions beside Christianity, are scattered throughout the long article on New Testament morality (Section 2, Article 4); they often merge into simple anti-clericalism. The objects of the most frequent expressions of disapproval are institutions like celibacy, which are contrary to ordinary notions of social welfare, and Old Testament justifications of wars of conquest. But the Militaire philosophe does not make a complete separation between religion (in the broad sense) and morality, since in the 'Quatrième cahier' he is to base his own system of morality on a particular concept of God, not on the purely secular needs of society. In Montesquieu and Voltaire, the secularism is more clear-cut.

A last series of arguments is directed against Christian dogmas, especially those which the Militaire philosophe sarcastically calls 'les admirables découvertes des philosophes chrétiens par les lumières de l'Evangile' (p. 295), namely Original Sin, the Redemption, and the notion of grace, together with accounts of the Devil and the Fall of Man. These form a theological conception of human nature which the Militaire philosophe combats by a kind of humanism, reinterpreting the Christian concepts in secular terms. 'Il ne faut que la constitution de notre machine pour nous tenter, voilà le diable, il ne faut que notre raison pour nous engager à résister au désir des actions honteuses, voilà la grâce' (p. 266). He sees nothing supernatural about what are supposed to be the consequences of the Fall, mortality, sexual shame, work and the pains of childbirth. Death is 'un accident nécessaire'. Wild animals and peasant women suffer less in giving birth than domestic pets and duchesses, which proves that labour pains can be explained without recourse to scriptural dogma (p. 219).

There are some criticisms of Christian concepts which do not fit into this pattern. On the Trinity or the Last Judgment, for instance (pp. 259, 262), the Militaire philosophe includes textual arguments about the Bible, and rational argument about metaphysical impossibilities. But the most striking feature of his discussion of doctrine is the prevalence of a kind of philosophical optimism, usually associated with a later period of the eighteenth century (although it is also found in Gilbert). 'Les hommes sont ce qu'ils doivent être par leur nature' (p. 295): this, occurring in a passage which mentions the alleged 'contrariétiés' of human nature, reads like Voltaire refuting Pascal at the end of the *Lettres philosophiques*.[18] Resistance to Jansenist or Augustinian pessimism about humanity seems to be a recurrent theme in deistic thought.

Before the conclusion of 'E', the Militaire philosophe adds a rather miscellaneous section on 'la sainteté du culte' (p. 303). Here anti-clericalism goes hand in hand with social protest – the poor are dragged to the communal burial pit, the rich pay for Masses to send their souls to Heaven. There are also belittling comparisons between Christianity and paganism. Probably the most significant argument, which throws light on similar passages in Montesquieu or Voltaire, is a rejection of all types of ritual – material things can have no relation to the spirit; a man consecrated by 'cérémonies burlesques' has no power to change the Communion wafer into the Infinite Being (p. 304). After this section, the Militaire philosophe repeats in formal terms the eleven proofs of Christianity which he has refuted, lists five apologias whose well-rewarded authors 'couvrent le faux de leur raisonnement par des fleurs' (p. 309),[19] and expresses courteous doubt

[18]   As regards Gilbert, see Chapter 8, pp. 122; on Voltaire, Chapter 14, pp. 258 (for instance on Remarque III of L. 25). The Militaire philosophe does not appear to have read Pascal; the idea of 'contrariétés' must come from another apologist, possibly Mauduit, whose *Traité de religion contre les Athées, les déistes et les nouveaux pyrrhoniens*, 1677, utilizes Pascal and may be the object of a reference by the Militaire philosophe (see next note).

[19]   The apologias listed, without authors' names, do not all have identifiable titles; see Mortier edition, p. 308 and nn. 2–6. The only title quoted word for word is the *Incrédulité des déistes confondue par Jésus-Christ*, 1706, by Louis Bastide. Others are probably by Abbadie and Bernard Lamy and possibly by Mauduit.

whether even Malebranche will be able to answer him.[20]

A SYSTEM OF DEISM BASED ON JUSTICE

The last part of the *Difficultés,* subtitled 'un système de religion fondé métaphysiquement sur les lumières naturelles, et non sur des faits', exemplifies very clearly the process by which rational 'natural religion' was transformed into the constructive side of deism. Philosophically, it is more interesting than any of the early deist works except those of Montesquieu and Voltaire. Indeed, in his own sphere of metaphysics the Militaire philosophe is arguably superior to either in his handling of certain thorny problems, despite some inadequacy over freewill and the afterlife.

The *Quatrième cahier* is also better arranged than most of the critical parts of the treatise. The principal subjects of natural theology are dealt with in turn, first the existence and attributes of God, then the spirituality and immortality of the soul. But in the course of the longest section, 'De la morale', it becomes obvious that the central concern is moral thought. The Militaire philosophe explains that metaphysics is not valuable for its own sake, but for the practical truths to which it leads: morality is founded on the justice of God. The basic principle is: 'qu'il nous jugera avec une souveraine et précise équité, et que par conséquent notre unique affaire est la pratique de la vertu' (p. 326). The articles of Section 2, in which this statement occurs, lead up to a fuller exposition of the idea of justice in Article 4, 'De la cause finale de l'homme'.

The beginning is almost a matter of routine: the proving of the existence of God. The Militaire philosophe, for once independent of the Cartesian tradition, avoids ontological proofs, which he considers unnecessarily subtle; there is no value in proving our own existence (p. 324). He prefers arguments from 'la fabrique du monde', which will persuade one and all. However, the idea of God seems to be innate: 'Cet Etre que tous les hommes ont présent à l'esprit et au coeur sans presque s'en apercevoir se fait sentir très vivement au moindre avertissement. Ensuite une attention médiocre nous fait trouver que c'est l'Etre nécessaire, l'Etre indépendant, l'Etre immense, l'Etre éternel,

---

[20] With his habitual bluntness, the Militaire philosophe later comments on Malebranche's apologetic work: 'Pardonnez-moi, M.R.P., je ne vous excepte point de la foule sur cet article, vous allez vous casser le nez comme les autres. Quand il faut en venir à la preuve de la religion chrétienne, de la trinité, de l'incarnation, et à celle de tous les dogmes particuliers: du péché originel, de la grâce etc., vous dites des pauvretés, des puérilités à faire pitié à un écolier de troisième. Ce n'est pas votre faute, c'est qu'il n'y a que cela à dire' (p. 318). For a sample of the arguments which may have given rise to these forthright remarks, see the last of the *Entretiens sur la métaphysique* (XIV: '... L' incompréhensibilité de nos mystères est une preuve certaine de leur vérité. Manière d'éclaircir les dogmes de la foi. De l'Incarnation de Jésus-Christ. Preuve de sa Divinité contre les Sociniens. Nulle créature, les Anges mêmes, ne peuvent adorer Dieu que par lui. Comment la foi en Jésus-Christ nous rend agréables à Dieu').

l'auteur de toutes choses, qui est lui-même l'essence de toutes choses, qui pénètre l'univers sans l'occuper, qui le borne et le passe' (p. 320). The series of adjectives denote, we are told, only the most obvious of the divine attributes. The *Militaire philosophe* selects those of power and wisdom for emphasis; they are bound to 'nous ravir en admiration et (...) nous imprimer de profonds respects, avec une souveraine vénération mêlée de crainte et d'une espèce de joie et de plaisir' (p. 323).

The proof of the spirituality of the soul proceeds straightforwardly, on Cartesian lines. The body is a machine, but 'I' am not only mechanical; I fear, hope, remember, deduce, and in such acts there is nothing material.[21] But the problem of immortality is no so easily solved, as with Gilbert's Cartesian *Avaites* in a similar situation. Although the *Militaire philosophe* keeps to the principle that the soul is a spiritual entity, he cannot explain what it might become when it is free of the body, and after a long and unconvincing struggle ('Solution des difficultés', pp. 330–336), he takes refuge in lyricism: 'ce mot de mort bien entendu ne signifie autre chose que l'instant où mon âme, le véritable moi, se trouve dans un état simple et naturel, comme un oiseau dont on brise la cage' (p. 336).

The freedom of the will is another element in his system which is proved less by demonstrative argument than by hopeful assertion. He depends heavily on the evidence of introspection, in a way which recalls Malebranche's 'sentiment intérieur':[22] 'dans le même temps que j'agis, emporté par la passion la plus violente, je sens et je vois, pour peu que j'y pense, que je me retiendrais si je voulais; de même quand je me retiens, je sens que je suis le maître d'agir et je le vois distinctement' (p. 342). We know that men are free, but not machines; otherwise, we should allow ourselves to get angry with a clock. 'Je menacerai bien quelqu'un de lui donner un coup d'épée, je ne le menacerai point de lui donner la goutte' (p. 344).

Before the article on freewill, the *Militaire philosophe* has defended the reality of moral values, against the incipient nihilism of the sceptics, who assert that they vary from country to country. Everyone has a sense of justice, independently of any laws, according to Article 2 of Section 2; even children or savages, or a man who has grown up in isolation from others. The good lies in freedom, truth, helping our fellows; actions such as murder, rape, or breaking a promise are always bad. The 'essence' of a human being, then, is to possess a material body and a spiritual soul, which is free and has the knowledge of good and evil.

---

[21] This leads on to what must be one of the most idiosyncratic proofs ever devised: 'qu'une femme d'honneur ait été trompée sous l'apparence de son mari, loin d'avoir senti quelque douleur corporelle, elle aura senti le plus vif des plaisirs; cependant elle souffrira une peine mortelle en découvrant la fourberie, fût-ce dans le temps de l'action. Qui peut être la partie souffrante en cette occasion? Ce n'est assurément pas le corps (...)' (p. 330). Perhaps the *Militaire philosophe* had been watching *Amphitryon*; there are several appreciative references to Molière in the *Difficultés,* one being in this passage.

[22] For instance, *Recherche de la vérité*, Premier éclaircissement.

This definition points the way towards solving the problem of the creation of mankind. Men's existence was necessary in order that God's justice should not remain unexercised. 'Je suis bien livré à de cruelles tentations pour le vice, par le goût des plaisirs et la crainte des douleurs, mais je connais parfaitement mon devoir sans équivoque et sans obscurité. (...) Je suis donc un être capable d'exercer l'Etre parfait d'une manière digne de lui, puisqu'il n'y a qu'un Etre infini qui soit capable de connaître et de combiner les différentes circonstances de chacune des mes actions pour en décider le point de bonté ou de malice' (p. 348).

How will the omniscient and just God reward and punish us? The Militaire philosophe makes no claim to answer with certainty. He points out that the mere existence of men, as the proper objects for the exercise of divine justice, need not strictly speaking entail any consequent rewards or punishments. In a most original passage, he attacks the majority's belief in providence: 'il leur faudrait une providence humaine, indéterminée et qui s'accordait à leurs désirs insensés, qu'on gagnât par prières, par cérémonies, par amis et par corruption, une providence humaine vague, prodigue et avare, telle que les plus rusés et les plus importants en profitassent aux dépens des autres' (p. 381). However, he would like to think that God wants all men to be happy, and again relies on introspection in support; he has found that he can wish for justice to be done and, at the same time, for a particular individual to be happy. The illustration is artless. Once he was in charge of a lottery for a horse, which a friend of his needed. There were no witnesses, and he could have drawn out his friend's name; 'je ne le fis cependant pas, l'équité me le défend'. By analogy, we may suppose the same about God, but in God's case, presumably, the desire for the happiness of mankind will be effective. Whatever happens, it is at least certain that men will be treated with complete justice, and our attention should be directed to fulfilling God's requirements, as revealed by reason and conscience. The Militaire philosophe declines to decide about matters such as 'l'éternité des peines', although he regards this particular idea as implausible (p. 355).

The Militaire philosophe's conception of God is notable in at least two respects. First, as might be expected, God tends for him to be a personification of justice; his phraseology often evokes the image of a judge. The analogy is made explicitly in one passage, where it is explained that the relation of God to men is not one of love, but is 'le coup d'oeil pour ainsi dire dont il les regarde' (p. 371). Conversely, men cannot love such a deity, in the literal sense (the Militaire philosophe pours scorn on mystics and their ideas of loving God); neither, properly speaking, can they directly offend him. Their sins are 'fautes devant Dieu, et non envers Dieu' (p. 373).

Secondly, and in consequence, God is not to be regarded as 'good'. In an interesting discussion of the meaning of the word when applied to divinity, the Militaire philosophe find that 'bonté', in its ordinary sense of kindheartedness, is inappropriate. Since it involves a tacit comparison, it is inapplicable; there are not better or worse gods to be compared. In passing, we are told that Christ could be described as 'bon': 'il avait les intentions louables, mais beaucoup de petitesse et peu de capacité' (p. 367).

However, there are difficulties in the concept of a God of justice. Its abstraction conflicts with more personal aspects of deity. For instance, God cannot be said to 'want' men to perform their duty: 'Dieu ne veut ni ne demande rien, c'est l'ordre qui demande, et la justice divine punit ou récompense les êtres qu'il a formés avec la connaissance de l'ordre' (p. 373). Similarly, God may appear not to be free, since he is bound to follow the laws of his wisdom and justice.[23] For the Militaire philosophe, this is not a genuine problem. God is no less free than a man who, for example, has the power to stab a friend, but refrains out of affection and horror of crime (p. 374).

Again, the omniscience of God presents a threat to human freewill; but freewill is necessary if men are to be morally responsible beings, as the Militaire philosophe has already argued. Facing this problem, his idea seems to be that God will have foreseen all possible actions, yet that the will is autonomous. Commenting on Malebranche's theory of 'causes occasionnelles', he says that the human will must have 'quelque chose qui soit absolument à elle, quoiqu'un présent du créateur' (p. 385). In a passage on a related subject in theodicy, God's responsibility for human immorality, he admits that evil was bound to occur, but on the physical level was simply a possibility, foreseen as such, but not determined, by God (p. 389). On the moral level, actions are good or bad, but these qualities, apparently, are not the responsibility of God; his part is to judge them, according to transcendent criteria.

Towards the end of the *Quatrième cahier*, the Militaire philosophe admits, with the intellectual honesty which is one of his most appealing characteristics, that 'il y a encore une terrible difficulté que je ne veux pas dissimuler (. . .) si Dieu m'avait proposé ses récompenses et ses punitions, avec les violences qu'il me faut faire pour obtenir les unes et éviter les autres, j'aurais bien mieux aimé retomber dans le néant ou dans l'insensibilité' (p. 398). Having thus questioned the value of human existence and incidentally placed his entire philosophy in doubt, he reassures himself by a kind of rational act of faith: 'Il n'y a qu'une réponse, cela est sans doute et incontestablement, nous l'avons vu, donc cela est juste, et nous verrons cette justice clairement et sans ombre de difficulté lorsque nous serons au point de l'exécution'.

In his last section, on forms of worship, the Militaire philosophe agrees that public worship would be an excellent institution, provided it were confined to discourse on the greatness of God, exhortations to virtue and

[23] For Malebranche's discussion of this problem, see for instance the *Entretiens sur la métaphysique,* VIII, section xiii, on the relation between God and immutable order.

prayers asking forgiveness for weakness. But so simple a form of worship would almost certainly be corrupted by preachers wishing to distinguish themselves, who would in time found a regular clergy. It was by some such process, in the Militaire philosophe's opinion, that early Christianity must have declined into papism (p. 414). Consequently, he can only recommend private worship, 'le seul sentiment habituel de l'adoration de Dieu, et le dessein de ne faire que ce qu'il approuve' (p. 410).

An epilogue explains to Malebranche the purpose behind the four *cahiers*, claiming that the natural religion of the fourth is in essentials accepted by all mankind. 'Il n'y a de vrai dans toutes les religions que ce qui leur est commun, dont je prétends que tout ce cahier n'est que le fidèle rapport, mais paraphrasé, prouvé, éclairé' (p. 418). The Militaire philosophe wants men to live at peace; 'je voudrais qu'ils s'aimassent et s'entretraitassent avec justice comme la nature les y engage si fortement et si clairement'. If his religion were publicly adopted, there would be no more clergy to practise deceit and live in idleness; society's work would be done by everyone, 'ne rien faire ne sera plus le meilleur de tous les métiers' (p. 423). Finally he promises more works, on various subjects including magic, the great religious leaders and the beliefs of the 'religions factices', saying unconvincingly that all of this 'ne fera pas la dixième partie de ces quatre cahiers'.

The 'système' of the Militaire philosophe, if not the first full exposition of deism in French – Gilbert's *Histoire de Calejava* has the prior claim – is certainly the most important in the first twenty years of the eighteenth century.[24] Every part of it, as can be shown easily, is shaped by the idea of justice, the moral ideal to which men should aspire. As an attribute of God, justice supplies a reason for the existence of mankind, and is the standard by which God will assess men's merit. Much of what the Militaire philosophe says about the relationship between God and man is based on the pre-supposition that God is justice transcendent. Even the weaknesses of the system are governed by this concept, since where it is not relevant, as on the subject of creation, the Militaire philosophe comes close to admitting that he has nothing worthwhile to say. What then is the definition of justice?

We may perhaps look for an answer in the conclusion of Section 2, 'De la morale'. More fully than in other passages, the Militaire philosophe here expresses his most general moral injunction in words suggesting a version of the 'Golden Rule', a very popular moral axiom in deist writing:[25] 'je dois agir avec tous les autres hommes comme je sens qu'ils doivent agir avec moi, faire pour eux tout ce que raisonnablement je puis leur demander, et ne leur

---

[24]   Mortier's claim that the *Difficultés* comprise 'le premier système cohérent de déisme qui ait été conçu en France' (p. 32; cf. pp. 38, 59, 63), though understandable, cannot be accepted without strict reservations; besides Gilbert, there are Lahontan and Foigny's Austral deists to take into account, and probably the *Examen de la religion*, depending on its date (see Chapter 11, n. 6).

[25]   Its Christian form is found in Matthew 7. 12.

rien faire dont je me plaindrais justement si quelqu'un me le faisait' (p. 357). Applying this idea, he chooses a rather obvious example: 'Sommes-nous juges? recevons les plaideurs comme nous voudrions raisonnablement qu'on nous reçût (...)' (p. 358).

It is disappointing that this definition does not take us very far, despite its rational and logical appearance; we are not given any method of deciding what 'raisonnablement' or 'justement' would signify in practice. The Militaire philosophe has simply rephrased the idea that all men should behave justly to each other, with a hint that they may be encouraged to do so by reciprocity. He observes elsewhere that since men live in society, they are 'tenus à certains devoirs réciproques qui sont les règles de cette société' (p. 337). These duties are of a conventional nature; in many different passages, the Militaire philosophe refers to the obligation to avoid crime, to keep our promises, to be on our guard against vanity, greed, ambition and so on. Despite the metaphysical turn which he gives to the discussion, his moral values are defined in commonsense terms.

Because of the identification of God and justice in the Militaire philosophe's scheme of things, it might seem that in his view men should follow justice merely because, if they do not, they will suffer punishment. Although he may give such an impression at times, he protests against the Christian idea of Hell and the morality based on it (p. 390). He also gives a motive for right conduct which is free from self-interest. This is that we should always have God's approval in mind, which appears to mean feeling something akin to the love of God, at the same time as we should fear his perceiving injustice in our actions. 'C'est ainsi que notre vie sera une perpétuelle oraison sans en troubler les actions ni interrompre le cours de nos devoirs' (p. 359). In another passage, the Militaire philosophe suggests that the fear of God resembles our fear of harming a friend (p. 369). Such passages convey a more subtle idea of God than the simple 'Dieu rémunérateur et vengeur' of other deist writers, especially the later Voltaire.

Considered historically, the *Difficultiés sur la religion* strongly reinforces the conclusion to be drawn from Gilbert's work, that the earliest form of deism in France was closely related to the rationalism of late seventeenth-century Christian writers. The *Difficultés* reveal the paradoxical nature of the relationship more clearly than Gilbert, however, because the *Histoire de Calejava* is lacking on the critical side. As regards constructive deism, the Militaire philosophe takes much directly from the Cartesianism of Malebranche; this influence is most apparent in some of the *Vérités* of the first part of the treatise. Where criticism is concerned, the debt is equally great, but is owed to the writers of rational apologetics (including Malebranche), and results of course in refutation rather than imitation. The third part of the *Difficultés* depend on the apologists in the sense that, without their 'proofs', there would be nothing to write about except the defects in

Catholicism, and other religions, which the Militaire philosophe had observed for himself.

He also attacks another form of Christianity, fideism. Here, as with the apologists, his target is identifiable in general but not in particular, for he names no specific works. He seems unaware of Bayle, for instance, whose deep moral sense he shares, and even of Pascal and Montaigne. For the rest, his system appears to be the result of reflection on his experiences, in France and abroad. It seems unnecessary to look for any other source for his emphasis on justice and moral values. The tendency in the *Quatrième cahier* for secular morality to supersede reason as the guiding principle is paralleled in other writers of the time, from Bayle through to Montesquieu and Voltaire. Again, there is a resemblance to Gilbert in this respect. It should perhaps be said that in the Militaire philosophe secularism is still a tendency, not a completed process. His system of justice is too closely connected with the idea of God to be considered purely secular, even if the religious element is more a matter of intellect than feeling.

CHAPTER 11

THE *EXAMEN DE LA RELIGION* AND OTHER CLANDESTINE WORKS

The most widely disseminated and typical of the early eighteenth-century clandestine deistic works is one which is known in three different versions and goes under a variety of titles. The commonest, and the most appropriate for the content, is 'Examen de la religion', which was used after 1760 for printed editions. Another is 'Doutes sur la religion', sometimes with the insincere addition 'dont on cherche l'éclaircissement de bonne foi' (the purpose being not to resolve any doubts, but to increase them). Manuscript copies are found in libraries throughout France.[1] Its history is similar to that of the Militaire philosophe's *Difficultés;* having been copied and revised anonymously for many years, it was published during the *philosophes'* campaign against the Church. One publication was due to Voltaire, in his *Evangile de la raison*, in 1764.

The authorship of the *Examen* remains a mystery, although many more or less plausible rumours have been transmitted since the eighteenth century. From I. O. Wade's investigations of the extant copies, it appears that the different versions are not distinguished by their titles, but by the number of chapters they contain – eleven (or occasionally twelve); fourteen; or fifteen.[2] The order of chapters also varies. As regards content, the fifteen-chapter version includes a chapter on miracles which is absent from the others. Either the fifteen-chapter or the eleven-chapter version was almost certainly the original; the fourteen-chapter version is written in a more facile and disingenuous style, which strongly suggests that it is a late revision. A prefatory letter which accompanies it is dated 1739.[3] In studying the *Examen,* it is preferable to choose the fifteen-chapter version, because of the presence of the chapter on miracles. In addition, it seems

---

[1]   See Wade, *Clandestine Organization*, p. 13 and Pt. II, Ch. 3 (pp. 141–163).

[2]   The classification by the number of chapters is due to Wade (pp. 141–145); the difference of number results partly from the fact that single chapters in one version have the same material as two in others and partly from the presence or absence of a chapter on miracles. On authorship, see Wade, pp. 152ff.; he gives good reasons for rejecting a traditional attribution, to the Chevalier de La Serre, hanged in 1748 for spying. According to Wade's summary of his findings (p. 157) the work was attributed to Dumarsais more often than to the other two writers commonly suggested, Boulainviller and Mirabaud.

[3]   This of course proves nothing about the text which the letter precedes, but may indicate a date for the presumed revision of the text.

likely from internal evidence that the fifteen-chapter version was written before that in eleven chapters.[4] As for the date, the usual view, following Wade, is that it was written between 1710 and 1720, but this seems too late.[5] References in the text to events, publications and the date of writing indicate a date of about 1705.[6] The *Examen* may well antedate the Militaire philosophe's *Difficultés*, then, but only by a few years, and evidently the process of recopying and revision continued for some time.

In several respects the *Examen* is close to Gilbert's *Calejava*, but it is even more similar, especially in the critical chapters, to the Militaire philosophe's work and to other clandestine manuscripts, notably the *Religion chrétienne analysée,* written rather later than the *Examen.* All these works are rationalist, combining positive deism with objections to the current arguments in favour of Christianity. In the *Examen* a threefold plan can be discerned which is also the rough outline of *Calejava* and the *Difficultés sur la religion*: the early chapters define the rational approach to religion and proclaim the right to 'examine', a longer central section attacks the main proofs adduced by the defenders of Christianity, and in conclusion the writer gives his own religious philosophy.

Rationalist preliminaries
In the first years of the eighteenth century, the work's title was a bold one, for (without implying any Protestant influence) it assumed the right of the individual to decide for himself about religion, and denied the claims of

---

[4]   Borrowings from Fontenelle (see nn. 12 and 13 below) are found in many chapters, including the 15-chapter version's chapter on miracles. If we suppose that the 11-chapter version, with its borrowings, was the original, we have to make a further supposition which seems very improbable: that the writer who revised the 11-chapter version to form a 15-chapter work added a chapter on miracles which, coincidentally, contained borrowings from the same source.

[5]   Wade's dating (*Clandestine Organization,* pp. 149–152) is partly based on annotations to two manuscripts. Both put the date of the *Examen* more than thirty years previously, which is vague and unreliable evidence. The annotations themselves were made in 1741 and 1750; Wade also refers to resemblances between the *Examen* and another manuscript, *De la conduite qu'un honnête homme doit garder pendant la vie,* but these prove nothing about the relative priority of the two works. On this latter manuscript, see Rétat, *Le Dictionnaire de Bayle et la lutte philosophique,* pp. 87–88; he shows that it must be posterior to 1706. No doubt it copies the *Examen,* as well as Bayle. In the *Examen*, references *inter alia* to Fontenelle's *Histoire des oracles,* of 1686; to Admiral Russell's expedition to the Mediterranean, in 1694; and to the Bossuet-Fénelon controversy in 1697–1698 (Chs. 4, 5 and 1 of the 15-chapter version) concur with statements mentioning 1700 to suggest that the *Examen* was written shortly after that date. The time of writing is referred to in the phrase '1700 ou quelques années après' (Ch. 3), St Paul is said to have prophesied 1700 years previously (Ch. 5) and Catholicism to have last 1700 years (Ch. 8). These remarks admittedly do no more than emphasize the idea of the year 1700.

[6]   References are only to chapters, not to the pages of any particular copy or edition, because of the textual complexities. The copies consulted principally were manuscript 2091 of the Bibliothèque de l'Arsenal, entitled *Examen de la religion en quinze chapitres,* and two in the Bibliothèque nationale, n.a.f. 1902 and 10436.

authority to impose faith and submission on the loyal believer. Moreover, whereas the Militaire philosophe had addressed his treatise only to Malebranche, the *Examen* is addressed to anyone prepared to buy a copy or copy it himself. The first chapter is headed by a question: 's'il nous est permis d'examiner notre religion'. The answer is that a number of religions all threaten us with damnation: faced by the conflicting demands of Jews, Turks and pagans, as well as those of our own religion, we are obliged to try to find out the truth. The argument is easy but powerful. It contains the essence of the dilemma experienced by Marana's Spy in France, and a later reference suggests that the author might have read Marana; a Muslim, he says, would consider as silly the rites which sensible French people perform ('badiner avec un morceau de pain').[7] But Mahmut had only gradually moved away from ideas of loyalty to an established religion. The author of the *Examen* immediately declares his allegiance to a more abstract authority, that of reason: 'ce que nous croyons par raison ne saurait être faux, parce que la raison est une lumière qui vient de Dieu et Dieu ne saurait nous tromper'. This enormously simplified rationalism seems to come from Malebranche, to whom, as the author of the *Recherche de la vérité*, a reference is made. According to him, says the writer, all men's pronouncements must be subjected to the test of reason. This seems to be a genuine, not an ironic, statement of indebtedness to Malebranche.

The universality of rational principles means that variety of belief, as displayed by the established religions, is a mark of falsity.This is the affirmation made in the second chapter, 'S'il y a une véritable religion', which is full of assertions that God is veracious; if any one religion were true, he would have revealed it clearly. The only true religion, therefore, is that which is derivable from universal reason. On this basis, the writer rejects any beleif due to submission to authority, the kind found in children and 'le vulgaire' — recognizably a reference to fideistic Catholicism. He admits that such beleif is easier than the rigours of an all-embracing 'examination'.

The next chapter (or part of chapter, depending on the version) has a title which is again uncompromisingly rationalistic: 'Des preuves que doit avoir la véritable religion et des conditions que doit avoir ces preuves'. The treatment is rather less methodical than we might expect. The main theme is that the truths of religion should be clear, as we have read before, easy to understand, and convincing. Christianity, however, depends on facts, and fails to satisfy such criteria. Tha argument shows once more, after the Militaire philosophe and his attack on the 'religious factices', the essential opposition between Cartesian reason and factual truth. The writer

---

[7] This recalls Marana's letter describing the Communion service (*Espion turc*, I, L. 12; see Chapter 7, p. 100).

summarizes the history of Christ, which contains the facts in question, and asks how they support the claims of Christianity. Why did the miracles performed by Christ not convert the Jews, and why did the Romans not know of them? (The implication is that the 'facts' are untrue.) Some of the rest of the chapter pursues the same line of argument. Much in Christianity has changed — more facts, from the emendations made in sacred texts to the contrast between the pomp of modern bishops and the poverty of the apostles — whereas God is immutable, and 'ne se dément jamais'; consequently, he was not responsible for the establishment of the Christian religion. Another passage makes a contrast between what reason tells us about God and what Catholicism tells us. For the rationalist, God is (for instance) ubiquitous, not subject to emotion, and omnipotent, but the Christian is told that God had to look for Adam in the Garden of Eden, that he repented of making man, and that he has an enemy whom he can conquer only by the sacrifice of his son.

The preliminary chapters move towards the conclusion that, because of the disparity between what we expect of God and what we find in Christianity, the Christian religion is of human origin and can be accounted for in human terms. Malebranchian rationalism has developed into a statement of the imposture theory of religion. The core of the argument is the opposition between human and divine, and the method in subsequent chapters is to make constant reference to it, either explicitly or implicitly. It is the use of this method which endows the *Examen* with such unity as it possesses, since its content is often no more than a disconnected series of criticisms.

The critique of Christian proofs
The middle chapters, which contain the bulk of the critical material in the *Examen,* are those which differ most in the two early versions. The criticisms cover various aspects of the Christian revelation — two important dogmas, those of the Trinity and Original Sin; the 'external proofs' of miracles and prophecy; and supporting arguments such as the constancy of the martyrs. The author, or later editor, of the *Examen* seems to have had difficulty in deciding where to put what he had to say about the external proofs. In neither version is the order of chapters entirely satisfactory, and it seems best to ignore the numerical order and begin with the chapters on the subject of revelation.[8]

[8] The order of the middle chapters is as follows, in the 15-chapter version: Chs. 4, miracles; 5, prophecy; 6, the martyrs; 7, Scripture; 8, Christ; 9, the Church and its councils; 10, the Fathers of the Church; 11, the Trinity; 12, Original Sin, and in the 11-chapter version: Chs. 3, Scripture; 4, Christ; 5, the Church and councils; 6, the Fathers and martyrs; 7, prophecy; 8, the Trinity and Original Sin. The important chapters on Scripture and Jesus Christ are better placed in the 11-chapter version, but it omits the chapter on miracles (the subject-matter of which naturally accompanies that on prophecy) and its Chapter 6 is disjointed.

The chapter entitled 'De l'écriture sainte' is the first of these. It is directed against the idea that the Scriptures were written under divine inspiration, and argues, for example, that the authors of the New Testament themselves never claimed to be divinely inspired; the claim is therefore a modern one. Most of the chapter is a string of similar arguments. The Gospel, were it divine, should be sufficiently clear not to require interpretation by men; it should have consisted of the words of Christ (compare the Koran, written by Mohammed); it should have been comprehensible to one and all, and been both clear (according to one passage) and distinct (according to another). These and other criteria for divinity are scattered through the chapter and interspersed with remarks about the human inperfections of Scripture. There are copyists' faults; Hebrew is full of ambiguities; God is said, ludicrously, to do things like discussing Job with the devil. 'L'Ecriture sainte est pleine de contradictions, parce que l'esprit de l'homme qui en est l'auteur ne saurait se soutenir et avoir tout présent'. Matthew writes 'Zechariah' when he means 'Jeremiah'; the Gospels of Mark and Luke are irreconcilable as regards the times when Jesus was judged and executed.

On occasion the criticisms seem strained. One, for instance, is that if God made the rainbow as a sign of peace between himself and mankind, it ought not to be visible to criminals. Elaborate reasoning of this sort could be paralleled in many other chapters of the *Examen*. Perhaps the author was following his sources. He makes it quite plain that he obtained much of his material from Christian writers, presumably apologists or biblical commentators. He refers to an error in the Old Testament mentioned by Cajetan and to a remark by Gerson, that nothing is more perplexing than the account of Christ being tempted by the Devil. The observation about the time at which the Crucifixion took place seems to come directly from the apologist Mauduit.[9] Such passages recall the Militaire philosophe's observation that reading the defenders of Christianity did more than anything else to disabuse him. The author of the *Examen* ascribes his critical attitude to his respect for God: 'plus on a du respect pour la divinité, plus on doit éviter de s'exposer de prendre les fables des hommes pour la parole de Dieu'.

The same line of argument, broadly speaking, continues for three further chapters, against the divinity of the Christian revelation. The abrupt beginning of the chapter on Christ is typical: 'Jésus-Christ était un homme comme Mahomet'. It goes on to list the ways in which Christ was inadequate as bearer of a revelation and as redeemer. He had only a few disciples, taught moral precepts which the pagans had anticipated, and did not mention dogmas such as the Trinity which are the foundation of the

---

[9] In Chapter 7 (Arsenal 2091, f. 373) there is a discussion of the apologists' defence of the discrepancy, that it was due to a copyist's error. The reference given is to a dissertation of the Gospels by Mauduit, which must be Michel Mauduit, *Analyse de l'Evangile selon l'ordre historique de la concorde, avec des dissertations sur les lieux difficiles,* first published in 1694 and many times later.

Catholic religion. As for the redeeming sacrifice of Christ, it was unnecessary (God could have saved all men had he wished) and conveys an unfitting idea of God (only men, not God, are to be appeased by sacrifice). This chapter in particular, together with those on the Trinity and Original Sin, would justify the association between deism and Socinianism, often made at the time, as in the review of Lahontan's *Dialogues curieux* by the *Journal de Trévoux*.[10] The extreme Arian statement of Christ's humanity, criticism of the idea of sacrifice, anti-trinitarianism, and denial that human nature is sinful are all typical of radical rationalist sects such as the Socinians and Arminians. But the influence, if any, seems likely to have been filtered through the apologists who, in devising answers to radicals' objections, often disclosed what the objections were.

Humanity and the weakness of humanity, again, are what the *Examen's* author sees in the Church, its councils and the Fathers. 'L'Eglise n'est autre chose qu'une société d'hommes': the truism means that the councils were wrong in claiming to have received divine guidance. Much of the argument in the chapters on these subjects is undistinguished. There are facile criticisms concerning such things as disputes between the Fathers, the divisions in the Church, including the schism of Avignon, and the gradual development of Christian doctrine over the centuries; all this is contrary to the author's ideal of immutability in religion. It is interesting that a similar line of argument had been developed by Bossuet, denouncing the variations of the Protestant Churches in the name of the unchanging Catholic religion, and it is also Bossuet whom the author of the *Examen* seems to have in mind when he attacks the view that the establishment of the Christian religion followed a providential plan. This was the idea expounded by Bossuet in the *Histoire universelle*.[11] The author of the *Examen*, for his part, thinks that Christianity succeeded for more ordinary reasons, such as the popular fondness for marvels, the zeal of preachers and the example set by the martyrs.

At this point, another and less orthodox presence begins to obtrude, that of Fontenelle, in the form of borrowings from the *Histoire des oracles*. The author maintains, continuing with his argument about the spread of Christian belief, that if he himself had a dozen apostles he would be just as successful if he set out to persuade people that the sun gave no light. This is

[10] See Chapter 9, p. 136. There is a curious reference to 'un Indien de bon sens' in the manuscript (Arsenal 2091, f. 371): the Scriptures should have been written by Christ and be clear and distinct, 'autrement un Indien de bon sens ne peut les regarder que comme des livres à l'ordinaire', which closely resembles the objections made by Lahontan's friend Le Rat. This could mean that the author had read Lahontan, the title of whose *Dialogues* refers to 'un savage de bon sens qui a voyagé'. If so the *Examen* was written, or perhaps revised, after 1703.

[11] The *Histoire universelle* was published in 1681, the *Histoire des variations des églises protestantes* in 1688. Jurieu, answering the latter work in his *Lettres pastorales*, had countered with the argument that doctrines accepted by the Catholic Church were also variable, not immutable, having developed historically; this could be a source of the *Examen's* arguments.

what Fontenelle had said, give or take half a dozen, and the *Examen* proceeds to utilize Fontenelle's explanation, in terms of gases exhaled from the earth, of the origins of the oracles at Delphi, together with other passages from the *Histoire des oracles*.[12] These borrowings could have been interpolated into the original text (although they are found in both the eleven- and fifteen-chapter versions), so that it is not certain that the author himself, rather than a reviser, was significantly influenced by Fontenelle, but that there was such an influence on the *Examen* as we have it cannot be doubted. This is one of the comparatively rare cases in which Fontenelle's inflence can be documented; his reduction of the supernatural to the human, with regard to oracles, is often said to have been an anticipation of Enlightenment interpretations of religion in general. In another chapter of the *Examen,* its kinship with the *Histoire des oracles* is illustrated by a comparison between Fontenelle's explanations and the Old Testament prophecies.

The chapters on the external proofs, which relied on the idea that the Christian revelation was guaranteed by supernatural phenomena, complete the *Examen's* refutation of the apologists. The chapter on miracles found in the fifteen-chapter version begins with the argument that miracles are a poor method of inculcating religious truths: they can be no more than supporting evidence, other religions can have miracles also, the miracles ascribed to Christ failed to convert his Jewish and Roman contemporaries. Subsequent reflections imitate Fontenelle. They follow the order in which the relevant passages occur in the *Histoire des oracles,* which tends to imply that this part of the chapter at least was an addition to the first form of the *Examen.*[13] The theme is men's propensity to believe in the supernatural. On the prophecies, a previous type of argument returns: revelation through prophecy is too obscure; it cannot be divine. Divine prophecy would not need interpretation and would have converted the Jews. The discussion centres, as is normal, on the three prophecies expounded at the greatest length by apologists, Jacob's 'The sceptre shall not depart from Judah', Isaiah's 'Behold, a virgin shall conceive' and the so-called 'seventy weeks' of Daniel.[14] Once more the author of *Examen* finds the biblical commentaries an easy target as he explains, for instance, the ambiguities of the word 'sceptre'. He also records that a friend of his made some prophecies in the vein of Nostradamus and saw them all come true in a few years.

[12]   *Histoire des oracles,* Première dissertation, Ch. 11, on the Delphic oracle; I, Ch. 13 and II, Ch. 4 are the sources of borrowings in the *Examen's* chapter on the Church and its councils.
[13]   The borrowings are mostly from the first Dissertation. Before and after the section containing them, the first and last parts of the chapter are free of any borrowings.
[14]   See Genesis, 49. 10; Isaiah, 7. 14; Daniel, 9. 24–26. The apologist Louis Ferrand provided the fullest treatment of the prophecies, and was used as an authority by other apologists (Monod, *De Pascal à Chateaubriand,* p. 72).

In these chapters criticizing revelation, the author composes his attack, indefatigably, by choosing features of Christianity apparently at random, and rejecting them because they do not match up to the 'divine' standard of perfection which he demands. He tends, like the Militaire philosophe, to assume that the Christian revelation is a series of logical propositions. In this, he seems to have been influenced by the apologists more subtly than when he is simply reversing their arguments.

The later chapters of the *Examen* cover a rather heterogeneous group of subjects, mainly the doctrines and moral values of Christianity. The section or chapter on the Trinity is short, but contains several powerful arguments: the doctrine is contrary to a rational idea of God; it was not mentioned by the earliest Fathers of the Church; its source lies in pagan thought. What is said about Original Sin, by contrast, is notable for the positive point of view which it implies, and which is humanist or optimist, as in other writers of this period. The writer begins as before, appealing to a principle of divine perfection (God is too just to punish children for the misdeeds of their parents), and then gives an explanation in human terms for the existence of a doctrine of Original Sin. He sees it as an interpretation of the problem of suffering: unable to find a reason for suffering, and yet needing to believe that it was in some way deserved, men have imputed the fault to their first ancestor. But the author of the *Examen* prefers another view. Pain, he says, is God's way of showing us what we must avoid for our own good. The optimism of this becomes more apparent in the arguments that the misfortunes of poverty are imaginary and that death is a lesser evil than commonly thought, since it is necessary in the order of nature (hence it is not a punishment for Adam's sin). On a more intractable problem, that of moral evil or wrongdoing, the writer simply denies that it is a problem at all. Men have no bad inclinations: 'tous nos penchants sont bons parce qu'ils viennent de Dieu'; 'l'homme est tel qu'il est par sa nature; la nature est l'ordre que Dieu a donné et établi, qui par conséquent ne peut être mauvais'. In these reflections the dominant influence seems again to be that of Malebranche, perhaps at one or two removes.[15]

By this stage, the initial purpose of the 'examination of religion', to decide in which religion we shall be saved, has been lost to sight in the profusion of detailed criticisms. But before passing on to describe the religion he desires to see, orientated towards secular values, the writer recalls his first arguments about the need to find salvation. He now denies that the idea of salvation itself has any meaning, in a passage of radical deistic determinism. All things depend on God; all events occur according to his laws. Consequently, as regards God, no actions can be either good or bad, even though created

[15] The notion of 'ordre', in such a context, always suggests Malebranche, and the idea of the natural utility of pain is also favoured by him; see for instance *Recherche de la vérité*, L. I, Chs. V, X.

may do good or harm to each other. 'Le voleur fait le bien et le mal, le bien par rapport à lui, le mal par rapport aux autres, et rien par rapport à Dieu. Immoral or illegal conduct is exclusively the business of society; a thief, for example, should be removed from society as if he were 'une machine mal montée'. As for our salvation in the afterlife, which apparently depends on following one particular form of worship, the *Examen* argues that if God had wished us to keep to one religion he would have revealed it from the beginning, instead of giving the Jewish and then the Christian law. Belief in God, like reason, exists universally; so too would all the articles of any religion instituted by God. The conclusion, in blunt terms, is that 'il n'y a donc pas de religion' – in the sense, presumably, of one true established religion.

Catholicism replaced by rational secularism

The penultimate chapter is a statement of the conflict between Catholic and utilitarian values, entitled 'Que la religion catholique[16] n'est pas nécessaire pour la société civile, qu'elle tend à la détruire, et de retenir dans de légitimes bornes moins de personnes qu'on ne pense' – a reply to the argument for Christianity based on the social value of religion. The *Examen* notes that the Catholic Church condemns worldly pomp and pleasure, sex and money-making, which for the author comprise the sum of social activity. Monastic society, he says, is the Catholic ideal, and he proceeds to denounce monasticism in the name of society and the deistic God. On one side he sets celibacy, asceticism and the exclusive concern with our happiness in Heaven; on the other, the continuation of the human race, natural instincts and social activity for the happiness of all. The author of the *Examen* believes, like Gilbert, that God wants men in general to be happy, and that if we are useful to others we will ourselves be contented and prosperous.

In this attack, 'monasticism' is an exaggerated distortion of Christian morality. It is not a convincing representation of the state of contemporary Catholicism, but an effective instrument of polemic, driving home the basic distinction between religious and secular. The lesson is completed by the outline of a secular morality in the final chapter, which is entitled 'Qu'il y a un être supérieur, et de la conduite qu'un honnête homme doit garder dans la vie'; part of it is also found as a separate manuscript work.[17] It is one of the classic statements of positive or constructive deism, consisting in three basic elements, belief in reason, belief in God, and a code of morality.

The writer starts by proving, in the manner common to both Christian and

---

[16]   The 11-chapter version has 'la religion chrétienne'.

[17]   *De la conduite qu'un honnête homme doit garder dans la vie,* referred to in n. 5 above. It is the fifth item in a collection, ms. 1194 of the Bibliothèque Mazarine. It consists of the second half of the chapter in the *Examen* and a large number of borrowings from Bayle.

deistic exponents of natural religion, that God exists. The argument on this occasion is that the marvels of the world are beyond human comprehension (the writer instances the tides, light and colour, the movements of the stars and the coordination of animals' bodies), and their creation must have been due, not to chance as the atheistic theory has it, but to 'un être sage et tout-puissant'. Thus the deity is seen as an inventor of scientific technology at a more than human level, and the universe as a superior sort of machine: 'une structure admirable où la disposition des parties répond à une fin est assurément l'effet d'une cause intelligente'.

Once the question of creation has been settled, however, God is regarded as reason divinized; his perfections are the absence of contradiction and inconsistency. Reason in man comes from God, and is particularly the mark of the chapter's hero, the 'honnête homme', here a name for the ideal deist. The 'honnête homme' will not follow other people's views (those of the Church) concerning his duties unless they conform to the 'lumière claire et évidente' of reason. He will believe in the infinite divisibility of matter because, although we cannot understand such a thing, it agrees with clear and evident principles; but he will not believe in Christianity because of its inadequacies. Harking back to previous passages on changeable historical religion and imperfect sacred texts, the author predictably concludes with the extreme form of his constant assumption about 'human' and 'divine' — religion is an imposture, devised by its founders in their own interest; a human phenomenon, and due, moreover, to the less admirable elements in human nature.

The rational 'honnête homme', having given up Christianity, is faced with the problem of a replacement for its morality of salvation. The author of the *Examen* supplies the solution by making reason into a moral authority. There are some people, he says, whose disbelief is no more than disbelief in Hell; they have been brought up to fear damnation, and when in adult life they lose their fears, they lose their moral scruples also. But the 'honnêtes gens qui ne croient pas la religion catholique par raison' have a moral guide of their own: 'l'esprit d'ordre les fait agir, et la raison leur persuade par cet esprit d'ordre combien il leur importe d'avoir de l'honneur et de la probité'. The 'spirit of order' looks very like a descendant of Malebranche's fundamental virtue in the *Traité de morale*, 'l'amour de l'ordre', but if Malebranche is the source he is soon abandoned. The precepts which make up the *Examen's* moral substitute for Christianity are typically deistic. The 'honnête homme' should profess his belief in God, and do his best to please God; he should follow the Golden Rule, behaving towards others as he would want them to behave to him — a maxim which the author prefers to consider as pagan rather than Christian.

Instead of Christian worship, the *Examen* recommends a purely intellectual form of 'estime intérieure', consisting in the knowledge of God and his attributes. There should be no public worship, but rather conduct suitable to the essence of God and our dependence on him. These enigmatic phrases seem to refer again to moral conduct: we should use all things as God intended, not to excess and not to our own detriment. The writer's last reflections turn to social considerations, as, on the basis that God wants the good of men generally, he calls for mutual assistance between men. We should love others as ourselves; but the Christian precept has been converted into enlightened self-interest, since our reward, according to the *Examen*, is that we are assisted by others in our turn.

To summarise: the *Examen's* intellectual affiliations are Cartesian, as is shown by the frequent, but not always expert, use of terms such as 'clear and distinct' or 'evident', and at a deeper level by the writer's assumption that reality is governed by reason. Like Gilbert and the Militaire philosophe, he appears (when not criticizing Christianity) to be closer to Malebranche than to Descartes himself, for he refers several times to the author of the *Recherche de la vérité*. He is basically making the same attempt as Malebranche, but much more crudely, to combine reason and religion. For the most part, he remains at the stage of supposing reason to be logical consistency. While this provides a powerful critical weapon, especially when turned against the rational apologists, it is less fruitful on the positive side.

The *Examen* is a second-rate work, not only because the writing is often disorderly and confused, which might be due, at least in part, to the vicissitudes of clandestine drafting and copying, but because the rationalism is superficially and naïvely expressed, without moderation or nuance. Nor does the writer show any great learning. Nonetheless, his treatise has great importance as testimony to what might be called popular deism, showing how Cartesian rationalism could easily become, even in the hands of an inexpert thinker, the foundation for a completely anti-Christian work. Its lack of distinction also suggests that its attitudes could well have been widespread, while its plain speaking can be a valuable guide to the greater subtleties of Montesquieu and Voltaire.

THE *EXAMEN* AND OTHER DEIST MANUSCRIPTS

The many resemblances, general and specific, between the *Examen de la religion* and the Militaire philosophe's *Difficultés sur la religion* raise the question whether there was a direct relationship between them. The uncertainty of date is such that either could conceivably be the source of the other. The overall arrangement of the material is the same, except that the *Examen* lacks a separate section on faith; there is the same Cartesian rationalism, the same appeal to a criterion of divinity and the same utilitarian, secularist tendency. Both writers argue that 'examination' is necessary because our salvation is threatened by choosing a wrong religion, and both are indebted to Malebranche and other apologists. However, more detailed comparison reveals notable differences. In refuting the affirmation that Christianity is based on fact, the Militaire philosophe develops an ingenious and lengthy argument, but the *Examen's* treatment is rudimentary.[18] Although both writers attack a series of apologetic proofs, the Militaire philosophe faces a larger number than the *Examen,* which has nothing on such matters as the 'miracle' of the Jewish Diaspora and discusses fewer Christian dogmas.[19] On the other hand, the author of the *Examen* appears to be better read in scriptural interpretation. He knows more about the prophecies and the discrepancies between the Gospels. Detailed similarities, such as references to Nostradamus or the recourse to the Golden Rule as a moral axiom, could easily be mere coincidence.

The evidence points to the hypothesis of common sources (obviously the Cartesian tradition and the apologetic literature of the seventeenth century, perhaps assisted by sermons) rather than the direct influence of one work on the other. Moreover, in the *Examen* there is no trace of the coherent deistic system of divine justice worked out by the Militaire philosophe in his *Quatrième cahier.* If the *Examen* was written after the *Difficultés* and if its author knew them, he omitted the most original section entirely and replaced it with deistic banalities. Conversely, if the Militaire philosophe knew and imitated the *Examen,* he took little from it except a general outline and some characteristics, such as secularism in ethics, which are shared by many other writers of the time. It remains possible that one work influenced the other in some such manner, but both give the clear impression that they are the independent reactions of rationalists to the pressures of Christian propaganda.

The other clandestine work which the *Examen* resembles in scope and content is known either as the *Analyse de la religion* or as *La religion chrétienne analysée.*[20] In this treatise the author 'analyses' the Old and New

---

[18] The writer merely says that the 'truths' of established religion 'ne sont point innées et métaphysiques ni éternelles, ce sont des vérités qui dependent des faits, et ce sont même des vérités que je ne dois pas croire légèrement de peur de rendre à Dieu un culte qu'il n'approuve pas' (Arsenal 2091, f. 319 (start of Ch. 3)). He then passes on to the history of Christ and the early martyrs, stressing the doubtfulness of events remote in time.

[19] *Difficultés sur la religion,* Mortier edition, pp. 290–292 ('La dispersion des Juifs'); on various doctrines the *cahier* 'E', Section 2 (the Messiah, the Redemption, the Trinity, the resurrection of the dead, predestination, etc.) and 10 (the Redemption, Original Sin, etc).

[20] See Wade, *Clandestine Organization,* Pt. II, Ch. 4. Like the *Examen,* the *Analyse* was published by Voltaire, in 1763 or 1764, and has therefore been attributed to him. See Pomeau, *La religion de Voltaire,* p. 175, rejecting the attribution. The manuscript which I have used is that of the Bibliothèque nationale, f. fr. 13353, entitled *Religion chrétienne analisée.* A note in a separate hand on its first page reads: 'C'est le vrai manuscrit sur lequel l'ouvrage attribué à V*** a été

Testaments, picking out many errors and inconsistencies. He is a more learned and able critic than the author of the *Examen,* and his argument, while not entirely free from repetition, follows a well-planned course throughout. In general terms, it begins with considerations designed, as in the *Examen,* to justify the critical enterprise, and in the body of the work the writer tests the authority of the Bible by applying one standard after another: first the criterion of divinity (similar to that used by the Militaire philosophe and the *Examen*), in order to show that the Scriptures cannot have come directly from God; then the criteria of internal consistency, plausibility and verifiability, by which ordinary histories are judged. Apologists' arguments are discussed whenever they present a serious objection to the criticisms. From about two-thirds of the way through the *Analyse,* its main subject is the theological meaning of the Crucifixion, the sacrifice of the Son of God for the redemption of mankind, a subject neglected by the author of the *Examen.* The *Analyse* attacks it as a 'mystery', by means of rational argument, but the author recognizes that despite its illogicality it is still believed. In consequence he then sets about demolishing supporting proofs, of prophecy, martyrdom and miracles, and concludes that the Christian religion has nothing to distinguish it from other religions. Thus although he deals with many of the same subjects as the *Examen,* his criticisms are not disconnected, following the order of proofs in a typical apology, but are incorporated into a coherent plan.

The greater professionalism of the *Analyse* is also displayed in the discussion of many points of detail. The author is able to compare the chronology of the Vulgate and the Septuagint, for example, or to show that historians contemporary with Christ do not report the extraordinary events of the New Testament, such as the Massacre of the Innocents. Where he and the *Examen* both make the same criticism, he will do so more thoroughly; he mentions the confusion between Zechariah and Jeremiah in Matthew, but also gives the Old Testament reference and deduces, more exactly than the author of the *Examen,* that either the text of the Old Testament or that of the New must be incorrect.[21] He is well versed in ancient authorities, Christian and pagan, and with some of the modern writers on Scripture, such as Spinoza, [22] Richard Simon, Dom Calmet and Houtteville. (The reference

imprimé. Il a fait beaucoup de bruit'. One of its many corrected passages (p. 135) indicates that it was first written about 1730, at the time of the faith-healing at the tomb of the Jansenist curé Pâris, in the cemetery of Saint-Médard. The original text refers to 'guérisons miraculeuses', then to 'ce que nous voyons arriver aujourd' hui'. This last clause is deleted, and replaced by a reference to Saint-Médard; i.e. the original writer did not need to explain what he meant because of the notoriety of the events, but the reviser felt that an explanation was called for.

[21]   Loc. cit., p. 66; Matthew 27. 9 refers to a statement which is in Zechariah 11. 12, but ascribes it to Jeremiah.

[22]   He is referred to (p. 37) as the Jewish author of a *Traité des cérémonieuses superstitieuses des Juifs,* which is one of the titles under which Saint-Glain's French version of the *Tractatus theologico-politicus* was published.

to Houtteville fixes the date of the *Analyse* after 1722, the year of his *La religion chrétienne prouvée par les faits.*) The author of the *Analyse* uses Fontenelle, like the author of the *Examen*, but recalls that Fontenelle himself was adapting Van Dale.

Apart from the extremely competent destructive criticism there is little in the *Analyse de la religion chrétienne.* An ingenious calculation at the beginning proves that only one part in 160 of the world's population is Catholic, a reckoning later supplemented by another, showing that only one person in four thousand can be saved. The doctrines attacked are regularly described as 'mysteries', but the standpoint from which the author writes is not that of the metaphysical rationalist, like the Militaire philosphe or the author of the *Examen*; reason in the *Analyse* is more in the nature of the critical faculty or common sense. As regards deism, what is more relevant is that the author does not clearly reveal that he believes in God. He often refuses to accept the Scriptures can be divine, which might indicate that his own position is theistic, but could equally well be a debating stance modelled on the claims of the apologists. The practical consequences he draws from his criticisms are secular and conformist: 'Eloignons donc pour jamais un respect servile (. . .); ayons pour la religion chrétienne le même oeil et le même sens commun que pour les autres; suivons extérieurement le culte établi dans les lieux où le hasard nous a fait naître; regardons ce culte comme faisant partie des lois civiles'.[23]

Although, therefore, the *Analyse* could be said to belong to a French tradition of critical deism (to use Leslie Stephen's term),[24] its tendency is probably atheistic. Its importance is almost entirely as an anti-Christian work. Nothing can be affirmed definitely about the relationship between it and the *Examen*; it could be a much improved version of the *Examen's* critical chapters, as the similarity with one of its titles suggests. The *Examen* must have circulated for some time before the *Analyse* was written. But if the writer took the idea of a critical survey of Christianity from the *Examen*, he carried it out with considerably greater skill.

---

[23]   In the Bibliothèque nationale ms. 13353, this is not the final passage, but is followed by another, an addition to the original text. Here religion is seen in moral or social terms; 'le peuple ignorant et grossier' is prevented from plunging into crime by the fear of hell (as well as by 'les roues et les gibets'), while 'l'homme raisonnable et instruit' will follow the Golden Rule, a universal maxim which 'suffit pour maintenir les liens de la société'. There is also a postscript, addressed to one Adélaïde, 'plus intéressante encore par votre âme que par des attraits périssables'; she is advised that it is risky to enlighten the masses about religion: 'ils nous traiteraient injurieusement, et les noms les plus odieux nous seraient prodigués'. Religion was established for political reasons and should be permitted to subsist as popular belief.

[24]   *History of English Thought in the Eighteenth Century*, Ch. IV, on a group of writers including Charles Blount, Anthony Collons, Thomas Woolston and Peter Annet.

The clandestine manuscripts of the early eighteenth century span a wide range of unorthodoxy, from the mild *Le Ciel ouvert à tous les hommes* of the priest Pierre Cuppé to the anonymous *Traité des trois imposteurs,* the title of which refers to Moses, Jesus and Mohammed.[25] Before about 1750, they are as typical a means of communicating free-thought as the propaganda of d'Holbach's 'atelier' or Voltaire's campaign against 'l'infâme' was in later decades. In this movement of religious opposition — since its variety and extent give it the status of a movement — the most important of the deistic works are the *Examen de la religion* and the Militaire philosophe's long treatise. The *Analyse de la religion,* being almost exclusively critical, belongs to an ambiguous category, on the border between deism and atheism. The complementary but less radical category of works which could be either Christian or deistic is best represented, before 1715 or 1720, by several essays or treatises, most of them interrelated, which are connected with the Comte de Boulainviller.

Henry de Boulainviller or Boulainvilliers (1658–1722) came from a distinguished family and had scholarly inclinations.[26] He was known in his day for independence of mind and for proficiency in astrology. In politics he was an ardent advocate of the cause of the *noblesse d'epée.*[27] His present reputation where religion is concerned is that of a Spinozist.[28] For a year, at the Oratorian school at Juilly, he was a pupil of Richard Simon.[29] He figures in the memoirs of both Saint-Simon and Mathieu Marais, the latter having reservations about his religious ideas.[30] However, both report that at

---

[25]   On the former, see Wade, *Clandestine Organization,* Pt. I, Ch. I. Written before 1716, it was published in 1768. On the latter, see in addition to Wade (Pt. II, Ch. II) the edition by P. Rétat (Lyon, 1973); it had originally been published in 1719. Another interesting manuscript, of 1703–1705, is the deistic *La religion du Chrétien,* by Yves de Vallone (1666 or 1667–1705), a monk of the Congrégation de France who went over to Calvinism. His work was totally unknown until discovered by James O'Higgins, S. J.; see his *Yves de Vallone: The Making of an Esprit-Fort* (The Hague, 1982), which appeared too recently for me to take account of it in this study.

[26]   See Renée Simon, *Henry de Boulainviller, historien, politique, philosophe, astrologue, 1658–1722* (Paris, n.d. (1939)), for biographical information and full summaries of his writings, both published and manuscript.

[27]   In his *Essais sur la noblesse de France,* 1732; Simon, op. cit., pp. 70 ff.

[28]   See Vernière, *Spinoza et la pensée française,* Vol. I, pp. 306–322.

[29]   Simon, *Henry de Boulainviller,* p. 25. She mentions (p. 28) that one of his sons was in the same class as Montesquieu when at Juilly.

[30]   Saint-Simon, *Mémoires,* edited by Gonzague Truc, Bibliothèque de la Pléiade, 7 vols. (Paris, 1957–1961), Vol. IV (1958), pp. 685–686, Vol. VII (1961), p. 178; *Journal et mémoires de Mathieu Marais,* edited by E. Lescure, 4 vols. (Paris, 1863–1868; reprint, Geneva, 1967), Vol. II, pp. 212–214 (on the *Vie de Mahomed:* 'il faut lire ce livre avec quelque précaution, à cause de certaines critiques indirectes de la religion chrétienne, et il n'appartient pas à tout le monde de manier des matières si hautes et si délicates', pp. 213–214); Vol. IV, pp. 143, 361. Saint-Simon says that 'il était curieux au dernier point, et avait aussi l'esprit tellement libre, que rien n'était capable de retenir sa curiosité' (Vol. IV, p. 685); but this may refer only to astrology.

his death his conduct was Christian, and several of his works reveal obviously Christian feelings.[31] He wrote much but published virtually nothing; some years after his death the politico-historical works, the *Vie de Mahomed* and the Spinozist *Essay de métaphysique* appeared, but much else remained in manuscript.[32]

The clandestine works associated with Boulainviller are all of a kind which he had the knowledge to write, since they are concerned with the religious ideas of antiquity, especially those of the Egyptians, Hebrews and Greeks. This subject is important in his *Abrégé d'histoire ancienne,* one of his surviving manuscripts, which was itself copied and circulated.[33] Probably the first in date of the manuscript works in question is the *Lettre d'Hippocrate à Damagette,* which also appeared in print, with the date of 1700.[34] It is a report of an interview between Hippocrates and Democritus, the atomist philosopher. He has however abandoned, in the letter, the materialism usually ascribed to him, and now has a philosophy of religion based on the belief in God. This belief, he says, is natural and universal; it is fortified by reason, and also by organized religion, which is instituted for moral and social ends by wise 'politiques'. Among the benefits of religion are that it encourages good citizenship and a sense of national unity.[35] Democritus seems to accept that religions normally contain a degree of falsity, and can decline into superstition, but argues that they have impressive advantages in utilitarian terms. He briefly surveys the Egyptian, Chaldaean and Hebrew

[31] See for instance, in Henry de Boulainviller, *Oeuvres philosophiques,* edited by Renée Simon, 2 vols. (The Hague, 1973–1975), cited henceforth as Simon edition, I or II, his *Réflexions sur les principes de la religion chrétienne suivant la méthode de St. Ignace* (II, pp. 64–101; written in 1697, according to Mme Simon (p. x)), and his treatise *De la persévérance* (II, pp. 102–113).

[32] *La Vie de Mahomed par Monsieur le Comte de Boulainvilliers,* London and Amsterdam, 1730 (with a second edition in 1731); the last of the three parts is not by Boulainviller. The *Essay* was published under the disingenuous title *Réfutation de Spinoza,* in a volume entitled *Réfutation des erreurs de Benoît de Spinoza* (Brussels, 1731); the title 'Essay de métaphysique dans les principes de B. de Sp.' is that of the manuscript copies.

[33] See Simon, *Henry de Boulainviller,* Pt. II; Wade, *Clandestine Organization,* pp. 106–111.

[34] The published title was *Traduction d'une lettre d'Hypocrate à Damagète,* with the date of 1700; see Wade, op. cit., pp. 104–106. The *Journal de Trévoux* of March 1705 (see Simon edition, I, p. 134) mentions a report that the publication was done at Rouen, which is near where Boulainviller lived. The article's date and phraseology ('il s'est répandu ici depuis peu une traduction . . .') suggest that the date of 1700 on the title-page might be false. (Compare the publication dates of Tyssot de Patot's book; Chapter 13, n. 6.) The idea of a letter about Democritus, sent by Hippocrates to Damagettus, must be based on the letter attributed to Hippocrates in collections of his works, but the two pieces have nothing in common as regards content.

[35] It is because of religion that the state 'ne fait qu'un même corps et que les particuliers pénétrés de zèle public y sacrifient jusques à leurs propre intérêts'; the whole passage is interesting and unusual. See Simon edition, I, p. 338.

religions, approving of each, but he reserves the greatest praise for Moses.[36]

The *Lettre*, which is incomplete,[37] has been attributed to Boulainviller because one of the manuscripts known is in his handwriting.[38] It is therefore possible that he wrote it (and did not simply copy it himself out of interest), although the favourable treatment of Moses and the Jews is not typical of Boulainviller in other pieces; he often seems to have been influenced by Spinoza in this respect, as in others.[39] On the other hand, the *Lettre's* views on the value of religion resemble those put forward by Boulainviller elsewhere.[40] He regarded man as a 'religious animal', and might perhaps have chosen to develop his ideas through the *persona* of Démocrite.[41] A basic assumption made in the *Lettre* is that, apart from the religious instinct, everything in religion is the result of deliberate human invention. This might seem close to deism, but the author affirms that the belief in God alone is inadequate as a religious attitude;[42] hence, although the *Lettre* contains a passage of natural theology proving God, its argument is not intrinsically deistic.

The other works attributable to Boulainviller are the series of 'Opinions des anciens': three essays on the soul, the creation and the Jews.[43] Another traditional attribution is to Jean-Baptiste de Mirabaud (1675–1760), which seems less plausible on general grounds; Mirabaud was the translator of Tasso's *Gierusalemme liberata* and a secretary of the Académie française.[44]

---

[36]   He is described as a man of 'une haute et sublime intelligence, et qui me paraît supérieur à tous ceux qui se sont distingués dans le cours des siècles' (Simon edition, I, p. 329); 'ce grand législateur dont le nom n'est connu que dans le secret de leur sanctuaire. Il leur a présenté des lois qu'il leur a certifié avoir reçu' (sic) 'de l'Eternel, après une communication sensible avec lui. Mille prodiges ont paru ou aux yeux ou à la crédulité de ce peuple, qui ont éternisé le respect de ses paroles' (p. 330); the Mosaic religion can be said to have 'plus d'excellence' than all others (p. 331).

[37]   Hippocrates begins by asking Democritus about three matters, of which the first, 'ce que vous pensez de l'auteur de la nature et des religions qui nous engagent à des devoirs envers lui' (ibid., p. 318), is dealt with in what was apparently intended to be the first of three sections, but is almost the entirety of the *Lettre* as we now have it; it breaks off after four short paragraphs of a second section, on physiological and rational factors in human behaviour (p. 339). The third should have been on the soul and the afterlife, the subject of Hippocrates' third question.

[38]   Simon edition, I, p. 315.

[39]   Vernière, *Spinoza et la pensée française*, Vol. I, pp. 308–320, shows that Boulainviller at first reacted with indignation to Spinoza's ideas, in a critique of six chapters of the *Tractatus*, *Extrait du Traité théologo-politique de Spinoza*, written in the 1690s (text: Simon edition, I, pp. 10–82); but he was gradually won over, and the *Essay de métaphysique* is a sympathetic consideration of parts of the *Ethics*. It probably dates from 1712 (Simon, *Henry de Boulainviller*, p. 457, n. 2).

[40]   See for instance the fragment entitled *Histoire de la religion et de la philosophie ancienne* (Simon edition, I, pp. 307–313), which, Mme Simon suggests, may have been the draft of a preface to a full-length study. On 'l'utilité de la religion vraie ou fausse', Boulainviller remarks that 'C'est par la religion que leurs espérances s'animent, que leurs passions s'adoucissent, que leur fierté souffre d'être désarmée; c'est la religion qui a formé les liens de la société; c'est elle qui a accoutumé les hommes à la compassion; c'est elle qui a défendu l'homicide chez toutes les nations, et qui par ce moyen a conservé l'espèce humaine, conjurée pour sa propre ruine' (p. 308).

One of the treatises, 'sur la nature de l'âme' (the others being 'sur le monde' and 'sur les Juifs'), is found among Boulainviller's manuscripts, but only in a collection of summaries and notes, *Extraits des lectures de M. le comte de Boulainviller avec des réflexions.*[45] All three are clear, impartial and well-documented studies of their subjects, and constantly skirt the edge of free-thought. The *Opinions des anciens sur le monde,* for instance, argues that the modern concept of creation, that is creation *ex nihilo* by God, was unknown in antiquity. Boulainviller makes the same point in some *Notes* added in 1700 to an early work, *Idée d'un système général de la nature.*[46] It is a sound Christian argument when, as in the *Notes,* there is no doubt of the writer's Christian belief, but, when there is, the same argument might imply the view that matter is eternal, the Averrhoist idea typical of free-thought.[47] In the *Opinions des anciens sur le monde,* there is little or nothing by way of Christian reflection to counterbalance the authority of the early philosophers whose theories are the subject of investigation.

In the *Opinions des anciens sur la nature de l'âme,* the aproach in the first chapters (there are five) is the same as in the treatise on creation: to ascertain when and where a modern conception, in this case that of the immortal, spiritual soul, can be said to have originated. The conclusion of the second chapter is that men naturally wish to believe themselves immortal, 'mais cette opinion eût toujours été en eux une croyance confuse ou un désir inquiet plutôt qu'une véritable certitude si d'habiles législateurs

---

[41]   In the *Essay de métaphysique,* Boulainviller glosses 'cette ancienne définition qui nous apprend que l'homme est essentiellement un animal religieux' as follows: 'c'est à dire qu'il est formé dans une telle disposition qu'il ne saurait refuser son culte à certains objets qu'il ne connaît point, mais que son imagination lui représente à la discrétion de sa propre crédulité, mélangée de toutes les passions auxquelles elle se joint dans l'ordre commun' (Simon edition, I, p. 204).

[42]   The writer affirms that the main value of religion is to 'déterminer le coeur', by which he apparently means that it canalizes natural religious feelings into a structured set of beliefs, which may be true or only plausible ('des vérités, ou des vraisemblances équivalentes'); he continues by saying that 'l'idée de la Divinité est trop abstraite, elle a trop peu de rapport aux sens et à la raison ordinaire des hommes pour les rendre attentifs et les occuper. Il a fallu introduire des mystères, inventer des faits, proposer des doctrines, imposer des lois, établir une morale, tout cela pour remplir l'homme qui serait demeuré vide s'il n'avait eu que la Divinité pour objet' (ibid., p. 337).

[43]   See Wade, *Clandestine Organization,* Pt. II, Ch. VI (written on the assumption that the works are by Mirabaud) for the distribution and titles of the manuscripts and published editions.

[44]   See Paul de Mirabaud and Léon-Frédéric Le Grand, *Notice sur J. -B. de Mirabaud* (Paris, 1895).

[45]   The text, under the title *Histoire des opinions des anciens sur la nature de l'âme,* is in the Simon edition, I, pp. 253–291.

[46]   Simon edition, II, pp. 145–267; *Notes* ('sur le premier traité, du monde'): pp. 268–276. The same idea is found in the *Abrégé d'histoire ancienne* (Simon, *Henry de Boulainviller,* p. 322).

[47]   See for instance Busson, *Rationalisme,* pp. 201–203 (Vicomercato's Averrhoist views on God, the creation and 'l'éternité du monde').

ne l'avaient pour ainsi dire consacrée par la religion.'[48] The list of able lawgivers which follows includes Orpheus, Pythagoras, the Mages and the druids. Another chapter collects evidence for the view that the concept of the spiritual soul is comparatively modern, and notes that some early Christian thinkers, although admirers of Plato, believed the soul to be material.[49] As the treatise continues, its tendency to unorthodoxy becomes more noticeable; the last chapter advances the Baylian argument that disbelief in the soul, among the Romans, did not make the disbelievers morally worse.[50]

As with the *Opinions des anciens sur le monde,* the *Opinions* on the soul need not be anti-Christian, although the writer conceals his own viewpoint with a degree of prudence which is suspect in itself. Moreover, the dissemination of the work through manuscript copying indicates that it was considered free-thinking. The series of all three *Opinions des anciens* — almost certainly the same author was responsible for the third, on the Jews, which gives reasons why the Jews were hated in antiquity and catalogues doctrinal differences between Jews and Christians — contain many ideas which were to become the stock-in-trade of deist or atheist propaganda against Christianity. We should not infer too hastily, however, that the author was himself a deist, or even necessarily anti-Christian. His ideas are compatible with enlightened Christian belief, of the sort which regards the philosophers of antiquity as pagan, interesting, no doubt, but without relevance to the truths of faith; there is an obvious parallel with Bayle's *Dictionnaire.*

Whether Boulainviller was the author of the *Opinions* or not, a fragment by him entitled *Histoire de la religion et de la philosophie ancienne* contains interesting similarities. Boulainviller here argues that, although modern rational philosophy provides more elevated conceptions of God and men's dependence on him than 'aucun des anciens législateurs', it was nevertheless providential that the early religions should have given men some notion of God, because of the value of religion generally, in personal, social and

---

[48]   Simon edition, I, p. 266. Compare the similar reflections concerning the notion of God quoted from the *Lettre d'Hippocrate à Damagette* in n. 42 above.

[49]   'Jamais le platonisme n'a été plus en vogue qu'au temps où l'on commença à goûter l'Evangile, et peut-être jamais les hommes n'avaient-ils eu une notion si imparfaite de l'esprit' (Simon edition, I, p. 277). Boulainviller's examples include Irenaeus, Tertullian, Arnobius and Lactantius. If Voltaire read this passage it might perhaps have given him the idea for the mocking list of 'opinions des anciens sur l'âme' which opens L. XIII of the *Lettres philosophiques.*

[50]   Bayle, *Pensées diverses sur la comète,* edited by A. Prat, 2 vols. (Paris, 1911–1912), Vol. II, pp. 5 ff. (Chs. 133 ff., *Septième preuve,* 'L'athèisme ne conduit pas nécessairement à la corruption des moeurs').

moral terms.[51] There are, from this point of view, advantages even in the defects of Egyptian, Greek and Chaldaean religions, which, 'ayant réveillé l'attention des sages, sont devenus la cause de la découverte de la vérité'.[52] These remarks, which are made from a Christian standpoint, show by analogy that the standpoint could have been the same in the *Opinions des anciens* series of treatises.

The sequel of the fragment is even more illuminating about the degree of apparent free-thought which could be accommodated within a Christian scheme. Boulainviller strongly criticizes the idea of revelation, and the Old Testament as an instrument of revelation. The nature of God, as implied in Scripture, is that of 'un père tendre et équitable pour ses enfants', who reveals his attributes ('son unité, sa toute-puissance, sa spiritualité')[53] to mankind in order to provide a certain guide and remove the aberrations of polytheism; but the world as a whole, excluding the Christians, has received little benefit. Boulainviller goes on to criticize Bible stories – the Fall, the Flood and others – and the inadequacy of the idea of God found in some passages of the Old Testament. His comments resemble those found in the *Examen de la religion* or the Militaire philosophe's *Difficultés;*[54] the Jewish revelation, he says, produced no clear advantages for the Jews themselves – rather the opposite, indeed, since the possession of revealed truth resulted for them in 'vengeance, punitions célestes, accablement d'esprit et de courage, ignorance, présomption'.[55]

Boulainviller then faces directly the question which must arise from these observations: was the Jewish revelation false, or inferior to the religious truths knowable rationally, and is it less valuable than ancient pagan religions? His answer is firm: 'Non, sans doute; l'avantage des Juifs est grand (...) ils ont été les dépositaires de la vérité, ils ont préparé la voie à la seconde révélation qui a dissipé les ténèbres de la

---

[51] See n. 40; Boulainviller remarks that 'l'existence et l'infinté de l'Etre suprême, notre dépendance à son égard, la raison des lois morales, etc., sont rendues bien plus probables par les démonstration d'une bonne métaphysique que par les expression de Moyse' (Simon edition, I, p. 308). Nonetheless, he goes on, in view of primitive man's inability to reason adequately, the Mosaic revelation was justified.

[52] Ibid., pp. 309–310.

[53] Ibid., p. 310.

[54] How can a revelation of such kind, he asks, convey the spirituality and immensity of God? 'Ne semble-t-il pas plutôt qu'elle combat tous ses attributs, quand elle nous dépeint le vrai Dieu montant au ciel ou en descendant, se promenant à la fraîche dans un jardin, s'irritant, se repentant, délibérant, punissant rigoureusement, faisant peu de bien et beaucoup de mal, surtout lorsque cette révélation nous cache à nous-mêmes ce que nous sommes, qu'elle ne parle point de l'immortalité dont la philosophie nous flatte, et qu'elle ne nous propose point l'espérance ou la crainte d'une autre vie?' (Simon edition, I, p. 311). Compare the chapter 'Des preuves que doit avoir la véritable religion' in the *Examen,* mentioned above, and in the *Difficultés* the long first section, 'Des livres des Juifs', of the *cahier* 'E' (e.g. 'J'y vois Dieu de mauvaise humeur, se fâchant, se dépitant, se repentant, s'apaisant comme un enfant pour des bagatelles, le voilà de figure humaine, changeant de place etc.'; Mortier edition, p. 204).

[55] Simon edition, I, p. 312.

première'.[56] Even if this conclusion now seems curious, or inconsistent, its sincerity cannot easily be impugned, since Boulainviller must have been writing for himself alone, clarifying his thoughts by putting them down on paper.

Other works of his also show that he was willing to explore unorthodox ideas without appearing to regard them as incompatible with allegiance to Christianity. In the *Essay de métaphysique,* he is constantly concerned to decide whether the Spinozist philosphy which he is in the process of explaining involves the rejection of Christianity. Having worked through the arguments of the first part of the *Ethics* and reached the conclusion, with Spinoza, that 'Dieu et l'universalité des choses sont le même', he asks whether the conventional religious ideas he has held hitherto should be abandoned.[57] In the same way as with the question of the Jewish revelation, he replies negatively; conceiving God in Spinozist terms preserves, and even increases, the obligation to obey, love and worship God. As regards 'le culte', Boulainviller observes that 'l'idée de Dieu comprise sous celle de l'univers' makes him prefer the religion in which he was born above all others, while purifying it of the inhuman zeal and bigotry 'qui accompagnent la religion vulgaire'.[58] Another sacrifice which he is prepared to make is that of belief in the Creation.[59] Near the end of the *Essay,* after a severe analysis of the irrationality of religious faith, he nonetheless seems to accept that 'les hommes sages et vertueux' can reasonably continue to accept the doctrines of their own religion, at least in part.[60]

There can have been few readers of Boulainviller, in manuscript or print, who were able to follow him in combining Spinozist metaphysics with Catholic faith, as he seems to do; Spinoza was generally regarded as an atheist, and the greatest enemy that Christianity had to face. In any case, whether we regard the Spinozism alone, or the unorthodox Catholicism, or a combination of both, as representing Boulainviller's real position, he seems not to have been a deist. Voltaire's 'Comte de Boulainvilliers', for whom philosophy is rudimentary deism, 'l'amour éclairé de la sagesse, soutenu par l'amour de l'Etre éternel, rémunérateur de la vertu et vengeur du crime',

---

[56] Ibid.

[57] Simon edition, I, p. 102, and on how to reinterpret the ordinary notion of God's omnipotence in Spinozist terms, pp. 102–103.

[58] Ibid., p. 103.

[59] Ibid., pp. 112–115. The metaphysical arguments against the concept of creation are different from, but compatible with, those implied in the *Opinions des anciens sur le monde.*

[60] Ibid., p. 206; the conclusion of a passage of which the starting-point seems to be the *Ethics,* III, 52, on the 'admiration' or wonder aroused by individual things. Boulainviller's reflections concern credulity, which he connects with the human disposition towards religion; while accepting that imagination, hope and fear play a large part in religious belief, he also affirms that religions can all claim an appearance of rationality and all include moral principles (p. 205).

is a misrepresentation, no doubt deliberate or heedless.[61] The real figure was more complex and interesting; like Saint-Evremond before him, he demonstrates that the distinction between Catholic belief and free-thought is not at all straightforward. His rationalism and complete freedom from prejudice might appear to make him predisposed to deism, and much of what he wrote could have come from a deist. The same applies also, whoever wrote them, to the *Opinions des anciens* treatises, which became part of the clandestine movement of religious criticism. Giving little indication of their author's positive beliefs, but moderate in tone, they come to be associated with deism almost by default, since they certainly appear to be by a free-thinker, and deism was the moderate form of contemporary free-thought.

CHAULIEU AND LA FARE

An entirely different form of deistic writing, still in a sense clandestine, comes from two society poets who were close friends, the Abbé de Chaulieu (1639–1720) and the Marquis de La Fare (1644–1712). Even if they had wished to publish their poems on religion (and aristocratic writers were usually not eager to publish at all) the censorship would certainly have prevented them at the time when the poems were written. La Fare's most interesting deistic poem was not published until this century, although his and Chaulieu's poems, mostly *salon* verse or love-poetry, but some of a moralizing turn, appeared in print together in 1724.[62] They represent the religious attitudes of the 'libertins du Temple', a centre of free-thought even during a time of great devoutness, and form a link between Saint-Evremond, who figures in the 1724 collection, and Voltaire, who knew Chaulieu and wrote a humorous epitaph for him.[63]

The date of La Fare's *Ode à l'honneur de la religion* is unknown. The

---

[61] Le Comte's second speech in *Le Dîner du Comte de Boulainvilliers* (*Oeuvres complètes de Voltaire*, edited by Louis Moland, 52 vols (Paris, 1877–1885), Vol. XXVI (1879), p. 532).

[62] The standard edition of La Fare's poems was formely the *Poësies de monsieur le marquis de la Farre* (Amsterdam, 1755), but the number of poems known to be by him was more than doubled by the discovery of the manuscript f. fr. 15029 of the Bibliothèque nationale. See F. Lachèvre, *Les derniers libertins*, Le libertinage au XVIIe siècle, XI (Paris, 1924), pp. 215–254, *Poésies libertines et philosophiques* (*en partie inédites*) *de La Fare*; *Poésies inédites du Marquis de La Fare (1644–1712)*, edited by Gustave L. Van Roosbroeck (Paris, 1924), cited henceforth as Roosbroeck edition.

[63] See Pomeau, *Religion de Voltaire*, pp. 78–79. In one of La Fare's poems, *Epître satirique à Mr l'abbé de Chaulieu*, 'Je ne me connais plus, moi dont l'âme tranquille' (Roosbroeck edition, pp. 43–47), the tone is that of social protest rather than merely free-thought, with attacks on hypocrisy and corrupt leaders (including Louis XIV, apparently: 'A la tête est monté le poison qui nous tue (...) Se plaindre en de tels maux est réputé pour crime', p. 45), and a defence of Fénelon, if he is the prelate of pure life who seeks to 'élever notre faible nature Jusqu' à des sentiments qui soient dignes de Dieu' (p. 46) but finds that even Rome is hostile to him.

theme is indifferentist. God is 'universel'; distinctions of worship ('culte') do not matter provided the individual believers are fervent:

> Des soupirs enflammés de leurs âme brûlantes,
> Du mélange confus de leurs voix différentes,
> Il se forme un concert encore plus précieux.
> Tout hommage est reçu pourvu qu'il soit sincère,
> Les hommes sont nés tous enfants du même père (...).[64]

Such sentiments make La Fare a deist in Furetière's sense, 'qui reconnaît seulement un Dieu, sans lui rendre aucun culte extérieur'.[65] While being more emotional than most rationalists, he also rejects, in the name of reason, the Christianity of the fideists, with their mysteries of dogma:

> Qui pensent que ce sont les choses impossibles
> Et les évènments les moins compréhensibles
> Que font le digne objet de la religion.

Reason, on the other hand, is an innate light, divine in nature, and should be revered like God. These ideas are almost as plain an expression of deistic rationalism and indifference as in the *Examen de la religion,* and it is understandable that even in 1724 they were not thought fit for publication.

Chaulieu's verse is better and more complicated. He wrote three poems which he called 'trois façons de penser sur la mort'. In a preface he explains that each expresses a different outlook, Christian, deist and Epicurean. The first, dated 1695, begins 'J'ai vu de près le Styx, j'ai vu les Euménides'. Chaulieu has been ill, and fears death and judgement, especially since a threatening voice has warned him that his misdeeds will be punished by 'un Dieu vengeur (...) sans grâce et sans clémence'. This must be the God of Jansenism, replacing the Greek terrors of the first line. The poet prefers a kindlier deity, beneficent and merciful, 'qui jamais à mes voeux ne fut inexorable'. Pursuing his self-interested plea, Chaulieu maintains that his sins were merely 'vains plaisirs', about which it would be wrong to be severe, and reminds us that the God of the Old Testament forgave the Jews, heaping them with gifts and even working miracles on their behalf. The poem ends with another hint of an argument against Jansenist predestination:

---

[64] Roosbroeck edition, p. 37 (verses 8–9). As Roosbroeck observes (p. 11), the poem contains a strong plea for tolerance. God 'ne veut point qu' à son culte on donne des limites'; religion should bring peace, not war (verse 6, p. 36).

[65] Furetière, *Dictionnaire universel,* 1690.

> Trop sûr de ses bontés, je vis en assurance
> Qu'un Dieu qui par son choix au jour m'a destiné
> A des feux éternels ne m'a point condamné.[66]

The contrast between the harsh God of judgement and Chaulieu's gentler 'Dieu que je chéris' excludes any reference to Christ, which makes it difficult to understand Chaulieu's statement, in his preface, that he was writing 'dans les principes du Christianisme'.

The next poem of the sequence is the Epicurean version, of 1700, which is a simple piece of hedonism, denying that there is an afterlife, counselling wisdom in enjoyment of the passions, and paying tribute to Epicurus, 'cet esprit élevé'. The deistic poem is dated 1708, and in its opening lines it may contain a reference to the other two poems; Chaulieu says that he now has no doubts, 'Je ne suis libertin, ni dévot à demi'. It returns to former themes, the innocence of natural pleasures and the beneficence of God. There is also a passage in which, having just referred to the miracles of the Old Testament, Chaulieu says that God can take the form of Apollo, Mars and Ceres. Whether this comparatist approach is intended to be deistic is not clear; the most obviously deistic passage comes next:

> Après tant de bienfaits, quoi! j'aurai l'insolence,
> Dans une mer d'erreurs plongé dès mon enfance
> Par l'imbécile amas de femmes, de dévots,
> A cet Etre parfait d'imputer mes défauts,
> D'en faire un Dieu cruel, vindicatif, colère,
> Capable de fureur, et même sanguinaire,
> Changeant de volonté, réprouvant aujourd' hui
> Ce peuple qui jadis seul par lui fut chéri!
> Je forme de cet Etre une plus noble idée;
> Sur le front du soleil lui-même l'a gravée:
> Immense, tout-puissant, équitable, éternel,
> Maître de tout, a-t-il besoin de mon autel?

Again, as in the 1695 poem, we have a contrast between two conceptions of God, and again Chaulieu seems to be protesting against Jansenist strictness, here put in Old Testament terms; Jehovah can plausibly be said to be capable of fury. The same sentiments are found in the *Examen de la religion*, which probably dates from the same time. Chaulieu's 'noble idée' of God is

---

[66] Quoted from: *Oeuvres de Chaulieu, d'après les manuscripts de l'auteur*, 2 vols. (The Hague, 1777). The three poems on death are the first in the collection. See also Lachèvre, *Derniers libertines* (pp. 143–200: Chaulieu's *Poésies libertines*; the three poems are pp. 145, 150, 170).

conveyed in the string of epithets favoured by rationalists. Towards the end of the poem, Chaulieu concentrates on divine justice as well as goodness. His argument is that a just God is not moved by expensive offerings, but attends only to the morality of human actions. Chaulieu has a clear conscience, and can face the prospect of judgement without fear.

In his comments on the three poems on death, Chaulieu makes a distinction between his own beliefs and the 'principles' behind each poem, as if he could adopt at will any of three conventions: 'J'ai fait la première (...) dans les principes de Christianisme (...) sans être par malheur dévot. J'ai fait la seconde dans les principes du pur déisme, sans être Socinien; la troisième dans les principes d'Epicure, sans être athée. (...) Ferme dans les principes de ma religion je n'ai point prétendu dogmatiser le libertinage'. This implies that the poet, enjoying greater freedom than the prose writer, can take up an attitude which he recognizes as deistic or Epicurean without feeling committed to it personally. Nonetheless, the unity of tone and attitude in the poems is such that they seem to reflect Chaulieu's own convictions. As for the reference to Socinians, he probably had in mind the denial of eternal damnation, for which they were notorious;[67] this is also a point of contact between Chaulieu and the only professedly 'deist' work of the early seventeenth century, the *Anti-bigot,* which is primarily concerned with repudiating the threat of hellfire. Whether Chaulieu had read the poem (or Mersenne's paraphrase) is unknown, but his 'J'ai vu de près le Styx' belongs to the same *libertin* tradition of poems expressing doubt about the afterlife.[68]

When all due allowance has been made for the uncertainty surrounding the contemporary meanings of 'déisme', it remains true that from 1700 until about 1712 a series of writings appeared which created deism in France, in the sense defined at the beginning of this study — a religious attitude or philosophy which in appearance at least is independent of Christian belief, since it incorporates a generalized critique of Christianity, while retaining the belief in God as its basis. Historically speaking, the fact that French deism first appeared in a comparatively large number of different writings, over

[67]   See D. P. Walker, *The Decline of Hell: Seventeenth-Century Discussions of Eternal Torment* (Chicago, 1964), Ch. V, especially pp. 77–78. Chaulieu's remark needs to be interpreted in the light of the history of the word 'déisme':he is aware that 'déiste ou Socinien' is a standard phrase and wished to avoid it. By the words 'pur déisme' he means what would now be termed theism, the belief in some kind of God; there are no implications of hostility to Christianity.

[68]   The tradition is best exemplified in the later seventeenth century by the poems of Mme Deshoulières; see Lachèvre, *Derniers libertins,* pp. 67–104. Another *libertin* poet, François Payot de Lignières (ibid., pp. 3–21) wrote in a self-portrait: 'La lecture a rendu mon esprit assez fort Contre toutes les peurs qu'on a de la mort, Et ma religion n'a rien qui m'embarrasse. Je me ris du scrupule, et je hais la grimace' (hypocrisy); 'Quoique je n'aime pas à prier nuit et jour Les heureux habitants du céleste séjour Je ne prétendrais pas avoir l'âme moins bonne, Et je ne voudrais pas faire tort à personne' (p. 13).

about ten or fifteen years, is fundamental; among the consequences which follow are, for example, that seemingly deistic writings which date from before 1700 must be regarded as more or less isolated precursors, and that the books so often regarded as the earliest works of the Enlightenment, Montesquieu's *Lettres persanes* and Voltaire's *Lettre philosophiques,* were written when the first phase of French deism had come and gone.

Considered *en bloc,* the first deistic writers share few social characteristics. The most that can be said is that all are educated laymen. Even this statement has to be qualified, since Lahontan's collaborator Gueudeville had been a monk, like Foigny, Chaulieu was an *abbé,* and it is possible that the author of the *Examen de la religion* was a cleric (like the atheist Meslier). Gilbert was a provincial lawyer, Lahontan an aristocratic adventurer, the Militaire philosophe a professional soldier; at the social level, there seem to be no connecting links. However, the factors which are important for the works before 1700 which tend towards deism remains so after that date; they are the experiences of travel and of the divisions within Christianity, together with the idea of natural religion. The continuing influence of Cartesian thought reinforces the last factor. To schematize, natural religion had been combined with Cartesianism in a large number of rationalist but Christian works (the example considered previously is that of Régis),[69] and in writers such as Gilbert and the Militaire philosophe this combination accounts for the positive side of their deism. Gueudeville, Lahontan and the Militaire philosophe all travelled, the last two to North America, and witnessed or experienced the conflicts produced by dogmatic intolerance backed by the resources of the nation-state. Gueudeville renounced Catholicism and joined the Protestant propagandists in Holland (and his contribution to deism seems to have been very largely critical), Lahontan observed the Canadian situation in which the native religion was confronted by both Anglicans and Catholics, and the Militaire philosophe in addition took part in the repression of the Huguenots in France, which seems to have affected him deeply. Gilbert appears not to have done any travelling, but the Huguenot overtones of his book indicate that for him also the background of religious conflict was important; his characters leave France because of the persecution in the 1680s. The *Examen de la religion* makes some use of the argument that the very existence of competing religions tends to disprove their specific claims, but nothing can be deduced certainly about the author's personal experiences. Chaulieu and La Fare, the least significant of the group, seem to have been genuine *libertins,* rebelling against the threatening morality of Jansenism.

Taken in conjunction with the related facts in the lives of the precursors

---

[69]   See Chapter 6, pp. 78.

of deism, Saint-Evremond, Veiras, Foigny and Marana, all religious exiles, these points strongly suggest that one of the originating causes of French deism was the desire to avoid the religious intolerance and conflict of the time. The influence of travel seems subordinate. It can be a preliminary to observing confrontation between religions and, of course, was usually part of the process of changing religion. In itself, travel no doubt weakens the attachment of individuals to the religion in which they are born.

Given the existence of the concepts of natural religion and reason, which were assumed to be universally valid, it was a comparatively simple matter for these writers (whatever the original motive for their break with Christianity) to devise forms of rational religion which, if adopted, would have eliminated interdenominational tolerance and conflict. Materials for the attack on Christianity, a necessary part of establishing a universal religion, were available in the very numerous apologetic works of the period; all that had to be done, in order to elaborate a comprehensive critique, was to reverse the apologetic process, so that the arguments which are objections for the apologist to surmount become, for the deist, a means of attack. This is particularly noticeable in the array of objections set out by the author of the *Examen* and the Militaire philosophe.

CHAPTER 12

TYSSOT DE PATOT: TYPES OF DEISM AND RELIGIOUS CRITICISM

In the decade between the Militaire philosophe's treatise and the *Lettres persanes,* the Jansenist controversy gained in intensity, before and after the death of Louis XIV in 1715; the influence of Fénelon superseded that of Malebranche and Bossuet; and the English deists, notably Anthony Collins, began to be known in France — well after French deism had been created, despite the long-standing scholarly myth that it came from England.[1] But the more general association, that with Protestantism, is maintained in the most important French deistic work of these years, another anonymous travel-story, the *Voyages et avantures de Jaques Massé,* full of characters with unorthodox or anti-Christian opinions. Simon Tyssot de Patot, its author, was born in England of Huguenot parents in 1655. He was brought up in France and spent his adult life in north Holland, mostly in the small town of Deventer, where he taught French and mathematics. His biography has been investigated by Aubrey Rosenberg, who shows that Tyssot's life was uneventful, apart from a struggle to establish himself professionally, until disaster came in old age: the publication of his *Lettres choisies* in 1726 caused a scandal.[2] He was accused of expressing irreligious views, Spinozist and immoral. In 1727, by way of defence, he prefaced his *Œuvres poétiques* with a dissertation proving 'l'existence d'un être souverainement parfait, comme aussi l'immatérialité et l'immortalité de notre âme'.[3] However, all efforts to clear his name having failed, Tyssot was dismissed from his post as professor of mathematics and left Deventer. He died in 1738.

Apart from the *Voyages de Jaques Massé* the ill-fated volume of letters is his most interesting book. In it he discusses materialist topics and conveys

[1] See G. Bonno, *La culture et la civilisation britanniques devant l'opinion française de la paix d'Utrecht aux Lettres philosophiques* (Philadelphia, 1948), pp. 107–111, and the comments in Chapter 15, p. 269.

[2] See A. Rosenberg, *Tyssot de Patot and his work, 1655–1738* (The Hague, 1972). The pioneering study, as with so many writers of this period, is in Lanson, *Origines de l'esprit philosophique* (pp. 227–238).

[3] The dissertation (published by Lachèvre in his *Les successeurs de Cyrano de Bergerac,* together with Tyssot's preface — another self-justification — to his *Œuvres poétiques* of 1727) is in the form of a letter to a friend, and is very strongly influenced by Descartes. It ostensibly defends the two basic truths of natural theology, but there are many hints of scepticism.

185

his personal religious opinions, many of which are reflected in his novels.[4] His second attempt at this *genre, La vie, les avantures, et le voyage de Groenland du Révérend Père Cordelier Pierre de Mesange,* 1720, was less successful in every sense than the first. A Franciscan monk finds an underground society in Greenland, which is primitive and virtuous. The prevailing religion is Spinozist, but other views are tolerated; a religious impostor, who claims to have returned from the abode of the blessed, causes serious disturbances. The book gives some reason for supposing that Tyssot was himself a Spinozist.[5]

It used to be accepted that the *Voyages de Jaques Massé* had been published in 1710, as stated on the title-pages of the four editions which give that date. Rosenberg has shown conclusively that they were antedated; the novel was first published a few years later, between 1714 and 1717.[6] The story of the novel covers some fifty years of the seventeenth century, from about 1640 to 1690. Its fictional element is slight, at times providing little more than interludes between the series of discussions about religion, between Massé as narrator and an assortment of acquaintances in different lands, which form the real content of the book. The variety of points of view put forward in the discussions gives Tyssot's work an eclectic quality which is quite unlike the deistic works immediately preceding it chronologically, the clandestine treatises and Gilbert's *Calejava,* of which Tyssot can have had no knowledge. On the other hand, the *Voyages* has close links with works of a previous period, by Veiras, Foigny and Marana, which were in more general circulation. Tyssot borrowed freely; several important episodes of his novel seem to be deliberate imitations of previous deistic work, especially in the chapters on the Austral Land.

The first two chapters concern Jaques Massé's youth and education. He is brought up as a pious Catholic in Abbeville, and as a young man in Paris meets unbelief for the first time. Having read and admired Descartes, he is told that Copernicanism in physics is the way to atheism ('Cologne, Kainkus' edition, p. 10).[7] The possible conflict between science and religion is to be a theme of the book. Having a desire to see the world, Massé makes his first

---

[4] The *Lettres,* like Tyssot's other works except for *Jaques Massé,* are rare. Rosenberg (*Tyssot de Patot,* Appendix G) lists library holdings, and gives summaries (Chs. 5, 9, 11), as does Atkinson for the two novels (*The Extraordinary Voyage in French Literature from 1700 to 1720* (New York, 1922), Chs. 4, 5; cited henceforth as *Extraordinary Voyage 1700–1720*). Tyssot also wrote a discourse on chronology; his first publication was a work on sense-experience.

[5] This is Rosenberg's view (Ch. 4). Tyssot certainly puts forward determinist ideas in his letters, and the Gascon met by Massé is given some Spinozist arguments, but in discussing God and nature Tyssot does not seem to go as far as to identify them. He was deeply interested in Spinoza, however, and Rosenberg may be right in suggesting (p. 66) that he concealed the full extent of his agreement with Spinoza.

[6] See Rosenberg, ibid., Ch. 6, 'The Publication of *Jaques Massé*'.

[7] I quote from one of the editions dated 1710, described by Rosenberg as Edition C, which has the false imprint 'A Cologne, chez Jacques Kainkus'.

voyage in 1643, after an encounter at Dieppe with the 'Wandering Jew', about whom he tells the same legend as Marana.[8] The ship has a Huguenot captain and bears a student, presumably a Huguenot also, whose conversation does much to diminish the Catholic Massé's respect for the saints. The ship is wrecked, Massé is providentially rescued, and at the beginning of Chapter 2 finds himself in Lisbon.

His first acquaintance in Portugal is another Protestant, a surgeon who gives him a job. Massé is tolerant about working for a heretic, saying that he is no bigot, but when his master gives him the Bible to read his reaction is stronger. 'Il ne faut pas mentir, la première fois que j'en fis la lecture, (...) je la pris pour un roman assez mal concerté (...). La Genèse, selon moi, était une pure fiction; la loi des Juifs et leurs cérémonies un badinage et de vaines puérilités; les prophéties un abîme d'obscurités et un galimatias ridicule; et l'Evangile une fraude pieuse, inventée pour bercer des femmelettes et des esprits du commun' (pp. 22–24). Such is the result, we are perhaps intended to think, of a Catholic upbringing combined with the scientific influences of Cartesian philosophy and the practice of surgery; in terms of the history of thought, the young Massé's remarks actualize in fiction the warnings of apologists who had been shocked by the implications of Spinozist scriptural criticism.[9]

Massé gradually becomes reconciled to the Bible – his master gives him Calvin to read, which helps (pp. 43–44) – but not before he has made many detailed objections to the Old Testament. His main argument is that the pains of childbirth cannot be a punishment for Original Sin, because in certain climates women in labour feel little pain (pp. 26–27).[10] When he sees the body of a black man dissected, it occurs to him that the Book of Genesis does not account for the existence of all the races of mankind (p. 33); he also hears a doctor discourse learnedly about epistemology, on nominalist lines. Not everyone, says Massé, would have grasped the implications of what he said. This enigmatic comment means that the doctor's ideas (for instance, that animals can reason) are destructive of rational proofs of the soul. The influence here is that of Hobbes.[11]

---

[8]   In *L'Espion turc*, II, L. 39. See S.G. Andrews, 'The Wandering Jew and the *Travels and Adventures of James Massey*', *Modern Language Notes* 72 (1957), 39–41. Pinot (*La Chine et la formation de l'esprit philosophique*, pp. 234–235) notes passages about dissections of black men, with similar 'Preadamite' implications, in both Marana and Tyssot (p. 33).

[9]   See Chapter 6, e.g. p. 81 (Huet's remark that Spinoza's *Tractatus* tended to demolish the foundations of Christianity).

[10]   Other objections are scientific (how could light be created before the sun and stars?) or moral (criticism of the actions related in the stories of Lot and Sarah). There is also a long defence (pp. 27–29), perhaps from Bayle and in any case with a Protestant air, of those who swim against the current of tradition.

[11]   See David Rice McKee, *Simon Tyssot de Patot and the Seventeenth-Century Background of Critical Deism* (Baltimore, 1941), p. 83, who shows that Tyssot used Hobbes' objections to Descartes's *Meditations*.

The young Massé is a different character from the mature man who travels the world; Tyssot used the same device as Voltaire in *Candide,* criticizing through a character who is innocent and seemingly free from malice. By the end of the second chapter, Massé has become a man of critical temper but of settled Christian faith. He could be said to express rationalism, but of the scientific rather than the metaphysical variety, another difference from the deists like the Militaire philosophe. He is supposed to remain Catholic, but (a point not stressed by Tyssot) his beliefs and attitudes are markedly Protestant.

Austral deists again

In his travels Massé meets deism first in the Austral Land, where a judge expounds natural religion and a priest criticizes Christian belief; then in Goa, where non-sectarian Christianity is professed by a Chinese convert with Arian ideas; and in Algiers a Gascon renegade parodies Christianity in a 'fable des abeilles'. From the Austral Land also comes a history of its religion, while the description of the Inquisition in Goa is horrific. In almost all his encounters, Massé is faced with more or less hostile criticisms of the Bible, which he defends as best he can. A prefatory letter states about these attacks that Massé stays firm, which is true, and that he exposes their weakness, which is not.

The destination of Massé's second voyage is the East Indies, but after a long storm with water-spouts, scientifically described, the ship makes a landfall in the far south. Massé and two companions, La Forêt and Du Puis, go exploring and have weird and exciting adventures, some of which, to do with opiate fruits and attacks by birds, recall Foigny's earlier version of the Austral Land.[12] In Chapter 5, they discuss religion. Du Puis inclines to sun-worship, which he believes to be more natural than theism (an echo of Veiras): 'si je n'étais pas né sous des climats où les peuples sont assez heureux pour avoir été instruits dans la connaissance de leur créateur, et que je n'eusse jamais ouï parler de l'Etre des Etres, le flambeau des cieux serait sans contredit la seule et unique divinité que je croirais digne de mes adorations' (p. 83).[13] The accommodating Massé is sympathetic, offering a list of countries and philosophers who support sun-worship, but La Forêt, who is another Huguenot, thinks it idolatrous: 'si j'ai de la vénération pour les créatures, ce n'est que par rapport au Créateur' (p. 85). Massé discourses

---

[12]   *Jaques Massé*, Ch. 4; *La Terre australe connue,* Ch. 4.

[13]   The discussion between Du Puis and La Forêt is a watered-down version of that between the sun-worshipper Sévaris and the theist Giovanni in the *Histoire des Sévarambes* (see Chapter 5, p. 67); Massé's providentialism and well-intentioned deceit also recall the history of Sévarias. On borrowings from Foigny and Veiras, see Atkinson, *Extraordinary Voyage 1700–20,* pp. 95–96, and Rosenberg, *Tyssot de Patot,* pp. 103, n. 10, 105, n. 17, and 106, n. 26.

on Copernican astronomy (further indirect support for sun-worship) and other scientific matters, until the explorers are held up by impenetrable geographical barriers. To encourage them, Massé tells them that God is watching over them. This is a statement of the providentialism which recurs intermittently throughout his adventures, as with his rescue off Portugal. But he also tells them, falsely, about a dream he has had, prophesying eventual success, and this may be an insinuation about the impostures, not always blameworthy, of religious leaders.

Unfortunately Du Puis is lost when he disappears into a pit, perhaps because he is a sun-worshipper and not under God's protection (or because of his name), but La Forêt and Massé win through to an inhabited country where they are received suspiciously by goatherds. They learn the language, which is rationally structured, witness seasonal rites, tour the country, which has outsize sheep and villages geometrically planned, and on a visit to the mines are surprised when the guide slips, falls and exclaims 'Christ!' The explanation, as Massé is later told by the judge who looks after him, is that three or four centuries earlier a Christian friar had arrived with several other outsiders, and had gone about preaching the history of Jesus and the life after death. The Australians had tried and punished him for blasphemy, giving him a life-sentence in the mines, since when it has been traditional for miners to use the name of Christ as an expletive. The whole episode is an interesting adaptation of narrative for purposes of religious satire.

The unknown country where the status of Christianity seems to be that of criminal blasphemy has other un-European features, but there are fewer marvels than in Foigny or Veiras. The mines and agriculture are normal, indeed primitive; it is La Forêt who makes a clock for the villagers.[14] Politically, the country is an elective monarchy. There is no capital punishment, which, like the penalties for blasphemy, is justified by the Australians' deistic beliefs: since a human life depends directly on God, it is not man's prerogative to end it (pp. 148–150); but blasphemy against God is the worst of crimes. When Massé says that capital punishment is prescribed in Christian laws, the judge retorts that they must be 'des ordonnances d'un tyran dénaturé' (p. 149). The judge thinks that the reason for sentencing the friar so harshly was political, to avoid disruption from new ideas, but adds that in any case 'ce Christ (...) embarrasse prodigieusement la raison' (p. 155). Massé's reply is unpersuasive fideism: 'J'avoue, lui dis-je, que c'est un mystère incompréhensible; nous le croyons pourtant (...) il nous est avantageux de le croire, parce que cela influe dans l'économie du salut'.

We are now approaching the first and longest of the book's three full-scale

---

[14]   Later, La Forêt's ability earns him the post of royal clockmaker; the details, according to Pinot (*La Chine et la formation de l'esprit philosophique*, p. 231, n. 75) are taken from Athanasius Kircher's account of the mission of Père Ricci to China.

religious debates, Austral deism against Massé's Christianity. The judge ironizes about Christian claims to a unique revelation; the deity is 'un esprit universel' and 'immuable de sa nature' (pp. 155, 159); everything related to such a God must be entirely general in application. Thus the Australians have no particular day for worship and believe that prayer is useless, since God's will cannot be changed. They worship God in their churches for an hour each day, and do not fail to 'méditer à chaque moment sur sa grandeur, et d'admirer sa bonté envers toutes les créatures' (pp. 158–159). The judge sums up in a deistic credo which is so representative of the literature of deism that it is worth quoting in full: 'Je crois une substance incréée, un esprit universel, souverainement sage, et parfaitement bon et juste, en Etre indépendant et immuable, qui a fait le ciel et la terre, et toutes les choses qui y sont, qui les entretient, qui les gouverne, qui les anime; mais d'une manière si cachée et si peu proportionnée à mon néant que je n'en ai qu'une idée très imparfaite. Cependant, voyant la nécessité de son existence, et la dépendance où nous sommes à son égard, nous croyons être dans un obligation indispensable de lui rendre nos hommages et nos adorations, de ne parler de lui qu'avec respect, et de n'y penser même qu'en tremblant; ce qui fait la principale partie de notre culte. L'autre est de lui rendre continuelle-ment nos actions de grâces pour tous les biens qu'il nous a faits, sans aucune prétention pour l'avenir, et bien moins après la mort, puisqu'alors n'existant plus nous n'aurons absolument besoin de rien' (pp. 157–158).

The resemblances between this and the beliefs of Foigny's Australian spokesman, Suains, are very close; if any readers believed in Foigny's Austral Land they would have had their belief confirmed by Tyssot. The 'universal' creator God who is gratefully worshipped, and the denials of Christian revelation, prayer and the afterlife, are virtually the same in both writers.[15] In the ensuing discussion, which includes an Austral priest, one of the main issues is the same as in Foigny, the question of providence, or God's relationship to man. The discussion begins with some criticisms of the Bible (to be dealt with later), and works round, by way of arguments against the resurrection of the body, to the question of the soul. This is a concept which the priest does not understand. He attributes it to wishful thinking; 'des esprits d'un ordre commun' like to believe that they will survive after death (p. 184). He also denies that men can be damned as a result of Original Sin, or disobedience to God: 'je nie que personne soit capable de faire du bien ou du mal par rapport à Dieu' (p. 185), a view found in the Militaire philosophe and the *Examen de la religion*.[16] Crime, according to the priest, is not an

---

[15] See Chapter 5, pp. 61–62.

[16] See Chapters 10 and 11, p. 153, 164. This is not evidence that Tyssot knew the clandestine manuscripts, since for all three writers the same idea is a natural deduction from the concept of an immutable, perfect God, a concept which they owe chiefly to Descartes.

offence against God, but against the rules of society, which were instituted to protect the weak or the virtuous (p. 191). More radically, he says that no action has any moral significance in itself, but becomes good or bad only 'par rapport à de certaines institutions' (p. 190). This moral positivism, reminiscent of Hobbes or Spinoza,[17] is the priest's alternative to Christian morality, but also contradicts theistic morality. Massé asks if he believes that God prescribed maxims and laws to man, and the priest concedes only that 'il lui a donné une volonté et un entendement pour se conduire, comme vous voyez que nous faisons'. Massé, still defending providentialism, says that God is the father of mankind, as both the Bible and 'le bon sens' agree.[18]

The difference between Massé and the Austral priest, fideistic Christianity with providence as against deism without, it less pronounced than that between Sadeur and the Australian Suains; in Foigny, the assurance of Christian salvation had been opposed to the Australian belief in mortality. Tyssot's priest, instead of believing in rewards and punishments after death, is content with the laws and sanctions of society, while Massé treats the Chrisitian revelation essentially as an assurance that God is directly concerned with human activities. As with the God of Gilbert's *Calejava*, it is clear that the rational conception of God as 'universal' and 'immutable' was virtually impossible to reconcile with the particularities of human affairs; hence, however constantly the Australians worship their God, he remains remote and almost indifferent, like the deity ascribed to Epicureans.[19]

A Chinese anti-trinitarian in Goa

Massé and La Forêt, after a stay at court, have to leave because La Forêt has a love-affair with one of the king's wives. The Frenchmen escape through a tunnel, providentially, and find the shipmates whom they had left behind years earlier. The reunion calls forth more thanks to God (p. 351). In due course the sailors are rescued, by a Spanish ship, and Massé makes his way to Goa, arriving there in 1663. Many different creeds co-exist in Goa, but Catholic worship is the only one permitted in public. Massé finds the clergy stupid and intolerant, the people superstitious and criminally inclined.[20] He

---

[17] *Leviathan*, Pt. I, Ch. XV; *Ethics*, IV, 37, Scholium 2. Again, however, there may be no particular source.

[18] 'Il en est le père; il en veut être aussi le directeur et le conservateur', says Massé; about the Bible, he exclaims: 'Plût à Dieu (...) que vous la puissiez voir, cette Parole; elle porte tant de marques de celui qui l'a dictée, que vous seriez le premier à la lire avec vénération, si elle vous tombait entre les mains' (p. 191).

[19] Not all the Austral clergy share the priest's views. When Massé is at court, he hears a sermon in which the preacher emphasizes the greatness of God and the nothingness of man, but says that divine providence takes care of all created beings (p. 244).

[20] Tyssot probably used the *Voyages de Mr. Dellon, avec sa relation de l'Inquisition de Goa*, 1709, for the Goan episode (Atkinson, *Extraordinary Voyage 1700–1720*, pp. 89–91).

imprudently makes some pointed jokes on these matters, with the result that he ends up in the evil-smelling prisons of the local Inquisition.

One of his fellow-prisoners is a stoical Chinese, who tells Massé that he is 'résigné aux decrets de la Providence' (p. 412), and unconcerned about what men can do to him. This immediately starts another discussion, Massé inquiring which religion the Chinese professes. 'Je suis, me dit-il, universaliste, ou de la religion des honnêtes gens; j'aime Dieu de tout mon coeur, je la crains, je l'adore, et je tâche de faire aux hommes, sans exception, ce que je souhaite que l'on me fasse à moi-même.' His ready answer is one which might have come from Parisian 'honnêtes gens' also.[21] It does not satisfy Massé: to which 'communion' does the Chinese belong? This is the crux of the matter; the answer is: 'Je ne fais aucune différence d'une société à l'autre; il n'y en a un point qui n'ait ses beautés et ses tâches, et je suis persuadé qu'il n'y a point de route où l'on ne se puisse damner ou sauver' (p. 413). The language of Massé's new friend is exactly that of Marana, and the next remarks exchanged by the two, about the variety and changeability of men's views on religion, recall a common strain in L'Espion turc.[22] When the Chinese recounts his story he describes himself as a Chrisitian; he seems to be Tyssot's version of Tite de Moldavie, the role adopted by the Turkish Spy in disguise, but is more radical than Tite in denying the divinity of Christ.

The story of his life resembles Massé's early history, but is made more definitely anti-Catholic. It begins with an attack on Jesuit missionaries in China (pp. 415–416). In Goa, the Chinese had been instructed in religious matters by another Portuguese, a doctor, who is outwardly Catholic but conforms only for safety's sake. Privately he is indifferentist: 'il est indifférent dans quelle église et avec quels peuples on adore Dieu, moyennant qu'on le serve avec respect et vénération. Lui seul est le père commun de tous les hommes; il veut leur accorder à tous le salut. Ce n'est ni le nom de catholique, de calviniste, de luthérien, ou d'anabaptiste qui sauve les gens, c'est la foi et les bonnes oeuvres. Celui qui vit bien est agréable à Dieu, en quelque endroit qu'il se trouve' (pp. 425–426). Faith and works here must be non-sectarian. When the doctor remarks that 'il est aisé de marcher avec les sots, et d'imiter même leurs grimaces extérieures, sans participer à leurs sentiments ridicules', he is referring to Catholicism in Goa.

The Chinese prisoner had found this attitude reasonable and had adopted it, except for the 'external' profession of attachment to a particular church. He regards Christ as a moral paragon rather than as divine, but insists that he himself is a Christian. The Inquisition, which imprisoned him for objecting

[21]   Compare the last chapter of the *Examen de la religion* ('Qu'il y a un etre supérieur et de la conduite qu'un honnête homme doit garder dans la vie'); see Chapter 11, pp. 165–7.
[22]   The theme is especially noticeable in Volume V, e.g. Ls. 41, 42, 62, 67. The basic idea of a Chinese character in Goa came however from Jean Mocquet, *Voyages,* 1616, according to Atkinson (*Extraordinary Voyage 1700–20,* pp. 91–92).

to the Incarnation, presumably regards him as a heretic. The appropriate description for his attitude seems to be Christian theism, since in outline he believes in salvation through conduct pleasing to God, respects Christ and affirms the Golden Rule as a Christian precept. Like the Austral deists, he emphasizes the universalist aspect of his religion. Massé implies, by his first questions, that adherence to a particular church is necessary if one is to be a Christian, but the Chinese apparently rejects this. In broad terms he seems to represent a free-thinking variant of the moralizing, anti-trinitarian Christianity of the radical sects, such as the Arminians, of Tyssot's adoptive country, Holland.

A Gascon renegrade in Algiers

The last we see of the Chinese is at his trial, when his defence (devised by Massé) is successful. Massé himself moves on to his next round of discussions. He is sentenced to the galleys, largely because he persists in his open disapproval of Goan religion, and so embarks on further adventures, involving pirates and slavery, which bring him to Algeria, his final destination before he returns to France. Massé is well treated by the Algerians, whom he finds as charitable, humane and sincere as Europeans, 'et même, si je l'ose dire, davantage' (p. 445). But although they are virtuous, these pagans make mock of the Crucifixion, and Massé has many a dispute with them. He expresses more deeply-felt dislike for the renegade Christians whom he meets, converts to Islam. Among them is 'un proposant gascon, qui était bien le plus hardi athée, ou déiste, que j'aie vu de mes yeux' (p. 455), a description which may seem contradictory. It must derive from the accusations made against Spinozist Biblical criticism, which had been said, for instance by Le Clerc, to lead to deism and atheism.[23] The former Huguenot theological student ('proposant') conforms to Le Clerc's description of deists as those who consider Scripture to be exclusively human and full of lies; his role is entirely critical.

The Gascon says that he has examined all the religions that have come to his notice, but 'il n'avait rien trouvé dans aucune qui pût satisfaire un homme raisonnable; et (...) il ne voyait rien qui dût empêcher un homme sage de se conformer, pour le moins extérieurement, à la religion dominante du pays où il demeure' (p. 457). He has therefore become a Muslim, finding himself in Algeria, the more willingly because the Christian religion is 'cent fois plus absurde et impertinente' (p. 458) than Islam. His attitude is similar to that of the Portuguese doctor in Goa (who had said that it is found in Polybius): wise men have no need of religion, but the fear of Hell keeps the

---

[23] See Chapter 6, p. 86.

masses in check, while their superiors accommodate themselves to whatever religious circumstances may obtain.

The Gascon and Massé, naturally, soon move into position for a set battle, and the Gascon demolishes Massé's proofs of Christianity, without making it clear whether he does so from a deistic or atheistic standpoint.[24] His unscrupulous conformism suggests the latter, but since Tyssot does not use the term 'déiste' about any of the other characters the question remains a little obscure. Bayle's well-known category, the 'virtuous atheist', might well include him, since he is of an eminently gentle disposition (pp. 455, 456), and has good reasons for being hostile to religion, for his father, a Catholic, was murdered on a pilgrimage, and his mother, a Huguenot, died as a result of the 'dragonnades' (which incidentally is an anachronism in the narrative).[25]

The renegade's importance, in any case, lies in his thoroughgoing rejection of Christianity as an imposture. By the time he has finished his anti-Christian parable, the 'Fable des abeilles', which Massé calls 'impertinent et ridicule' (p. 476) and which we shall consider later, it is too late at night for Massé to start on a reply. He does not have another chance, for a few days afterwards the Gascon is killed in an accident. A divine chastisement, perhaps? Massé says so, to some other free-thinkers of this acquaintance; but they laugh at him (p. 477).

The end of the novel returns more definitely to providentialism. Its last episode is the story of Pierre Heudde, illustrating divine judgment on iniquity. Heudde had first appeared in Chapter 2, when he had cheated a friend of Massé's. Some fifteen years after the Gascon's death, Massé meets Heudde again, repenting a lengthy career as confidence trickster, and asking God's pardon. Having pretended to be a convert to Judaism in order to marry the daughter of a rich Jew, he managed to defraud his father-in-law, but was caught and sent to the galleys. As he reiterates that he is suffering divine retribution, Massé expresses awe and amazement at 'la sage conduite du Tout-Puissant' (p. 502). Thus his argument against the Austral priest, when he had defended the cause of providence, is vindicated, as it had been on the many occasions throughout the book when, safe after some narrow escape, he has given thanks to God for his deliverance.[26]

The prevalence of this theme calls for comment, although it hardly seems to be a serious contribution to religious discussion. It conveys a positive but

---

[24] Massé later reflects (p. 477) that the best way to re-convert the Gascon would be to reach agreement on the existence of the Creator and continue from there, but this does not reveal whether the Gascon already believes in the Creator or not.

[25] The 'dragonnades' began in 1680, but Massé must have met the Gascon before then (pp. 441, 478 and 503 for the dates).

[26] For the sake of completeness I give the references: pp. 4, 21, 244, 351, 379, 389, 399, 412, 445, 456, 477.

vague religious belief, which, if the implications were drawn out, would presumably be that there is a deity who protects the virtuous (or virtuous theists, if the Gascon is an atheist) and punishes the wicked. Perhaps this should be related to Le Clerc, who in 1685 had said that the aim of the writers of the Bible had been to inculcate similar lessons about providence.[27] Narrative providentialism is common in the fiction of the early eighteenth century, including the *Lettres persanes*,[28] and reinforces the contemporary tendency to emphasize the moral side of religion; Pierre Heudde's misdeeds are obviously criminal, not doctrinal.

THE POLITICS OF RELIGION: WAR, IMPOSTURE AND INTOLERANCE

In most deistic texts in letter or novel form, the author not only gives us his theological ideas, which Tyssot does through the Australians and the Chinese, but also says something of the social or political aspects of religion. These are the subjects of a discussion between Massé and the king of the Austral Land, in Chapter 9. Early in the country's history, its first dynasty of kings had ruled by a kind of divine right based on sun-worship, as in Veiras' Sévarambe. They had claimed to be 'fils du soleil et de la terre' (p. 209) and made free with the womenfolk and property of their subjects, from whom they had also demanded worship.[29] Talking with the present king, Massé is told that the priests had so strong a hold over the people that any critics would have been mobbed; opponents of the régime were brought to trial, and after a prayer that whoever was guilty should be punished (in words like those of Voltaire's impostor Mahomet),[30] a secret trapdoor precipitated the unfortunate rebel to his doom (pp. 237–239). There was also a device for producing fake oracles; Tyssot had no doubt read Fontenelle as well as Veiras.

These horrors had been abolished when the impostures were exposed. A Portuguese (the nation's role in Tyssot seems to be to proclaim truth) had arrived in the country after being shipwrecked and journeying along a subterranean river. His appearance, seemingly miraculous but easily explained, proved to the Australians that not all of mankind was descended from

[27] See Chapter 6, p. 85, on Le Clerc's mouthpiece 'M. N.''s view about the Bible in the *Sentiments de quelques théologiens de Hollande*.

[28] For instance in Prévost, Marivaux and Voltaire (especially *Zadig*). Compare *Lettres persanes*, L. 67 and L. 143.

[29] Similar details are found in the Stroukarambe episode of the *Histoire des Sévarambes*; see Chapter 5, p. 70.

[30] *Mahomet* (1741), Act V, Sc. iv. Voltaire presumably read Tyssot's book in about the year of the play; in the 1742 edition of the *Lettres philosophiques*, Massé's name appears in a revised passage in L. 13 (Lanson/Rousseau edition, 2 vols. (Paris, 1964), Vol. I, p. 175, variants).

common ancestors, as was alleged by the sun-priests.[31] The people realized that their rulers were 'des fourbes et des scélérats' (p. 212), a revolution followed and a new monarch was elected, his family retaining the throne as long as they remained virtuous and just.

The conversation between Massé and the king brings the implications nearer home when the king is told about European war, which Massé locates in Spain, although the reference is clearly to France. The Christian God authorizes war (a blasphemy, says the king), and it can be caused by religious differences; in 'Spain' the church exacts payments for prayers on behalf of the souls in Purgatory and 'engage à confesser que Jésus-Christ est vivant, en chair et en os, et aussi grand qu'il était quand il a été crucifié, dans une hostie ou morceau de pâte de la grandeur de la paume de la main' (pp. 224–225). Some cannot believe such things, and there is war, which Massé describes emphasizing its bloodshed and waste.

The king is properly shocked by this (and presumably unaware that, though nominally Catholic, Massé's account of the Real Presence has a heavy Protestant bias), and comments that Christians are slaves, victims of the self-interest and ambition of their kings, whom he compares with the early Austral kings. Some remarks about royal caprice as a cause of war (pp. 219–220) strongly imply, when taken with the anti-Catholic propaganda and the association with sun-kings, that Tyssot is making an attack on Louis XIV.

In contrast to this talk of conflict, the coastal encampment of the ship-wrecked sailors, whom Massé and La Forêt rejoin after escaping from the Austral court, is a model of peaceful co-existence. Each morning and evening their leader Le Grand 'faisait une prière, où tous assistaient; car encore qu'ils fussent pour la plupart catholiques, ils vivaient ensemble comme s'ils avaient été d'une même religion. Ils faisaient tous profession d'aimer Dieu et leur prochain autant qu'eux-mêmes' (p. 378). They keep careful guard; each takes his turn with duties; 'la moindre parole deshonnête' is forbidden. The deism of the encampment is an extreme simplification of Christianity: natural religion without revelation and with eirenic overtones. The contrast with the preceding conversation about European conflict and the situation in Goa, which comes next, suggests that the sailors' encampment portrays a deistic, anti-clerical ideal society.

In Goa, clerical dominance, superstitious practices and the oppressive Inquisition create a sort of nightmare for Protestants. The narrative shows Massé standing up bravely against this tyranny. The remark which gets him into prison is directed against Catholic moral laxity, specifically the use of confession: he jokes about 'ces mangeurs de crucifix et avaleurs d'images, qui

---

[31]   The episode of the Portuguese traveller is a re-working, in fictional terms, of criticisms voiced previously by Massé, concerning the origins of mankind as described in the Book of Genesis. See Pinot, *La Chine et la formation de l'esprit philosophique*, pp. 231–232.

croyent pouvoir faire couper une bourse d'une main, pour ainsi dire, pourvu qu'ils tiennent un chapelet de l'autre' (p. 410). At his trial he expresses himself even more vigorously, saying that Goans, devout as they are, are prone to 'se vautrer dans l'ordure des plus infâmes vices' (p. 440). He also rejects Purgatory, 'puisqu'il suffit à un Chrétien d'être persuadé que le sang du Sauveur le nettoie de tous ses péchés', together with the infallibility of the Inquisition, since according to Scripture all men err, and God alone is infallible. The chapter ends with more propaganda, when an octogenarian is sent to the stake; he had dared to complain of some monks who cheated him of an inheritance, and they brought a false accusation against him.

The Goan episode seems to be an attack on Catholicism rather than a plea for tolerance. Tyssot does not appear to have any doctrine of tolerance, although the idea had been developed recently in Protestant countries, especially in works by Bayle and Locke. The assumption in the *Voyages de Jaques Massé* seems to be that each state has its religion and its law about other religions, but that there is no natural right to freedom of conscience. The Chinese theist seems not to expect toleration, although there is officially freedom of conscience in Goa. In the Austral Land, where the missionary friar had been severely punished, Massé and La Forêt are not molested, because they put their views forward only in private. On their departure, they hear some Australians saying they they must have escaped in order to practise their religion freely (pp. 334–335). But individual characters always respect each other's opinions, even when finding them scandalous. The best example is Le Grand's encampment. In sum, private unorthodoxies are acceptable, if combined with outward conformity. Despite his speculative audacities, Tyssot never seems to claim the right to publicize one's opinions.

ATTACKS ON THE BIBLE AND BIBLICAL DOCTRINES

Although there are many passages against Catholic 'superstition', Protestantism fares no better in Tyssot's novel; criticism of the Bible occurs throughout. Often the criticisms are rebutted, but not always convincingly. There is always a potential conflict between the religious and scientific sides of Massé's personality. A clear example is provided by the lessons he gives to the Frenchmen in the coastal encampment. Argument arises concerning three points on which science and Scripture are at odds: heliocentrism, the Flood, and the size of the Ark. In the first lesson, Massé states that the earth revolves around the sun; he is contradicted in the name of Scripture, and replies that the purpose of Scripture is not to be scientifically accurate (p. 381). He instances the account of the Creation and Solomon's 'molten sea', which involves the ratio of circumference to diameter in a circle.[32]

[32]   I Kings 7. 23, in which the approximation, three to one, is used. McKee (*Simon Tyssot de Patot*, p. 22) observes that the example is found both in Thomas Browne's *Religio medici* and Spinoza's *Tractatus theologico-politicus;* the latter is much the more likely source.

'Dieu bégaie avec nous; pour se rendre intelligible, il s'accommode au langage des hommes; lorsqu'il parle à sa manière, il nous est impossible de l'entendre; ce qu'il dit sont des mystères que nous ne saurions pénétrer' (p. 382).

On the Flood, Massé argues differently, saying that science and the Bible can be reconciled. The questions are whether the Flood covered the whole earth or only a part, and whether the Ark could have held every type of animal.[33] Massé eventually propounds a compromise solution; the Flood was not universal 'par rapport à la terre, mais seulement à l'égard de l'homme'. God caused only the inhabited regions to be inundated, and Noah took on board only the local species of animals (p. 393).

The interpretation of Scripture is also an important subject in the three major religious debates in the book, and in these Massé reaches agreement less easily. The Austral priest, commenting on the Old Testament, makes no allowances for Moses' lack of science: 'Cette Création (...) est une pure allégorie, que je trouve assez grossière dans son genre, et fabriquée par un auteur fort ignorant de la nature des choses' (p. 169). He has already asked, like Lahontan's Indian friend Adario,[34] whether Massé himself witnessed the miraculous events he relates, but has apparently been silenced by the reply that the 'facts' in question are certified by wise and pious men and 'des nuées de témoins' (p. 167). He has nothing to say against Massé's scientific explanation of one miracle, the pillar of fire which guided the Israelites in the desert.[35] However, he later returns to such questions more insistently. Brushing aside the argument that the progress of technology ('les arts') suggests a world history extending over about six thousand years, he asserts that the discovery of a ship's anchor on top of a mountain is evidence that there have been geological revolutions occurring over huge spans of time, the present mountains having once been the sea-bed (p. 178).[36] (Massé later witnesses a similar vast upheaval, when a mountain is transformed into a lake (p. 378) — perhaps a confirmation of the priest's argument.) Massé tries to defend the official Christian chronology, based on Genesis, but himself tells

---

[33]   See Pinot, op. cit., p. 241, on Tyssot's *Discours au sujet de la chronologie,* of 1722, in which scepticism about the Ark accompanies speculation about the age of the earth. Pinot considers that Tyssot believed in a creator God.

[34]   Lahontan, *Mémoires,* p. 122; see Chapter 9, pp. 132. Another possible borrowing from Lahontan is the character of a Portuguese doctor, who argues (*Nouveaux voyages,* Lettre 24, pp. 249—250) that Red Indians cannot be descended from Adam; but in *Jaques Massé* a similar character expresses materialist views, while the argument concerning race, occurring in the same passage (pp. 33ff.), is Massé's own.

[35]   McKee (*Simon Tyssot de Patot,* pp. 44—45) traced the explanation to John Toland's *Hodegus,* a part of his *Tetradymus.* In the *Voyages,* Tyssot refers to Toland in a note (p. 168) as 'un savant Anglais'. *Tetradymus* was not published until 1720, but Toland showed the manuscript to friends of Tyssot's in 1708, at The Hague. See also Rosenberg, *Tyssot de Patot,* p. 16.

[36]   See Pinot, *La Chine et la formation de l'esprit philosophique,* pp. 229ff., especially pp. 232—233, on the chronological arguments based on the progress of 'les arts'. Tyssot may have been using Abbadie (*De la vérité de la religion chrétienne,* Livre I, Ch. 9) as a source for Massé's Christian viewpoint.

the priest about Chinese annals going back much longer. He also tries to explain why, in Genesis, God is said to have created light before the sun and stars, but the priest laughs at him, as he does at the idea of the resurrection of the body (p. 179).

The priest's uncompromising rational and scientific approach to Scripture is in sum victorious. He seems to accept Massé's views about the pillar of fire in the desert, but they constitute a scientific explanation. When Massé has a discussion with the Austral judge, the roles are reversed. Massé accounts in non-miraculous terms for an Austral myth about volcanoes; for him, the myth shows simply that the manufacture of glass was once known in the Austral Land (pp. 193–196). As the arguments swing to and fro, alleged miracles being interpreted as natural processes and religious writings being defended against science, Tyssot's characters seem to be living out the early history of geological studies and the consequential adjustments to religious ideas. Two resultant tendencies emerge: to reconcile the contradictions and to abandon, or at least modify, religious belief when faced with scientific criticism.[37]

Massé's conversations with his fellow-prisoner in Goa include not only the subject of Scripture, but also that of doctrines such as the Trinity. The Chinese tells Massé of some criticisms which had been made by his father. He had denied the Trinity on the grounds of the distinction between spirit and matter, expressing himself in unitarian terms: 'Surtout, me disait-il, je frémis lorsque l'on me veut persuader qu'un Etre souverainement parfait et immatériel engendre un autre Dieu corporel, égal à lui, de toute éternité, et qu'il y a encore un autre Dieu, esprit indépendant, qui procède du Fils et du Père (. . .). Assurément c'est faire une étrange chimère de l'être du monde le plus simple et le moins divisible' (pp. 415–416). The Jesuit missionary with whom he was arguing had tried to preserve the concept of the Trinity by means of a comparison: the three persons are like the trunk, branches and fruit of a tree.[38] The Chinese accepted this, so that theological dogma has been replaced by analogy; as with Old Testament miracles, discussion ends with concessions to rational criticism.

The Chinese anti-trinitarian's son is more receptive than his father, but is troubled by chronology (p. 423), a special interest of Tyssot's, and also criticizes Trinity doctrine, but from an Arian point of view: 'Quelque grand homme qu'ait été ce divin prophète, il suffit de le croire fils de Dieu par excellence, et c'est lui faire une injure de l'imaginer capable de s'attribuer ce titre par nature' (p. 427). This must mean that Christ's moral excellence and role as prophet (moral teacher?) are divine in some metaphorical sense.

---

[37] On the developments during the first half of the century, see Ehrard, *Idée de nature,* Vol. I, pp. 199–210.

[38] The source, if any, of this analogy has not been traced; perhaps Tyssot is satirizing the Jesuit presentation of Christianity, often accused of conceding too much to natural reason.

Similarly on the Redemption: a dogmatic mystery becomes a moral concept when the Chinese asserts that Christ mediates between man and God by showing 'la voie du salut', with no reference to sacrifice. Orthodox formulations of dogmas, the Trinity and the Virgin Birth, are mentioned only to be rejected (p. 428), the Chinese affirming that passages from Scripture used to support them have been interpreted in too far-fetched a manner.[39] He regards the miracles of the New Testament as parables of faith or virtue; Peter walking on the waves represents the believer having faith, as for Gilbert's character Christofile.[40]

These ideas, which like other given to the Chinese theist seem to be an extreme development of Socinian or Arminian views, evoke from Massé the non-committal comment that he has raised many questions for discussion. The end of their conversation shows Massé hesitating about scientific materialism, on the subject of gall-flies, creatures whose religious significance is that they were supposed to originate in pure matter.[41] To believe this, says Massé, is to 'faire, avec Lucrèce, le soleil et la terre les seuls auteurs de tous les animaux sans exception, ce qui serait injurieux à Dieu' (p. 438). Whether the possible insult to God is a sufficient reason for deciding against spontaneous generation is left in the air, as often happens when Tyssot's characters make objections to orthodox belief. There can be no doubt that he invented the Chinese in order to put forward these objections in the guise of a 'real' person met in the East by Massé.

The Gascon who delivers the novel's last onslaught on the Bible is a rationalist but not a scientist. He denies a particular revelation – the idea that God communicated religious truth to only one part of humanity, the Jews and Christians. God's will, he says, is the order of nature in general; he would not have entrusted revealed truth to 'des gens obscurs, ignorants, ou fanatiques' in preference to 'les nations savantes et polies' (pp. 465–466). It cannot be proved that the books of the Pentateuch, supposedly by Moses, were written before the time of Ezra;[42] the miracles and prophecies (which Massé regards as proof of divine inspiration) are known only from the very books which they are supposed to authenticate; in themselves the miracles are implausible, nature being constant, and the prophecies vague; the canon is insecurely based (pp. 461–436). Massé can do no more than express astonishment at the Gascon's wide knowledge, and on arguing that Christian

---

[39]   'Sa morale est incontestablement pure, sa vie sainte, et ses enseignements divins; il en a confirmé la vérité par sa mort. Mais qu'il soit Dieu tout-puissant et éternel, la même essence qu le Père, et cependant personnellement distinct de lui, et engendré de toute éternité, conçu immédiatement du Saint-Esprit, ou de Dieu lui-même, et né d'une vierge immaculée, c'est ce qu'il n'a pas prétendu' (pp. 427–428).

[40]   *Histoire de Calejava*, pp. 66. See Chapter 8, p. 120.

[41]   Following observations made by Anthony van Leeuwenhoek. See McKee, *Simon Tyssot de Patot*, p. 71, Rosenberg, *Tyssot de Patot*, pp. 62ff.

[42]   Spinoza's argument, in the *Tractatus*, which is a reason for supposing that the epithet 'déiste ou athée' applied to the Gascon implies Spinozism.

belief is the gift of grace he is told that the same argument could be applied to the Koran. The Gascon concludes like the Austral priest, that the Christian revelation is 'une imposture, fondée sur la faiblesse des hommes en général, et inventée par ceux qui voulaient leur imposer dans de certaines vues et pour certains desseins' (p. 467).

The sinister designs are revealed in the Gascon's 'Fable des abeilles', one of the best examples of the imposture theory.[43] It tells how a false religious revelation is created by the drones (the clergy), who foist their story on the other bees and are thus enabled to live a life of idleness. 'Toute leur occupation consiste à inventer de quoi faire peur aux abeilles et les tenir dans la dépendance' (p. 474). They usurp authority and stir up trouble between different hives.

This biting anti-clericalism is accompanied by satire of the doctrines of Original Sin and the Redemption. In the Gascon's parody, the God of the Bible becomes the omnipotent king of an island populated by bees. They are punished for disobedience, having taken nectar from flowers forbidden to them, but are redeemed when the king's son takes the form of a bee. He teaches morality, but is mocked and stung to death. The king is dissuaded from taking revenge on the bees through the intercession of his son, deciding to forgive those who 's'attachent entièrement à son fils' (p. 472). Believers will be rewarded and unbelievers punished. There is even a satirical reference to proofs of the immortality of the soul in Christian apologists. The drones claim that when bees die, only their bodies rot; 'leur bourdonnement, qui est quelque chose de différent de ces corps, va jouir des récompenses ou souffrir les peines dont ils les ont menacés'.

The Gascon's attacks on Scripture differ from others in the novel in method and targets. No character had previously dismembered the standard apologetic arguments for the divinity of the Christian revelation, or used satire and parody. There is nothing in the 'Fable des abeilles' relative to the conflict between religion and science, a theme of earlier discussions, nor is there any possibility of compromise or conciliation, as there had been when this conflict was evoked; the Gascon's attitude is total negation. It is hard to see how Massé could have answered the fable; the Gascon's sudden death is scarcely a reply.

---

[43]   That Bernard Mandeville used the same title, *Fable of the Bees,* for the second version of his poem on the theme 'private vices, public virtue', seems to be no more than a curious coincidence. Mandeville's new title appeared in June 1714, the earliest year in which *Jaques Massé* could have been published.

With travel-stories by writers such as Foigny or Gilbert, we can reasonably ask whether the author himself sides with the Christian or the non-Christian characters, but in the *Voyages de Jaques Massé* the variety of opinions is such that the only possible question is whether any of them is Tyssot's. Apart from Massé's own attitude, there are three forms of belief: the deism of the Austral judge and priest; the non-sectarian Christianity of the Chinese in Goa; and the violently anti-Christian attitude of the Gascon renegade. Minor characters, the Austral king, the father of the Chinese and the assortment of Portuguese and Huguenots, contribute their own important ideas.

The attempt to create a composite attitude out of all these attitudes simply reveals their incompatibility. The Gascon's aggressiveness is at odds with the semi-deistic Christianity of the Chinese, which is also differentiated from the anti-Christian deism of the Austral Land. Nor do there seem to be good reasons for picking out any one character as Tyssot's mouthpiece. The Australians have most to say, the Gascon is the last and most original, and the Chinese closest to what might be expected in early eighteenth-century Holland with its radical sects. As for Massé, he is an all-purpose instrument, a vehicle for anti-Catholic propaganda, scientific criticism of Scripture, weak fideism or providentialism. He usually behaves like a modern figure, the interviewer, bringing out other people's ideas by putting to them a conventional Christianity, provoking disagreement and reacting with facile surprise.

The only conclusion to draw is that the variety of opinions represents a deliberate choice on Tyssot's part. This is supported by his use of sources. Atkinson, McKee and others have shown that Tyssot took much from earlier books, most of them unorthodox, some of them deistic — works by Foigny, Veiras, Marana and Lahontan. Descartes, Hobbes and Spinoza loom in the background, and probably Bayle and Fontenelle, as well as less predictable influences like that of John Toland.[44] However, no single influence is dominant; Tyssot takes fragments from many works. Rosenberg gives many examples of the way in which he worked incidents and names from his personal experience into his novels; in the same way, the intellectual content of the *Voyages de Jaques Massé* is a series of borrowings — Austral deism after Foigny and Veiras (with references to sun-worship from the latter); Chinese 'Christianity', if such it can be called, after Marana, the missionary accounts of the Far East and perhaps the Dutch radical sects; criticisms of

---

[44] One of the few instances of the 'English influence' on French deism. Lanson (*Origines de l'esprit philosophique*, p. 235) took the view that Tyssot was influenced by various writers including Locke and Collins, but this is not borne out by more recent research. Tyssot did however use Hobbes. See McKee, *Simon Tyssot de Patot*, especially pp. 83 and 93 ff., and Atkinson, *Extraordinary Voyage 1700–20*, pp. 88–96.

the apologists' arguments from Spinoza and others, and presumably the apologists themselves; propaganda against the Inquisition from Dellon and against other aspects of Catholicism from Huguenot preaching or polemical works. Ths list could be lengthened. Tyssot does include ideas which he advances himself in his letters or other works, but they are given no particular prominence.[45] It would seem, then, that he did not intend to convey any one positive religious attitude, but to produce a readable and audacious survey of contemporary deistic ideas by borrowing lavishly from his predecessors. And because the positive elements in religion, the various types of deism or Christianity in his book, tend to cancel each other out, the cumulative effect of the critical passages is greater. They add up to almost a complete rebuttal of the Christian religion. The Austral priest denies belief in the soul and other elements in Christian doctrine or practice, such as prayer; the Chinese revises, and almost dissolves, the dogma of the Trinity; the Gascon refutes some of the most important apologetic proofs, denies revelation, and satirizes the Redemption and the clergy. Other criticisms, mainly against the Bible, come from minor characters, including Massé as a young man. On the whole, the critics do not repeat each other, and as their objections continue, less and less of Christianity remains immune. Massé believes firmly in little except providence. These is no character to put the case for atheism, so that the range of positive attitudes is limited to shades of undenominational Christianity and deism, but these combine to give only a vague impression, while the impression left by the innumerable criticisms is one of firmly based hostility to Christianity.

Tyssot has no clearly defined positive doctrine of his own, then, but by taking the most typically deistic elements from earlier works he provides a statement of deistic and related doctrines in about 1715. His survey has one great omission: the rational deism, complete in all aspects, constructive, critical and moral, of the French clandestine works produced just before the *Voyages de Jaques Massé*. Tyssot appears not to have known them; occasional resemblances of ideas are probably coincidental.

The causative factors behind Tyssot's novel continue the same as before, though modified to some extent. The factor of travel is important for his characters rather than himself, since he led a settled life after his early years, but almost all his characters (apart from the Australians) are exiles or travellers, who know at least two religions by experience. Natural religion is of lesser significance. Theologically, it is the same as the deism of the Austral Land, which however is organized and has a clergy, making it much more realistic than the deism of Foigny's Austral hermaphrodites. As for the third factor which usually has some influence on deistic thought, that of religious conflict, it is relevant not because deism in Tyssot has any obvious eirenic aim, but because his book appeared at the end of the long period of war

---

[45]   See Rosenberg, *Tyssot de Patot*, pp. 61 ff.

between France and the Protestant powers. This probably accounts for several passages of anti-Catholic propaganda — Massé's conversation about religious war with the Austral king, the experiences of the Chinese with missionary Catholicism and the Inquisition, and the family history of the Gascon renegade. The pattern of the book, the recurrent confrontations between representatives of Christian orthodoxy and its critics, is obviously related to such factors, but seems to be due to Tyssot himself, perhaps because (as suggested by Rosenberg's study)[46] he was discontented with his life in northern Holland.

---

[46] Ibid., pp. 44 ff., on the effect that Tyssot's desire to be famous had on his writings.

Part IV

Deistic ideas in the early works of Montesquieu and Voltaire

CHAPTER 13

MONTESQUIEU: *LETTRES PERSANES*

In 1721, the year of the *Lettres persanes,* the *Dictionnaire de Trévoux* defined a deist as follows: 'Homme qui n'a point de Religion particulière; mais qui reconnaît seulement l'existence d'un Dieu, sans lui rendre aucun culte extérieur'. This is Furetière's definition of 1690 almost *verbatim.* It is followed by a slightly argumentative article on deist belief, which is interesting mainly because it confirms that the connection between deism and natural religion had become an accepted fact. Deists wish to return to 'la simplicité de la nature', they 'rejettent toute révélation, croyant seulement ce que la lumière naturelle démontre, qu'il y a un Dieu, une providence, des récompenses pour les bons, et des châtiments pour les méchants; qu'il faut honorer Dieu, mais chacun à sa manière et selon sa volonté, comme on convient, disent-ils, que les premiers hommes l'ont fait jusqu' à Moïse'.[1] The inclusion of an outline of natural religion gives deism a more respectable status than the mere 'belief in God' mentioned by previous dictionaries; the author complains about the deists' attitude to revelation and their repudiation of fideism ('la nécessité qu'on leur impose, de croire des mystères inconcevables'), but is not at all derogatory. This could reflect Jesuit policy towards theists and natural religion. In any case, it eliminates the connections with Socinian heresy, plots to subvert Christianity and the Epicurean denial of providence, all of which had often featured in previous accounts of deism.

A year later the most successful and competent apologia of the time appeared. The Abbé Houtteville's *La religion chrétienne prouvée par les faits* is directed, according to the title-page, against the deists. From the Livre troisième, which consists of answers to twelve deistic objections, it emerges that he thinks of deists primarily as those who deny the divinity of Christ.[2] The burden of his argument is that biblical miracles and prophecies, being facts of a supernatural order, prove that Christ alone, of all religious

---

[1]   *Dictionnaire universel françois et latin,* 5 vols. (Trévoux, 1721), Vol. II.
[2]   About two-thirds of Livre III is on the question of prophecies concerning the Messiah. See for instance p. 357, repudiating the objection that Christ cannot have been the Messiah and so was not divine.

leaders, is divine. Deist arguments, it seems, are (for instance) that the resurrection of Christ should have been an event as public as the Crucifixion if it were to be believed, which is very like the arguments of the clandestine manuscripts.[3] 'Un Etre infiniment bon et sage doit employer pour l'avancement de sa gloire et pour le bien des hommes la méthode la plus directe et la plus efficace':[4] against such principles Houtteville writes without indignation, as if he accepted, or at least understood them. He is much more hostile to those whom, like Spinoza or Toland, he regards as materialist atheists. He was taken to task by reviewers for reducing the area of disagreement between deism and Christianity, and it seems likely that the reviewers were right.[5]

The Trévoux definition and Houtteville's apologia together indicate that deism was now well understood, and regarded with much less alarm than previously. Christians and deists shared a rational conception of the divinity,[6] unlike the materialists whose views were also being promulgated in the clandestine works of the period. This slackening of tension between deism and Christianity is manifested also in the *Lettres persanes.* Montesquieu published the work when he was thirty-two. A gentleman from a leading *parlementaire* family in Guyenne, he had married a wife of Huguenot descent and for several years had held the important post of *président à mortier* in the Parlement at Bordeaux. However, he showed less interest in his legal duties than in intellectual matters. He was one of the first members of the Académie de Bordeaux, and had written a number of short pieces for it. Nothing seems to have suggested that he was to become the author of a best-seller which has established itself as the most representative work of the Regency of Philippe d'Orléans and the first major work of the French Enlightenment.[7]

The book's fame puts it in quite a different category from the more or less minor and obscure works which precede it in the history of deism. To them, except for the *Espion turc,* Montesquieu owes little, yet he writes as though the deistic attitude was nothing unusual. His cool assumptions about religion led Emile Faguet to describe him as 'l'âme la moins religieuse qui

---

[3]   In the Militaire philosophe's *Difficultés sur la religion,* see on the 'divinity' of the Old and New Testaments Mortier edition, pp. 197–212, 230–235; in the *Examen de la religion,* the chapter 'De l'écriture sainte'; in the *Analyse de la religion* or *La religion chrétienne analysée* Arsenal ms. 2091, ff. 19–41 (Old Testament), 42–83 (New Testament); and above, Chapters 10, p. 145; 11, pp. 161, 169.

[4]   *La religion chrétienne prouvée par les faits,* p. 316.

[5]   See Monod, *Pascal à Chateaubriand,* pp. 230–231.

[6]   Cf. Pomeau, *Religion de Voltaire,* p. 112, on Asselin's *La religion, poème, avec un discours pour disposer les déistes à l'examen des vérités de la religion,* 1725; Ehrard, *Idée de nature,* Ch. VII; and for the preceding period, Tocanne, *Idée de nature en France,* Pt. II, Ch. VI.

[7]   Robert Shackleton, *Montesquieu: A Critical Biography* (Oxford, 1961; cited henceforth as *Montesquieu*), Ch. 1. On the success of the book, see pp. 27–28.

soit'; against this, there is the evidence of Montesquieu's addresses to God in his personal writings.[8] However, the viewpoint from which he writes, both in the *Esprit des lois* and the *Lettres persanes*, is undoubtedly secular, although the Persians are presented as devout Muslims. Montesquieu's attitude was well defined by Joseph Dedieu as that of the legal theorist, 'qui, indifférent au contenu de la croyance, s'inquiète uniquement de son utilité sociale'.[9] This is typical of Roman writers, such as Cicero, whom Montesquieu greatly admired, and of the man of the world or *honnête homme*, a type well exemplified by Usbek and Rica despite their ostensibly Oriental birth. The urbane style of their comments often recalls an earlier *mondain*, Saint-Evremond, who also professes loyalty to his religion, while appearing more sensitive to political or social requirements than to matters of belief.

Montesquieu's Roman affinities are shown in the only important piece concerning religion that he wrote before 1721, a *Dissertation sur la politique des Romains dans la religion*, read to the Académie de Bordeaux in 1716.[10] In the first sentence he refers to the social importance of religion, and later gives many examples to demonstrate that Roman policy was to subordinate religious interests to those of the state. In the course of the discussion, many concepts typical of the imposture theory of religion appear – the credulous and superstitious mob, the enlightened minority, the strife caused by priests – but Montesquieu does not go on to denounce Roman religion; he

---

[8] Emile Faguet, *Dix-huitième siècle: études littéraires* (Paris, n.d. (1890)), p. 142. Compare Lanson: 'Il est foncièrement irréligieux; il ne comprend pas plus le christianisme que l'islamisme. Le principe intérieur de la religion lui échappe' (*Histoire de la littérature française*, 6th edition (Paris, 1901), p. 702). Perhaps the best-known passage showing religious sentiment in Montesquieu's personal works is that concerning *De l'esprit des lois*, which ends 'Dieu immortel! Le Genre humain est votre plus digne ouvrage. L'aimer, c'est vous aimer, et, en finissant ma vie, je vous consacre cet amour' (*Mes pensées*, No. 1805; quoted from *Oeuvres complètes*, Caillois edition (on which see n. 10), Vol. II, p. 1041). The question of Montesquieu's private religious opinions is beyond the scope of this study. See *inter alia*: Roger Caillois, 'Réflexions pour préciser l'attitude de Montesquieu à l'égard de la religion', *La Table ronde* 90 (1955), 138–150; Sergio Cotta, *Montesquieu e la scienza della società* (Turin, 1953), Ch. 1 (on the *Lettres persanes*, see pp. 26–34); R. Shackleton, 'La religion de Montesquieu', in *Actes du congrès Montesquieu réuni à Bordeaux du 23 au 26 mai 1955* (Bordeaux, 1956), pp. 267–294). On the *Lettres persanes*: Pauline Kra, *Religion in Montesquieu's Lettres persanes* SVEC 72 (1970) (considering the work largely in the light of the Bible), and on the Muslim aspects: Ahmad Gunny, 'Montesquieu's view of Islam in the *Lettres persanes*', SVEC 174 (1978), 151–167.

[9] J. Dedieu, *Montesquieu, l'homme et l'oeuvre* (Paris, 1943), p. 109.

[10] Montesquieu, *Oeuvres complètes*, Collection de la Pléiade, edited by Roger Caillois, 2 vols (Paris, 1949–1951), Vol. I, pp. 81–92. References are to this edition, cited as Caillois edition, for works other than the *Lettres persanes*. For these, reference is normally made only to the individual letters, numbered as in modern editions. Reference is also made when necessary to two critical editions, those by Paul Vernière, Classiques Garnier (Paris, 1961) and Antoine Adam, Textes littéraires français (Geneva, 1954). Both are based on the 1758 edition of Montesquieu's works, on which see Vernière edition, pp. XXXVIII–XLI. For eight other fragments, see Elisabeth Carayol, 'Des *Lettres persanes* oubliées', RHLF 65 (1965), 15–26. It should perhaps be added, with reference to the fourth of the fragments concerned, that it is not evidence of religious sensibility on Montesquieu's part, but a parody of it, disguising the true subject, an attack of sea-sickness.

recognizes that it contained many artificial elements (among which the belief in God seems not to be included), but praises Roman skills in creating and maintaining a form of worship which served state ends.[11] In the *Lettres persanes,* the Persians do not seek to reform or refute Christianity and Islam, but treat them as permanent elements in the life of the community, which have both good and bad points in the light of society's needs.

GOD AND JUSTICE

The apparent lack of structure in the *Lettres persanes* adds to the impression of casual detachment and seems to exclude methodical discussion, except within the limits of a letter. Yet the Persians make their views known on virtually the whole range of religious issues: not only their conception of God and the worship due to him, which are the subject of the best-known letters on religion, but also the question of the soul and survival after death, providence, the clergy, the Bible, religious authority and tolerance. It is noticeable that questions of proof, which were so important for the rational deists, have little place, while much greater attention is given to the social or political issues raised by religion. This is because the work is in essence an informal survey of a particular society in all its aspects.

On the subject of God, however, Montesquieu is enough of a rationalist to write in metaphysical style, though he apologizes for it.[12] He abandons the central concept in the rationalist philosophy of religion, the relationship between God and truth. For Usbek, in L. 83 and L. 69, it is the relationship between God and justice which has to be defined. His position is that the two are separable only in thought: 'S'il y a un Dieu, mon cher Rhêdi, il faut nécessairement qu'il soit juste (...)': the bold opening of L. 83 does not mean that the existence of God requires to be proved, but that justice is the one attribute which is fundamental. Yet justice in itself is a social ideal, rather than a religious one, and Montesquieu does not entirely dispel the impression that for him the social ideal comes first.

The letter is of complex design, since, while asserting the indivisibility of God and justice, it refutes two bodies of opinion which have nothing in

---

[11]   The aim of Roman legislators in establishing religion, says Montesquieu, 'était d'inspirer à un peuple qui ne craignait rien la crainte des dieux, et de se servir de cette crainte pour le conduire à leur fantaisie' (Caillois edition, Vol. I, p. 81). He later mentions Cudworth, and explicitly follows him in saying that 'ceux qui étaient éclairés parmi les païens adoraient une divinité suprême, dont les divinités du peuple n'étaient qu'une participation' (p. 87). This seems to come from the *True Intellectual System of the Universe,* Ch. IV, perhaps section XXXIV.

[12]   L. 69 is introduced as 'ce débordement de ma philosophie'. The second paragraph is critical of metaphysics, referring to rationalist philosophers who ascribe all possible perfection to God, 'sans songer que souvent ces attributs s'entr' empêchent'.

common except that they both seem to make God and justice separate. Usbek refers to them rather late in the letter. The first is almost certainly that of Thomas Hobbes, that justice depends on 'conventions humaines', instead of being transcendent or of divine origin; phrases in the summary of Montesquieu's lost *Traité des devoirs,* of 1725, show that in it he refuted Hobbes in the same terms as L. 83.[13] The second opinion is held by theologians, 'docteurs', according to whom God seems to be unjust, 'un être qui fait un exercice tyrannique de sa puissance'. Much of the argument in L. 83 is determined by the need to answer Hobbes and the theologians; the answers are distributed in alternating paragraphs. For Hobbes, there is no need to explain why men act unjustly, because it is their nature to do so; but Montesquieu has to explain it because he has stated that justice is real, and in theory always perceptible by men as a guide to conduct. His explanation comes in the remarks about self-interest, which can overcome the impulse to act justly.

The contrast made subsequently, between men and God, the former being unjust out of self-interest and the latter necessarily following justice, is directed against Montesquieu's other opponents. He says to them, in effect, that belief in God ought to involve believing in a just God, whereas they represent him 'tantôt comme un être mauvais, tantôt comme un être qui hait le mal et le punit'.

The requirements of debate are also the reason for the supposition made initially, that God may not exist. Hobbes was one of the famous atheists, according to his reputation, and in order to defeat his arguments Montesquieu must place himself on the same ground.

The identity of 'ces docteurs' with whom Usbek disagrees is less certain. From the references to punishment and tyranny we can deduce that the subject is damnation; and from the obscurity of the passage, that Montesquieu was being cautious because he was dissenting from a common Christian opinion. Probably, then, Usbek is criticizing the doctrine of punishment for Original Sin, on the grounds that ideals of human justice do not accord with the idea of the damnation of mankind on account of Adam's disobedience. L. 83 also manifests a degree of optimism about human nature — men can achieve justice by dominating self-interest — which is at odds with Original Sin; other deistic works reveal the same

---

[13]   See Caillois edition, Vol. I, pp. 108–111 (p. 109: 'L'auteur (...) fait voir que la Justice n'est pas dépendante des lois humaines, qu'elle est fondée sur l'existence et la sociabilité des êtres raisonnables, et non pas sur des dipositions ou volonté particulières de ces êtres. Cette question conduit l'auteur à la réfutation des principes d'Hobbes sur la morale'). The summary was published anonymously in J. -F. Bernard's *Bibliothèque françoise* in March 1726.

212

attitude.[14] Since it was the Jansenists who put the greatest emphasis on sinfulness and the likelihood of damnation, it is they who are the most likely target of the arguments in L. 83.[15]

The definition of justice itself, 'un rapport de convenance qui existe réellement entre deux choses', resembles the definition of law which Montesquieu was to give in *De l'esprit des lois*.[16] The concept is that of a transcendental value akin to Malebranche's 'ordre' in the *Traité de morale*.[17] God is just in the sense that his actions correspond to 'convenance', which can be expressed as an exact relationship; again, this resembles Malebranche's view that the order of values can be calculated rationally.[18] The idea is illustrated in L. 102, when Montesquieu writes of 'la proportion qui doit être entre les fautes et les peines', and once more attacks tyrannical punishments.

The resemblance to Malebranche's phraseology does not mean that the Oratorian philosopher was the source of Montesquieu's emphasis on the divine attribute of justice. The idea of justice as a moral ideal was common at the time, no doubt because of the social importance of the *noblesse de robe* and the pervasive influence of legal thought.[19] The idea in Montequieu

---

[14]   Notably L. 25 of Voltaire's *Lettres philosophiques*, but also the rational deists (Gilbert, *Histoire de Calejava*, Livre 10, Troisième dialogue, Quatrième dialogue (pp. 230 ff.); the Militaire philosophe's *Difficultés, cahier* 'E', section 10 (Mortier edition, pp. 295 ff.); the *Examen de la religion*, 15-chapter version, Ch. 12, 'Du péché originel').

[15]   Adam (his edition, p. 216, n. 8) suggests that Montesquieu was arguing against Calvinism, but the emphasis on Original Sin was no less characteristic of Jansenism, and there seems to be no particular reason why he should have been mainly concerned with Protestant attitudes (unless it is that his wife came from a Huguenot family).

[16]   'Les lois (...) sont les rapports nécessaires qui dérivent de la nature des choses'. In this sense, says Montesquieu, 'la Divinité a ses lois' (*De l'esprit des lois*, Livre I, Ch. I; Caillois edition, Vol. II, p. 232).

[17]   Alessandro Crisafulli, 'Parallels to Ideas in the *Lettres persanes*', PMLA 52 (1937), 773–777 (pp. 773–774), suggests that the definition of justice might have come from Malebranche or Leibniz, but the arguments of André Robinet, 'Malebranchisme et Régence', in *La Régence*, edited by Henri Coulet (Paris, 1970), pp. 263–275, in favour of the former as the source, are more convincing.

[18]   In his later works (e.g. *Entretiens de métaphysique*, VIII; *Méditations chrétiennes*, IV) Malebranche's preferred phrase is 'rapports de perfection', a concept used in the *Traité de morale* to indicate that moral duties can be arranged according to priorities demanded by 'l'amour de l'ordre': 'Puisque la *Vérité* et l'*Ordre* sont des rapports de grandeur et de perfection réels, immuables, nécessaires, rapports que renferme la substance du Verbe Divin; celui qui voit ces rapports, voit ce que Dieu voit: celui qui règle son amour sur ces rapports, suit une loi que Dieu aime invinciblement' (*Traité de morale*, I, i). Compare Montesquieu's phraseology in L. 83: 'ce rapport est toujours le même, quelque être qui le considère, soit que ce soit Dieu, soit que ce soit un ange, ou enfin que ce soit un homme. Il est vrai que les hommes ne voient pas toujours ces rapports (...)'. Vernière (his edition, p. 174, n. 4) also cites the *Traité de morale*.

[19]   The best example among earlier deists is the Militaire philosophe's God of justice (in his *Quatrième cahier*), but justice as an ideal is found in very different places, for instance in Boileau's *Satires* and *Epîtres* or in La Bruyère's chapter *Des esprits forts* in the *Caractères*. For many examples, see Sheila M. Mason, *Montesquieu's Idea of Justice* (The Hague, 1975), e.g. pp. 15, 20, on the ideal in Malebranche and Bossuet (pp. 149 ff. on L. 83 of the *Lettres persanes*).

is an aspect of his secularism; the person of God seems less important than the secular value in the abstract. When Usbek reflects on the two possibilities, the non-existence of God and the non-existence of justice, his style shows that the latter prospect is worse; 'Quant il n'y aurait pas de Dieu, nous devrions toujours aimer la justice' displays less anxiety than his reaction to the thought that justice might depend on human conventions: 'ce serait une vérité terrible, qu'il faudrait se dérober à soi-même'.

In less metaphysical moods, however, the Persians refer to God as habitually and casually as most other deists. In one of the pieces in the form of Persian letters which Montesquieu did not publish, Rica attacks the 'athéisme brutal' of a young man whom he meets, commenting that there are some blasphemies which 'm'élèvent vers le Créateur comme des hymnes que j'entends chanter'.[20] The reflections of L. 83 exemplify a phenomenon which is typical of Montesquieu, the conceptual separation of the religious and the secular, God and justice, with the implication that the former is subordinate to the latter; nonetheless there is the manifest intention of uniting the two and eliminating any possible conflict.

The same conciliatory intent is visible in L. 69. It is less difficult than L. 83, although the subject is more intricate -- God's foreknowledge of human actions. This metaphysical puzzle was much discussed, notably by Bayle and Leibniz.[21] The crux was the opposition between omniscience and human freewill: an act does not appear to be free if it has been foreseen by God; yet if God is unable to foresee it, he is not omniscient. Usbek's solution is a compromise. He says that God cannot foresee something which does not exist, but that he can know the future when he wishes to, because he can force men to act in a certain fashion ('déterminer les créatures conformément à sa volonté'), as a king can oblige his ambassadors to carry out his orders.

As presented by Montesquieu, the problem is to reconcile omniscience with divine justice, rather than with human freedom. The point is that, for God to behave justly, in other words for him to reward the virtuous and punish the wicked, men ought to have freewill. Montesquieu says that God usually leaves men the freedom to act, in order that they should be capable 'de mériter ou de démériter'. Evidently he does not accept Jansenist, or

---

[20] Adam edition, pp. 418–419; Vernière edition, p. 345.
[21] It enters into the problem of theodicy, as propounded by Bayle in articles in his *Dictionnaire* such as 'Manichéens', to which Leibniz furnished an answer in his *Théodicée* (1710). However, Montesquieu seems not to have read Leibniz (for the contrary view, see Vernière edition, p. 147, n. 1, etc.); among other points, Leibniz denies that there is any real conflict between God's prescience and human freewill (*Théodicée*, Pt. I, section 37, etc.), but L. 69 is written on the assumption that there is such a conflict.

Calvinist, doctrines of predestination (another link with L. 83).[22] From the strict Christian point of view, he is guilty of the heresy of Pelagianism; no doubt it is for some such reason that he expresses himself abstractly and with circumspection. Yet at the end of the argument, which rests on the implicit conflict of interests between divine omniscience and human freewill, Usbek's compromise is an attempt to avoid the theoretical conflict. At the same time, his preferences lie as it were with the human side; freewill is maintained except when God wishes otherwise.

In 1754, Montesquieu added an additional paragraph in conclusion, which is almost a retraction of his metaphysical speculations about God: 'Nous ne le connaissons bien que dans ses préceptes'.[23] However, there is little doubt that the precepts, had he listed them, would have concerned virtue and justice. Passages concerning God in other letters confirm the close relationship between socio-legal and religious concepts. Rica, when faced with the young atheist, emphasizes divine punishment and does not bother with rational proofs: 'Cet Etre suprême qui ne voit un insecte comme vous que parce qu'il est immense saura bien vous punir'. In L. 97, God is 'l'auteur de la nature', but Usbek's admiration is reserved especially for the 'lois générales, immuables éternelles, qui s'observent sans aucune exception, avec un ordre, une régularité, et une promptitude infinies, dans l'immensité des espaces'. In L. 135, Rica comments disparagingly on physicists who fail to feel the same admiration and wonder.

The concept of God which is implied by L. 83 and L. 69, and reinforced by these passages, is not at all complicated, despite the metaphysics and the occasional obscurities of expression. It resembles that expounded by the Militaire philosophe in his *Quatrième cahier*: God is just, and men are free to earn his approval or disapproval by following or neglecting the dicates of justice; they will not be punished for other reasons. The question naturally arises how any rewards or punishments will be carried out. Is there some form of survival after death? Alternatively, does God providentially ensure that the good and the bad are treated as they deserve during their earthly lives? Or, finally, does Montesquieu leave the whole question uncertain?

---

[22]   Cf. Roger Oake, 'Montesquieu's Religious Ideas', JHI 14 (1953), 548—560 (p. 559), on L. 69 as a denial of predestination. Adam (his edition, p. 186) relates it to one of Montesquieu's *Pensées* (Caillois edition, Vol. I, p. 1178; No. 674), headed 'Doutes', which begins: 'S'il arrive quelquefois que Dieu prédestine (ce qui ne peut arriver que rarement: car il n'arrive que rarement que Dieu nous ôte la liberté), il ne peut jamais nous prédestiner qu'au salut'.

[23]   This paragraph, like other revisions done for the 1754 edition, was no doubt influenced by Montesquie's desire to counter the attack made anonymously by the Abbé Jean-Baptiste Gaultier, *Les Lettres persannes* (sic) *convaincues d'impiété*, 1751. Gaultier devotes much space to L. 69, and objects chiefly to the denial of God's prescience, which, he says (quoting St Augustine, the standard authority for Jansenists), is equivalent to denying God's existence: 'Qui peut douter de l'athéisme de cet homme?' (p. 26).

To the first of these questions the answer is simple: there is no evidence that the Persians believe in any meaningful form of afterlife. In several letters, the beliefs of Orientals about the afterlife are treated with humour and fantasy, and the only explicit reflections on the soul, in L. 76, tend to deny its existence.

The Oriental material is among the most entertaining in the work. In L. 35, the tone of which is set at the beginning by a query about 'les infidèles turcs, qui serviront d'ânes aux juifs, et les mèneront au grand trot en enfer', Usbek tells a dervish, who is his cousin, that the Christians hope for a bodily resurrection in Paradise, 'où ils goûteront mille délices'.[24] The vision is exemplified in L. 141, in the tragi-comic story of the virtuous Anaïs, stabbed to death by her brutal husband. The delights are indeed bodily, Montesquieu's sources having informed him (in accordance with European tradition) that the Muslim afterlife is sensual rather than spiritual. In L. 125, Rica observes, with satirical examples, that every religion has difficulty in describing the pleasures 'destinés à ceux qui ont bien vécu' — those who, like Anaïs, will be rewarded if God is just. Rica also has a story (based on reality) of an Indian widow, who is about to immolate herself with her husband's body.[25] She changes her mind when she learns that in Paradise she will be reunited with him, and ends by treating the belief about the afterlife as an imposture.

The flippant tone makes it impossible to suppose that in Montesquieu's view the reward for virtue took the form of physical resurrection. As for the survival of the soul, Usbek in L. 76 is seeking to justify suicide, and faces Christian arguments that it contravenes God's will: 'Dieu a uni votre âme avec votre corps, et vous l'en séparez'. Replying, Usbek seems first to suggest that the human person is wholly material, as he talks of 'les modifications de la matière', but later he adopts the assumption that the body is united with the soul. His body, he thinks, might become 'un épi de blé, un ver, un gazon' (so much for bodily resurrection, when Montesquieu is writing seriously). As for the soul, he only asks a question: 'Pensez-vous (. . .) que mon âme, dégagée de tout ce qu'elle avait de terrestre, soit devenue moins sublime?' This is so vague, indeed almost meaningless, that it must be tactful evasiveness, disguised as pious rhetoric. At best it is a statement of

[24] In the *Spicilège*, one of his notebooks, Montesquieu records some jokes about the resurrection of the body, made by Fontenelle in a letter to La Fare; they convey a clearer impression of disbelief than in the *Lettres persanes* (Caillois edition, Vol. II, p. 1295; pp. 261–263 of the manuscript).

[25] See Vernière edition, p. 263, n. 1, for the reference to the *Voyages* of François Bernier, which seems to be the origin of the anecdote.

agonsticism. The latter as a whole has a Stoic rather than a Christian ring.[26]

The question of providence is more complicated. The idea appears sporadically throughout the *Lettres persanes*, and plays a significant part in the famous sequence of letters about Troglodytes. In L. 59, the word is a synonym for God, as it is in the letter on suicide; but in L. 35 'l'ordre de la providence' is considered unsympathetically as a Christian cliché, in L. 98 those who benefit from sudden prosperity are said ironically to attribute their good fortune to providence, and in L. 130 the purvevors of news are described, again with irony, as 'marchant au-devant de la providence'. When Rica and Usbek are speaking as good Muslims, they claim that the purpose of providence is to further the interests of Islam (L. 35, L. 39, L. 123), and here too there is a degree of satire. By contrast, Montesquieu's tone is one of approval when providence means divine retribution. In L. 121 Usbek notes that among the *conquistadores,* of whose exploits he disapproves, many died, which is 'une fatalité que je ferais mieux de nommer une justice divine'. In a fragment left unpublished, about the success of rebels in Persia, it is suggested that the rebellion was divine retribution for the misdeeds of the Persian despots.[27]

The letters on the Troglodytes are a mixture of economics and ethics in the form of a parable. They answer a question from Usbek's friend Mirza: does happiness come from pleasure or 'la pratique de la vertu'? Virtue turns out to be synonymous with justice, and so has close connections with the concept of God in the metaphysical letters. According to Usbek, as Mirza tells us, justice is innate in men; in L. 83 it is inherent in God. Usbek's reply to the question, in L. 11 to L. 14, tells how the first generation of Troglodytes, most of whom were individually selfish to the point of destroying their society, was replaced by a new generation who based society on virtue (or justice); they became happy and prosperous in consequence.

The history emphasizes the value of economic cooperation and is not providentialist; the actions of the Troglodytes themselves, not the gods, are the cause of their sucess. However, providentialism dominates the comments which they or others make on their history. A doctor who had not been paid for treating the first selfish Troglodytes is called in a second time, to cure a new epidemic; but he refuses to help, asserting that the disease is sent by the gods: 'je croirais offenser les dieux, qui vous punissent, si je m'opposais à la justice de leur colère'. Yet the real punishment is his

---

[26]   In the 1754 edition, an answering letter, L. 77 of modern editions, was added. It seems at first sight to be a defence of laws against suicide, but avoids making the admission that such laws are justified.

[27]   Adam edition, p. 423; Vernière edition, p. 349.

own refusal of treatment. Similarly, the second generation of Troglodytes, whose own 'virtue' brings affluence, celebrate 'les grandeurs des dieux, leurs faveurs toujours présentes aux hommes qui les implorent, et leur colère inévitable à ceux qui ne les craignent pas'. Usbek, as narrator, confines himself to the remark that 'un peuple si juste devait être chéri des dieux', which leaves it nicely ambiguous whether the gods did in fact cherish them. It seems more likely that their morally-based economy was the deciding factor.

As with the discussion of God and justice in L. 83, the history of the Troglodytes enables secular and religious elements to be distinguished, economic decline and prosperity appearing to depend on human decisions, but being interpreted as if they were the result of divine action. Montesquieu again seems to want to unite the two orders of events, human and divine, but the providentialism here, like the comment of the *conquistadores*, is little more than a pious hope.

A similar conclusion can be drawn from the ending of an even more fanciful tale, on Arabian Nights lines, the story of Anaïs and the two Ibrahims in L. 141. Anaïs too has hopes of providence; as she dies, stabbed by the first Ibrahim, her husband, she exclaims to his other wives: 'Si le Ciel a pitié de ma vertu, vous serez vengées'. In due course they, and she, are indeed revenged, when from Paradise she sends one of her angelic lovers to impersonate Ibrahim. The consequences are comic, but not trivial, since the subject is virtue rewarded, and vice punished, by divine agency. The narrator Zulèma, who is learned in all religious matters, has 'un certain caractère d'esprit enjoué, qui laissait à peine deviner si elle voulait amuser ceux à qui elle parlait, ou les instruire'. This could be a self-description of Montesquieu himself. But assuming that the tale is meant to instruct, the moral is that 'le Ciel' will punish barbarity towards wives and, it seems, failure to beget children. The false Ibrahim frees the wives, satisfies their natural desires and fathers numerous offspring. Hence the simple lesson for men, repeated in another Oriental tale, L. 67, and in the letters on depopulation, especially L. 116, is that they should love their wives and propagate the species. (The contrast, incidentally, is furnished by the disastrous events in Usbek's harem, the account of which ends the book.) The providentialism of L. 141, therefore, is merely a means of communicating a moral message about human behaviour, not a representation of the action of God on earth.

Whether metaphysical or narrative, these letters do not show that divine justice produces any specific effects. Both damnation and heavenly bliss are treated in the sceptical mode, and any hints about rewards and punishments on earth are found to have little substance when real causes are analysed. Justice, then, although the first attribute of deity, is not a genuine power in the world, but an ideal to be aimed at. Usbek ends L. 83 with the words: 'si j'étais sûr de suivre toujours inviolablement cette équité que j'ai devant les yeux, je me croirais le premier des hommes'.

SECULAR AND UTILITARIAN VALUES

The moral ideal of justice is made more explicit in the most famous of the letters on religion, L. 46. This contains, first, a statement of moral and religious precepts which correspond, at the practical level, to the ethical theory of L. 83, and secondly a rejection of the 'ceremonies', or ritual, of established religion. Usbek begins on the Christians and their controversies, principally, no doubt, the Jansenist dispute; he deplores the social and ethical results for the Christians as citizens, even though he is a Muslim: 'Car, dans quelque religion qu'on vive, l'observation des lois, l'amour pour les hommes, la piété envers les parents, sont toujours les premiers actes de religion'. Right from the beginning the movement from a religious to a secular viewpoint is clear; the acts which Usbek affirms to be 'religious' are essentially those which are morally or socially valuable. Citizenship matters more than the profession of any particular religion.

In order to carry the argument through, Usbek nonetheless puts himself in the position of 'un homme religieux', which he is himself, since he remains loyal to Islam throughout. The man who believes in his religion[28] must also believe, if he is consistent, that God wishes men to be happy, and he should act accordingly: be charitable and humane, and not break the law. The reasoning seems obvious, even pointless; but it has a definite purpose, that of suggesting a solution to the religious disputes in Christianity. The 'homme religieux' here is the man whose convictions will make him intolerant, if he believes that his religion alone is the right one. Usbek wishes to convince him that God desires all men to be happy, not only those who profess his particular religion. Thus the grounds for intolerance and conflict will be removed.

These ingenuities are followed by a more effective plea for tolerance, but one which is more destructive of religious loyalties, when Montesquieu reduces religious differences to a matter of 'cérémonies'. He imagines a

---

[28] This is a paraphrase of the curious beginning of the sentence 'en quelque religion qu'on vive, dès qu'on en suppose une, il faut bien que l'on suppose aussi que Dieu aime les hommes, puisqu'il établit une religion pour les rendre heureux'. What does 'dès qu'on en suppose une' mean? If one belongs to a religion, one must already 'suppose that a religion exists'. Unless the text is faulty (which is not unknown in the *Lettres persanes*), it seems to be an abbreviated way of saying 'if one supposes that only one religion is instituted by God' – the basic principle of intolerance. If so, Montesquieu is arguing against those who hold such a principle, and in order to make his argument effective he is placing himself on the same ground as they. This is a method adopted also in L. 83 when apparently atheistic suppositions are made.

little scene in which a man is confronted by threats of damnation (another form of intolerance) unless he makes the correct choice of religion. But this choice, which for Marana's Spy had been a lengthy and anxious examintion of alternatives, is reduced by Usbek to ludicrous proportions: should a man sit or kneel when praying, should he refrain from eating rabbit-meat? The Oriental setting, the imaginary dialogue and the wit have the same function as in L. 125, that of satirizing the orthodox belief that salvation may be achieved only in one religion. The scene is a rare but significant example of a resemblance between the *Lettres persanes* and the clandestine deist works, since the *Examen de la religion* also utilizes threats of damnation as a pretext for destructive criticism.

Montesquieu's imaginary individual, who is almost without characteristics except that he has to eat, finds a solution to his problems in the universal certainties of the ethical code (Marana's solution), now with a more deistic ring; a man's decision to act morally is made in order to please God, who is responsible for the existence of men as citizens and fathers. Here there is an echo of the concept of justice, in the sense of reciprocity in the performance of good actions, which is the Toglodytes' code; just actions are done in return for the benefits of existence, received from God. The ending of the letter, in an indifferentist mode found in Saint-Evremond as well as Marana, conveys once more that differences between religions are less important (to the point of triviality) than the moral element in religion.

As a document in the history of deism, the contribution of L. 46 as a whole is the skill with which Montesquieu expresses the idea that conflict between religions should be superseded by humane tolerance. This necessarily involves a movement towards theistic morality, and here, in contrast to other latters, it is harder to separate the religious and moral elements. Humaneness and obedience to law are seen as religious acts, since morality is the manifestation of belief in God.

It would be a mistake to conclude, from the indifferentism of L. 46 or the fact that the *Lettres persanes* is preceded chronologically by anti-Christian deistic works, that it is regularly hostile to established religion. The book's range of comment extends from complete rejection of some aspects, such as monasticism, to indifference or even approval, as with the Muslim ban on wine; the profession of secular values can also be compatible with approval for institutional religion as a whole.

The leading example of the conflict between secular and religious is constituted by the series of letters on depopulation.[29] In this compressed survey of world history, the value in question is utilitarian; all customs are

---

[29]   On these see D. B. Young, 'Libertarian Demography: Montesquieu's Essay on Depopulation in the *Lettres persanes'*, JHI 36 (1975), 669–682.

judged according as they encourage or discourage the growth of population. Both Christian and Muslim beliefs and institutions are found defective. At the beginning of L. 114, Usbek compares them to the religion of the Romans: 'il s'en faut bien que ces deux religions soient aussi favorables à la propagation de l'espèce que celle de ces maîtres de l'univers'. The bulk of the letter demonstrates a paradox, with sophistry and many quotations from the Koran: Muslim polygamy does nothing to increase the birthrate. L. 116 gives a similar demonstration for the Christian ban on divorce, which according to Usbek causes conjugal detestation, prostitution and barrenness. He says finally that he cannot understand what Christian marriage consists in, which for him is a serious criticism; he means that he can find no useful purpose in it. The next letter condemns monasticism in even more sweeping terms, opposing 'l'utilité publique' to 'ce métier de continence'. Monks and priests are 'eunuques'. Usbek again fails to understand the virtue of celibacy, 'ne sachant ce que c'est qu'une vertu dont il ne résulte rien'. Monasticism produces no children, but also no wealth for the national exchequer. Catholic decline will be accompanied by Protestant dominance: 'Le commerce ranime tout chez les uns, et le monachisme porte la mort partout chez les autres'.

Even in the later eighteenth century, there can have been few clearer statements that religion is detrimental to material economic progess – the affluence of the Troglodytes, and of more modern times. Montesquieu even seems to be blaming the monks for the loss of the War of the Spanish Succession. We may deduce, from the frankness with which he gives his views (there are some token Persian phrases, but the concern for the future of Catholic countries is not Persian), that he did not regard them as particularly daring, or that he expected them to be shared by his readers.[30]

Where doctrinal belief is concerned, the comments are milder. L. 119 contains some favourable remarks on the Jewish doctrine of a Messiah (it encourages women to have children) and on the religious beliefs of the Chinese and the Gabars. There is also a short critique of the otherworldliness of Islam. Belief in the afterlife, 'toute sainte qu'elle est', causes useful work in agriculture and building to be neglected. The ostensible reference to Persia is emphatic, to compensate for the real reference to Christianity.

In all this, opposition to religion is selective; specific criticisms, sometimes harsh, but not total condemnation. Moreover there is no clear statement of principle, but only the thematic repetition of terms concerning utility. The formulation of a doctrine came later, in the *Esprit des lois*. In 1721, Montesquieu seems to have had only a sense of priorities, dictating

---

[30] The Abbé Gaultier (*Lettres persannes convaincues d'impieté*, pp. 82–93, on L. 117) seems resigned to facing attacks on monasticism, saying that they are found in many works by deists and Spinozists (among them being the *Esprit des lois*).

his responses to the various aspects of religion which were relevant.

The Gabars[31] mentioned with approval in L. 119 are also the subject of an enigmatic story of love and marriage in L. 67. Aphéridon persuades Astarté, by religious arguments, to leave the Muslim eunuch whom she has been forced to marry, and they elope. They are married according to the rites of their religion, and have a daughter. The problem of interpretation is that Aphéridon and Astarté are brother and sister; L. 67 is an apologia for sibling marriage, which in Montesquieu's view is virtually an article of the Gabar religion: 'ces alliances saintes, que notre religion ordonne plutôt qu'elle ne permet'. The justification is that such marriages are natural, 'des images si naïves de l'union déjà formée par la Nature'. At the end of the story, the ideal of unity is realized, 'l'union régne dans ma famille'. Marriage between brother and sister is good because, apparently, it combines romantic love with the affection natural within the family, and the Gabar religion is good because it encourages such feelings as well as the procreation of children, which had been impossible in Astarté's first marriage, to the eunuch.[32]

The attack on monasticism in the letters on depopulation is complemented by numerous jokes about monks elsewhere, in which social uselessness is the prevalent theme. Rica is impatient with a Capuchin, in L. 49, largely because the project of founding a mission in Persia is pointless ('très utile et à l'Europe et à l'Asie'). The humour about the unchastity of monks at the beginnings of L. 57 and L. 82 may owe something to the principle that increasing the population is a useful act, which seems to be reflected in an innuendo in L. 82 about depriving monks of 'tout ce que leur profession leur rend inutile'. Another monk who symbolizes uselessness, being rude, ignorant and greedy, unconsciously reverses the idea when he describes the abbey librarian as 'bon à rien (...) parce qu'il ne travaille point pour le couvent' (L. 133). We later find that the librarian is helpful to the public, as represented by Rica, and has important views on freedom.

It is not that Usbek cannot understand the justification of the monastic life (although he says that he cannot in L. 117). Writing to his brother, a holy man, in L. 93, he treats him as one of the pure souls whose prayers and

---

[31]   Or Ghebers. They profess 'le culte de ces anciens mages' — a form of sun-worship, the original religion of Veiras' hero, Sévarias.

[32]   Montesquieu's chief source of information about sibling marriage among the Gabars was certainly Thomas Hyde, *Historia religionis veterum Persarum* (Oxford, 1700); see Adam edition, pp. 180—181 and Vernière edition, notes to pp. 137 ff. It is strange that the story in L. 67 should be set in modern times (it concerns a friend of Usbek's correspondent Ibben). In the *Esprit des lois,* Montesquieu explains the incest taboo by the need for purity within a household, and expresses astonishment that some religions have encouraged the 'égarements' of incestuous marriage (L. XXVI, Ch. XIV). See Jeannette Geffriaud Rosso, *Montesquieu et la féminité* (Pisa and Paris, 1977), pp. 367—369, 507—513.

austerities protect 'tant de peuples rebelles' from the wrath of Allah. Usbek also gives a moralizing explanation of Christian legends about the hermits of the Thebaid, to whom he seems sympathetic. But the letter is not free from irony, and in L. 123, to a 'Mullah', we hear that the prayers of holy men are ineffective; despite 'les jeûnes des immaums, et les cilices des mollaks',[33] the Turks have suffered defeat. Usbek ends with a pious hope that the Turkish and Persian branches of Islam may be reunited, 'par les larmes des saints', which does not seem to be intended ironically. The impression given by the passages on the religious life is mixed, but on the whole the criticisms are moderate, if compared with L. 117. Attacks on monks in writers such as Voltaire or the Militaire philosophe are much sharper.

The other area of religion in which uselessness is the main theme of criticism is ritual observance, the 'exercices' which for the believer should be the outward expression of worship. The tendency in the Lettres persanes, as in virtually all deist thought, is to emphasize only the inner attitudes to God, gratitude, respect and wonder, and to play down ritual as being meaningless; L. 46 is typical. The Catholicism of Spain, in L. 29, is entirely a matter of ritual, which serves only to convince the Inquisition that one is orthodox: 'Quand on tombe entre les mains de ces gens-là, heureux celui qui a toujours prié Dieu avec de petites graines de bois à la main, qui a porté sur lui deux morceaux de drap attachés à deux rubans (...)'. The French writer to whom L. 78 is ascribed has a similar view of Spain, attacking 'de petites pratiques monacales'.

Sometimes the Persians make an effort to explain ritual. Usbek cannot understand why he is prevented, as a Muslim, from eating pork, since material substances are not in themselves pure or impure; nor why he should wash in order to purify his soul.[34] The question about pork is tentatively answered in L. 17, but in L. 18 we are also given the answer of a 'mullah', a repellent tale about the Ark; pigs were created from animal excrement.[35] The legend is probably a satire of Old Testament stories. To the rational moralist, such as Usbek's friend Mirza, who in L. 10 complains of mullahs 'qui me désespèrent avec leur passages de l'Alcoran', it merely repeats what is in question, and in a most uncivilized manner to boot. Montesquieu's

[33] Montesquieu's faulty spelling is habitual; there are several such instances with Oriental words. A mullah is a theologian in the language of the Lettres persanes, or here, perhaps, a hermit.

[34] Usbek nonetheless understands the symbolism of purity in L. 2, when he exhorts his wives to wash, cleanliness being the 'image' of moral purity; the situation is similar to that with L. 93 and L. 117 as regards understanding monasticism.

[35] One of Montesquieu's Pensées (Caillois edition, Vol. I, pp. 1556–57; No. 2147) records his answer to a question about impurity from Fontenelle; Montesquieu relates it to the Cartesian principle that corporeal and spiritual things should be rigorously distinguished. Before the principle was established, he thinks, physical aversion naturally influenced moral ideas.

implication is that pork is obviously useful, as food, and so should be permitted.

The wearing of amulets and talismans, on the other hand, is acceptable, as Rica explains in L. 143. The theme of the letter, which includes a long satire on the Jesuit writer Caussin and other religious persons, is that 'l'arrangement de certaines lettres' has no material effect; if it had, amulets would truly be able to ward off danger and illness. Montesquieu is attacking the lingering belief in magic, but Rica's conservatism in the matter of the 'chiffons sacrés' which he carries about him implies that religious observances need not be abandoned if they do no harm, even though they may be superstitious. In the same way, the objection to Spanish Catholicism in L. 78 is not that ritual is bad in itself, but that it should be thought to have some effect.[36]

Most of Montesquieu's religious satire or criticism attacks more than one object, and it is difficult to separate them in analysis. The Persians' resistance to ritual observance leads, by way of the justifications for ritual found in religious texts or legends, to the subjects of revelation and the Bible. Montesquieu does not discuss the general principle of revealed truth, nor does he embark on a methodical critique of the Bible, as rationalist deists habitually did; he comments piecemeal, as the occasion arises. Usually he treats the Bible as a source of explanation, concluding that as such it is deficient; this is part of the criticism implied in L. 18, on the origin of the prohibition of pork. The same is true of L. 143, on the subject of military victory. According to Rica, 'les livres sacrés de toutes les nations' explain it in supernatural terms,[37] while his Jewish correspondent believes that magic spells can cause defeat and victory. Rica, displaying the young Montesquieu's interest in historical causation, prefers to look for natural and human factors, which he lists – the terrain, the quality and number of the soldiers, and the experience of their leaders.

With causation in science, in L. 97, the tone is more satirical, but the burden of the argument similar. Usbek tells the 'sage dervis' that European philosophers are far superior to Muslim theologians or the Koran as regards scientific knowledge. They can calculate annual rainfall, the speed of sound and light, or the best shape for a boat's hull. He limits the appeal of the 'Koran' (his remarks apply equally well to the Bible) to the aesthetic domain. It is full of useless trivialities, 'petites choses', he says, conceding

---

[36] Writing now in the *persona* of a French visitor to Spain, Montesquieu would like to see a new form of Inquisition, 'non pas contre les hérétiques, mais contre les hérésiarques, qui attribuent à de petites pratiques monacales la même efficacité qu'aux sept sacrements' (i.e. effectivemess in achieving salvation). The subject is again utility, but of the religious kind.

[37] Sacred books are 'remplies de ces terreurs paniques ou surnaturelles', a cause of defeat; the references must be to the origin of the word, that the god Pan inspired terror. Kra, *Religion in Montesquieu's Lettres persanes,* p. 161, also relates the passage to biblical incidents, victories by Gideon and Judas Maccabaeus (Judges 7. 3–7; I Maccabees 3. 56).

only that they are 'relevêes par la force et la vie de l'expression'. The combination of triviality and fine style characterizes a letter of a different type, the devout L. 39, from Hagi Ibbi, on the miracles which attended the birth of Mohammed. Some of them are ludicrous ('il vint au monde circoncis'), but the letter contains another legend which has considerable poetic appeal. It was translated by Montesquieu from his Latin source with great attention to prose rhythm.[38] The concluding ironies ('il faut avoir un coeur de fer pour ne pas croire sa sainte loi') are aimed at the apologists' principle that religion can be 'proved' by retailing miracles from sacred texts.

The Bible, it seems, lacks one of the qualities possessed by the moralizing story in L. 141, told by the wise Zulêma; she can both divert and instruct, but the Bible has no degree of utility and at best can only divert. Even so it is not subjected to any very severe criticisms. In L. 113, Montesquieu disagrees with the biblical account of creation. 'Des philosophes' (or, in the first edition, 'Ceux qui connaissent la nature et qui ont de Dieu une idée raisonnable') say that the world was created before mankind. Usbek adds that, since 'tous les historiens nous parlent d'un premier père', Adam was perhaps the survivor of some universal catastrophe, like Noah after the Flood. These remarks, which are accompanied by signs that Montesquieu considers them audacious,[39] seem to be intended to reconcile his own scientific and historical knowledge with the biblical chronology and version of creation, which gave a world history of six thousand years.[40] We might infer that Montesquieu does not believe in the truth of the Bible, which would hardly be surprising in 1721, yet he takes the trouble to devise a theory which protects it from the suggestion of falsity. The situation is the

[38]   For instance: 'une voix du Ciel fut entendue, qui termina toutes les diputes: 'Il ne sera point ôté d'entre les mains des mortels; parce que heureuses les mamelles qui l'allaiteront, et les mains qui le toucheront, et la maison qu'il habitera, et le lit où il reposera'''. Adam (his edition, p. 105) notes that the letter imitates Marana's style (Espion turc, V, L. 51), and considers that Marana's treatment was bolder.

[39]   Many of his remarks are put tentatively, in the form of questions, and the arguments inply only that the world was created 'dès le commencement' (not that it was coeternal with God, as Vernière seems to suggest; his edition, p. 238, n. 1). The sentence found in editions prior to 1758, 'il ne faut donc pas compter les années du monde; le nombre des grains de sable de la mer ne leur est pas plus comparable qu'un instant', seems to make a similar implication, expressed in 'Muslim' style so as to reduce the degree of boldness. The fragment in the Pensées entitled Histoire d'une île (Caillois edition, Vol. I, p. 1034; No. 489) is apparently an attempt to imagine a way in which a mythological account of the first men, as in Genesis, could have been invented and passed on in good faith; this too is perhaps intended to protect the Bible from criticism.

[40]   The accepted chronology since James Usher, Annales Veteris et Novis Testamenti, 1650–1654. Bossuet had used it in his Discours sur l'histoire universelle, but it appeared less and less certain. The works which seems most important in the background of L. 113 are the Espion turc, Thomas Burnet's Telluris theoria sacra, 1681, and La Peyrère's Preadamitae, 1655; see Pinot, La Chine et la formation de l'esprit philosophique, pp. 193 ff., Adam edition, p. 287, notes, and Vernière edition, notes to pp. 236–238.

same as with Tyssot's Jaques Massé a few years previously, but Massé's answers to objections to the Bible are more suspect than Usbek's speculations.[41]

THE CLERGY

If the theme of the jokes against monks is that they serve no useful purpose, with the secular clergy the main subject is the authority to which they lay claim. The very presence of jokes shows disrespect for authority. Imitating Marana, who often writes fulsomely to religious dignitaries, Usbek addresses the 'Mollak Méhêmet-Hali' in flattering terms in L. 16, but the underlying irony is easy to perceive; it continues through Usbek's question and the mullah's reply in the next two letters. In L. 125 the Indian widow snubs the 'bonze', and L. 46 is almot as irreverent concerning a Brahmin. In such passages about countries other than France, Montesquieu can allow himself considerable latitude. Apart from some straightforward humour about wordly clerics, a safe target, in L. 28 and L. 48,[42] passages of irreverence towards the French clergy are more complex.

The letter which best defines Montesquieu's attitude is L. 61, which is not humourous. Visiting Notre-Dame, Rica meets a civilized ecclesiastic who is prepared to talk about his calling. He admits that the clergy is intolerant, and explains the difficulties of winning respect in 'le monde' when endeavouring to instil morality. His conception, which must also be Montesquieu's, of the clergy's role is conveyed in two contrasting anecdotes about St Ambrose. In one, the saint heroically rebukes the emperor Theodosius for carrying out a massacre; in the order, he forbids the emperor to sit in the place reserved for priests, and here the comment is that he acted like a fanatic.[43] The contrast which is made between socially valuable morality and trivial religious observance corresponds to those made in L. 46, with the clear implication that the clergy should employ their authority only to impose moral standards. Another example comes in L. 33, about the

---

[41]   Jaques Massé, pp. 168–169 (creation), 174–179 (chronology); see Chapter 12, pp. 197ff. Massé himself gives the Austral priest, with whom he is supposed to be arguing, evidence from Chinese chronology and Greek writers which would overturn the Old Testament chronology, but says that it is impossible to doubt Moses, and produces obviously feeble arguments against the non-Christian material (pp. 175–176).

[42]   The accusation is immorality, as is self-evident with the *abbé* in L. 28 who makes an opera-girl pregnant, and slightly less so with the 'directeur' in L. 48; he is too ready to excuse women's sins.

[43]   The text of editions prior to 1758 was stronger: 'un fanatique et un fou'. Gaultier (*Lettres persanes convaincues d'impiété*, p. 101) said that the remarks about St Ambrose displayed 'l'impudence d'un Déiste' (though on p. 102 Montesquieu is said to be a Spinozist).

religious law of Islam, 'faite pour nous rendre plus justes'; in the context, being just means avoiding intemperance and the crimes to which it leads.

The attitudes of L. 61 underlie the more entertaining and varied criticisms made of bishops and the Inquisition in L. 29 and the casuist in L. 57. The casuist finds ways of evading God's commands. The bishops do much the same, by dispensing Christians from their due obligations of marriage and other promises. L. 29 is written with imitation 'Persian' naïvety, so as to present the Christian religion as the opposite of what it should be, if it conformed to the moral ideals of L. 46 and L. 83: it is full of 'une infinité de pratiques très difficiles', meaningless ritual, and unintelligible and pointless disputes. For the 'dervis' of the Inquisition, these constitute the sum total of religion.

The beginning of L. 29, about the Pope, makes a different accusation, attacking the secular power of the Church. When Rica says that the Popes could depose kings with ease, he is not expressing approval of their power. The criticism is developed in L. 24 in relation to the Pope and Louis XIV. Rica claims that the Pope's magic extends to making the king accept items of dogma and decrees against the Jansenists. In this letter, the message is conveyed through ironic astonishment; whatever Rica finds extraordinary is to be understood as being unbelievable or deplorable, for instance the king's ability to cure scrofula or his monetary measures. Rica's opinion, half-hidden by this convention, is that the Pope should not have any power over kings, or (put more abstractly) that religious values, represented by curious dogmas and anti-Jansenist intolerance, should not take precedence over secular. His view is reiterated in L. 100, where Montesquieu describes the adoption by the French of 'toutes les constitutions des papes' as a new form of servitude.

In historical terms, Montesquieu's attitude in L. 24 is a version of Gallicanism, the principle that the Church in France should conduct its affairs without ultramontane interference. In the *parlementaire* circles from which he came, Jansenism and Gallicanism were indistinguishable at the period of the *Lettres persanes*.[44] There may also be the implication that the king should be the head of the Church, as Voltaire later implied in the *Lettres philosophiques* (L. 6). However that may be, Gallican feeling, or at least resistance to papal influence, is more clearly discernible in L. 24 than any sympathy for Jansenism. In the burlesque account of the reception in France of the decree against the Jansenists, Montesquieu is probably attacking clerical propensities to persecution, as in several other letters. Similarly, L. 102 contains a witty satire of an anti-Jansenist bishop, but gives no sign of pro-Jansenist sentiment.

This is not the only area of obscurity in L. 24. The notorious remarks

[44] Shackleton, *Montesquieu*, p.17.

about the Trinity and the Real Presence, doctrines said to have been foisted on the French king by the Pope, are unusual for their boldness. Although both were often criticized by deists, the *Lettres persanes* make few references to Christian dogma, and none are so obviously derogatory. The remarks may have been an objection to Montesquieu's membership of the Académie française,[45] and he presumably had them in mind when defending himself in the *Quelques réflexions sur les Lettres persanes*, in 1754.[46] Perhaps Montesquieu simply miscalculated the degree of impertinence which would be tolerable, meaning to make a joke like that about the 'Vierge qui a mis au monde douze prophètes' in L. 1. If so, he was misled by the Turkish Spy's example; he had also expressed 'Muslim' surprise about the doctrine of the Eucharist, calling it mad, 'fou'.[47]

In many of these letters, L. 24, L. 29, L. 61 and L. 101, anticlericalism goes hand in hand with the presentation of religion as a source of strife. Perhaps the most telling comment is in L. 29: 'il n'y a jamais eu de royaume où il y ait eu tant de guerres civiles que dans celui du Christ'; here the protest is made in the name of Christian pacifism. In some ostentatiously Muslim passages, Rica and Usbek praise the peacefulness of Islam, for instance at the end of the same letter. Apart from any feelings of pacifism attributable to Montesquieu himself, the suggestion is that religion harms the state by encouraging conflict, as the cleric of L. 61 says.

No doubt it is for the same reason, regard for the utilitarian interests of society, that the issues at stake in religious disputes are said or implied to be unimportant. In L. 24 the dispute concerns women's right to read the Bible. In L. 36, like L. 29, conflicts are started, apparently for no reason at all, by theologians talking Latin: 'une autre sorte de disputeurs, qui se servent d'une langue barbare, qui semble ajouter quelque chose à la fureur et à l'opiniâtreté des combattants'.[48] Policies of intolerant persecution are

---

[45]   Ibid., pp. 86–89.

[46]   In the *Réflexions,* Montesquieu says: 'Il y a quelques traits que bien des gens ont trouvé trop hardis', and excused himself on the grounds that the Persians had to appear ignorant of French customs in the interests of realism. 'Bien loin qu'on pensât à intéresser quelque principe de notre religion, on ne se soupçonnait pas même d'imprudence. Ces traits se trouvent toujours liés avec le sentiment de surprise et d'étonnement (. . .)'; the Persians 'trouvent quelquefois nos dogmes singuliers' (Adam edition, pp. 4–5; Vernière edition, pp. 3–5). The *Réflexions* must have been written as a response to Gaultier's attack in 1751. In his *Avertissement* (p. ii), Gaultier had written that 'le Persan qui parle, est un Français très connu qui met dans la bouche du Persan ce qu'il pense lui Français en matière de religion', but did not mention L. 24 in his criticisms.

[47]   *Espion turc,* I, L. 12, in later editions; see Chapter 7, p. 100.

[48]   The relation between trivial issues and conflict is put in the form of a law in an unpublished fragment ('Haggi Ibbi à Gemchid, derviche de la montagne de Jaron'; Adam edition, pp. 419–420, Vernière edition, p. 347): 'En matière de religion, plus le sujet de la dispute est léger, plus elle devient violente'. The example is the division between the Shiite and Sunni branches of Islam. See Carayol, '*Lettres persanes* oubliées', pp. 25–26 and p. 25 n. 3, for an additional draft, concerning a more definitely trivial issue, from Germany − also no doubt a disguised version of the real issues in French religious history which Montesquieu must have had in mind.

regularly pursued, according to the Persians, for petty reasons, not only by the Spanish Inquisition in L. 29 and L. 78, but also by the French Church. In L. 61 the cleric admits that 'nous troublons l'Etat (...) pour faire recevoir des points de religion qui ne sont point fondamentaux'. A measure of Montesuqieu's indifferentism, as compared to the seventeenth century's passionate involvement in religious issues, is given by the style of reference in L. 60 to the persecution of the Huguenots: 'on s'est mal trouvé (...) en France, d'avoir fatigué des Chrétiens dont la croyance différait un peu de celle du prince'.

The positive side of such criticisms is found in L. 85, the famous letter to which the *Lettres persanes* owes much of its reputation for tolerance. The subject is again the Huguenots, but in Oriental disguise; Montesquieu had found incidents in Persian history resembling the persecution and emigration of the Protestants in France. Usbek argues that intolerant policies harm the state. Persia has lost its farmers, and may lose its artisans and merchants also. Conversely, toleration benefits society: 'ceux qui vivent dans les religions tolérées se rendent ordinairement plus utiles à leur patrie (...) toutes les religions contiennent des préceptes utiles à la société'. The argument is designed to appeal to the makers of policy; it is not based on the rights of conscience. Montesquieu accepts that it is wrong to 'affliger la conscience des autres', and ends the letter with a vehement attack on 'l'esprit d'intolerance', but seems not to be in favour of strong religious convictions, which would be contrary to the prevalent mood of indifferentism.

In other letters, he criticizes 'une certaine envie d'attirer les autres dans nos opinions' (L. 61), one of Montesquieu's periphrastic understatements, meaning religious zeal, or in L. 49 a project to send missionaries to Persia; but he also comments unfavourably on persecuted Jews who display 'une obstination invincible pour leur religion, qui va jusqu' à la folie' (L. 60). Thus the plea for tolerance has a secular basis, being founded in feelings of humanity and religious indifference. In this respect Montesquieu differs greatly from his predecessor in the advocacy of tolerance, Pierre Bayle.[49]

On the subject of Judaism, Montesquieu observes with satisfaction that persecution is on the wane in Europe. The theme of L. 60 is religious unity, the connections between Judaism, Christianity and Islam, and it ends with the hope that the divisions within Islam may be removed. A letter which is more difficult to interpret, L. 35, develops the same theme with regard to the resemblances which Usbek finds between Islam and Christianity. The letter neatly reverses the assumption that Christianity is the standard religion, and is probably a satire of reports on primitive nations by missionaries hoping to convert them. Usbek's tone of naïve enthusiasm as he

---

[49]   See especially, on the rights of the individual conscience, the *Commentaire philosophique sur ces paroles de Jésus-Christ: 'Contrains-les d'entrer'* (1686).

lists the resemblances, some of which are comic, recalls that of collections such as the *Lettres édifiantes et curieuses*.[50] The letter begins with an implied attack on intolerance (the Christians have never heard of Ali, 'qui était le plus beau de tous les hommes', so how can they be blamed for unbelief?); its ending is more fanciful than L. 60 but looks forward to the same prospect: 'tout les hommes seront étonnés de se voir sous le même étendard: tout, jusques à la Loi, sera consommé (...)'. This must mean that the individual religions will merge into one, but if 'la Loi', the law of Islam, is consumed, presumably that religion will be universal and not Muslim. There is a contrast with L. 123, in which Usbek tells a mullah that 'tu voudrais les voir réunis sous l'étendard d'Hali'. The ending of L. 35 represents, in obviously Oriental style so as to disguise the relevance for Europe, the logical conclusion of Montesquieu's protests against conflict.

CONCLUSIONS

The accepted view of the letters on religion used to be that their criticisms denoted general hostility. In recent scholarship the tendency is different. Shackleton admits that Montesquieu is a deist, but does not think that deism and Christianity are necessarily enemies; Vernière and Adam both emphasize the positive values in the *Lettres persanes*.[51] What cannot be denied, where established religion is concerned, is the preponderance of critical passages. On occasion, there is approval: the Koran can be admired for its style, Rica meets a helpful monk, St Ambrose imposes penance on a cruel emperor. But usually, in passages of satire or argument, religions are shown to be opposed to ideals of social utility and justice. Most monks are idle, theologians stir up strife, the Pope wrongfully claims secular power, intolerance damages the economic interests of the state, ritual observance is pointless. However, many of the more biting attacks are made against targets far from home, the priests of the East or the Spanish Inquisition.

This atmosphere of criticism does not mean that the Persians regard themselves as free-thinkers or *libertins*. In L. 75, Usbek deplores the fact that the French are unfaithful to their own religion, and describes free-thinkers as fickle, irrational and rebellious. He also disapproves of those Christian kings who obey the precepts of their religion only when it suits

---

[50] See Pinot, *La Chine et la formation de l'esprit philosophique*, pp. 158 ff., on these collections of reports from all over the world.

[51] See Shackleton, 'La religion de Montesquieu' (partly reproduced in his *Montesquieu*, pp. 350 ff.); Adam edition, pp. XXI ff. ('une pensée nullement sceptique, et tout au contraire occupée de maintenir les valeurs spirituelles'); Vernière edition, pp. XXXII–V, on Montesquieu's 'ordre idéal'.

them to do so on political grounds. In L. 61, he seems sympathetic towards the cleric who has to face controversy and unbelief.

Further indications concerning the book's general attitude to Christianity are provided by many passages in which Montesquieu adopts the Oriental *persona*. Often this is done for the sake of criticism, as in L. 24 or L. 85, but Montesquieu also gives the Persians frequent expressions of allegiance to Islam. If the same principle of interpretation is applied as for the critical passages, the conclusion must be that Montesquieu wishes to preserve traditional respect for religion. For instance, at the end of L. 97, after a critique of the Koran which must be directed also against the Bible, Usbek declares that his reservations have not affected his Muslim faith: 'l'esprit n'a pas corrompu le coeur; et, tandis que je vivrai, Hali sera mon prophète'. The conventional view of this and similar passages is that they are mere camouflage, and that the criticisms represent Montesquieu's real position. But such an interpretation is more like an assumption than an argument.

It is true that the Persians are not particularly consistent in their Islamic *persona*, especially as regards their attitude to Christianity. In L. 35 Usbek is tolerant, hoping to see the Christians converted; in L. 106, he hopes that they will be confounded. Rhédi regrets in L. 31 that the lack of fresh water in Venice prevents him from performing his ritual ablutions, but in L. 75 Usbek tells him that the Muslims are silly to allow this obstacle to deter them from capturing the city. On occasion the Oriental style is used to ironic effect, as in L. 16 or L. 93. But as a rule the Persians, even when critical of their own religion, remain loyal. In this respect, Rica's attitude to Muslim charms and amulets in L. 143 is the same as Usbek's in L. 97 to the Koran; no irony is perceptible. At the end of L. 60, which being a plea for tolerance has to be taken seriously, Usbek says, of the founders of the two branches of Islam: 'Je voudrais qu'on les honorât par des actes de vénération et de respect, et non pas par de vaines préférences; et qu'on cherchât à mériter leur faveur, quelque place que Dieu leur ait marquée (...)'. Whether transposed into Christian terms or not, this is a repudiation of interde-nominational conflict, combined with a statement of respect towards religious leaders. In the preceding passage, Usbek distinguishes between 'le zèle pour les progrès de la religion' (which he often attacks) and 'l'attachement qu'on doit avoir pour elle'. Those of greater piety than Montesquieu may find that to write of religious allegiance as if it were a duty is inadequate, just as Rica's conformism where amulets are concerned does not suggest that his feelings from them go very deep, but the Persians do seem to accept religion, and the profession of one's own religion, as a normal part of life. They do not appear to harbour any thoughts of replacing their Muslim faith with anything less conventional. The furthest Usbek goes is to hope for some future unification of religions and for the toleration of several religions within the state, since all contain 'des précepts utiles à la société'.

The work's most radical implications are made in L. 46. The man who prays to God and who lives in the East ('il m'arriva l'autre jour de manger un lapin dans un caravansérail'), desires to please God by living as a good citizen and father, and seems to reject allegiance to the established religions. Introducing the prayer, Usbek expresses great hesitation over 'les cérémonies', though his remarks could be read as implying doubt rather than total rejection.[52] The Troglodytes, however, create a religion which largely consists of 'cérémonies' — festivals, sacrifices and thanksgiving at temples. Their worship is a celebration of 'les faveurs des dieux', providential dispensation of rewards for virtue. This somewhat resembles the deistic forms of worship invented by writers like Veiras or Tyssot de Patot for their imaginary lands. Thus L. 12 or L. 143 imply that the element of worship in religion should be preserved, even if, in L. 46, some rituals seem meaningless, or in L. 78 lack 'efficacité'. Such conservatism on Montesquieu's part illustrates his general attitude: despite the criticisms and the satire, there is little evidence of any destructive or subversive intent, and much to show acceptance of religion as part of the established order.[53]

Against this it might be argued that the utilitarian tendency of the *Lettres persanes* is entirely irreligious. In the *Esprit des lois*, Montesquieu explicitly states the principle which underlies many passages in the early work, when at the beginning of the section on religion he says: 'Je n'examinerai donc les diverses religions du monde que par rapport au bien que l'on en tire dans l'état civil'.[54] His many examples show that religion may be valuable in society, but often is not. He claims also that with Christianity, 'la vraie religion', his intention is not to 'faire céder ses intérêts aux intérêts politiques, mais les unir'. This too clarifies the unifying tendency of the *Lettres persanes*, although in them it is moral values rather than political interests which are united with religion. The desire to unify, however, whether it involves God and the ideal of justice in L. 83, or the competing religions in L. 35, seems to spring from the awareness that secular ideals of usefulness and avoidance of conflict are intrinsically damaging to religious

---

[52] 'Les cérémonies n'ont point un degré de bonté par elles-mêmes; elles ne sont bonnes qu'avec égard et dans la supposition que Dieu les a commandées. Mais c'est la matière d'une grande discussion; on peut facilement s'y tromper; car il faut choisir les cérémonies d'une religion entre celles de deux mille'. Until the last clause, this seems to reflect caution rather than the spirit of criticism.

[53] Despite the rumours about the difficulties which the *Lettres persanes* caused Montesquieu (Shackleton, *Montesquieu*, pp. 85 ff.), the book was not subjected to any criticism until Gaultier's in 1751, which was a by-product of Jansenist and other attacks on the *Esprit des lois* (ibid., p. 364). Gaultier explains the fact that the book had not aroused censure when published by the obsesstion at the time with the Jansenist controversy (*Lettres persanes convaincues d'impiété*, p. ii), but whatever the reason there is little evidence that in 1721 Montesquieu was considered as an enemy of religion.

[54] *De l'esprit des lois*, L. XXIV, Ch. I; Caillois edition, Vol. II, p. 714.

loyalties. Although the Persians profess respect for religion, they do so from a secular standpoint. Religion must be justified in secular terms if it is to have any real value.

The intellectual categories appropriate for the description of earlier deist works cannot be applied to Montesquieu. The definition of deism given in 1721 by the *Dictionnaire de Trévoux,* quoted at the start of this chapter, adequately sums up the main characteristics of the rational natural religion of the clandestine manuscripts, but nothing like it is to be found in the *Lettres persanes.* The fundamental distinction between natural and revealed religion, reason and faith, has become irrelevant; a related distinction, the division into constructive and critical deism, is scarcely more helpful. The epistolary *genre* of the *Lettres persanes* entails the comparison of religions, but there is no confrontation between Utopian and Christian, as there had been in Foigny, Gilbert and Tyssot, who had thereby distinguished rational from fideistic religion with the utmost clarity. The society of the Troglodytes may be Utopian, but it does not exemplify natural religion.[55] Even less does Montesquieu adopt the rationalist mode of presentation by which the *Militaire philosophe* and the author of the *Examen de la religion,* among others, had methodically expounded their form of deism. The metaphysics of the *Lettres persanes* is not the work's best feature. Allowing for difference in literary ability, the *Militaire philosophe's* discussion of the concept of a God of justice is more interesting than Montesquieu's.

Seen in relation to Montesquieu, therefore, it is as if the deistic works of 1700 to 1715 had not existed. The immediate and lasting success of the *Lettres persanes* placed the earlier works inside a kind of parenthesis of intellectual history, from which they were not recovered until this century. Montesquieu's only direct precursor among the works studied above is Marana, whose attitude is not definitely deistic. From him Montesquieu took the literary conventions of the letter-series and the foreign *persona,* besides may features of style and approach. There is nothing in Marana, however, which resembles Montesquieu's secular ideals of justice and utility. There are some passages of indifferentism, but in this respect Montesquieu seems closer to the elegant tone of Saint-Evremond, with whom he also shares a certain air of conformism, the secular reduction of religious allegiance.

---

[55]   In the sense of religion acquired independently of revelation. An ambiguous sentence in L. 12 prevents us knowing whether, for the Troglodytes, knowledge of the gods is natural: 'Dès qu'il ouvrit les yeux pour les connaître, il apprit à les craindre, et la religion vint adoucir dans les moeurs ce que la nature y avait laissé de trop rude'. This suggests that religion is not innate. The remarks about religion in the chapter on the laws of nature in the *Esprit des lois* (L. I, Ch. II; Caillois edition, Vol. II, p. 235) are even more ambiguous. In any case, Montesquieu is not given to theorizing about origins.

In the history of deism, then, the *Lettres persanes* is a work which, in many important respects, is entirely original; in almost every respect, it marks a break with the traditions of deism which had already developed clandestinely or outside France. From Foigny to Tyssot, a constant progression in audacity can be traced in published work, and in the clandestine manuscripts any destructive implications were made quite explicit. Montesquieu, however, makes implications about the Bible, for instance, which are less far-reaching than those in Tyssot, and almost negligible in comparison with the Militaire philosophe's attack. There is almost nothing on doctrinal belief in the *Lettres persanes,* apart from the unfortunate witticisms in L. 24 which apparently caused so much trouble, and nothing concerning the history of Christ; on this subject Montesquieu was even more prudent than Marana.[56] The two main areas of criticism are ritual and the clergy, but there is no suggestion that either should be abolished, whereas such a suggestion is commonplace in clandestine and Utopian writings. Montesquieu's strongest condemnation is of intolerance and monasticism. On the positive side, he does not set up an artificial religion as a rival to Christianity, unlike the deists who developed the idea of natural religion. Instead, it seems that the established religion should remain, but should be tolerant, and that (as implied in L. 29 and L. 61) the clergy's role should be moral and social, not political. The only religious belief firmly stated in the *Lettres persanes* is the belief in God, and for this reason and the work's secularism it is certainly to be regarded as a deistic work, but its deism can coexist with Christianity, or at least with liberal Christianity, just as the Persians can acclimatize themselves in France.

[56] In L. 18 it is significant that, as Vernière points out (his edition, p. 45), Montesquieu omits all reference to Christ, who is mentioned in his sixteenth-century source. Similarly, although L. 39 resembles a letter about Mohammed in the *Espion turc* (V, L. 51), Adam observes (his edition, p. 105) that there is no parallel in the *Lettres persanes* for a subsequent, and similar, letter about Christ in Marana's work (V, L. 69).

CHAPTER 14

VOLTAIRE: *LETTRES PHILOSOPHIQUES*

BETWEEN CHRISTIANITY AND DEISM: RAMSAY AND LASSAY

To judge from the number of apologias published in the period from the *Lettres persanes* in 1721 to the *Lettres philosophiques* in 1734, free-thought was either on the retreat or only in mild disagreement with orthodoxy. The number rises continuously until 1720, and falls from 1725 until 1745.[1] From about 1715, moreover, works in defence of Christianity are of small distinction, except for Houtteville's in 1722. There is one outstanding figure, or rather reputation: Fénelon had died in 1715, after years of provincial exile at Cambrai, defeated by Bossuet's intransigence over Quietism, but his writings were extremely influential and did much to create a philosophic, liberal Christianity which is sometimes difficult to distinguish from deism.[2] His classicizing, moralizing novel *Télémaque,* of 1699, was one of the eighteenth century's favourite books and influenced Montesquieu in his allegory of the Troglodytes;[3] it shows the religion of classical antiquity as a vague and idealized worship of 'les dieux'.[4] His *Traité de l'existence de Dieu* (1715) greatly strengthened the concept of natural religion, which was common ground for deists and Christians.[5]

After Fénelon's death his ideas were ardently promulgated by a Scottish disciple, Andrew Michael Ramsay (1686–1743), who is best known as a founder of French freemasonry.[6] He edited and published some of Fénelon's

---

[1]   See the frontispiece of Monod, *Pascal à Chateaubriand,* a graph based on his bibliography of apologetic works.

[2]   Cf. Elie Carcassonne, *Fénelon, l'homme et l'oeuvre* (Paris, 1946), p. 115: Fénelon 'succédait à la primauté morale' which had been Bossuet's until he died in 1704. On Fénelon's influence, see Albert Chérel, *Fénelon au XVIIIe siècle en France* (Paris, 1918).

[3]   *Lettres persanes,* Vernière edition, notes to pp. 31, 36, 37.

[4]   Tocanne, *Idée de nature en France,* p. 260, observes that although Fénelon refuted deism in the *Lettres sur la métaphysique,* insisting on the necessity of adherence to a church, the setting of *Télémaque* led him to describe countries ruled by 'des rois philosophes qui reconnaissent l'existence des dieux, mais n'invoquent pas le nom du Christ'.

[5]   Pomeau, *Religion de Voltaire,* p. 52: 'Le sujet même du traité empêchait Fénelon de pousser l'apologie à son terme; démontrant l'existence de Dieu par des arguments purement rationnels, il n'établit que la vérité du déisme' (presumably in the sense of 'theism').

[6]   See A. Chérel, *A. -M. Ramsay, un aventurier religieux au XVIIIe siècle* (Paris, 1920; a revised and abridged version of part of his *Fénelon au XVIIIe siècle*) and G. D. Henderson, *Chevalier Ramsay* (Edinburgh, 1952).

works, in which it is not always clear whether the opinions expressed are Fénelon's or his own. For instance, Ramsay wrote that Christianity, in Fénelon's view, 'n'ajoute rien au pur déisme que le sacrifice de l'esprit', to which is added a mysterious quality called 'la catholicité'.[7]

This is from Ramsay's *Histoire de la vie de Fénelon* (1723), to which he appended a *Discours philosophique de l'amour de Dieu.* According to the *Discours,* 'le pur amour', the central concept in the Quietist controversy, was Fénelon's most important doctrine. It is the source of all virtues, human and divine, and is found in religious philosophies of all times and places, including those of the ancient Persians, Plato and the Stoics. Ramsay emphasizes the moral aspects of the doctrine, which at one point resembles the creed of the Troglodytes: 'tous les législateurs païens, et tous les philosophes, ont supposé comme un principe fondamental de la société, aussi bien que de la morale, qu'il faut préférer le bien public à soi'.[8] This 'sublime' morality avoids both superstition and unbelief, and is rational: 'La raison universelle, qui éclaire tous les esprits, enseigne les mêmes vérités à tous ceux qui la consultent avec attention'.[9] These generalities relegate such matters as the choice between religions to a lower plane. Theoretically Ramsay's lofty principles are compatible with Christianity, being common to all religions, but taken in isolation they are a sentimental form of deism.

Even if there had been no encouragement for deism in Fénelon's work, Ramsay's creation of the 'Fénelon legend', that of a generous Christian dignitary whose Catholicism was merely one variety of universal religious aspirations, would have blurred the differences between deism and Christianity. Ramsay's own background, including travel and the experience of different churches, was typical of the early deists: a strongly Protestant childhood in Scotland, against which he rebelled, a stay in Holland where he was influenced by the pietist Pierre Poiret, and conversion to Catholicism by Fénelon (the account of which is the culmination of the *Histoire de Fénelon*). His most famous work, the *Voyages de Cyrus,* was published in 1727. In this the young Cyrus is taken for a long tour of the Middle East, like Télémaque, and discusses religion, politics and other subjects with eminent figures such as Nebuchadnezzar, Pythagoras and Daniel. They can be identified as spokesmen for common contemporary opinions. Nebuchadnezzar is a repentant Epicurean hedonist or *libertin* and Daniel personifies Christian apologists who proved the divinity of Christ through prophecy. According to Ramsay's preface to the 1730 edition, Hermès, Pythagore and Zoroastre are 'déistes', which must signify believers in a god. Pythagore defeats Anaximandre, who represents Bossuet, in a long debate.[10]

---

[7]   Quoted here from A. Chérel, *De Télémaque à Candide* (Paris, 1958 edition), p. 184.
[8]   Cf. *Lettres persanes*, L. 12.
[9]   *Discours de l'amour de Dieu,* X (*Histoire de Fénelon* (Paris, 1724), pp. 194–198).
[10]   Although Pythagore is said to be a deist, he resembles the Fénelon of Ramsay's biography. Chérel (*A. -M. Ramsay*, p. 151) says that the characterization of Pythagore 'associe, que Ramsay l'ait voulu nettement ou non, l'idée de Fénelon, dans l'esprit des lecteurs, à l'idée d'un philosophe déiste'.

The education of Cyrus ends with Daniel's vision of the coming triumph of a religion which, the reader realizes, is Christianity. However, Ramsay's syncretism, both in the novel and the accompanying *Discours sur la mythologie des anciens,* is so heavily emphasized that it conceals any intentions he may have had of writing a fictional Christian apologia. The overriding impression is of eclectic religiosity which can absorb any and every religious belief or institution, provided they are interpreted allegorically.[11] The only exclusions are the doctrines of Fénelon's and Ramsay's opponents, Jansenists, Spinozists and Bossuet.

Another writer for whom deism and Christianity are not wholly antagonistic is the Marquis de Lassay (1652–1738), although with him deism is certainly in the ascendant. In 1726 he published privately a two-volume miscellany entitled *Recueil de différentes choses.*[12] It includes a sketch of a Utopian society, the 'Royaume des Féliciens', again set in the Austral Land. This time, however, there is no doubt that the beliefs of the Féliciens are also those of their creator, since they recur in the later description of his own religion, 'réflexions faites par un homme né dans un royaume chrétien, qui raisonne suivant les lumières de la raison, indépendamment de la religion à laquelle tous les raisonnements doivent être soumis'. Submission here is superficial, for Lassay's view is clear: the world's religions were founded for political motives, under the guise of divine revelation; if there were only one true religion, it would have been revealed to all men, because 'il ne serait point de la bonté et de la justice de Dieu de permettre que ses créatures trompées par de fausses révélations fussent entraînées dans des malheurs terribles et éternels' (II, p. 314). This may seem familiar, since it is very like arguments used in the *Examen de la religion* and by the Militaire philosophe and Chaulieu. Lassay had been taught to believe in God, the afterlife, and the truth of the Christian religion, but has not retained everything: 'La raison qui est mon guide, après avoir examiné les preuves qu'on me donne de tout cela, me fait croire sans peine à un Dieu, maître et créateur de tout'; reason also tells him that religions were invented by men. The Christian religion, which has the advantage of a 'morale admirable', is based on Original Sin. This, like other doctrines which he is required to accept, he has found impossible to believe.

Lassay's attempts to prove the immortality of the soul end in professions of agnosticism and good resolutions. Having provided as typical an example as could be wished of deism, he then affirms that he should behave as if he were a Catholic, without any sign that he regards this as hypocritical: 'Je suis pourtant persuadé que je dois me soumettre, quant à l'extérieur, à la religion

---

[11] See D. P. Walker, *The Ancient Theology,* pp. 240ff., especially p. 246, on Ramsay's syncretism, he was much indebted to Ralph Cudworth.

[12] The first edition, undated, is rare. I quote from the copy in the Bibliothèque nationale, Réserve Z. 1164–65, which has manuscript annotations presumably by Lassay. Many later copies omit the *Réflexions* on religion.

de mes pères, et du lieu dans lequel je vis, sans jamais parler contre cette religion, la regardant comme une loi du pays, et même la première' (pp. 318–319). His attitude is akin to that of Boulainviller and almost identical to that expressed at the end of the *Analyse de la religion*,[13] except that he displays no contempt for the religion of the majority; rather the reverse. His frankness may cast some light on the status of the criticisms in the *Lettres persanes*, which also do not seem to entail rejection of the 'religion of one's fathers'.

VOLTAIRE'S RELIGIOUS POEMS BEFORE 1734

Writers such as Lassay and Ramsay indicate that in the 1720s there was a convergence of opinion towards a form of Christian belief including certain important elements – rationalism and the emphasis on morality – which do not seem to be more Christian than secular. Voltaire's early works on religious subjects are in harmony with this mood. They are deistic, but only occasionally do they go beyond the limits of the territory on which deist and Christian could meet, and this occurs mainly in passages which were not intended for publication or were revised after Voltaire visited England in 1726–1729. However, an underlying current of tension, notably absent from Lassay or Ramsay, can be discerned.[14]

There are two important religious works before 1734: the poem usually known as the *Epître à Uranie* and the *Henriade*. Apart from his plays, Voltaire before 1726 is primarily a writer of verses in which there are few indications of depth. In several such pieces, he is thoroughly disrespectful about Christianity, mocking the Old Testament, the religious aspects of the war against the Turks, or the devoutness which discourages women from yielding to their natural desires.[15] He exhorts his reader to take pleasure in this life and to resist fears of later eventualities. If such fears arise in illness, as in the *Epître à Génonville*, they seem to disappear on recovery, and prospects after death are again a subject of humour (*Epître au duc de Sully;*[16] Voltaire almost corresponds to the *libertin* in L. 75 of the *Lettres persanes*, whose beliefs depend on his state of health.[17]

[13] Bibliothèque nationale ms. f.fr. 13353, pp. 138–139; see Chapter 11, p. 170.

[14] The emotional content of Voltaire's religious writings is a main theme of Pomeau's *Religion de Voltaire*, e.g. Pt. I, Ch. 3, on *Œdipe* (1719) and the *Henriade*.

[15] Epître VI, 'A une dame un peu mondaine et trop dévote'; Epître VII, 'A M. le Prince Eugène'; Epître XII, 'A Madame de G**' (*Œuvres complètes*, Moland edition, Vol. X, pp. 222; 225; 231).

[16] Epître XVII (ibid., p. 245) and Epître XX (p. 249). In the latter, Voltaire writes on Chaulieu: 'Et si d'une muse féconde Les vers aimables et polis Sauvent une âme en l'autre monde, Il ira droit en paradis'.

[17] 'Quand le médecin est auprès de mon lit, le confesseur me trouve à son avantage. Je sais bien empêcher la religion de m'affliger quand je me porte bien; mais je lui permets de me consoler quand je suis malade (...)'. The joke was an old one.

The *Epître à Uranie* is to some extent of similar inspiration. It seems originally, perhaps in 1721, to have been an answer to the poem *La grâce* by Louis Racine.[18] As we now have it, the *Epître* also imitates Chaulieu's 'trois façons de penser sur la mort', especially the first; it is to this poem that Voltaire seems to owe the idea of opposing a gentle to a fierce God.[19] Later in its history the *Epître* was given a new title, *Le pour et le contre,* which refers to the poem's two interpretations, favourable and unfavourable, of Christianity.

The first begins with forbidding images from Old Testament, and makes some direct criticisms, like Chaulieu's: the Lord is inconsistent, creating men only to punish them (by the Flood), and then creating a race worse than men, the giants (ll.32–45e).[20] The criticisms continue on the New Testament, with objections to the Redemption (ll.59–76). The more favourable 'portrait' of Christianity is much shorter. Voltaire refers to the usual proofs of the divinity of Christ, from prophecy to the more-than-human quality of his moral teachings (ll.103–8), but adds a reflection which at best is equivocal:

> Et si sur l'imposture il fonde sa doctrine
> C'est un bonheur encore d'être trompé par lui (ll.110–1).

The most famous lines come at the turning-point of the poem, after the first 'portrait'. 'Cette indigne image', says Voltaire, destroys his belief in Christianity, but he still remains sincere – presumably, sincere in his belief in God and inability to accept Christian belief:

> Mon incrédulité ne doit pas te déplaire,
> Mon coeur est ouvert à tes yeux;
> On te fait un tyran, en toi je cherche un père;
> Je ne suis pas chrétien, mais c'est pour t'aimer mieux (ll.93–96).

This is followed by an evocation of Christ in glory, which fails to dispel the impression that Christianity has been decisively rejected.

This would be valuable evidence about Voltaire's religious attitudes before the visit to England if we could be sure that the lines were written before 1726. However, it is not certain that they were present in the poem before about 1730, between the dates of the *Henriade* and the *Lettres*

---

[18] Pomeau, *Religion de Voltaire*, pp. 99–101.
[19] See Chapter 11, p. 180.
[20] Quotations are from the critical edition, with a long introduction, by I.O. Wade: 'The *Epître à Uranie'*, PMLA 47 (1932), 1066–1112.

philosophiques.[21] Leaving the question of date on one side, the *Epître à Uranie* in any case conveys the view that natural religion and morality are sufficient to please God, that Jansenist Christianity, with its 'tyrannical' God, is repugnant, and that the poet believes in God and admires Christ without committing himself to belief in Christ's divinity.

The *Epître à Uranie* still bears traces of its source, the *libertin* tradition with its somewhat apprehensive resistance to threats of hellfire. In his major work of the 1720s, the *Henriade,* fear of the evil aspects of religion (a permanent feature of Voltaire's work) is transferred from the other world to this, from punishment in Hell to the sixteenth-century religious wars and their consequences for society. These include, in a series of *tableaux* which are the most memorable passages in the poem, the assassination of Henri III by Jacques Clément, the Massacre of St Bartholomew's Day, a black Mass, and the scene in Chant X when a starving mother eats her dead child. By contrast, God is portrayed as remote and equitable. There are maleficent deities, called La Discorde and La Politique, but they are far removed from the Old Testament God whom the *Epître à Uranie* repudiates.

The narrative is largely concerned with the fact that, as a Protestant, Henri de Navarre cannot succeed to the throne of France. Before the ending, when Voltaire arranges for his hero to perceive the truth of Catholicism, Henri seems agnostic rather than Calvinist. His conversion occurs notwithstanding the almost constant insinuation in the preceding cantos that Catholicism, or at least the Catholicism of the *ligueurs,* is a priestly imposture. The Parisians besieged by Henri's forces are a credulous mob, gulled by scheming, fanatical and politically ambitious leaders into believing that their cause is the true one. It is not at all clear why Henri should change his religion, except for the sake of preventing further bloodshed and horror, a highly desirable aim, but one which is human rather than religious. The ending of the poem is in effect a lesson in indifferentism. Although the words in which Henri's conversion are narrated are carefully orthodox, the belief in Transsubstantiation seems unimportant in comparison with the atrocities of which we have read previously.[22]

[21] See Wade edition, pp. 1103–1104, and Pomeau *Religion de Voltaire,* pp. 109–110. Pomeau's arguments that the final version of the Epître dates from before 1726, an essential point in the debate over the genesis of Voltaire's religious ideas, are insubstantial. They are based partly on suppositions about what Voltaire might have inserted in a revision, if it had occurred after the return from England, and partly on the fact that in 1722 Voltaire is known to have been concerned with Louis Racine's poem *La grâce.* This consideration is irrelevant, since the question at issue relates to revisions, not the the first state of the poem. In any case, Pomeau accepts that 'il n'est pas possible de démontrer qu'aucun des manuscrits connus soit antérieur à 1731', which tends to contradict the idea that, before 1726, Voltaire was 'un rimeur anti-chrétien', the title of Part I of Pomeau's study.

[22] 'Le Christ, de nos péchés victime renaissante, De ses élus chéris nourriture vivante, Descend sur les autels à ses yeux éperdus, Et lui découvre un Dieu sous un pain qui n'est plus' (Chant X, ll.489–492). Quotations are from *La Henriade,* critical edition (second) by O. R. Taylor, in Voltaire, *Œuvres complètes,* edited by Theodore Besterman (Geneva, 1968–), Vol. II (1970). The *Henriade,* of 1728, was originally *La Ligue* (1723).

The portrayal of the bad side of religion is evidently Voltaire's chief purpose in *La Henriade*, but there is one canto, the *Chant Septième*, which contains a sort of deistic theology. St Louis shows Henri round the celestial realms, where Death conducts men of various faiths before 'Cet Etre infini qu'on sert et qu'on ignore' (VII, 1.73); not an exclusively Christian deity, it seems. Will they be punished by the divine judge? Not for their 'ignorance', that is, not for belonging to another religion than the true one.[23] They will apparently be judged according to their obedience to the laws of morality, the natural law, which is an idea expressed in the *Epître à Uranie*, but also has a long history in the debate over the 'salut des païens'.[24] Nature guides and enlightens us; 'De l'instinct des vertus elle aime à nous remplir' (VII, 1. 93, variants). It also seems, because Voltaire is poetically ambiguous, that the laws of nature, rather than creed, determine God's judgements on 'us', the Christians, as well as those of other faiths.[25]

Stripped of all its equivocal phrasing, this passage of Chant VII is advancing the deistic view that all religious creeds are regarded with equal tolerance, or indifference, by God, and that men of all religions should try to be virtuous rather than believe all that the priests tell them. In 1728, the change of emphasis from doctrine to morality was far from new as a religious opinion, but it was an innovation to convey it in official poetry at its most elevated, a national epic.

Henri's task in the eighth canto is, therefore, to demonstrate his virtue, a more important qualification for the French throne, or so we understand, than the Catholic faith which is added later. Examined in his task by St Louis (VIII, ll.439–442), Henri pardons the vanquished instead of punishing them, 'tel qu'un père attentif' (1.476). In the last canto the same thing happens, when he offers food to the starving Parisians instead of slaughtering them (X, ll.333–378). The priests claim that Henri is trying to make them all into heretics (ll.379–410),[26] but St Louis intercedes with

---

[23] See Taylor edition, pp. 514–516, for three versions of the relevant passage. The line quoted, 1.73, echoes La Fare's 'Cet Etre universel qui du rivage More Promène ses regards aux climats de l'aurore', in his *Ode à l'honneur de la religion*; see Chapter 11, p. 179.

[24] To mention only works considered already, it is a theme of Marana's *Espion turc*, appears in the *Lettres persanes* (L. 35), and is La Mothe le Vayer's argument about theists in *De la vertu des païens*. See Capéran, *Salut des infidèles, passim*.

[25] The final text, dating from after 1730 for this passage, favours natural religion more clearly than the 1728 version; but as Henri soliloquizes about the pagans, deftly converting them into Christians on the basis of their virtue ('Et si leur coeur fut juste, ils ont été Chrétiens', 1.111), he is warned by a voice of thunder not to rely on his reason. This should be interpreted as reflecting Voltaire's view of what it was and was not permissible to print in about 1730 in a verse epic.

[26] The lines on the Trinity are: 'La puissance, l'amour, avec l'intelligence Unis et divisés, composent son essence' (ll.425–6). The author of a letter to the *Journal de Trévoux* in 1731 complained that this was a bad definition, the terms being 'plus propres à altérer le dogme qu'à l'établir et l'enseigner' (quoted by R. E. Florida, *Voltaire and the Socinians*, SVEC 122 (1974), pp. 78–79).

God, saying that so good a man should not be abandoned to error. His intercession is successful. Responding, God speaks and Henri sees the truth:

> Il avoue, avec foi, que la religion
> Est au-dessus de l'homme, et confond la raison (ll.483—484).

In other words, he accepts the fideistic Catholicism of Charron's time, which means that he can become King of France. Voltaire repeats that Henri's new religion is anti-rational; he submits to 'ces mystères dont son esprit s'étonne' (1.494).

In the *Henriade,* then, as in Marana, Montesquieu and the *libertin* poets, morality counts for more than belief. A just God rewards the good and punishes the bad; Henri the virtuous Calvinist is granted a Catholic kingdom. However, nothing that Voltaire writes, taken strictly, is necessarily un-Christian. There are hints of natural religion, but as in the *Epître à Uranie* Voltaire pays homage, in some degree, to Christianity. He also conveys that the true religion is usually perverted by political and religious impostors.

As regards degrees of speculative unorthodoxy Voltaire's early works are rather less advanced than the universalist Ramsay or the conformist deist Lassay, but the tension and conflict which are lacking in these writers, and not at all prominent in Montesquieu, are found anew in Voltaire. He does not attack Christianity as he did after 1760, during the campaign against 'l'infâme', or as the clandestine manuscripts had already, but he treats religious matters with an intensity which is always perceptible, even when the tone is ambiguous, outwardly orthodox or flippant. In the *Lettres philosophiques,* which were probably being written soon after the final versions of the *Epître à Uranie* and the *Henriade,*[27] the same elements of secular morality, theism and indifferentism reappear, in a form which is both clearer and more elaborately camouflaged.

THE *LETTRES PHILOSOPHIQUES*: THE LETTERS ON THE QUAKERS

In broad terms, the work known also as the *Lettres anglaises,* first published in England in 1733 under the title *Letters concerning the English Nation,* contains Voltaire's considered reaction to his experiences in England from 1726 to 1729, after the humiliating fiasco of his quarrel with the Chevalier

---

[27] Lanson's opinoin was that Voltaire wrote most of the *Lettres* from 1729 to 1731, and revised them during 1732 (Introduction, pp. XXXV—XL, to his critical edition of the *Lettres philosophiques,* first published Paris, 1909). André M. Rousseau gives reasons for supposing that the earliest drafts went back to 1727. See the *Notes complémentaires* in his re-issue of Lanson's edition, 2 vols. (Paris, 1964), Vol. II, pp. 309—312. Quotations here are from the re-issue, cited as Lanson-Rousseau edition.

de Rohan and his vain attempts to seek redress.[28] The book has the air of consummating Voltaire's break with the French society in which his previous career had been so brilliant. No longer is he a poet; even tragic or epic verse is less weighty than the subjects to which he now addresses himself, which include politics, science and philosophy, as well as religion and literature. Between 1729 and 1733 he had made another new start, as a historian, with the *Histoire de Charles XII,* which was bold enough for the police to confiscate it in 1731. His tragedy *Zaïre,* of 1732, the heroine of which is caught in the mutual intolerance of Muslims and Christians, was also controversial; it has some notorious lines about religion being a matter of local education,[29] and as a whole it repeats the lesson of the *Henriade,* that virtue (touchingly portrayed) is more important than creed. The *Lettres philosophiques* take the audacities of the works around 1730 considerably further, and give them the status of mature reflection, rather than occasional flashes of irreverence or heterodoxy.

Lanson's celebrated description of the book, 'la première bombe lancée contre l'Ancien Régime',[30] may be exaggerated, but there is no doubt that a new set of values is being propounded, utilitarian and secular, as in Montesquieu, and more or less overtly in opposition to the aristocratic and Chrisitian values of the seventeenth century. Unlike Montesquieu, who scatters passages on religion through all his letters, Voltaire groups the letters on religion at the beginning, and then allows the subject to fade out gradually in two letters about politics. Thereafter, apart from some isolated passages, we have only a philosophical letter on the soul ('Sur M. Locke') and the last-minute 'twenty-fifth letter', the hostile commentary on Pascal, added for the French edition in 1734.

The *persona* adopted is that of a cultivated Frenchman reporting on a strange country which is both admirable and barbarous. This is the situation of missionaries, or of Lahontan in his *Mémoires,* confronted with noble savages. In this case they are Quakers. Voltaire's reason for beginning with four letters about them was no doubt that he knew the Quakers of London, who had impressed him, and the letters seem designed to overcome the

---

[28]   For the details see Besterman, *Voltaire* (3rd edition, Oxford, 1976) pp. 113–116. On Voltaire in England, ibid., pp. 117–130; A. M. Rousseau, *L'Angleterre et Voltaire,* SVEC, 145–147 (1976), P. I, section III; etc. On the *Lettres philosophiques,* see also Pomeau, *Religion de Voltaire,* Pt. II, Ch. I; the editions by Raymond Naves (Classiques Garnier, 1964 issue) and F. A. Taylor (Oxford, 1943) have valuable annotation. On Voltaire's English version see W. Harcourt Brown, 'The Composition of the *Letters concerning the English Nation',* in *The Age of the Enlightenment,* Studies presented to Theodore Besterman, edited by W. H. Barber and others (Edinburgh and London, 1967), pp. 15–34, and A. M. Rousseau, 'Naissance d'un livre et d'un texte: les *Letters concerning the English Nation',* in *Voltaire and the English,* Transactions of the Oxford Colloquium from 26 to 28 May 1978, SVEC 179 (1979), pp. 25–46 (volume cited henceforth as *Voltaire and the English*).

[29]   *Zaïre* ruefully remarks that 'les soins qu'on prend de notre enfance Forment nos sentiments, nos moeurs, notre croyance. J'eusse été près du Gange esclave des faux dieux, Chrétienne dans Paris, Musulmane en ces lieux. L'instruction fait tout (...)' (Act I, sc.i).

[30]   Lanson, *Voltaire,* p. 52 (Paris, 1960 edition).

prejudices of the French public also.[31] The Frenchman takes a condescending interest in 'un peuple si extraordinaire', and goes to observe one of them. He is mildly shocked and amused by the Quaker's social non-conformity, rebuked for swearing when he hears that the Quaker is not baptized, defeated in argument by New Testament erudition and, finally, given a lecture on the moral significance of Quaker customs, such as the use of 'thou' and avoidance of ornament in dress, which had struck him as comical.

In this first letter especially, every word is charged with meaning. The stylistic method employed is to draw contrasts between the externals of human behaviour (by describing it in an ironically naïve, uncomprehending manner), and the true values which the behaviour obscures. Insincere French politeness, for example, is described from outside, as it were, as 'l'usage de tirer une jambe derrière l'autre, et de porter à la main ce qui est fait pour couvrir la tête'; the Quaker by contrast reveals genuine friendship in 'l'air ouvert et humain de son visage'. The Quaker in turn draws contrasts between the outward show and inner reality: the empty pastimes of social life, 'les assemblées de plaisir, les spectacles, le jeu', as opposed to 'des coeurs en qui Dieu doit habiter'; or, in the superb final image which is a cluster of such contraries, religious thanksgiving for military victory as opposed to the brutal realities of war.[32] If we follow the series of contrasts through the letter, we find that the values attributed to the Quaker are humanitarianism, sincerity, tolerance, learning and pacifism.

This technique of style, similar to the way in which Montesquieu's Persians (or Marana's Spy) describe unfamiliar things in France, is virtually an automatic method of giving true moral values primacy over the rituals of society and religion. The Quaker treats the sacrament of baptism as a pointless charade: 'nous ne pensons pas que le Christianisme consiste à jeter de l'eau froide sur la tête, avec un peu de sel'. For him Christianity is spiritual, and the sacraments are 'des cérémonies judaïques'. The difference between Montesquieu and Voltaire is that the latter's spokesman is firmly Christian, at least in his own eyes — it would be ingenuous to suppose that the Frenchman's Catholic disapproval of him is meant seriously. However, it is hard to find any specifically Christian elements in the positive tenets his words imply.

[31] On Voltaire and the Quakers, see E. Philips, 'Le Quaker vu par Voltaire', RHLF 39 (1932), 161–177; W. H. Barber, 'Voltaire and Quakerism: Enlightenment and the Inner Light', SVEC 24 (1963), 81–109; Pomeau, *Religion de Voltaire*, pp. 131–137; and the editions by Lanson-Rousseau, Vol. I, pp. 19–22, and Naves, pp. 182–190.

[32] 'Notre Dieu qui nous a ordonné d'aimer nos ennemis et de souffrir sans murmure ne veut pas sans doute que nous passions la mer pour aller égorger nos frères, parce que des meurtriers vêtus de rouge avec un bonnet haut de deux pieds enrôlent des citoyens en faisant du bruit avec deux petits bâtons sur une peau d'âne bien tendue, et lorsqu'après des batailles gagnées tout Londres brille d'illuminations, que le Ciel est enflammé de fusées, que l'air retentit du bruit des actions de grâces, des cloches, des orgues, des canons, nous gémissons en silence sur ces meurtres qui causent la publique allégresse'.

The second letter, in which Voltaire goes to a Quaker service, is more straightforward. There is a new subject, that of revelation, and the issue is whether it is the individual or the Church who can rightfully claim true knowledge of God. The French visitor is again put off by indecorous Quaker behaviour, and on this occasion the Quaker's defence is less convincing. He admits that the Quakers do not know if a member of the congregation who rises in order to bear witness will be 'inspiré par l'esprit ou par la folie'. When the Catholic naturally inquires why they have no clergy (instead of relying on doubtfully valid inspiration), he is met with a powerful piece of anti-clericalism, emphasizing the fact that priests receive money for their duties. Unable to counter this, he nonetheless remains sceptical about the radical Protestant principle of 'révélation immédiate'. He is to be silenced only when the Quaker resorts to philosophical theism, in a passage of metaphysics based on the premiss that the mind receives all its ideas from God: 'tu n'as donc qu'à ouvrir les yeux à cette vérité qui éclaire tous les hommes, alors tu verras la vérité et la feras voir'. Some Malebranchian expressions ('tu vis dans Dieu, tu agis, tu penses dans Dieu') cause the Frenchman to comment that this is 'le Pére Malebranche tout pur'.

Coming after the rejection of the Catholic and Protestant authorities for religious belief, the Church and the Bible,[33] this passage is the nearest approach in the *Lettres philosophiques* to the rationalist deists' affirmation that each individual has innate knowledge of God. It is interesting that, like Gilbert and the clandestine authors, Voltaire is open to Malebranche's influence.[34] The Quaker's last speech, which has some resemblances with L. 13,[35] might perhaps represent Voltaire's own opinion, but there are some contrary considerations. In L. 13, he calls Malebranche's ideas 'illusions sublimes'. In the third chapter of the *Traité de métaphysique,* written soon after the *Lettres,* Voltaire pursues a line of reasoning about ideas which is almost identical to that in L. 2, and which he presents as a summary of Malebranche, but it is then criticized radically. Voltaire says that it is unintelligible and involves an absurd kind of pantheism.[36] The *Traité* is not necessarily a guide to the

---

[33] According to the Quaker, 'Quiconque (...) priera Dieu de l'éclairer, et qui annoncera des vérités évangéliques qu'il sentira, que celui-ci soit sûr que Dieu l'inspire'. But Gospels truths are immediately lost to sight in the following 'Malebranchian' passage. Lanson's notes (Lanson-Rousseau edition, Vol. I, p. 30, n. 11, etc.) give material from Robert Barclay which might be Voltaire's source.

[34] See Chapter 8, pp. 119, etc., Chapter 10, p. 140, etc., Chapter, pp. 159, 160, etc.; Pomeau, *Religion de Voltaire,* pp. 95, 135–136.

[35] The Quaker denies that we can move or have ideas through our own agency (Lanson-Rousseau edition, Vol, I, p. 25); in L. 13, Voltaire emphasizes that we cannot understand how bodies have ideas (ibid., p. 173, e.g.).

[36] On the date of the *Traité,* 1734 to 1737, see I. O. Wade, *Studies on Voltaire, with some unpublished papers of Mme du Châtelet* (Princeton, 1947), pp. 56–114, and Pomeau, *Religion de Voltaire,* pp. 191–192. Referring to Malebranche's theory of vision in God, Voltaire comments that 'pour réduire le système du père Malebranche à quelque chose d'intelligible, on est obligé de recourir au spinosisme, d'imaginer que le total de l'univers est Dieu, que ce Dieu agit dans tous les êtres, (...) est pensée et caillou, a toutes les parties de lui-même détruites à tout moment, et enfin toutes les absurdités qui découlent nécessairement de ce principe' (*Traité de métaphysique,* edited by H. Temple Patterson (Manchester, 1937), p. 25).

meaning of the *Lettres,* but the third chapter does imply that if Voltaire accepted Malebranche's principles in 1734 he must have abandoned them shortly afterwards. The conclusion of the chapter in the *Traité* is scepticism. and (to return to L. 2) a similarly non-committal conclusion seems to be intended when the Frenchman fails either to agree or to disagree explicitly with the Quaker; all he does is to note the similarity with Malebranche.

The doctrine of the Quakers in L. 1 and L. 2 can briefly be described as dependence on God and adherence to a moral code which is presented as Christian. In their history, which occupies L. 3 and L. 4, the persecution which they face, and eventually overcome, is related in a manner consistent with these principles. In L. 3, the story tells how George Fox established Quakerism. Underlying the frequently absurd and caricatural account is an important issue, the question of the causes of religion. Commentators have noted the way in which Voltaire utilizes New Testament phraseology so as to assimilate Fox to Jesus, with bad implications for Christianity: 'délivré de sa prison, il courut les champs avec une douzaine de prosélytes, prêchant toujours contre le clergé, et fouetté de temps en temps'.[37] These and other phrases[38] do not only satirize Quakerism and the New Testament; they also suggest how a new religion spreads. Voltaire's reasons are that 'les persécutions ne servent presque jamais qu'à faire des prosélytes' and 'l'-enthousiasme est une maladie qui se gagne'. ('Enthusiasm' in the sense of religious fervour.) He does not, of course, acknowledge the spirital force of Fox's message. Fox's 'grande habitude d'inspiration' is described in the same way as the Quaker meeting in L. 2, from the viewpoint of the enlightened man of the world contemplating lower-class superstition. The model might well have been Saint-Evremond narrating the adventure of the Irish faith-healer.[39] But despite the ironies, Fox is sincere and pacific, like the Quaker in L. 1, and earns sympathy as a victim of intolerance.

Much of L. 3 is devoted to denouncing the clerical authorities who are responsible for the persecution. The narrative shows how suitable retribution overtakes Fox's persecutors; an Anglican vicar is pilloried in Fox's place, and a magistrate dies of apoplexy just as he is sending some Quakers to prison. The neat providentialism recalls that of some tales in the *Lettres persanes,* such as L. 141. The use of humour conveys indifference to religion by making the convictions both of Fox and the Anglicans seem trivial.

The end of the narrative comes when Robert Barclay appeals directly to Charles II. Voltaire translates part of his letter, asserting that 'la persécution

---

[37] Lanson-Rousseau edition, Vol. I, p. 36; Naves edition, p. 179; Pomeau, *Religion de Voltaire,* p. 132. Pomeau and Barber ('Voltaire and Quakerism', p. 86) also note resemblances with the Jansenist *convulsionnaires,* as did Voltaire himself in a letter to Cardinal Fleury (Besterman D. 761, 23 June 1734).

[38] Fox 's'avisa de prêcher en vrai apôtre à ce qu'il prétendait, c'est à dire sans savoir lire ni écrire'; 'Fox tendit l'autre joue'.

[39] See Chapter 4, p. 48; Saint-Evremond, *Œuvres en prose,* Ternois edition, Vol. IV, pp. 71–89.

cessa', which is doubtful.[40] Perhaps Voltaire wanted to think that a letter to a king from 'un particulier obscur' could be effective. In L. 4, Quakerism acquires prestige; according to Voltaire, leading Quakers are patronized by kings. His style reflects their new-found respectability; he continues to adapt the New Testament ('les amis semèrent aussi en Allemagne, mais ils recueillirent peu'), but without any sharp ironies. Nor is there any more persecution, except that William Penn's father, driven to despair by his son's refusal to 'vivre comme un autre' and address royalty in the proper manner, expels him from the paternal home; but later comes a touching death-bed reunion. Previously, the theme has been Penn's success in polite society, both with men and women, for different reasons.[41] He and Fox also manage to impress the aunt of George I, 'femme illustre par son esprit et son savoir'.

This emphasis on the social advance of Quakerism shows that, once persecution is removed, a religion can be absorbed into society and will no longer cause disruption. The best possible relationship between religion and society is shown when Penn founds Philadelphia, the Utopian community which is Voltaire's counterpart to the imaginary lands of earlier deistic works. The element of absurdity, so prominent before, is almost absent here. In Pennsylvania, the first law is tolerance, the second fraternity to all theists; equality and pacifism, not the priesthood, are in command ('un gouvernement sans prêtres'). The state is still Christian, or so it seems from references to 'les autres chrétiens', but its religion is one of social and moral values, like that of Montesquieu's Troglodytes.

The remainder of the history tells of tolerance in England and prosperity in Pennsylvania, until it concludes, rather surprisingly, with Quakerism in decline, at least in London. This apparently pessimistic ending to the success-story is in fact the completion of the process of secularization. The young generation of Quakers are becoming infected by the values of society, and want to 'jouir, avoir des honneurs, des boutons et des manchettes, ils sont honteux d'être Quakers, et se font Protestants pour être à la mode'. Conformism and indifference have replaced religious conviction.

The metamorphosis of Quakerism related in these two letters, personified in the contrast between the graceless Fox of L. 3 and the upright Penn of L. 4, is essentially the loss of those elements in Quakerism which had repelled the Frenchman of L. 1. The idiosyncrasies of behaviour gradually disappear, but pacifism, integrity, tolerance and belief in God remain. It is the same with the evangelicalism of the first two letters. By the end of L. 4, Quakerism has become, in the contemporary phrase, 'la religion des honnêtes gens', or of the Quaker at the very beginning of the *Lettres,* whose air is 'noble' and 'engageant'. If original Quakerism is ludicrous and fanatical, like

---

[40] See Lanson-Rousseau edition, p. 44, n. 38.

[41] Needless to say, the reasons are human, not divine. Men are influenced because Penn has 'de la noblesse dans sa physionomie et dans ses manières'; women, because he is 'jeune, beau et bien fait'.

(so Voltaire implies, rather obviously) early Christianity, we may assume also that the final state of Quakerism is what Voltaire would like to see as the final state of Christianity: theistic secularism.

The first letters describe a religion of which Voltaire approves, on the whole. The sequence of letters which follows, interrupted by L. 7, on a different subject, does the opposite: they attack the power of the clergy and of established religion generally.[42] The unifying theme is indifference, in an exact sense. Religion is indifferent, both for laity and clergy, because – as presented by Voltaire – it has no influence on behaviour. The free Englishman chooses his religion at his pleasure, 'va au Ciel par le chemin qui lui plaît', and refuses to let the Puritans spoil his Sunday, when the entire nation 'va au sermon, au cabaret, et chez les filles de joie'. Members of the Stock Exchange are also 'content' with their various meaningless ceremonies, which are described in the manner of baptism in L. 1, and do not permit these trivial differences to interfere with business.[43] The nature of the clergy's faith is indicated by a definition given in passing: 'leur véritable religion, celle où l'on fait fortune'. As for the pleasures of life, the English clergyman is chaste because, unlike the French *abbé* at the end of L. 5, he has missed the training afforded by the company of worldly women, and the Scottish clergyman is hostile to luxury only because he is poorly paid.

In these and similar examples, the irony lies in the implication that the clergy, despite its position, would behave in as un-Christian or immoral a way as anyone else if it had the chance. Montesquieu's jokes had been confined to monks and *abbés*; Voltaire's are more subtle and of wider scope.

Voltaire is also protesing against the clergy's attempts to regulate secular living. The English Sunday is a notorious instance; but the Scottish Presbyterians had also tried to impose their authority on a king, Charles II, who 'se lassa bientôt d'être roi de ces pédants', and escaped from them. Weightier ecclesiastical claims to authority are the subject of the central

---

[42] There is some reason to think that L. 5 and L. 6 originally formed a single letter, and were separated after the addition of three long paragraphs about Whig policy, now in L. 5. See Lanson-Rousseau edition, Vol. I, p. 77, n. 13, and Vol. II, p. 303. Voltaire also put some anti-clerical remarks into his 'translations' from the English in the letters on literature; Hamlet's 'To be or not to be' soliloquy, in Voltaire's version, contains the line 'De nos prêtres menteurs bénir l'hypocrisie' (L. 18), and a piece on Italy in L. 20, attributed to Lord Hervey in later editions (Lanson–Rousseau edition, Vol. II, p. 120, variants) has the lines: 'L'extravagante comédie Que souvent l'Inquisition Veut qu'on nomme religion Mais qu'ici nous nommons folie'; the domination of the priesthood causes the economic desolation of the country. Other such translations were added in later editions; see Lanson-Rousseau edition, Vol. II, pp. 83–87, variants.

[43] This passage is the subject of a penetrating commentary by Erich Auerbach, *Mimesis* (Princeton, 1953; German original, Berne, 1946), Ch. 16, pp. 353–356.

portions of L. 5. Here, the clergy act in accordance with their ostensible beliefs, for once, but again in an anti-social manner: imbued with a spirit of intolerance, they do their best to stir up sectarian conflict. As Voltaire describes it, Anglican influence still presents a threat to civil peace, and he reports favourably on the Whig policy of reducing Church power, on the purely nominal authority of the bishops in Parliament, and on the fact that the clergy have to swear to obey the Church 'as by law established'.[44] His version of the Whig attitude to the question of the relation between Church and State explicitly gives the principle of secular control of religion (the Whigs 'aiment mieux même que les évêques tirent leur autorité du Parlement plutôt que des apôtres'). The preceding passage about strife shows that behind this statement lies the fear that, without such control, religion will be disruptive of civil peace.

The subject of relgous conflict continues in L. 8, 'Sur le Parlement', which is largely a historical treatment of civil war. It reiterates the message that while religion was at one time a cause of war, it is no longer. In L. 5, Voltaire had said that 'la rage des sectes a fini en Angleterre avec les guerres civiles'; now he adds that the English have no desire to 's'égorger dorénavant pour des syllogismes'. More plainly put, the English have become indifferent to religious quarrels. Like Montesquieu, Voltaire decries the triviality of the issues at stake. The sensible Romans, he says, 'ne se battaient point pour décider si le *Flamen* devait porter sa chemise par-dessus sa robe, ou sa robe pardessus sa chemise, et si les poulets doivent manger et boire, ou bien manger seulement, pour qu'on prît les augures'. As is confirmed by a pun on the word 'espèce' in the next sentence, this is a parody of the 'kinds' of communion in Catholicism and Protestantism and on differences in the dress of clergymen.[45]

In the rest of L. 8 Voltaire makes an indifferentist point almost undetectably, by failing to mention religion when it is a natural part of the subject. On the wars between England and France, he writes in such a way as to exclude entirely the idea that any religious factors were involved, and about the Wars of Religion in the sixteenth century his observation (in an astonishing contrast with the *Henriade*) is that 'il s'agissait seulement de savoir si on serait l'esclave des Guises'. In the Fronde, cardinals are military leaders, but are not fighting about religion. There is a kind of logic about this perverse treatment of war. Civil war can sometimes be justified, it seems, on secular grounds, as when the English fight for 'une liberté sage', but it is always wrong when undertaken for religious reasons. Whenever possible Voltaire explains war in non-religious terms, even though he obviously fears the power of religion to cause strife.

[44]   See Lanson-Rousseau edition, Vol. I, p. 68, n. 20, and Vol. II, p. 303, note to p. 65, 1.4, on contemporary French disputes between 'Parlements' and clergy.

[45]   The pun on 'espèces' is also in the *Lettres persanes*; the Pope makes the King believe 'que le pain qu'on mange n'est pas du pain, ou que le vin qu'on boit n'est pas du vin, et mille autres choses de cette espèce' (L. 24).

The next letter, L. 9, returns to the relation between religion and politics. The history of the English government shows the nation shaking off ecclesiastical domination as it makes its way to what Voltaire sees as modern freedom and prosperity. Here he attacks medieval Church power openly and vehemently; druids, bishops and popes are lumped together with barons and other nobles as oppressors and exploiters of 'le peuple'. The popes 'firent trembler les rois, les déposèrent, les firent assassiner, et tirèrent à eux tout l'argent qu'ils purent de l'Europe', which is an almost exact repetition of the accusations made in the *Lettres persanes.*[46] Montesquieu's comment about the Pope, 'on ne le craint plus' in L. 29, would serve as a summary of the remainder of L. 9; the time of the Church's secular power is set firmly in the past. This does not fit in very well with what L. 5 had said about the dangers to peace resulting from the propensities of the clergy, but both letters convey that religion has lost ground. History is being used in a quasi-providentialist way to drive home a secular moral. There can be no doubt that the progress of secularism is something of which Voltaire greatly approves and which he wishes to encourage. He relates that England has achieved freedom from religion, as from other forces; what he implies is that it must be right because it has happened, and that it should happen in other countries as well.

Taken as a group, the four letters from L. 5 cover the interconnected subjects of persecution, intolerance, conflict and the power of the clergy, which are also treated inseparably in many passages of the *Lettres persanes.* As is indicated by the many similarities of detail, Voltaire is close to Montesquieu on the undesirability of religious war, the pettiness of its causes, the part played by the clergy in starting it and, in general, on the disadvantages of allowing religious authorities to exercise temporal power. Voltaire's attack is the more concentrated, however, and there are no signs, as there are in Montesquieu, of any desire to be conciliatory towards the Church. In the *Lettres persanes* the clergy is satirized, but we can infer that it might fulfil a valuable moral and social role; in the *Lettres philosophiques,* Voltaire apparently shares the Quaker's view (in L. 2) that the clergy is unnecessary.

L. 7 AND L. 13, DR CLARKE AND MR LOCKE

In the dialogues with the Quaker in L. 1 and L. 2, Voltaire touches on theological questions, but such matters were extremely delicate, and in the two letters devoted to them he takes even greater stylistic precautions than

---

[46] L. 29: formerly, popes deposed kings with ease; the succession from St Peter is rich, since the Pope has 'des trésors immenses, et un grand pays sous sa domination'. Montesquieu makes no reference to assassination.

elsewhere. As a result, L. 7 on the Trinity and L. 13 on the soul require considerable care in analysis. In both, Voltaire pretends to be flippant, and communicates his own opinion obliquely by reporting the opinions of eminent Englishmen.

In L. 7 the issue is stated clearly enough to start with: is God the Father 'plus grand' than the Son? But the formulation is vague. The question for Voltaire and his contemporaries can also be simply stated, although he refers to the technical terms of 'consubstantialité' (which he gets wrong);[47] it was whether Christ was human or divine. There can be little doubt that in Voltaire's eyes Christ was the human founder of a world religion, and that the doctrine of the Trinity was a theological fabrication. What L. 7 actually suggests is much less audacious: that God may be 'greater' than Christ, if the Arians are correct, and should be treated with more honour. This is the meaning of an anecdote about a bishop and an emperor which displays little respect for the Son.[48] It is also suggested that the Trinity doctrine cannot be reconciled with reason. The remark about Newton, 'ce philosophe pensait que les Unitaires raisonnaient plus géométriquement que nous', means that the idea 'three in one' is rationally speaking absurd.[49] Finally, what we are told about the public's reception of books by Samuel Clarke, who had some influence on Voltaire himself, indicates that the existence of God can be proved, though with difficulty, that the truth of Christianity cannot, and that 'les Unitaires', who believe only in the divinity of God, have the evidence from early Christianity on their side.[50] This last insinuation is reinforced by a reference soon after to 'trois cents ans de triomphe' enjoyed by the Arian movement, which considerably overstates its success.

The second half of the letter is indifferentist. Clarke's Arianism lost him an archbishopric: Voltaire comments that he should not have been so scrupulous, 'il valait mieux être primat d'Angleterre que curé arien'. Theological issues are unimportant now, 'on est si tiède à présent sur tout cela': here Voltaire is anticipating his historical sketch in L. 8 by asserting that the time for religious wars is over, and implying that philosophical opinions will

---

[47] Voltaire wrote 'consubstantiation'. The error was noted by Lanson (Lanson–Rousseau edition, Vol. I, pp. 81–82).

[48] The bishop, in order to persuade the emperor that his son deserves respect, tweaks the boy's nose, and when the emperor is angry takes his anger as proof that the son should be respected. However, the anecdote itself, confusingly, suggests disrespect for the son.

[49] The first draft of L. 13 included a remark that the mysteries of the Trinity and the Eucharist are 'contraires aux démonstrations connues' (Lanson-Rousseau edition, Vol. I, p. 201); in the 1734 version, the corresponding passage is less pointed (ibid., p. 175).

[50] 'C'est lui qui est l'auteur d'un livre assez peu entendu, mais estimé, sur l'existence de Dieu, et d'un autre plus intelligible, mais assez méprisé, sur la vérité de la religion chrétienne (...) il s'est contenté de faire imprimer un livre qui contient tous les témoignages des premiers siècles pour et contre les unitaires, et a laissé au lecteur le soin de compter les voix et de juger'. See W. H. Barber, 'Voltaire and Samuel Clarke', in *Voltaire and the English*, pp. 47–61, on Voltaire's use of Clarke's arguments.

not be so contentious. This is followed up by the ending, which, like that of L. 13, contrasts philosophical views and religious movements with regard to keeping the peace; the former present no danger to society. The accusation which Voltaire is answering here has not been mentioned; it is that the unorthodox views of Newton and Clarke are dangerous because they damage the Christian religion, which is the basis of social order. As we have seen from L. 8, not to mention the *Henriade,* Voltaire's own belief is that it is Christian fanaticism which presents the real threat to peace.

One of the problems with L. 8 concerns the history of deism in England and Voltaire's reaction to it. The movement is commonly considered to have begun at about the same time as in France, in the 1690s, with the publications of Charles Blount and John Toland, and even if Voltaire knew nothing of any published work he knew Bolingbroke, whose ideas were deistic, as a personal friend and patron.[51] Yet instead of saying anything about the English deists, he confines himself to 'une petite secte composée d'ecclésiastiques et de quelques séculiers très savants' to which he gives the old-fashioned name of 'Sociniens, ou Ariens, ou anti-trinitaires'. As far as it goes, his report on them is correct; Newton and Clarke held anti-trinitarian views, and Clarke's contribution to the Arian debate was controversial.[52]

The problem is complicated by a conversation Voltaire had with a Quaker, Edward Higginson, the record of which has fortunately been preserved.[53] Voltaire said that he was a deist, 'adding, so were most of the noblemen in France and in England'.[54] This is a most valuable piece of information, but needs care in interpretation. What did Voltaire mean by 'deist'? It has been generally assumed that he used the word as it is used by modern scholars about him, to denote one who criticizes Christianity from the standpoint of an independent theistic philosophy. This assumption is probably false. Voltaire's meaning, almost certainly, was that he did not believe Christ to be divine; he was using 'deist' in the heretical sense which had been current right from the beginning of the word's history in 1564. This was the meaning for Houtteville in 1722, and ironically enough for Père Catrou, in a comment

---

[51] On Voltaire and Bolingbroke, see Lanson-Rousseau edition, Vol. II, p. 313, n. 8; A. -M. Rousseau, *L'Angleterre et Voltaire,* pp. 58–63; Pomeau, *Religion de Voltaire,* pp. 91–92, 126–127; Charles Dédéyan, *Voltaire et la pensée anglaise* (Paris, 1956), Pt. VI. On the whole question of the alleged influence of English deism on Voltaire see Norman L. Torrey, *Voltaire and the English Deists* (New Haven, 1930; pp. 135–153 on Bolingbroke), the burden of which is that he used the English works to a significant extent only much later than the *Lettres philosophiques,* and chiefly after 1760; and on Voltaire's 'Socinian' interpretation of Newton and Clarke, Florida, *Voltaire and the Socinians,* pp. 123–132.

[52] See Lanson-Rousseau edition, Vol. I, pp. 82–83, nn. 6, 7; Taylor edition, notes to pp. 152–153.

[53] Lanson-Rousseau edition, pp. 19–22.

[54] Ibid., p. 21.

on George Fox, in 1733.[55] That Voltaire's sense was the heretical, Arian one is confirmed by the continuation of Higginson's report of their conversation: 'deriding the account given by the four Evangelists concerning the birth of Christ, and his miracles, etc., so far, that I desired him to desist; for I could not bear to hear my Saviour so reviled and spoken against'.

It is unnecessary, therefore, to look for reasons why Voltaire avoided writing about deists in the *Lettres philosophiques;*[56] he did write about them, but for him the word meant those who denied the Trinity or the divinity of Christ, a meaning found much later in his writings. He did not write about those whose works constitute, for modern scholars, the deist canon, Toland, Collins, Tindal and the rest, because it was not until John Leland published his *View of the Principal Deistical Writers* in 1754 that the modern assumption, that deism is a scular religious movement critical of Christianity, was firmly established.[57] Earlier in the century 'déiste' was still a pejorative term, and would not have been appropriate in L. 7 for figures like Newton and Clarke, whose opinions Voltaire wished to support when he refers to ecclesiastics and 'quelques séculiers très savants'.

The other letter about a fundamental doctrine, L. 13, is one of the longest, and is known in three versions, of which that published in 1734 is the second

---

[55]   On Houtteville, see Chapter 13, pp. 207–208. Pomeau (*Religion de Voltaire*, p. 135) mentions, with signs of puzzlement, that in Catrou's *Histoire des Trembleurs,* 1733, deism is ascribed to Fox and Penn. This does not mean that Catrou regarded them as anti-Christian, nor as mere theists (although there may be some such implication about the tendencies of their attitude); he is accusing them of believing that only God the Father is divine, like the 'deists' described by Du Préau in 1569 or Florimond de Raemond in 1605. Lanson notes that Clarke also was accused of having Socinian and deist ideas (Lanson-Rousseau edition, Vol. I, p. 83, n. 7), again in the sense of extreme Arianism. Voltaire preserved the heretical sense much later, as witness a passage from the *Essai sur les moeurs,* Ch. CXXXVI, on 'ceux qu'on appelait alors anabaptistes en Angleterre', sixteenth-century precursors of the Quakers: 'ce qui est très extraordinaire, c'est que, se croyant chrétiens, et ne se piquant nullement de philosophie, ils n'étaient réellement que des déistes: car ils ne reconnaissaient Jésus-Christ que comme un homme à qui Dieu avait daigné donner des lumières plus pures qu'à ses contemporains', etc. Here deists are not Christian, it seems, but also not 'théistes', from whom Voltaire subsequently distinguishes them; 'théistes' reject revelation and ecclesiastical authority (Moland edition, Vol. XII, pp. 320–321).

[56]   Lanson wrote: 'Voltaire n'a pas parlé des déistes anglais. C'était probablement trop dangereux' (Lanson-Rousseau edition, Vol. I, p. 81). A. -M. Rousseau thinks the reason was 'l'ignorance ou la méconnaissance' (ibid., Vol. II, p. 316). Voltaire mentions Toland, Collins and Shaftesbury at the end of L. 13, in a famous and often revised list of philosophers whose ideas are not inflammatory, which shows that he had some idea of their importance in 1734.

[57]   John Leland, *A View of the Principal Deistical Writers that have appeared in England in the last and present century,* 2 vols. (London, 1754–1755). Vol. I covers Herbert, Hobbes, Blount, Toland, Shaftesbury, Collins, Woolston, Tindal, Thomas Morgan, Chubb, Bolingbroke and several pamphlets; Vol. II is devoted almost entirely to Hume and Bolingbroke. For Leland, deists are those who 'reject all revealed religion, and discard all pretences to it as owing to imposture or enthusiasm'; they also profess esteem for natural religion (Vol. I, p. 3; cf. Vol. II, p. 641). He regards the deists described in 1563 by Viret, whom he paraphrases after Bayle, as being essentially the same as the deists of his own time (Vol. I, p. 2).

in order of composition. It was probably written in 1732.[58] It is not a genuine summary of Locke's philosophy; Voltaire selects a particularly controversial statement by him, which implies that there is no such thing as the soul, and skilfully comments on it so as to bring out the destructive implications while appearing to preserve a more or less orthodox position. We may be reasonably certain of Voltaire's personal views about the soul from the *Traité de métaphysique,* written for his own use not more than five years after the letter on Locke. In the sixth chapter he concludes that 'je n'assure point que j'aie des démonstrations contre la spiritualité et l'immortalité de l'âme; mais toutes les vraisemblances sont contr'elles'.[59]

L. 13, after an initial tribute to Locke, attacks dogmatic opinions about the soul by means of a lengthy parade of Greeks, Scholastics and moderns whom Voltaire ridicules.[60] He takes the opportunity of pronouncing Aristotle to be unintelligible and of noting that some early Church Fathers believed the soul to be material. St Bernard receives special attention, probably for preaching the Crusades rather than for his theology. More detailed comments are made on Descartes, Voltaire quoting and re-stating one of Locke's most important contributions to philosophy, his criticism of innate ideas. Only then do we reach the letter's main issue, presented as a quotation from Locke about the limits of human knowledge. Thenceforward L. 13 concerns both Locke's opinions and the fears expressed about them by theologians.

Locke had said, in Voltaire's words (following Pierre Coste's translation): 'nous ne serons jamais peut-être capables de connaître si un être purement matériel pense ou non'. This had been received as a statement of irreligious materialism, 'une déclaration scandaleuse, que l'âme est matérielle et mortelle'.[61] Voltaire explains lucidly that there is a distinction to be drawn between what Locke had said and the implications which had been seen in it. His reason for mentioning the theologians' interpretation is to let us know that, if we agree with Locke, we shall be inclined to disbelieve in the soul and the afterlife. We have already been made to realize, however, that Locke is a great philosopher, with whom it would be natural to agree. Despite Voltaire's denials that the statement from Locke can affect faith ('il ne

---

[58]   The first version (Lanson-Rousseau edition, Vol. I pp. 190ff.) was not published till 1738. In 1748, Voltaire greatly extended the 1734 text (ibid., pp 205ff.), which itself, on the evidence of a letter to Formont in November 1732, must have been written earlier that year (ibid., p. 176, n. 2). Lanson also notes (p. 179) that L. 13, with L. 25, was one of the main causes of the measures taken against the *Lettres philosophiques* by the authorities.

[59]   *Traité de métaphysique,* Patterson edition, p. 42.

[60]   Had Voltaire come across clandestine manuscripts which do the same? Besides the *Opinions des anciens sur l'âme* (see Chapter 11, p. 175 and n. 49), there were other similar works which reviewed ideas on the soul, with destructive intent; see Wade, *Clandestine Organization,* pp. 211–217.

[61]   See Lanson-Rousseau edition, Vol. I, pp. 182, n. 21, and 185, n. 46, on Voltaire's reliance on Coste. By the reference to theologians he means Edward Stillingfleet, Bishop of Worcester, with whom Locke was engaged in controversy in 1697–1699.

fallait qu'examiner sans aigreur s'il y a de la contradiction à dire: la matière peut penser'), his manner of presenting Locke's philosophy reveals that the issue is as fundamental to the Christian religion as in L. 7, where the true subject is also half-concealed.

Voltaire's own philosophical contribution to the debate is the idea, used frequently in later works, that God can give to matter the faculty of thinking. The possibility is always formulated indirectly, as in: 'qui osera assurer, sans une impiété absurde, qu'il est impossible au Créateur de donner à la matière la pensée et le sentiment?'. This mode of argument, whatever its philosophical soundness, has the considerable merits of supporting Locke's statement, of being eminently defendable (as we have just seen, Voltaire can accuse critics of impiously denying the power of God) and of not resolving the question. 'God can give' thought to matter; but we do not know whether he did so, or whether 'matter', the human body, has in itself the capacity of thought. Voltaire's argument is both a debating position and an expression of agnosticism. Although he appears for once to be arguing on his own account, he avoids pronouncing for or against the existence of the soul, and leaves the reader to reflect on the threats to religion perceived by theologians.

In two passages Voltaire acknowledges the significance of the implied threat. One is a paragraph of fideism, or rather pseudo-fideism, in which his words come to mean, on examination, the opposite of what they had seemed to mean at first: 'La raison humaine est si peu capable de démontrer par elle-même l'immortalité de l'âme, que la religion a été obligée de nous la révéler'. For those whose are true fideists, a dying breed in 1734, and accept the authority of the Church, this will pass;[62] but those who are not may be led to suspect that the doctrine of the soul has simply been invented. And Voltaire immediately gives the reasons for inventing it: 'Le bien commun de tous les hommes demande que l'on croie l'âme immortelle, la foi nous l'ordonne, il n'en faut pas davantage, et la chose est décidée'. This could be fideism, but it has a utilitarian air. Voltaire does not say that the doctrine is an imposture, but does suggest that its social value should be the measure of its truth. To judge by later works, he recognized the social risks of disbelief in the soul (no deterrent for evil-doers), and was half in agreement with traditional fideism on the subject.[63]

---

[62] Lanson relates this passage to ideas expressed by Anthony Collins (Lanson-Rousseau edition, Vol. I p. 184, n. 44) but the tradition of agnosticism on the soul was so ancient and widespread that it would be pointless to look for any one source.

[63] Voltaire is usually agnostic on the soul, but also tends to think that the people should believe in punishments in the afterlife. Cf. the second and seventeenth dialogues in *L'A, B, C,* of 1768–1769 (Moland edition, Vol. XXVII, pp. 327, 390), and Voltaire's comments on the second, in a letter: 'Toutefois il est fort bon de faire accroire aux hommes qu'ils ont une âme immortelle, et qu'il y a un Dieu vengeur qui punira mes paysans s'ils me volent mon blé et mon vin, qui fera rouer là-bas ou là-haut les juges des Calas, et brûler ceux d'Abbeville' (Besterman D. 15600, 20 April 1769, to d'Argental).

The other passage which assumes that the ideas of Locke are 'dangerous' is the end of the letter, designed to show that 'il ne faut jamais craindre qu'-aucun sentiment philosophique puisse nuire à la religion d'un pays'. Again we are told that trouble has been caused by trivial religious disputes; philosophers by contrast are insignificant and pacific. Voltaire writes as if what he was concerned about was the danger of sectarianism ('jamais les philosophes ne feront une secte de religion') and allays any fears by affirming that 'philosophical' ideas — in the context, these ideas must concern religion closely — will have no effect on society. The conclusion which the reader naturally draws is that men such as Locke (there is a list, much varied in different editions, reflecting Voltaire's sympathies) should be allowed to go on philosophizing in peace. Yet, as we have seen, Voltaire has taken care to show just where the danger to religion lies if we accept Locke's argument about matter and thought. Voltaire wants to have it both ways: to make anti-religious implications, but to be left in peace while he does so. At bottom, however, his attitude is consistent. For him the only real danger is social disorder; metaphysical debates are indifferent, provided they do not disturb society; and since organized religion is a source of conflict, philosophers whose ideas might reduce religion's power should be allowed to disseminate them. The overall message of L. 13 is that we should not regard the existence of the soul or the afterlife as demonstrated and that it does not matter if we therefore reject Christianity; even if, we do, we should regard belief in the soul as socially useful and preserve it on that account.

THE ATTACK ON PASCAL

In the *Lettres philosophiques* as a whole, religion begins by dominating the scene, and then is gradually supplanted by secular concerns such as politics, commerce and science, according to the indifferentist schema which diminishes the importance of anything religious. But at the end religion again appears, in the formidable figure of Pascal, as if Voltaire felt that it has not yet been finally dismissed.[64] In the commentary on the *Pensées,* 'mon petit anti-Pascal', he selects for comment the fragments in which the apologist is vulnerable or can be wilfully misunderstood, but also those which are damaging to Voltaire's own worldly and philosophical religious views. On the whole he treats Pascal as a rationalist, a misrepresentation which enables him to claim to be a fideist himself and to criticize rational arguments for Christianity: 'C'est vouloir soutenir un chêne en l'entourant de roseaux; on peut écarter ces roseaux inutiles sans faire tort à l'arbre'. This dubiously

[64] Voltaire's attacks on Pascal in L. 25 and later writings have been much discussed; see François Mauriac, *Voltaire contre Pascal* (Paris, 1929); Jean-Raoul Carré, *Réflexions sur l'anti-Pascal de Voltaire* (Paris, 1935); Pomeau, *Religion de Voltaire,* pp 226 ff.

fideistic strain characterizes the early Remarques, during which the insincerity seems to increase. He pretends to see rationalist despair in Pascal because 'sa raison ne peut débrouiller le mystère de la Trinité' (R. 6), and contrives to be indifferentist about it (why be 'prêt à se pendre' for such a cause?). On the prophecy of the Second Coming of Christ, Voltaire comments 'si cela n'est point arrivé encore, ce n'est pas à nous d'oser interroger la Providence' (R. 13).

Protected by the shield of pseudo-fideism, Voltaire is free to criticize Pascal on rational grounds, taking refuge in piety if necessary. Another weapon employed is erudition, displayed impressively so as to make Pascal seem an amateur in historical studies (R. 7, R. 9). R. 31 uses the principle that Scripture was written in accordance with the state of scientific knowledge at the time, but also pokes fun at Biblical science, while R. 33 is sceptical about the Crucifixion. Pascal had given an opening to ridicule when he referred to the inconsistent genealogies of Christ in the Gospels of Matthew and Luke; Voltaire takes the opportunity in R. 17 and R. 18. A similar attempt to discredit Pascal's reliance on Old Testament prophecies is made in R. 15. The two other Remarques concerning prophecy, R. 12 and R. 14, accept that they were of significance to the Jews, but not to Christians.

The burden of Voltaire's attacks on the Christian proofs is that all the phenomena which apologists cite as evidence of the divine should be regarded as merely human. On miracles, for instance, in R. 41, he makes a point about credulousness in a meaningful analogy: 'Le premier homme qui a été malade a cru sans peine le premier charlatan'. Prophecies can be explained by a knowledge of Jewish history and customs (R. 12 and R. 14); martyrdom proves the fanatacism of the martyr, not the truth of his convictions. This is in R. 23, on Pascal's famous affirmation 'Je ne crois que les témoins qui se feraient égorger'. The tendency to reduce the supernatural to the natural (only a tendency: it is not a principle, as in the *Examen de la religion*) is somewhat more obvious when Voltaire is discussing the specifically Pascalian arguments about Original Sin and the distress of the human condition. Whereas Pascal sees human nature as a set of contradictory qualities, 'contrariétés', which can only be explained by recourse to the doctrine of the Fall of Man, Voltaire describes man in commonsense terms: 'Il est comme tout ce que nous voyons, mêlé de mal et de bien, de plaisir et de peine. (...) ces prétendues contrariétés que vous appellez contradictions sont les ingrédients nécessaires qui entrent dans le composé de l'homme, qui est ce qu'il doit être' (R. 3). On this theme, much of the 'anti-Pascal' consists of descriptions of ordinary life which make Pascal's metaphysical anguish seem exaggerated (R. 3, R. 4, R. 6, R. 28). The tone is comfortable, moderate and down-to-earth, denying both that man is 'une énigme' and that life is as bad as Pascal had made out.

The soothing style at times becomes the vehicle for a rudimentary form of utilitarianism and philosophical optimism.[65] When Pascal asserts that some human feature denotes frailty, Voltaire counters by saying that the feature in question has social or moral value. This is the pattern of R. 21 to R. 27. Restlessness is for Pascal a mark of 'misère', but for Voltaire it is the basis of social activity (R. 23); if a man remains inactive, he is 'un imbécile, inutile à la société', which is the same objection that Montesquieu had made against the purely religious life of monasteries.[66] In R. 11, self-interest, denounced by Pascal, is another basis of society. In R. 6 and R. 28, Voltaire complains of Pascal's pessimistic one-sidedness, and refuses to think of the human condition in Pascal's images of dungeons and desert islands; he prefers Paris or London, where 'les hommes sont heureux autant que la nature humaine le comporte'.

There is one passage of the *Pensées* against which Voltaire's ironies are ineffective: the 'argument du pari'.[67] He treats it with almost complete seriousness, for Pascal's analogy of the wager, to denote the decision to believe in Christianity, is a true and radical form of fideism which cannot be repudiated by the pseudo-fideism employed elsewhere. It could be met by genuine rationalism, but although Voltaire asks Pascal for proof he fails to indicate what any proof might consist in. He falls back on agnosticism, observing that genuine doubt is not catered for by the 'pari' and that 'l'intérêt que j'ai à croire une chose n'est pas une preuve de l'existence de cette chose' (R. 5). This line of reasoning leads him to the further observation that in Jansenism the belief that few are saved makes the proposed 'wager' less attractive than if salvation were more certain; and the Remarque turns into a protest against predestination. Jansenism makes us so fearful of damnation that 'votre raisonnement ne servirait qu'à faire des athées, si la voix de toute la nature ne nous criait qu'il y a un Dieu avec autant de force que ces subtilités ont de faiblesse'.

When he wrote the series of additional Remarques for the 1742 edition Voltaire was apparently much less shaken by Pascal's argument. In the fourth of the new series, he quotes Pascal denying that the existence of God can be proved rationally, 'selon les lumières naturelles', but instead of asking for proofs, as he had before, he provides them himself, in the form of the 'self-evident proposition' that 'j'existe, donc quelque chose existe de toute éternité'. This is an abbreviated version of the proof of God which Voltaire had taken from Samuel Clarke and expounded in the *Traité de métaphysique*

[65] Pope's *Essay on Man*, full of memorable statements of optimism, appeared while Voltaire was preparing the *Lettres philosophiques*; see Richard G. Knapp, *The Fortunes of Pope's Essay on Man in 18th Century France*, SVEC 82 (1971), pp. 79–122, on Voltaire's reactions to the poem (pp. 89–90 on parallels between it and L. 25).

[66] In L. 117 of the *Lettres persanes*; see Chapter 13, p. 220.

[67] *Pensées*, Sellier edition, No. 680 (Brunschvicg No. 233). See Carré, *Réflexions sur l'anti-Pascal*, Ch. II, pp. 25–43, who also discusses relevant passages in Gilbert, Lassay, etc.

(written between the dates of the two series of Remarques).[68] The increased confidence of the new R. 4, and R. 7 which supports it, is probably due to the discovery of reasons which were more satisfactory than the earlier 'voix de toute la nature'. Clarke's arguments strengthened the case for deism against faith, and made possible once again the affectation of indifference, which, exceptionally in the *Lettres philosophiques,* is lacking in the objections to the 'pari'.

There is little in the 'anti-Pascal' which is specifically deistic. The modern concept of deism, but not the word, occurs in passing in R. 29, when Voltaire observes that nowadays 'un homme qui viendrait enseigner l'adoration d'un Dieu, indépendante du culte reçu' would be persecuted. This might indicate Voltaire's awareness that in propagating what is now called deism he himself might run risks; apprehensiveness on behalf of philosophers like Locke or Toland is expressed at the end of L. 13. R. 43 complements the suggestion about theism in R. 29 with a universal rule of morality, the so-called Golden Rule, which deists favoured, 'cette seule maxime reçue de toutes les nations: "Ne faites pas à autrui ce que vous ne voudriez pas qu'on vous fît"'. From these Remarques we might deduce that Voltaire believes in God and an elementary code of morality, which roughly corresponds to the message of the letters on the Quakers, but, lost as they are among the other Remarques, these two carry no special weight.

THE DEISM OF THE *LETTRES PHILOSOPHIQUES*

Voltaire's deism in the *Lettres* — things were to be different later — does not appear to be a religious attitude independent of Christianity. Although L. 7 is ambiguous in its implications about Christ, combining respect and disrespect in about equal proportions, the image of English Christianity generally is not unfavourable. For a French public in 1734, Voltaire's limited approval for Quakers and Arians, heretical 'déistes' and outcasts from the Catholic point of view, probably seemed almost as outrageous or eccentric as an open presentation of anti-Christian deism, but the Quakers and Arians (not to mention John Locke) do not abandon Christianity, even if they make large revisions in its content. From the portrayal in the *Lettres* of radical or evangelical Christianity we can infer the values which we are meant to share. The Quaker of L. 1 rejects much of traditional Christian practice, mainly the use of the sacraments, and emphasizes the moral element in religion — humaneness, social equality, sincerity. His morality is not separate from his faith, unlike that of the clergy in the book; each moral value is backed by biblical authority. 'Notre Dieu qui nous a ordonné d'aimer nos

---

[68] *Traité de métaphysique,* Ch. III, 'Qu'il y a un Dieu'. See Barber, 'Voltaire and Samuel Clarke', pp. 58–59, who thinks that the chapter may antedate the first *Remarques.*

ennemis et de souffrir sans murmure ne veut pas sans doute que nous passions la mer pour aller égorger nos frères': although this combines what we may regard as a secular value, that of pacifism, with religion, in the same way as L. 46 of the *Lettres persanes,* the background is Christian, not merely theistic as in Montesquieu.

By the time we reach the fourth letter on the Quakers, their creed has become the foundation of an ideal state, which is tolerant, egalitarian and prosperous. Its first law, admittedly, is deistic rather than Christian, 'de ne maltraiter personne au sujet de la religion, et de regarder comme frères tous ceux qui croient un Dieu', but Voltaire calls the Quakers of Pennsylvania Christians. In the *Lettres philosophiques* the Quakers do not seem to be disguised deists (in the secular anti-Christian sense), but the kind of Christians with whom the reader is encouraged to sympathize, like the charitable Alvarez in the tragedy *Alzire,* contemporary with the *Lettres philosophiques.* [69]

However, it is always clear that for the French reader Voltaire is describing figures in a foreign land, which in L. 4 becomes remote and Utopian. The closer Quaker belief approaches to a deistic religion, the further removed it is from European reality. Moreover, the conclusion of all the letters containing opinions presented favourably, L. 4, L. 7 and L. 13, is that these opinions are of little significance. Even when Voltaire approves of some religious belief, he plays it down, minimizing the extent to which it is contrary to secular values and behaviour. The members of the Stock Exchange in L. 6, indifferent to each other's creed, are typical. Indeed, indifferentism is the central feature of the letters on religion. The attacks on the clergy, religious war and ecclesiastical authority are all, in essence, the denial that these things have any real importance. The clergy's efforts to persecute fail, their faith has no effect on their conduct, the conflicts they cause are intrinsically trivial, their authority is (rightly) limited by the secular powers.

Voltaire's attitude is of course only assumed indifference. If religion were really as unimportant as he makes out, there would be no need to belittle it. The discussion of civil war in L. 8 acknowledges, in a number of incidental remarks, that religion has in fact the power to cause social disorder; hence Voltaire's assertions that it is not worth fighting a civil war, except for a social value, that of political liberty. The indifferentist pose is thus deliberate, destructive also. Herein lies one of the main innovations of the *Lettres philosophiques*: the development of literary techniques which take the place

[69]   *Alzire, ou les Amériquains,* 1736. Alvarez, whose humanity is contrasted with the imperialist ferocity of his son Gusman, eventually moves him to mercy; Gusman forgives his assassin, the Inca prince Zamore, and so converts him to Christianity – or seems to: a note of Voltaire's in the 1736 edition points out that there is no miraculous conversion, which would be ridiculous in the circumstances; Zamore merely 'commence à respecter le christianisme' (Moland edition, Vol. III, p. 435, n. 1).

of the direct criticisms in a deist treatise like the *Examen de la religion*. The famous Voltairean irony is only one of these techniques; in addition, wit and humour deprive religious personages of their standing, and pretended fideism reduces faith to a comic sham. In descriptive passages, concentration on externals excludes religious meaning from rituals; in passages of history, statements of apparent fact carry indifferentist lessons of the progressive diminution of religion's power. Some of these techniques can be found in the *Lettres persanes*, but not continuously, and in Montesquieu's hands their effect is comparatively mild. Voltaire had found a method of criticizing religion in a published work, conveying his meaning by implications which were as destructive as the explicit arguments of the manuscript works.

These considerations are less applicable to the commentary on Pascal, which is another type of critical deism. There are hints of a doctrine of optimism and utilitarianism, in opposition to Pascal's pessimism, and a very unobtrusive reference to a form of deism in R. 29, but the main contribution of L. 25 is its refutation of the rational proofs of Christianity. Before he added the *Remarques,* Voltaire wrote to his friend Formont about the idea, in words which reveal the violence latent in his ironic style: 'je ne critiquerai que les endroits qui ne seront point tellement liés avec notre sainte religion qu'on ne puisse déchirer la peau de Pascal sans faire saigner le Christianisme'.[70] The claim that Pascal alone is the object of aggression is not implausible as regards the first few Remarques, since they criticize such typically Pascalian ideas as the wager argument and the 'contrariétés' in human nature. Even here, since Pascal was re-stating the doctrine of Original Sin, Voltaire necessarily attacks a basic Christian concept. However, these early Remarques might be thought compatible with a more worldly type of Christianity than Jansenism.[71] With the apologetic proofs of prophecy, miracle and so on the situation is different. They had been used by countless apologists besides Pascal, so that when Voltaire criticizes them in the *Pensées* he is refuting the rational Christianity of the apologists generally. A genuine fideist might do this for Christian reasons, but Voltaire's fideism, skilful and entertaining as it is, is destructive irony, the more so since it can easily be imitated.

If we put the Quaker letters and L. 25 together, we have approval for an undenominational, moralizing Christianity coupled with rejection of the rational, Jansenist Christianity of the selections from Pascal. This in outline is the pattern of the *Epître à Uranie.* The *Lettres* also make a perpetual effort to seem indifferent towards religion, particularly as it affects the life of society; Voltaire's resistance to those *Pensées* which conflict with social values is part of the same attitude. The impression is that religion is acceptable only under the condition that it should encourage, or at least not

[70]   Besterman D. 617; about 1 June 1733.
[71]   See Pomeau, *Religion de Voltaire*, p. 228, on the Jesuits' reception of the 'anti-Pascal'.

interfere with, the morality of worldly life.[72] The belief in God meets this condition, for the Quaker of L. 1 regards pacifism, humanity and truthfulness as divine commands. But the Whigs of L. 5 and the stockbrokers of L. 6 prefer religion to be kept out of the world of politics and commerce, and when Voltaire's Quaker extols the spirituality of his faith, 'une religion toute sainte et toute spirituelle', he seems to mean that it is uncontaminated by contact with the real world. Conversely, whenever religion intrudes into this world, Voltaire attacks it.

The letters on religion are therefore almost entirely critical of established religion. The attempt to extract from the *Lettres* a positive creed, comparable to the deism or natural religion of earlier writers, meets with failure; little is to be found except a few hints, which are made in opposition to some aspect of the Christianity which is under attack. The assertion that God can give matter the power of thought, to which the theory of the soul is reduced in L. 13, arises out of a denial of the Christian concept of the soul; the Malebranchian passage at the end of L. 2, about religious truth, is an answer to the Catholic's suggestion that an intermediary, the clergy, is required between God and man; and the secular moral code of L. 1 and L. 25 is opposed to ritual and the ideas of Pascal. Yet since the work's importance lies in its use of techniques of implication, to make religion seem absurd and irrelevant, the absence of a coherent system of deism does not diminish its stature. In another letter about his book, to La Condamine, Voltaire tried to explain 'ce qui a pu choquer si vivement les idées reçues'.[73] He concluded that the uproar was caused by his humourous treatment of respectable subjects. 'Si je n'avais pas égayé la matière personne n'eût été scandalisé, mais aussi personne ne m'aurait lu'. As usual, Voltaire plays down the affair, as if it was all a matter of style; but in this case the matter of style is fundamental.

---

[72] As Pomeau observes: 'Cette religion indulgente, si c'en était encore une, convenait à l'ère du capitalisme naissant' (ibid., p. 229). Cf. Auerbach, *Mimesis,* p. 354, on Voltaire's method of insinuating that business values should take precedence over religious.

[73] Besterman D. 759; 22 June 1734.

CHAPTER 15

CONCLUSIONS

In the confusing early history of deism, there are two separate subjects to be considered: the history of the contemporary meanings of the words 'déistes' or 'déisme' has to be distinguished, for well over a century, from the history of the ideas which directly anticipate deism in the form it acquired during the Enlightenment. The words basically refer, as in modern usage, to those who believe only in God; but this means different things in different contexts. In the theological context of debate concerning the Trinity, it means the neo-Arian or anti-trinitarian belief that God the Father alone possesses perfect divinity; the divinity of Jesus Christ is to some extent denied. This must have been the meaning intended by the unknown person who applied the term 'déistes' (or 'deistae') to an anti-trinitarian group in Lyon in the 1560s, a group denounced in forceful and misleading terms by the reformer Pierre Viret. But for another unidentified individual, the author of the *Anti-bigot* in about 1620, 'le vrai déiste' means 'he who believes truly in God'. According to the poem, such a deist does not believe in Hell. In both cases the meanings are justified etymologically, but apparently have no other connection, and from the appearances of the words we should not deduce that, in the 1560s or the 1620s, there were deists holding beliefs essentially the same as those whom we now term deists, the writers of the eighteenth-century Enlightenment.

In his eagerness to denounce his enemies, Viret made them out also to be enemies of Christianity. Such an accusation may have been plausible for those who thought that diminishing the divinity of Jesus is equivalent to subverting the Christian religion, but, again, the vigour of the accusation should not make us believe that Voltairean attacks on Christianity were being mounted in the seventeenth or sixteenth centuries. Henri Busson's account of early deism, largely based on Viret's report (which had been given credence by Pierre Bayle, an opponent of 'déistes' in his own time) and on the *Anti-bigot* (or 'poème des déistes', as Mersenne called it), is hard to accept.[1] It seems to involve the claim that anti-Christian theism, a form of

---

[1]   See the relevant chapters in his *Le rationalisme dans la littérature française de la Renaissance* and *La pensée religieuse française de Charron à Pascal,* and above, Chapter 1, nn. 4, 21; Chapter 2, n. 19, etc.

rationalism, had a continuous history back into the middle of the sixteenth century.

The difficulty arises chiefly from the virtual impossibility of identifying any individuals who were known to have held such an attitude, except by extending the meaning of terms almost beyond recognition. A kind of identification is sometimes provided by polemicists, alleging that those whom they attack are deists, as when Jean Filleau accused the Jansenists in 1654; but we cannot seriously ascribe deism to Jansenists. The only alternative is to suppose that 'déisme' and 'déistes' were names for heretical tendencies, well suited for being bandied about in the controversies of the time.

Equally, the words had a place in theoretical discussion, where their use corresponds to the modern use of 'theism' and 'theist'. Thus when in 1684 Jacques Abbadie defines four classes of 'déistes', he means four categories of belief in God, independently of persons and places. He can include notions dating from classical antiquity, such as those of the Epicureans, since for the apologists the denial of providence, equated with an Epicurean concept of God, was an issue of permanent relevance and still required consideration. The same applies to Pascal when he discusses deism in the *Pensées;* he is not reporting on the contemporary religious scene, but analysing a concept.

The absence of any agreed identity for the 'déistes' is confirmed by the frequency with which sixteenth and seventeenth century writers define the word, almost invariably finding it necessary to explain it. Towards the end of the century, while controversy between Protestants and Catholics intensifies, phrases such as 'déiste ou Socinien', 'déiste ou Epicurien', 'déiste ou Spinoziste' become prevalent. They indicate that the word could be a synonym for various attitudes which in themselves have little in common, except that the Socinians and Spinoza were considered, usually with polemical exaggeration, to have overthrown belief in the Scriptures by their rational methods of criticism. Similarly, for his enemies the Arminian Jean Le Clerc is a deist, as is the Catholic biblical scholar Richard Simon. In the case of the Socinians and Le Clerc, it may be that their views on the divinity of Jesus are in question. As for Spinoza, since the outrage occasioned by the *Tractatus* was superseded in 1677 by the greater horror felt at the *Ethics,* almost universally regarded as an atheist work, the apparently contradictory phrase 'déiste ou athée' can also refer to adherents of his views. The welter of pejorative meanings necessitated a new term to denote the belief in God when treated impartially and in isolation from any other belief; in this sense, 'le pur déisme' came to be used.

Although the frequent references to 'déistes' in the seventeenth century cannot be taken as evidence of a deistic movement, it remains possible, and even probable, that some individuals confined their beliefs to belief in God.

If they did, they very seldom committed themselves to paper on the subject. The musician d'Assoucy, who refers to 'déistes' in 1676, is one of the few likely cases, for a period in his life, the great Condé was perhaps another. After 1700, very gradually, the process by which the senses of 'déiste' merged into the modern meaning can be preceived in the reactions of reviewers and others to ideas and texts which may or may not now seem to exemplify deism. Lahontan, now regarded as one of the earliest deists, is also regarded as one by reviewers in 1703 and 1704, but in the Socinian sense; Montesquieu's *Lettres persanes* do not appear to have been attacked for deism until 1751, and then the accusation is combined with that of Spinozism. The most remarkable coincidence of meanings, however, occurs in connection with the *Lettres philosophiques*. When in England, Voltaire explained to one of the Quakers he met, Edward Higginson, that English and French nobles were deists, using the word to refer to the denial of the divinity of Jesus; the Quakers were accused by a Jesuit historian, Père Catrou, of being deists, in a similar sense; while the work in which Voltaire himself describes them, which does not mention deists as such, is a classic example of the modern sense of deism, a separate movement of religious secularism.

The proper guide to the antecedents of deism is the content of the first deists' works. Writing about fifty years before the peak of Enlightenment deism, Gilbert, Lahontan, the anonymous author of the *Examen de la religion* and the Militaire philosophe, to whom others such as Chaulieu should be added in some respects, compose a group of writers whose works are remarkably similar in dates and attitudes. As regards origins, their most important shared characteristic is that they expound forms of rational or natural religion, with universalist pretensions. They also criticize the apologists' proofs of Christianity and repudiate totally the concept of submissive faith.

The homogeneity of approach in these first deist writings, which is the more striking because, until Tyssot de Patot, the authors appear to have no sense that they might belong to a common tradition, suggests that they were subject to the same influences, whether positive or negative. On the positive side, the most notable is Malebranche. It may seem to be a sad irony that one of the most distinguished exponents of Christian rationalism should soon have found disciples who adopted his principles and employed them in opposition to Christianity, but such was the case with Gilbert's *Calejava*, the *Examen de la religion,* and above all the Militaire philosophe's *Difficultés,* which were actually sent to Malebranche. The importance of his thought in the background of early French deism is confirmed by passages in Montesquieu and Voltaire.

This does not mean that without the *Recherche de la vérité* deism would not have appeared. Malebranche's influence is simply the most important instance of a wider movement influencing the deists, religious rationalism generally. Rationalism in metaphysics, especially the classic formulation by Descartes, provided the basis of rational criticism in works by deists and others. The negative influences on them, those which they rejected, were in part also rationalist, that of the apologists who (again like Malebranche) had elaborated a structure of reasoned argument in favour of the Christian revelation; but the fideist tradition was also rejected, with its principle that Christian belief must be accepted on faith. Apologists needed to reconcile reason and faith; the deists sought to divide them.

The development of the concept of reason had meant that the concept of natural religion developed in parallel, since its tenets consisted in those truths which could be discovered or proved by the natural light of reason. Typically, these were the existence of God and the spirituality of the soul. Natural religion was far from being opposed to Christianity; it was usually considered, by Christian writers apart from the Jansenists, to be the first stage on the way to Christian belief. Since it was also considered as the theological condition of certain non-Christians, pagans who had lived before Christ or savages who lived outside the ambit of Christendom, the idea was current that religious belief could be confined to natural religion. The idea emerged clearly from the argument over the salvation of pagans.

However, after La Mothe le Vayer's treatise on the *Vertu des païens*, directed no doubt against the Jansenists and provocatively suggesting that natural religion sufficed for salvation, there was a long interval before Foigny's *Terre australe connue*, the first work in which natural religion appears in a more or less deistic guise. Following the normal theological suppositions, but in fiction, Foigny attributes a religion based on natural reason to an imaginary people in the Austral Land. Although his hero finds this religion unsatisfactory, the Australians fit into the category defined by the modern sense of deism, believers in God but critics of Christianity. Hence in 1676 Enlightenment deism existed at the conceptual level.[2]

Another of the religious uses of reason, in the seventeenth century, was eirenic, to find a method of overcoming sectarian divisions by devising basic religious tenets, on which all parties could agree. Such attempts to eliminate intolerance and conflict proved fruitless, but the impulse to universalize religion is strong in a variety of seventeenth-century works, among them those of Herbert of Cherbury, whose 'five articles', common to all religions, are always regarded as the first form of English deism. Campanella had

---

[2]   The fourth of Abbadie's categories of deists is 'ceux qui reconnaissent que Dieu a donné aux hommes une religion (...) qui en réduisent tous les principes aux sentiments naturels de l'homme, et qui prennent tout le reste pour fiction' (quoted above, Chapter 6, p. 84). This definition is vague enough to have been based on the religion of Foigny's Australisns, but could also refer to *libertins.*

sought to propagate a universal Catholicism; Spinoza, in the *Tractatus*, supports a faith valid for all Christians with a rigorous analysis of Scripture (which admittedly was generally regarded as destructive). A more limited type of eirenism, the effort to find a basis for unity between Catholic and Protestant, inspired the work in which the fideist Saint-Evremond most nearly approaches the deist viewpoint, his *Considèration sur la religion.* Saint-Evremond utilized some of Spinoza's ideas and knew the work of d'Huisseau and Bossuet, proposing grounds for agreement from opposite sides. Foigny's motivation may have been the same, since in his Austral Land God must not be spoken of, for fear of strife, and the Australians are especially critical of European religious conflict; they attack its theoretical basis, the intolerant principle that only one religion can claim exclusive truth. Veiras too apparently sought to avoid conflict, but in an entirely different manner, putting forward the idea of a religion virtually confined to ritual observance, combined with tolerance for divergences of belief.

There seems to be no direct connection between these eirenic endeavours and the work of the rationalist deists after 1700. In the historical situation to which the latter respond, projects for religious unity do not have any credibility, although passages deploring conflict appear in almost all deist writing, and are often prominent. Before and after 1700, the assumption inherent in such writings is one which deeply affected the history of the time also, putting an end to eirenism after 1685, namely that to dwell in a particular country necessitated belonging to its religion, if only in externals. Such conformity was expected at least as much for political as for religious reasons; Saint-Evremond's fideism, with its call for submission to authority, exemplifies what was required.

This assumption underlies much deistic and pre-deistic writing, especially that of the Utopists. As a rule, travellers to deistic Utopias either stay because they wish to practice the religion in force there, or else leave because they wish to practice their own religion in their own country. Marana's Spy is faced with a dilemma which is analogous; unhappily aware of the mutual intolerance of Muslim and Christian, he is constantly seeking to formulate principles which will enable him to reconcile and transcend the differences.

That such dilemmas were based on reality is confirmed by the limited evidence which is available about the authors' lives. Marana's life as an exile in France must be related to his character's problems, although the relationship is not entirely clear. In order to have changed his religion twice, Foigny must have been beset with doubts of the same order. From Gilbert's *Histoire de Calejava,* it can be deduced that his background is that of the Huguenots who were obliged to accept the official Catholicism of 1685; outwardly in the same position as the Turkish Spy, they had to conform to the religious practices of Catholic France. The older member of Gilbert's party of travellers is prepared to return to France, despite his Huguenot affiliations, but the younger generation remain in non-sectarian, rationalist Calejava.

After 1700 the pressure to conform appears to become greater. The quantity of apologetic work rises, though apparently not its quality, and all kinds of dissident religious opinions are suppressed. Richard Simon had never been able to publish his works of biblical criticism in France, but after the turn of the century less suspect figures are prevented from doing so; Boileau, for instance, because of his Jansenist sympathies, or Fénelon.[3] All the deist writers are affected by these circumstances, as is evident from the ways in which they seek to propagate their views. The clandestine manuscripts (including the poems of the *libertins du Temple*) demonstrate by their very existence that the ideas they contain were impossible to publish. Gilbert, having made plans for publication, had to abandom them. The first letters of Marana's *Espion turc* had been published in Paris in the 1680s, but most of the series was published in English and French outside France, in numerous editions; Lahontan's memoirs were transformed into the *Dialogues curieux* with Gueudeville's assistance, and also published in England and Holland; Tyssot de Patot's book was published in Holland, like the *Lettres persanes*. Even rather later, Voltaire's *Epître à Uranie* and *Traité de métaphysique* were clandestine productions, *La Henriade* (although a national epic) was published in England, and the *Lettres philosophiques* in England and secretly in Rouen.

Such facts imply that the works concerned formed a literature of protest, but the elements of the protest were various. Often it is rationalist in nature, as is to be expected; some of the deists were offended on the purely intellectual plane by being required to believe 'les choses impossibles', in La Fare's phrase. The Militaire philosophe's autobiographical sketch, as always, provides valuable testimony; he is indignant about the clergy and 'le joug que nous portons', but is also irritated by the logical inadequacies of Christian arguments.[4] In response he accumulates a vast number of objections, many of which are duplicated elsewhere, notably in the *Examen de la religion*. The efforts of the apologists seem to have rebounded: their defence of Christianity by rational means had, in some cases at least, an effect precisely the opposite of that intended. For his part Lahontan seems to have identified himself, to some extent, with the Red Indians he met who were faced with the arguments of missionaries. Apart from the content of the objections, the virulence with which they are expressed must be due to the degree of official intolerance which then prevailed. After the end of the

---

[3]   The twelth satire, 'Sur l'équivoque', was refused permission for printing in 1710 (Boileau, *Satires,* edited by Ch. -H. Boudhors (Paris, 1934), p. 313); on the works not published by Fénelon, some political as well as religious, see Lanson, *Origines de l'esprit philosophique,* pp. 293–296.
[4]   *Difficultés sur la religion,* Mortier edition, p. 94.

wars and the death of Louis XIV in 1715, the negative aspect of deist literature is less pronounced.

It is noticeable that early critical deism is voiced by writers of both Catholic and Protestant upbringing: Lahontan, the Militaire philosophe and (presumably) the author of the *Examen* on one side, Tyssot de Patot and (again presumably) Gilbert on the other. The English origins of French deism have been made much of in the past because of the influence of Voltaire.[5] Before his time there is very little to be said in favour of such an interpretation, since in the deist texts of 1700–1715 any traces of English influence are insignificant.[6] However, the wider question of a possible Protestant influence does at least deserve to be raised. It will be evident by now that the existence of a rival to Catholicism played an important part for individuals, since several deistic writers changed religion, and also as regards the publication of early deist works. However, the clandestine manuscripts, the basic texts in the earliest deistic literature in France, have nothing to do with Protestantism, which therefore was not a necessary element in the advent of deism. Even in apparently Protestant writers, the influence of their upbringing may not have been paramount. Tyssot de Patot was a scientific rationalist with Spinozist leanings, whose work is almost as hostile to Protestant Christianity as to Catholic.

The question of Protestantism is closely related to that of the influence of travel, a factor not to be underestimated in the origins of deism, but one which is difficult to separate from others. Travel is often a necessary part of the experience of religious divisions or conflict, an experience shared by all the deist writers and their precursors from 1675 except Gilbert and possibly the author of the *Examen*. However, these exceptions are important. Moreover, Tyssot de Patot had travelled only in childhood, and although Montesquieu's journey to Paris from distant Bordeaux may have inspired the idea of the Persians' journey to France, the idea of comparing Islam with Christianity must have come from a literary source, the *Espion turc*. The

---

[5]   The classic statement of the case was made by M. M Tabaraud, *Histoire critique du philosophisme anglais, depuis son origine jusqu' à son introduction en France, inclusivement,* 2 vols. (Paris, 1806). It is devoted to English thinkers from Hobbes to Tindal and Woolston and to the *Lettres philosophiques,* which according to Tabaraud introduced 'philosophisme' into France. The modern treatment of the question is in N. L. Torrey, *Voltaire and the English Deists*; see Chapter 14, n. 51, above.

[6]   See Gabriel Bonno, *La culture et la civilisation britanniques devant l'opinion française de la paix d'Utrecht aux Lettres philosophiques,* who examines the evidence for English influence in the Utopian travel-stories, including Lahontan, the clandestine works and early Montesquieu and Voltaire, and concludes that 'l'influence précise' is very small (p. 111). To his list of cases, which includes the fact that Boulainviller read Thomas Burnet, Tyssot's borrowing from Toland of an explanation of a miracle (see Chapter 12, n. 35) and translations of works by Collins, Toland and Woolston, can be added Gilbert's reference to Hobbes (see Chapter 8, n. 19) and Tyssot's use of the same thinker (see Chapter 12, n. 44).

Militaire philosophe mentions that experience of other religions weakens Christian belief, but lays no particular emphasis on it.[7]

The evidence is therefore inconclusive, but if the type of writing concerned, manuscript or published work, is also taken into account a certain regularity can be observed. Authors resort to the fictional use of travel to foreign countries, and employ foreign or exotic *personae*, in order to express deistic ideas when they intend publication, which in any case is usually anonymous, but not if they are writing privately or for clandestine circulation. Voltaire's *Traité de métaphysique* confirms the rule. Written for personal use, it begins in the *persona* of a visitor from outer space, but this convention is soon abandoned, and Voltaire adopts direct discourse in order to consider the questions of God, the soul and morality.[8] In the *Lettres philosophiques,* he discusses such matters by way of report on the opinions of notable Englishmen. Either because of the censorship, or because of their sense of what readers would and would not accept, authors prefer not to take responsibility in print for their deist views. This situation continued until Rousseau made an innovation by putting his name to the book containing a complete exposition of deism, *Emile,* in 1762, but even he ascribes it to the 'vicaire savoyard'. The habitual use of *persona* may reflect the feeling that deism was not a real option, but an ideal. Thus travel appears to be significant as regards the expression rather than the origins of deist ideas.

These considerations concerning the origins and causes of early French deism do not give support to a view which has been put forward from time to time, namely that deism as a movement lacks any unity: 'il affecte autant de formes qu'il existe de penseurs', in the words of Paul Hazard, apparently echoed by Jean Ehrard.[9] Such a view seems exaggerated. It cannot be expected, in the first place, that any great unity of belief should exist among scattered individuals owing no allegiance to an institution or leader, but apart from that the early French deists are in agreement on a wide range of issues. Where they differ, it is often a matter of emphasis. To demonstrate

---

[7] 'Enfin, ce qui a terriblement assailli ma prévention, c'est grand j'ai vu de grands peuples plus sages que nous, au moins mieux réglés dans leurs moeurs, être également persuadés de mille extravagances dont nous nous moquons' (*Difficultés,* Mortier edition, p. 90; see his Introduction, pp. 36–37, on the *Militaire philosophe's* travels).

[8] The supposition in the Introduction and Ch. I is that 'je descends du globe de Mars ou de Jupiter', but it is forgotten in Ch. II (*Traité de métaphysique,* Patterson edition, pp. 2, 6).

[9] P. Hazard, *La pensée européenne au dix-huitième siècle de Montesquieu à Lessing,* 3 vols. (Paris, 1946), Vol. II, p. 297 (contents list). Hazard's remark is based on a wide-ranging selection of examples, Bolingbroke, Pope, Voltaire and Lessing, the subjects of Pt. III, L.III of his study. For Ehrard's view, on a more limited period of time, see his *Idée de nature,* pp. 451–463: 'peu d'en faut qu'on ne doive alors compter presque autant de déismes que de déistes' (p. 451). However, citing Hazard's view (ibid., n. 10), Ehrard also expresses reservations: 'dans la première moitié du siècle au moins, l'unité d'inspiration l'emporte à notre avis sur la diversité des doctrines'.

this is any detail would be exceedingly repetitive; it must suffice to say that there are many variations of outlook — on the question of the soul, for example, there is hardly any reliable generalization to be made except that all recognize the difficulty of the subject — but within definite limits. In some deist texts organized worship is regarded as desirable, in others not, but the supposition is always that 'internal' worship, usually defined as gratitude and esteem towards the Creator, is preferable and fundamental. In the type of literary expression they adopt, their intellectual methods, and the influences which affect them, the early French deists display many close resemblances.

As for the equally great number of variations which can be found, the most far-reaching are those which separate Montesquieu and Voltaire from their predecessors. In the domain of expression, Voltaire's model is probably Montesquieu rather than anyone else; Montesquieu's is Marana, himself something of an odd man out among the deistic writers generally. Neither makes any acknowledgement of the work of the rational deists. It is not that the issues and concerns of before 1721 cease to be relevant, since in respect of both content and influences manifold similarities can be found. However, in the epistolary works by Montesquieu and Voltaire the very foundation of religious thought seems to have changed: now it is essentially secular moralizing, instead of the rationalism of previous writers. This approach neglects the question whether a particular belief is true or false, which is basic for the rationalist thinker. Montesquieu and Voltaire prefer to comment on the moral or social utility of the various aspects of religion, including the existence of God: 'S'il y a un Dieu, mon cher Rhêdi, il faut nécessairement qu'il soit juste'.[10] They write with approval of Muslim tolerance and Quaker pacifism, dismissively of controversial theology or Christian otherworldliness. Where style is concerned they choose obliquity, especially innuendo and ironic humour, instead of the direct discourse found in the clandestine treatises and the speeches made by spokesmen for deistic Utopias. Although Voltaire's Quaker is their direct literary descendant, the England in which he lives is realistic. Utopia appears only in passing, with the Pennsylvania of the Quakers and Montesquieu's Troglodytes.

The increase in realism is accompanied by a less critical attitude than previously to established religion. Compared to the author of the *Examen* and the *Militaire philosophe*, or even Tyssot de Patot, the early Montesquieu and Voltaire seem almost benign. This change should not be obscured by the violence of Voltaire's later onslaught on 'l'infâme', nor by the point that even mild criticisms in great writers may be more memorable than lengthy denunciations in the work of an amateur. The heroes of the *Lettres persanes*

---

[10] *Lettres persanes*, L. 83; but on the exact force of the hypothesis, see Chapter 13, pp. 210.

stay in France, while remaining loyal to Islam, in spite of their reservations about both the religions involved; in the *Lettres philosophiques,* the Quakers and the 'Sociniens, ou Ariens, ou anti-trinitaires' are Christians, though Voltaire's readers may have had difficulty in accepting it.

The most profound originality of the two writers, however, remains that they devised a mode of expression in which religion can be judged from a secular point of view without appearing to be the object of direct criticism. Furthermore, whereas the earlier deists had found considerable problems in incorporating morality into a rationalist scheme, Montesquieu and Voltaire are able to avoid the difficulty, by revising the basic assumptions. The new principle, laid down by Voltaire in the *Traité de métaphysique,* is that the measure of good and bad is social utility.[11] Thus the belief in God and other less fundamental features of religion are retained, but only on the condition that they are socially or morally valuable, or at least indifferent. For this change in attitude brought about by Montesquieu and Voltaire there seem to be no obvious sources. Although antecedents can easily be found, for instance in Bayle's concern with morality and the Militaire philosophe's God of justice, the importance of the innovations made in the *Lettres persanes* and the *Lettres philosophiques* seems greater than their indebtedness to earlier writings.

[11]   'La vertu et le vice, le bien et le mal moral, est donc en tout pays ce qui est utile ou nuisible à la société' (Patterson edition, p. 57).

Appendix

THE ATTRIBUTION OF THE *DIFFICULTÉS SUR LA RELIGION* TO ROBERT CHALLE

The most recent and detailed of the attempts to penetrate the anonymity of the 'Militaire philosophe' is the hypothesis advanced first by F. -L. Mars in 1974 and taken up by F. Deloffre and M. Menemencioglu in a number of publications, of which the most important are two articles by Deloffre, 'Robert Challe père du déisme français' and 'Une crise de conscience exemplaire à l'orée du siècle des Lumières: le cas de Robert Challe', together with a new edition of the *Difficultés*: Robert Challe (*sic*), *Difficultés sur la religion proposées au père Malebranche,* edited by F. Deloffre and M. Menemencioglu, SVEC, 209 (Oxford, 1982).[1] Challe, now best known as the author of the novel *Les illustres Françaises* (1713), was an obscure figure until his rehabilitation by Deloffre, who has carried out and inspired much research concerning him, and has edited, also in collaboration with Menemencioglu, his *Journal d'un voyage aux Indes orientales (1690–1691);*[2] an edition of his *Mémoires,* written in 1716, is also promised.[3]

Deloffre's hypothesis that the *Difficultés* were written by Challe is based first upon the parallels between the biography of Challe and the information found in, or deducible from the *Difficultés,* especially the introductory *cahier,* 'Ce qui m'a fait ouvrir les yeux', secondly on the resemblance between Challe's works and the *Difficultés* as regards such matters as literary and historical knowledge; and finally on the similarity of religious attitudes which Deloffre finds in Challe's personal works and the *Difficultés.*

BIOGRAPHY

The main reasons for identifying the two writers are that they must have been born at about the same time, saw military service, and visited both

[1] 'Challe père du déism': RHLF 79 (1979), 947–980; 'Une crise de conscience': *Transations of the Fifth International Congress on the Enlightenment,* Vol. III, SVEC 192 (1980), 1063–1071. The edition will be referred to here as FD/MM edition.

[2] Paris (Mercure de France), 1979. The introduction includes a 'Vie de Robert Challe' (pp. 16–36), referred to below as 'Vie de Challe', which assumes that he wrote the *Difficultés* and incorporates material from this work into Challe's biography; it should therefore be treated with caution.

[3] The available edition, referred to below as *Mémoires,* is: *Un colonial au temps de Colbert: mémoires de Robert Challes (sic),* edited by A. Augustin-Thierry (Paris, 1931), which Deloffre and others described as expurgated (see e.g. *Difficultés,* FD/MM edition, p. 531, n. 242).

Canada and India.[4] The relevant facts about the Militaire, which are few, are conveniently summarized by Mortier.[5] Challe's life is known largely from the *Journal* and *Mémoires,* but also from the researches of Deloffre and J. Mesnard.[6] He was born in 1659. The Militaire's date of birth must be such that he was at least eighteen by 1683, when the persecution of the Huguenots by soldiers, known as 'dragonnades', began. According to the *Difficultés,* he had serious doubts at eighteen ('environ dix-huit ans'), then left school; 'La persécution des Huguenots suivit ces premiers temps', a statement followed by the description quoted above, which must be of an episode during the 'dragonnades'. [7] This places his date of birth in, say, the years 1663 to 1665. However, the year 1659 is not impossible.

The Militaire mentions that he was tonsured, in other words that at one stage, presumably before the doubts became serious, he was preparing for a career in the Church;[8] nothing of this kind is known in Challe's biography. Both did the optional *philosophie* year at the end of their schooling,[9] after which both joined the army, in Challe's case for the 1677 campaign; his *Journal* says that he saw action at Mont-Cassel 'le jour de Pâques fleuries onze avril 1677'.[10] The treaty of Nijmegen in 1678 must have halted his military career, since we hear no more of it, and he turned to the law, having relatives in the profession.[11] Probably because of lack of money he did not pursue this either, but went to Canada in 1683 with a small share in a trading company which had just been set up, the *Compagnie des pêches sédentaires d'Acadie;*[12] in the years that followed, up to 1689, he made two or three more visits to Canada and others to various European destinations, apparently on the company's business.[13]

All of this makes it seem highly unlikely that Challe could have taken part in the 'dragonnades', in 1683–1685, as the author of the *Difficultés* did. The

[4]   For the original form of the hypothesis, see F. -L. Mars, 'Avec Casonova à la recherche du *Militaire philosophe.* Une conjecture raisonnée: Robert Challe', *Casanova Gleanings* 17 (1974), 21–30.

[5]   His introduction, pp. 36–38.

[6]   In addition to Deloffre, 'Challe père du déisme', see particularly his article 'A la recherche de Robert Chasles' (*sic*) 'auteur des Illustres Françaises', *Revue des sciences humaines* (1959), 231–254, referred to below as 'A la recherche de Chasles'; Jean Mesnard, 'L'identité de Robert Challe', RHLF 79 (1979), 915–939, referred to below as 'Identité de Challe'; Lois A. Russell, 'Robert Challe à Québec', ibid., 1003–1012. This issue of RHLF was devoted to Challe.

[7]   See Chapter 10 above, p. 139, for the passage in question. Deloffre and Menemencioglu (p. 450, n. 48) make the extraordinary claim that it does not refer to the 'dragonnades'; they disagree with a marginal note which makes the obvious identification in the main manuscript, Mazarine 1163.

[8]   Mortier edition, p. 82; FD/MM edition, p. 48.

[9]   Respectively p. 84 and p. 48 of the editions; Challe, *Journal,* p. 95, a remark made to him in conversation, 'vous qui avez fait votre philosophie'.

[10]   *Journal,* p. 259.

[11]   Mesnard, 'Identité de Challe', pp. 922ff.; *Journal,* p. 18 and p. 551, n. 23; p. 372 and p. 617, n. 692.

[12]   Mesnard, ibid., p. 934.

[13]   Russell, 'R. Challe à Québec', p. 1004.

Militaire's treatise suggests throughout that his whole career was spent in military service of one sort or another (it is not clear when he became an 'officier militaire dans la marine', in the terms of the manuscript's title). He also mentions being at a siege, named as that of Luxembourg in one manuscript and of 'L. . .' in another; the siege of Luxembourg took place in 1684, at a time when Challe was in Canada.[14] In order to explain how this information could be accommodated in Challe's biography Deloffre and Menemencioglu are obliged to make various more or less implausible suppositions.[15]

The presence of Challe and the Militaire in both Canada and India is certain, and as far as it goes provides one of the stronger arguments in favour of identifying them. Challe wrote about Canada in the *Mémoires* and the *Journal* and about India, where he went as 'écrivain du roi', not as an 'officer militaire', on an expedition led by Duquesne-Guiton, in the *Journal*. The Militaire refers to his North American experiences in several passages of the *Difficultés*.[16] In the course of an argument about race in which he lists Indians, Caribbeans ('Caraïbes'), Iroquois, Eskimoes and Negroes, he observes: 'Je ne parle que de peuples que j'ai vus chez eux'.[17] But this overall similarity does not extend to all the points of detail. Both writers refer to Quebec and Montreal, but only the Militaire seems to have reached the latter town, Challe having been forced to turn back after setting out to go there.[18] In India, the Militaire visited Goa, on the western or Malabar coast, but Challe's route did not take him to that side of the sub-continent.[19] Nor does he seem to have seen Negroes 'chez eux', as the Militaire claims to have done,

---

[14]   Deloffre and Menemencioglu admit that this is an objection: 'un document récemment retrouvé par Mrs R. Runte établit sa présence au Canada à la belle saison de 1684' (*Difficultés*, their edition, pp. 467–468, n. 157 to p. 109, which discusses the question of the siege).

[15]   See note 7 above, and *Difficultés*, FD/MM edition, p. 450, n. 49, suggesting that the passage about the 'dragonnades' is fiction, or, if not, that Challe might have been involved in the incident while on a journey between La Rochelle and Paris mentioned in a passage of the *Journal* (p. 353), which however does not give a date or refer to any such incident. On the siege of Luxembourg, they suggest an amendment or falsification of the manuscripts (*Difficultés*, pp. 467–468, n. 157). Their 'Vie de Challe' states (*Journal*, p. 21) that the relevant passage of the *Difficultés* is suspect, a statement for which there is no foundation.

[16]   Mortier, Introduction, p. 36–37, gives the references. However, contrary to what he affirms (p. 36), the Militaire does not say explicitly that he lived in Virginia (see Mortier edition, pp. 90–91, 108; FD/MM edition, pp. 53, 67).

[17]   Mortier edition, p. 218; FD/MM edition, p. 162.

[18]   Mortier edition, p. 142; FD/MM edition, p. 94. Note that although the information about the Jesuits implies personal knowledge, it might also have been gained at second hand. On Challe's failure through illness to reach Montreal, see FD/MM edition, p. 463, nn. 105, 106, and Russell, 'R. Challe à Québec', pp. 1005–1009.

[19]   Deloffre and Menemencioglu (p. 463, n. 104) accept this, while producing another odd argument to evade the problem. Their supporting reference to the *Journal*, p. '242', appears to be faulty; see *Journal*, pp. 23–25, summarizing the route Challe followed, and e.g. pp. 303, 426, indicating that he knew about Goa only from others.

a claim which might be substantiated by a reference to Angola in the same passage of the *Difficultés*.[20]

Nearer to home, both the *Difficultés* and Challe's personal works reveal knowledge of the Mediterranean,[21] but whereas Challe visited northern Europe there is nothing in the *Difficultés* about this region, except a remark concerning Danish history and an imaginary incident set in London.[22] Challe asserts also that he went to Smyrna, Constantinople, and Jerusalem, but the references in the *Difficultés* to the Middle East give no hint that the author had gone there.[23] Conversely, the Militaire relates an incident during a campaign in Piedmont, which Challe seems not to have visited.[24]

Challe returned to France in 1691 and was at the battle of La Hogue in 1692. He gives a vivid description of it in his *Mémoires*, of which only the first part, down to 1701, was completed (the title is slightly misleading, since most of the book is social history rather than autobiography). He presumably took to writing, since he applied for a 'privilège' for a continuation of *Don Quixote* which appeared in 1702.[25] In 1712 there is documentary evidence that he was married and had a minor clerical post; at intervals from 1713 to 1718 he corresponded *incognito* with the *Journal littéraire* of The Hague.[26] He died in 1721. The Militaire's biography is still more obscure, even the date of his death being unknown. The *Préface* to the *Difficultés* explains that any personal allusion that might identify him has been removed from the original manuscript, for fear of reprisals against his

---

[20]   He writes, on the question of the fixity of race, 'Les Caraïbes font des Caraïbes à Angola' (Mortier edition p. 218; FD/MM edition p. 163). As Deloffre and Menemencioglu observe (p. 484, n. 147), this need not mean, strictly speaking, that he went to Angola himself; but taken in conjunction with his remark that he saw Negroes 'chez eux', it does suggest that he visited the west coast of southern Africa.

[21]   *Journal*, pp. 110, 457. The references in the *Difficultés* to the Aegean, Rome, and Spain (Mortier edition, pp. 235, 78, 81; FD/MM edition, pp. 178, 45, 47) do not necessarily imply, however, that the Militaire went to these places by sea.

[22]   Mortier edition, p. 279; FD/MM edition, p. 231. The Militaire also refers to the Arminians and the Dutch (respectively pp. 174 and 293; pp. 124 and 245). For Challe's visits to Copenhagen and Stockholm, see *Journal*, p. 457. The imaginary example (Mortier edition, p. 129; FD/MM edition, p. 84) concerns a fraudulent claim: 'Pierre dit qu'il m'a trouvé à Londres, prisonnier de guerre (...)', and requests the return of money he says that he had loaned. Deloffre and Menemencioglu regard this (p. 460, n. 68) as confirmation that the Militaire was Challe, their reason being that in his *Journal* (pp. 97–98, 215) Challe describes being taken prisoner by the English in America and transported to London, where he saw Saint-Evremond. If there were any explicit indication in the *Difficultés* that the Militaire's example were based on his own experience, the coincidence might be significant, but there is not. He often invents such examples; see note 33 below.

[23]   For instance, he mentions Constantinople and Jerusalem (Mortier edition, pp. 90, 184; FD/MM edition, pp. 53, 132), but only as illustrations.

[24]   Mortier edition, p. 219; FD/MM edition, p. 164.

[25]   'Vie de Challe', in *Journal*, p. 29.

[26]   Mesnard, 'Identité de Challe', p. 938; F. Deloffre, 'Une correspondance littéraire au début du XVIIIe siècle; Robert Challes' (*sic*) 'et le *Journal Littéraire* de La Haye', *Annales Universitatis Saraviensis*, 1954, 144–182.

family;[27] this might explain why there is no overlap between the incidents related in the *Difficultés* on the one hand and Challe's personal works on the other, which in itself is an important objection to Deloffre's hypothesis. With Challe's *Journal* and *Mémoires* the situation is different, ideas and anecdotes being repeated from one to the other.[28]

Both writers, then, were much-travelled men, but the correspondence between their journeys is not at all complete. In matters of family, too, there are significant differences. No information is given in the *Difficultés* about the Militaire's parentage, but is reasonably certain that he was married, with at least one son. The anonymous Préface tells us that the author was survived by 'une pauvre veuve, chargée d'une grosse famille, à qui le père n'a guère laissé que l'honneur';[29] this could perhaps be an elaboration of the reality, as Deloffre and Menemencioglu argue,[30] but in the body of the work the Militaire mentions being a husband and father and gives illustrative examples involving his children.[31] In one version of the first of these the phrase 'mon fils qui est devant Barcelone' occurs, which in the context – the question whether he would believe the news that his son had been killed – must mean that the son was at a siege or battle.[32] These examples do not seem to be the purely imaginative kind employed by philosophers for purposes of illustration, some of which are however to be found in the

[27] The author of the preface writes: 'On a cru devoir retrancher certains traits historiques d'un grand poids, mais qui auraient pu caractériser l'auteur et attirer bien des maux à une pauvre veuve' (Mortier edition, p. 73; FD/MM edition, p. 40).

[28] Above all the animosity towards the Jesuits (for relevant passages in the *Journal* and *Mémoires*, see note 75 below), but also the interest in ministerial policies, especially as regards the prospects for French colonial projects.

[29] Mortier edition, p. 73; FD/MM edition, p. 40.

[30] Deloffre and Menemencioglu take the view that the preface is by Challe, and that the details it gives about the manuscript are fictional (like those habitually devised at the time by the authors of travel stories, etc.). The reference in the preface to a widow, which is on the face of it difficult to reconcile with the theory that it was written by the widow's husband, is 'sans doute pour Challe une amère préfiguration de ce qui se passera à sa mort' (FD/MM edition, p. 22). Most of the arguments advanced on the authorship of the preface (ibid., pp. 18–23) have no force against the obvious supposition that the author was a copyist of the *Difficultés*, not their author also.

[31] Mortier edition, p. 96; FD/MM edition, p. 57. Having rid himself of his former scruples, he is 'tout un autre homme à l'égard de mes devoirs essentiels, tout un autre père, tout un autre fils, tout un autre mari, tout un autre maître'. He adds: 'je serais tout un autre soldat ou tout un autre capitaine', the use of the conditional suggesting that he is writing after retirement and that what precedes – 'père', 'fils', etc. – refers to his present state. For the examples, see Mortier edition, pp. 134, 359, 384, 389; FD/MM edition, pp. 89, 303, 321, 325.

[32] See FD/MM edition, p. 461, n. 84, for the possible dates, 1701, 1705, or 1710–1711. The complete manuscript, Mazarine 1163, has 'mon fils qui est à l'armée', which when compared to the reading 'devant Barcelone' in the passage of the Sépher manuscript, seems to exemplify the removal of identifying data explained in the preface (see note 27).

Difficultés.[33] Assuming that they reflect reality, this would differentiate him from Challe, who appears to have died childless.[34]

LITERARY ALLUSIONS

Of the various kinds of evidence internal to the texts the parallels of ideas or subject-matter ('structures associatives') advanced by Deloffre and Menemencioglu in support of their hypothesis are too vague and few in number to weigh very heavily;[35] computer-assisted comparisons of vocabulary might be useful, but would be difficult to arrange and have not been attempted. References to the author's reading are perhaps the most likely kind of evidence to lead to definite conclusions. Deloffre's hypothesis is supported, in his view, by the fact that among the classical, Christian and modern authors cited in the texts a number appear in all three; thus he has established that of nine early Christian writers mentioned in the *Difficultés*, five are also in the *Journal* and *Mémoires*. However, detailed comparison reveals significant differences in the treatment of these writers. Challe displays a very good knowledge of St. Augustine,[36] whom he likes to quote in Latin, and is particularly impressed by his arguments for predestination.[37] The manner of the Militaire's references to Augustine, however, is very imprecise, as if Augustine's work was not familiar to him, and he attacks predestination.[38] With another saint, St. Bernard, the contrast is more striking, since he was one of Challe's favourite authors, while the only

[33] For instance: Mortier edition, pp. 120, 149, 192; FD/MM edition, pp. 78, 103, 139; see also note 22. Mortier (p. 36) gives an example which seems to me ambiguous (his edition, p. 110; FD/MM edition, p. 68: 'Je suis né à Paris, je suis papiste; (...)'), and disagrees with R. Brummer, who thought that the passage showed that the writer of it was born in Paris.

[34] FD/MM edition, p. 461, n. 84; 'Vie de Challe', in *Journal*, p. 29; Mesnard, 'Identité de Challe', p. 938.

[35] Their edition, p. 9, which is based on Deloffre, 'Challe père du déisme', pp. 961–966. The two most elaborate examples concern the soul and the colonization of America; but a comparison of the passages adduced as evidence (the soul: *Journal*, pp. 116–118 and *Difficultés*, Mortier edition, pp. 331–335; FD/MM edition, pp. 283–286; colonization: *Journal*, p. 100–101 and *Difficultés*, editions respectively pp. 294–295; pp. 245–246) will show that the general resemblance is counter-balanced by important differences, which would take too long to specify here – for instance on the subject of metempsychosis, the treatment of which in the *Journal* and the *Difficultés* can be followed through the index references given in the Deloffre/Menemencioglu editions.

[36] Deloffre and Menemencioglu have been able to identify the volume of selections from Augustine, Bernard and others which Challe took with him on his voyage (*Journal*, p. 574, n. 145). They also note that some of Challe's quotations from Augustine come from passages not found in the volume, which testifies again to his knowledge of the saint's works.

[37] *Journal*, p. 103.

[38] For imprecise references, see Mortier edition, pp. 184, 195, 288, 290, 301; FD/MM edition, pp. 132, 142, 241, 243, 260. For example (p. 301/p. 260): 'un père de l'Eglise a dit que les vertus des païens étaient des vices'.

comment about him in the *Difficultés* is that he was an impostor.[39] Among more modern writers, there is hardly any overlap in the references to religious authorities, with the notable exception of Pascal.[40] Without naming him the Militaire calls him 'un grand génie, mais papiste et cagot',[41] but Challe admired him greatly, and had 'lu et relu vingt fois' the *Lettres provinciales* (and other Jansenist works).[42] It should be added that Malebranche, whom the Militaire read twice, he says, 'contre mon génie et ma coutume', does not seem to be known to Challe.[43] As for Descartes, who in the *Difficultés* is 'le grand génie du siècle', he is regarded by Challe, in the *Journal,* with some contempt, because of his views on the souls of animals.[44]

The material concerning Latin poetry provides only slightly better evidence for Deloffre's hypothesis. Challe's knowledge of the classical poets seems, in the *Journal* especially, to be considerably greater than the Militaire's, but both writers quote from them reasonably often. In two cases the parallel could be significant. Usually, however, the position is the same as with St. Augustine: when both writers refer to the same poet the Militaire does so less often and more vaguely. Ovid, for instance, was a favourite of Challe's, as he says himself and there are many quotations to prove it.[45] When the *Difficultés* refers to Ovid, on the other hand, it is only in general terms (for example, in order to remark that the events recounted in the *Metamorphoses* are more credible than those in the New Testament).[46] There is one passage of Ovid which the Militaire knows well enough to adapt, but the quotation is from the famous *envoi* of the *Metamorphoses,* with which any educated person in the seventeenth century ought to have been familiar.[47] Another important figure in this connection is Lucretius. Although the Militaire is aware of his reputation as a source of free-thought, he denies having ever read him: 'Je n'ai pas seulement voulu jeter les yeux sur un Lucrèce qu'un de mes amis me laissa il y a quelques mois', he says, in a passage about unorthodox thinkers. [48] He does quote 'Tantum religio potuit

[39]   Mortier edition, p. 301; FD/MM edition, p. 261. See also a marginal note in Mazarine 1163 to the word 'fourberie', giving St Bernard as an example (editions respectively p. 87; pp. 51 and 451, n. 64).
[40]   The *Difficultés* refer (Mortier edition, p. 308; FD/MM edition, p. 267), mainly by title, to a number of minor apologists whom Challe probably did not know at all, and also (editions respectively pp. 83, 318; pp. 48, 273) to the successful *Délices de l'esprit* by Desmarets de Saint-Sorlin, which he could well have seen.
[41]   Mortier edition, p. 297; FD/MM edition, p. 250 and p. 510, n. 518.
[42]   *Journal,* p. 435.
[43]   Mortier edition, p. 74; FD/MM edition, p. 41.
[44]   Mortier edition, p. 327; FD/MM edition, p. 280; *Journal,* p. 343 (cf. pp. 351–352: the *cogito* is a 'ridicule syllogisme').
[45]   *Journal,* p. 75, and many other references (see index).
[46]   Mortier edition, pp. 123, 212; FD/MM edition, pp. 79, 157.
[47]   Mortier edition, pp. 227, 420; FD/MM edition, pp. 170, 348.
[48]   Mortier edition, p. 75; FD/MM edition, p. 41.

suadere malorum', the best-known tag from Lucretius (quoted also by Challe), but ascribes it merely to 'les anciens philosophes';[49] he also knows that Lucretius, like Epicurus and Democritus, did not believe in Providence and attributed events to chance, a point which is mentioned in many of the apologias of the time and was in effect common knowledge.[50] There is nothing here to make us reject his assertion that he did not look at Lucretius, yet Deloffre and Menemencioglu affirm in a note than 'En réalité, Challe' (sic; i.e. the author of the Difficultés) 'comme tous les libertins français, connaît Lucrèce depuis longtemps', citing Challe's Journal as proof.[51]

The two quotations which might support Deloffre's hypothesis come from Juvenal and Persius. Challe's Journal quotes a line from the former: 'o sanctas gentes quibus haec nascuntur in hortis/numina'.[52] In the Difficultés the same line is quoted, but inaccurately: 'On a dit d'eux: Sacra gens cui nascuntur in hortis numina'.[53] Presumably we are to think, if Challe wrote the Difficultés, that his memory had deteriorated in the time since the Journal, which however, according to Deloffre, was revised for publication after the date of the Difficultés.[54] There is a somewhat analogous situation with the other quotation, three words from Persius, 'ad populum phaleras'. Challe records it in the Journal as a retort by a Portuguese priest whom he meets, and cites it again in the Mémoires; both times correctly.[55] The Militaire also gives the quotation, but with the mis-spelling 'faleras'.[56] Admittedly, the error could have been made by the copyist, but it tends to confirm the impression that the Militaire's knowledge of literature was less sound than Challe's. In any case, even if the coincidence between Challe's and the Militaire's works were perfect, as regards these two quotations, it would be too slight a matter to provide much evidence in favour of Deloffre's hypothesis.

In the areas of modern literature, little is to be deduced either for or against the belief that Challe wrote the Difficultés. The work contains several allusions to Don Quixote, which might seem to be significant in view of the presumption that Challe wrote a continuation, but, apart from the fact that the book was very popular, one of the allusions contains a mistake, as Deloffre and Menemencioglu point out (a confusion between Don Quixote and Sancho Panza);[57] such an error seems more likely to have been made by

[49]   Mortier edition, p. 326; FD/MM edition, p. 279.
[50]   Mortier edition, p. 316; FD/MM edition, p. 272.
[51]   FD/MM edition, p. 444, n. 6, referring to the Journal, pp. 97, 295.
[52]   Journal, p. 304 (Juvenal, Satire XV, lines 10–11).
[53]   Mortier edition, p. 304; FD/MM edition, p. 264.
[54]   Deloffre, 'A la recherche de Chasles', p. 244; Journal, pp. 57, 560, n. 6, 631, n. 874.
[55]   Journal, p. 366; Mémoires, p. 189.
[56]   Mortier edition, p. 247; FD/MM edition, p. 189.
[57]   Mortier edition, p. 360; FD/MM edition, pp. 304 and 521–522, n. 106.

someone who had read the novel solely for entertainment than by the author of a continuation. For the rest, the Militaire's references to light literature, such as the tales published in the 'Bibliothèque bleue',[58] indicate that his taste was less sophisticated than Challe's, who was well acquainted with those seventeenth-century authors, like Racine and Boileau, who have since become classics; Molière is the only writer whom both quote with appreciation, and there is little in common between their references to him except an allusion to the *Malade imaginaire.*[59]

The Militaire's historical knowledge is also rather limited. He mentions various historical events in the course of argument, usually in order to denigrate the Church,[60] but nothing suggests that the basis of his knowledge was wider than what he could have acquired at school. As a good Cartesian, he distrusts factual evidence in any case. By contrast, Challe's *Mémoires* are largely concerned with recent French history from Richelieu to the end of the seventeenth century, about which he tells many detailed anecdotes; on occasion he is also capable of discussing fairly abstruse aspects of ecclesiastical history.[61] Nothing like this is to be found in the *Difficultés,* the author writing 'Je ne me pique pas de science historique (...) Le commun du monde est plus savant que moi sur ce chapitre'.[62] Conversely, the Militaire, who is generally supposed to have had the mathematical education of an officer in one of the technical branches of the armed forces, is able to refer to obscure mathematicians and scientists of antiquity, Diophantus, Archytas, and Proclus Diadocus, the first of whom he regards as fit to rank with Euclid and Aristotle.[63] It is hardly necessary to say that there is no trace of any such knowledge or interest in Challe.

RELIGIOUS ATTITUDES

If the religious outlook of Challe's personal works closely resembled that of the *Difficultés,* or even appeared a likely basis from which it might have

---

[58] Mortier edition, pp. 131, 210, 237, 272; FD/MM edition, pp. 86, 155, 180, 219.
[59] Mortier edition, pp. 173 (quotation from *Malade imaginaire*), 330 (*Pourceaugnac*), to which should be added p. 86 ('un air tartuffe'); FD/MM edition, pp. 123, 282, 50. *Journal,* pp. 82 (*Amphitryon* quoted), 131 (*Précieuses ridicules*), 235 (*Misanthrope*), 350 (*Amphitryon* quoted), 404 (*Tartuffe* quoted), 478 ('une conversation à être mise dans le *Malade imaginaire*'), 542 (*L'Avare*).
[60] E.g. in the fourth section, 'La manière surprenante dont le christianisme s'est établi' or the seventh section, second article, of the *Troisième cahier,* 'Les conciles' (Mortier edition, pp. 276–280, 286–289; FD/MM edition, pp. 227–232, 240–241).
[61] *Mémoires,* Ch.III (pp. 31ff.).
[62] Mortier edition, p. 100; FD/MM edition, p. 60. Deloffre and Menemencioglu, in their belief that Challe, who knew a good deal of history, is responsible for this remark, endeavour to cast doubt on its veracity (p. 456, n. 6). The Militaire also writes, in the preliminary letter to Malebranche: 'j'ai quelque teinture de l'histoire' (editions respectively pp. 76–77; p. 43).
[63] Mortier edition, pp. 289, 316, 422; FD/MM edition, pp. 242, 273, 349.

developed, the detailed factual evidence presented above might be set aside, but the opposite is the case. In the *Journal* Challe writes as a sincere Catholic, as is manifest from numerous passages, and even boasts of his reputation in this respect.[64] He does indeed make many criticisms of his fellow-Catholics, both laity and clergy, but the viewpoint is invariably that of a believer.[65] The *Journal* was written up for publication in about 1708, if we are to believe a statement at the beginning of the dedicatory epistle, though some later additions must have been made.[66] The *Difficultés* date from about 1710, perhaps having been written over a period of a few years, and are – the point should not need labouring – not Catholic, nor even Christian. In the *Mémoires,* of 1716, Challe writes again from the Catholic point of view, and again there are many separate passages to prove it. Despite this, Deloffre and Menemencioglu argue that there are so many resemblances between Challe's personal works and the *Difficultés* as to constitute an 'identité de doctrine'.[67] They are referenced in tabular form in the article 'Challe père du déisme', and mainly comprise criticisms of such matters as intolerance and superstition.[68] These criticisms are certainly to be found in Challe's work, and many of them, such as the criticisms of the papacy, can be paralleled in the *Difficultés.*[69] This does not amount to 'identité de doctrine'. The very considerable difference which separates the two writers can be gauged by comparing, for instance, a passage in the *Mémoires,* in which Challe expresses reservations about the custom of public prayer before battle, with the comments on the same subject in the *Difficultés.* Challe is ironical about the chaplain's sermon (it is on this occasion, before the battle

---

[64]   *Journal,* p. 300; expressing doubts about the virtues of certain saints, he says: 'si je n'étais pas connu pour aussi zélé pour ma religion que je le suis par la grâce de Dieu, on pourrait dire que ceci sent le libertinage, ou du moins le calvinisme', and defends himself against his self-criticism.

[65]   E.g. *Journal,* p. 245, regretting that Christians, who ostensibly believe that the tabernacle contains 'le Saint des Saints, le Créateur de toutes choses, en un mot Dieu lui-même', should behave with less respect for it than ignorant idolaters have for an animal's head which they worship.

[66]   *Journal,* pp. 57 and 444, a reference to the year 1713; and see note 54.

[67]   FD/MM edition, p. 10. The assertion which follows, that all the criticisms of Christianity found in the *Difficultés* can be found also in Challe's works, 'sauf sur certains points de dogme et les attaques contre la Révélation et ses instruments', is a good example of the question-begging method of argument adopted in this edition. It is precisely because (among other things) the *Difficultés* have criticisms of dogma and the concept of Revelation, which are very important matters, that they cannot be by Challe, whose mild criticisms are directed only against the clergy and relatively unimportant aspects of Christianity.

[68]   'Challe père du déisme', pp. 967–969.

[69]   However, the parallels are not as close as Deloffre implies; compare, for example, the first page of the *Difficultés* (Mortier edition, p. 78; FD/MM edition, p. 45) with the passages from the *Journal* (pp. 100, 125–126, 300) which are supposed to contain such parallels. Challe records that the Germans say that Clement VII had a mistress (p. 300), and he is hesitant over the question of infallibility (pp. 100, 125–126); the Militaire says that the Pope gave or withheld everything 'au gré de l'avarice de sa concubine, laquelle même durant ses délices décidait souverainement sur toutes sortes de matières, se trouvant ainsi l'oracle du St. Esprit'. Previously he describes 'cette Sainteté si révérée' as being often 'un vieux mangé de goutte et pourri d'ulcères qui suivent les plus infâmes maladies'. Such violence of tone is quite foreign to Challe.

of La Hogue, that he quotes 'Ad populum phaleras'), but concludes: 'Toutefois, je le répète encore, cette cérémonie, toute sainte qu'elle est, ne me plaît pas à l'instant d'un combat'.[70] The Militaire's attitude is as hostile as usual: 'Quoi de plus ridicule que ces prières pour la prospérité des armes, et ces Te Deum lorsqu'on est victorieux?'[71] Another passage from the Mémoires tells a humourous anecdote about Anne d'Autriche, on a pilgrimage to cure sterility; the story is at the expense of belief in a relic at Saint-Germain, but Challe's tone remains respectful.[72] As against this, the Militaire typically describes relics as 'os pourris', mocking the belief in them in the strongest terms.[73]

These are comparatively minor matters. A subject which is of quite a different order of importance, for Challe at least, is the Society of Jesus, a recurrent target for his hostility; in Deloffre's table of resemblances, nine references are given for the Journal and Mémoires. By contrast there are only three for the Difficultés (which, unlike the other two texts, is entirely devoted to religion). On inspection we find that, of these, two are entirely trivial, leaving as the Militaire's sole contribution to the question a comment on the luxury in which Jesuits live in Goa.[74] In Challe's Mémoires, criticism of the Jesuits plays an essential role in his argument about the decline of France – they are blamed for their pernicious influence on the King, La Chaise is said to have had an equally disastrous influence on James II (through the English king's confessor), they swindle when they get the chance (a long anecdote), they go to Canada for profit rather than to spread the word of God, they try to seduce Iroquois girls, and so on. Nor can this attitude be explained as a late development in Challe's life, since the Journal, written before the Difficultés, contains exactly the same kind of criticism; the index to the edition by Deloffre and Menemencioglu has thirteen entries under 'Jésuites', including the very lengthy conversation between Challe and François Martin, most of which concerns the misdeeds of the Society, and in which some of the detailed criticisms made in the Mémoires are also found.[75] Why Challe should have omitted all this material from the Difficultés, if he had written it, remains unexplained.

As regards positive beliefs, there are also significant differences between the Difficultés and Challe's works; the discourse which he attributes in the Journal to an abbé, proving the existence of God, the immortality of the soul, and the permanence of good actions, is not particularly close to the

---

[70] Mémoires, p. 188.
[71] Mortier edition, p. 269 (Mazarine 1163 version); FD/MM edition, p. 216 (Sépher ms. version, quoted here).
[72] Mémoires, pp. 55–56.
[73] E.g. Difficultés, Mortier edition, p. 304; FD/MM edition, p. 264.
[74] Mortier edition, pp. 142, 178, 249; FD/MM edition, pp. 94, 127, 192.
[75] Mémoires, pp. 8ff., 22–23, 45–47, 79, 88ff., 92ff.; Journal, e.g. p. 212, which refers forward to the talk with Martin, pp. 420–445; see especially pp. 444–445.

Militaire's positive deism in his 'quatrième cahier', although Deloffre considers it to be so;[76] but there is no value in discussing the matter, since it could be argued, in favour of Deloffre's hypothesis, that the likeness is slight because the discourse was an early form of the Militaire's deism. However, this argument cannot be used against the evidence for Challe's Christian convictions that is found in the *Mémoires,* since they were written after the *Difficultés.* They contain one passage dealing with a question which is fundamental to the Militaire's programme in the *Difficultés,* namely the institution of a religion in a new society. For Challe, the question arose in connection with the project for a French colony in the Mississippi region (i.e. the future Louisiana), and he devotes some time to giving advice and recommendations.[77] He states firmly that Catholicism, 'la religion catholique, apostolique, et romaine', must be the basis of the new society. It need hardly be said that this is in complete contradiction to the Militaire discussing, in the last section of his treatise, the subject of 'l'instruction et le culte'. For him, a brief deistic credo suffices, without any form of 'exterior' worship, nor any priests. Challe writes that, although he would ban Jesuits and monks, 'Il est cependant indispensable d'avoir des pasteurs'. They would be under secular supervision (an interesting example of Utopian Erastianism in 1716), but would have a church, a presbytery, and everything necessary for worship. Challe is specific: '. . . tels que sont les fonts baptismaux, les nappes d'autel, le missel, le lutrin, les lampes et les chandeliers ...', and so on, for three more lines. On one point he is strict, that there must be no burials inside the church: 'c'est une impiété, et même un sacrilège, de mettre la pourriture et le rebut de la nature, dans le même lieu où repose et où nous adorons le Saint des Saints'.

According to Deloffre's hypothesis, this was written by the author of the *Difficultés* a few years after he had completed his long anti-Christian manuscript and sent it to Malebranche. It is suggested by Menemencioglu, in order to understand how a *libertin* deist might have repented and returned to Catholicism, that we should regard as autobiographical the story of Gallouin, in the *Illustres Françaises,* who dies in the odour of sanctity after a life of debauch and irreligion.[78] All things are possible, but it remains preferable to believe that Challe and the Militaire were two men, one an unprejudiced Catholic of Gallican tendencies, the other a self-made deist hostile to Catholicism, and not a single individual who would be an incomprehensible mixture of both.

---

[76] 'Challe père du déisme', pp. 972–973, on the *Journal,* pp. 113–125.

[77] *Mémoires,* p. 252.

[78] Meláhat Menemencioglu, 'Gallouin-Don Juan, une clé pour Robert Challe', RHLF 79 (1979), 981–993. The article is of interest in that its quotations from Challe reveal his piety, belying what it is intended to prove.

Bibliography

1. MANUSCRIPT AND PUBLISHED WORKS DISCUSSED IN THE TEXT AS EXAMPLES OR PRECURSORS OF DEISM

Analyse de la religion chrêtienne: see *Religion chrêtienne analisêe*

L'Anti-bigot ou le faux dêvotieux ('Les Quatrains du dêiste'), in *Les Libertins au XVIIe siècle,* Textes choisis et prêsentês par Antoine Adam, Paris, 1964, pp. 90—109 (original in Bibliothêque nationale ms., fonds latin 10329; text also in Frêdêric Lachèvre, *Voltaire mourant, enquête faite en 1778,* Paris, 1908, pp. 110—136 and his *Le libertinage devant le Parlement de Paris: le procès du poète Theôphile de Viau,* Le libertinage au XVIIe siècle, I, 2 vols., Paris, 1909, Vol. II, pp. 91—126).

Bodin, Jean, *Colloque de Jean Bodin des secrets cachez des choses sublimes,* edited by Roger Chauvirê, Paris, 1914 (partial edition of 17th-century translation of the *Colloquium heptaplomeres*).

Colloquium of the Seven about Secrets of the Sublime by Jean Bodin, translated by Marion Leathers Daniels Kuntz, Princeton, 1975.

Boulainviller (or Boulainvilliers), Henri de, *Œuvres philosophiques,* edited by Renêe Simon, 2 vols., The Hague, 1973—1975.

Chaulieu, Guillaume Amfrye de, abbê, *Œuvres, d'après les manuscrits de l'auteur,* 2 vols., The Hague, 1777.

Poêsies libertines, in Frêdêric Lachèvre, *Disciples et successeurs de Théophile de Viau: les derniers libertins,* Le libertinage au XVIIe siècle, XI, Paris, 1924, pp. 143—200.

d'Assoucy, Charles Coypeau, *Pensêes dans le Saint-Office de Rome,* 1676, in d'Assoucy, *Aventures burlesques,* edited by Emile Colombey, Paris, 1858, pp. 339—398.

Examen de la religion en quinze chapitres, Bibliothêque de l'Arsenal, Paris, ms. 2091, ff. 305—438; Bibliothêque nationale mss., nouvelles acquisitions françaises 1902, 10436; etc.

Foigny, Gabriel de, *La Terre australe connue: c'est à dire la description de ce pays inconnu jusqu' ici, de ses moeurs et de ses coutumes. Par M. Sadeur,* Vannes (or rather Geneva), 1676 (second edition: *Les Avantures de Jacques Sadeur dans la dêcouverte et le voiage de la Terre*

Australe, Paris, 1692; 1676 edition, with variants from 1692 edition, reprinted by Frédéric Lachèvre in his *Les successeurs de Cyrano de Bergerac,* Le libertinage au XVIIe siècle, X, Paris, 1922).

Gilbert, Claude, *Histoire de Calejava ou de l'isle des hommes raisonnables. Avec le parallele de leur morale et du Christianisme,* s. l. (Dijon), 1700.

La Fare, Charles-Auguste de, marquis, *Poèsies inèdites du Marquis de La Fare (1644–1712),* edited by Gustave L. Van Roosbroeck, Paris, 1924.

Poésies libertines et philosophiques (én partie inédites), in Frédéric Lachèvre, *Disciples et successeurs de Théophile de Viau: les derniers libertins,* Le libertinage au XVIIe siècle, XI, Paris, 1924, pp. 215–254.

Lahontan, Louis-Armand de Lom d'Arce de, baron, *Nouveaux voyages de Mr. le baron de Lahontan dans l'Amèrique septentrionale,* 2 vols., The Hague, 1703 (Vol. II entitled *Mèmoires de l'Amèrique septentrionale).*

Dialogues de Monsieur le baron de Lahontan et d'un sauvage, dans l'Amérique, Amsterdam, 1704 (first edition: The Hague, 1703, entitled *Suplément aux Voyages du baron de Lahontan, où l'on trouve des Dialogues curieux entre l'auteur et un sauvage de bon sens qui a voyagé).*

Dialogues curieux entre l'auteur et un sauvage de bon sens qui a voyagé et Mémoires de l'Amérique septentrionale, edited by Gilbert Chinard, Baltimore, 1931.

La Mothe le Vayer, François de, *De la vertu des païens,* 1641, in *Œuvres,* 7 vols. in 14, Dresden, 1756–1759, Tome V, Pt. I (1757); reprint, 2 vols., Geneva, 1970, Vol. II, pp. 118–219.

Lettre d'Hippocrate à Damagette: see *Traduction d'une lettre.*

Lassay, Armand-Léon de Madaillan de Lesparre, marquis de, *Recueil de différentes choses,* 2 vols. in 1, s. l., 1727.

Marana, Giovanni Paolo, *"L'Esploratore turco" di Giovanni Paolo Maranna,* Letters 1–63, edited by G. Almansi and D. A. Warren, in instalments, *Studi secenteschi* 9 (1968) to 14 (1973); bibliography, 18 (1977); original in Bibliothèque nationale mss., fonds italien 1006–1007.

Marana, Giovanni Paolo, *L'Espion dans les cours des princes chrétiens, ou Lettres et mémoires d'un envoyé secret de La Porte dans les cours de l'Europe,* 14th edition, 6 vols., 'Cologne' (Amsterdam?), 1715–1716 (known as *L'Espion turc*; first full French edition 1696).

'Le Militaire philosophe', *Difficultés sur la religion proposées au Père Malebranche par M. . . . , officier militaire dans la marine,* Bibliothèque Mazarine ms. 1163, edited by R. Mortier, Brussels, 1970.

Montesquieu, Charles de Secondat de, baron de La Brède, *Lettres persanes,* edited by Antoine Adam, Textes littéraires français, Geneva, 1954.

Lettres persanes, edited by Paul Vernière, Classiques Garnier, Paris, 1960.

Opinions des anciens sur la nature de l'âme, Bibliothèque nationale ms., nouvelles acquisitions françaises 4369, pp. 1–169 (slightly different text in Boulainviller, *Œuvres philosophiques, supra,* Vol. I, pp. 253–291).

Ramsay, Andrew Michael (André-Michel), chevalier, *Discours philosophique sur l'amour de Dieu, in Histoire de Fénelon,* Paris, 1724 (1st edition: The Hague, 1723).

Religion chrétienne analisée ou Analise abrégée des fondemens de la Religion chrestienne, Bibliothèque nationale ms., f. français 13353; etc.

Saint-Evremond, Charles de Marguetel de Saint-Denis de, seigneur, *Œuvres en prose,* edited by René Ternois, Société des textes français modernes, 4 vols., Paris, 1962–1969.

Lettres, edited by René Ternois, Société des textes français modernes, 2 vols., Paris, 1967–1968.

Traduction d'une lettre d'Hypocrate à Damagette, 'Cologne' (Amsterdam?), 1700; and in Boulainviller, *Œuvres philosophiques, supra,* Vol. I.

Veiras (or Vairasse), Denis, *Histoire des Sévarambes, peuples qui habitent une partie du troisième continent, communément appelé Terre Australe,* 2 vols., Amsterdam, 1734 (first edition: 5 vols., Paris, 1677–1679).

Voltaire, François-Marie Arouet de, *Epître à Uranie,* in I. O. Wade, 'The *Epître à Uranie',* PMLA 47 (1932), 1066–1112.

La Henriade, second critical edition by O. R. Taylor, in Voltaire, *Œuvres complètes,* Besterman edition, *infra,* Vol. II (1970).

Lettres philosophiques, edited Gustave Lanson (first issue: 2 vols., Paris, 1909), re-issued by André-Michel Rousseau, Société des textes français modernes, 2 vols., Paris, 1964.

2. EDITIONS, USED FOR REFERENCE, OF WORKS BY MAJOR AUTHORS

Arnauld, Antoine, *Œuvres complètes,* 38 vols., Paris and Lausanne, 1775–1783.

Bayle, Pierre, *Dictionnaire historique et critique,* 4 vols., Basle, 1741 (first edition: 2 vols., 1697; second edition 4 vols. 1702).

Œuvres diverses, 4 vols., The Hague, 1727–1731.

Pensées diverses sur la comète, edited by Antoine Prat, Société des textes français modernes, 2 vols., Paris, 1911–1912.

Bèze, Théodore de, *Correspondance,* edited by H. and F. Aubert and others, Geneva, 1960–.

Calvin, Jean, *Institution de la religion chrétienne,* edited by Jean-Daniel Benoît, 5 vols., Geneva, 1957–1963.

Charron, Pierre, *De la sagesse, Trois livres,* edited by Amaury Duval, 3 vols., Paris, 1824.

Descartes, René, *Œuvres,* edited by Charles Adam and Paul Tannery, 11 vols., Paris, 1897–1909.

Encyclopédie ou Dictionnaire raisonné des arts, des sciences et des métiers,
edited by Diderot and d'Alembert, 35 vols., Paris, 1751–1780.

Fénelon, François de Salignac de La Mothe, *Œuvres complètes,* edited by
J. Gosselin, 10 vols., Paris, 1851–1852.

Lettre à Louis XIV, edited by Henri Guillemin, Neuchâtel, 1961.

Fontenelle, Bernard le Bouvier de, *Œuvres,* edited by G. Depping, 3 vols.,
Paris, 1818.

Textes choisis (1683–1702), edited by Maurice Roelens, Paris, 1966.

La Mothe le Vayer, François, *Œuvres,* 7 vols., in 14, Dresden, 1756–1759.

Malebranche, Nicolas, *Œuvres,* edited by André Robinet, 21 vols., Paris,
1958–1970.

Montaigne, Michel de, *Essais,* edited by Pierre Villey, 3 vols., Paris, 1922.

Montesquieu, Charles de Secondat de, baron de La Brède, *Œuvres
complètes,* edited by Roger Caillois, Collection de la Pléiade, 2 vols.,
Paris, 1949–1951.

Pascal, Blaise, *Lettres provinciales,* edited by Louis Cognet, Classiques
Garnier, Paris, 1965.

Pensées, edited by Philippe Sellier, Les Classiques du Mercure, Paris,
1976.

Rousseau, Jean-Jacques, *Œuvres complètes,* edited by Bernard Gagnebin and
Marcel Raymond, Collection de la Pléiade, 5 vols. planned, Vols. I–IV,
Paris, 1959–1969.

Voltaire, François-Marie Arouet de, *Œuvres complètes,* edited by Louis
Moland, 52 vols., Paris, 1877–1885. *Œuvres complètes,* edited by
Theodore Besterman and others, Geneva and Oxford, 1968–(in
progress).

Correspondance, definitive edition by Theodore Besterman, 51 vols., in
Oeuvres complètes, ed. Besterman, *supra,* Vols. 85–135, 1968–1977.

Traité de métaphysique, edited by H. Temple Patterson, Manchester,
1937.

Dictionnaire philosophique, edited by Raymond Naves, introduction by
Julien Benda, Classiques Garnier, Paris, 1954 (first issue: 2 vols. Paris,
1935–1936).

3. SECONDARY AUTHORITIES, CITED IN THE NOTES OR OF GENERAL INTEREST FOR THE
SUBJECT; EXCLUDING WORKS CITED IN THE APPENDIX

Actes du congrès Montesquieu réuni à Bordeaux du 23 au 26 mai 1955,
Bordeaux, 1956.

Adam, Antoine, *Histoire de la littérature française au XVIIe siècle,* 5 vols.,
Paris, 1949–1956.

Les libertins au XVIIe siècle, Paris, 1964.

Le mouvement philosophique dans la première moitié du XVIIIe siècle,
Paris, 1967.

The Age of the Enlightenment, Studies presented to Theodore Besterman, edited by W. H. Barber and others, Edinburgh and London, 1967.

Almansi, Guido, "'L'Esploratore turco" e la genesi del romanzo epistolare pseudo-orientale', *Studi secenteschi* 7 (1966), 35–65.

Almansi, Guido, and D. A. Warren, 'Roman épistolaire et analyse historique: l' "Espion turc" de G. P. Marana', *XVIIe Siècle* 110 (1976), 57–63.

Andrews, S. G., 'The Wandering Jew and the *Travels and Aventures of James Massey*', *Modern Language Notes* 72 (1957), 39–41.

d'Angers, Pierre-Julien-Eymard, *Pascal et ses précurseurs: l'apologétique en France de 1580 à 1670,* Paris, 1954.

Armstrong, Brian G., *Calvinism and the Amyraut Heresy,* Milwaukee and London, 1969.

Ascoli, Georges, 'Quelques notes biographiques sur Denis Veiras d'Alais', in *Mélanges offerts à Gustave Lanson,* Paris, 1922, pp. 165–177.

Aspects de la propagande religieuse, Etudies publiées par Gabrielle Berthoud (and others), preface by H. Meylan, Geneva, 1957.

Aspects du libertinisme au XVIe siècle, Actes du colloque international de Sommières, Exposés de Marcel Bataillon (and others), Paris, 1974.

Atkinson, Geoffroy, *The Extraordinary Voyage in French Literature before 1700,* New York, 1920.

    The Extraordinary Voyage in French Literature from 1700 to 1720, New York, 1922.

Auerbach, Erich, *Mimesis: The Representation of Reality in Western Literature,* Princeton, 1953 (German original: Berne, 1946).

Auvray, Paul, *Richard Simon (1638–1712), étude bio-bibliographique,* Paris, 1974.

Barber, W. H. 'Voltaire and Quakerism: Enlightenment and the Inner Light', SVEC, 24 (1963), Transactions of the First International Congress on the Enlightenment, 4 vols., Vol. I, pp. 81–109.

    'Voltaire and Samuel Clarke', in *Voltaire and the English, infra,* pp. 41–61.

Barber, W. H., ed.: see *Age of the Enlightenment.*

Barnaud, Jean, *Pierre Viret, sa vie et son oeuvre (1511–1571),* Saint-Amans (Tarn), 1911.

    'Pierre Viret à Lyon (1562–1565)', *Bulletin de la société de l'histoire du protestantisme français* 60 (1911), 7–43.

Barnes, Annie, *Jean Le Clerc et la république des lettres,* Paris, 1938.

Barnwell, H. T., *Les idées morales et critiques de Saint-Evremond,* Paris, 1957.

Barth, Paul, *Die Stoa,* third edition, Stuttgart, 1922.

Baruzi, Jean, *Leibniz et l'organisation religieuse de la terre,* Paris, 1907.

Besterman, Theodore, *Voltaire,* third edition, Oxford, 1976.

Blanchet, Louis, *Campanella,* Paris, 1920.

Boase, Alan, *The Fortunes of Montaigne: A History of the Essays in France, 1580–1669*, London, 1935.

Bonno, Gabriel, *La culture et la civilisation britanniques devant l'opinion française de la paix d'Utrecht aux Lettres philosophiques*, Philadelphia, 1948.

Bouillier, Francisque, *Histoire de la philosophie cartésienne*, third edition, 2 vols., Paris, 1868.

Brasart-de Groër, Georgette, 'Le Collège, agent d'infiltration de la Réforme: Barthélemy Aneau au Collège de la Trinité', in *Aspects de la propagande religieuse, supra*, pp. 167–175.

Bredvold, L. I., 'Deism before Lord Herbert', *Papers of the Michigan Academy of Sciences, Arts, and Letters* 4 (1924), 431–442.

Bremond, Henri, abbé, *Histoire littéraire du sentiment religieux en France*, 11 vols., Paris, 1915–1933.

Briggs, E. R., 'L'incrédulité et la pensée anglaise en France au début du XVIIIe siècle', RHLF 41 (1934), 497–538.

Brown, W. Harcourt, 'The Composition of the *Letters concerning the English Nation*', in *The Age of the Enlightenment, supra*, pp. 115–134.

Brummer, Rudolf, *Studien zur französischen Aufklärungsliteratur im Anschluss an J. -A. Naigeon*, Breslau, 1932.

Buckley, George T., *Atheism in the English Renaissance*, Chicago, 1932.

Busson, Henri, *Le rationalisme dans la littérature française de la Renaissance (1533–1601)*, Paris, 1957 (revised edition of his *Les sources et le développement du rationalisme dans la littérature française de la Renaissance (1533–1601)*, Paris, 1922).

La pensée religieuse française de Charron à Pascal, Paris, 1933.

La religion des classiques (1660–1685), Paris, 1948.

'Les noms des incrédules au XVIe siècle', BHR 16 (1954), 273–283.

Littérature et théologie: Montaigne, Bossuet, La Fontaine, Prévost, [Algiers,] 1964.

Caillois, Roger, 'Réflexions pour préciser l'attitude de Montesquieu à l'égard de la religion', *La Table Ronde* 90 (1955), 138–150.

Calvet, Jean, *La littérature religieuse de François de Sales à Fénelon*, Paris, 1956.

Cantimori, Delio, *Eretici italiani del cinquecento, ricerche storiche*, Florence, 1939.

Cantimori, Delio, ed.: see *Ginevra e l'Italia*.

Capéran, Louis, *Le problème du salut des infidèles*: (Vol. I) *essai historique*, (Vol. II) *essai théologique*, 2 vols., Paris, 1912.

Carayol, Elisabeth, 'Des *Lettres persanes* oubliées', RHLF 65 (1965), 15–26.

Carcassonne, Elie, *Fénelon, l'homme et l'oeuvre*, Paris, 1946.

Carré, Jean-Raoul, *La philosophie de Fontenelle ou le sourire de la raison*, Paris, 1932.

Réflexions sur l'anti-Pascal de Voltaire, Paris, 1935.

Cassirer, Ernst, *The Philosophy of the Enlightenment,* Princeton, 1952 (German original: *Die Philosophie der Aufklärung,* Tübingen, 1932).

Castiglione, Tommaso R., 'La "Impietas Valentini Gentilis" e il corruccio di Calvino', in *Ginevra e l'Italia, infra,* pp. 149–176.

Charbonnel, J. -R., *La pensée italienne et le courant libertin,* Paris, 1917.

Chérel, Albert, *Fénelon au XVIIIe siècle en France,* Paris, 1918.

   A. -M. Ramsay, un aventurier religieux au XVIIIe siècle, Paris, 1920.

   De Télémaque à Candide, Paris, 1913.

Chinard, Gilbert, *L'Amérique et le rêve exotique dans la littérature française au XVIIe et au XVIIIe siècle,* Paris, 1913.

Cognet, Louis, *Crépuscule des mystiques,* Paris, 1958.

Cohen, Gustave, 'Le séjour de Saint-Evremond en Hollande (1665–1670)', RLC 5 (1925), 431–454; 6 (1926), 28–78, 402–423.

Cotta, Sergio, *Montesquieu e la scienza della societá,* Turin, 1953.

Crisafulli, Alessandro, 'Parallels to Ideas in the *Lettres persanes*', PMLA 52 (1937), 773–777.

Dédéyan, Charles, *Voltaire et la pensée anglaise,* Paris, 1956.

Dedieu, Joseph, *Montesquieu, l'homme et l'œuvre,* Paris, 1943.

Delvolvé, Jean, *Religion, critique et philosophie positive chez Pierre Bayle,* Paris, 1906.

Denonain, J. J., 'Le *Liber de tribus impostoribus* du XVIe siècle', in *Aspects du libertinisme, supra,* pp. 215–226.

Desautels, Alfred R., S. J., *Les Mémoires de Trévoux et le mouvement des idées au dix-huitième siècle,* (Vol. I) *1701–1734,* Rome, 1956.

Ehrard, Jean, *L'Idée de nature en France dans la première moitié du XVIIIe siècle,* 2 vols., Paris, 1963.

Erba, Luciano, *Magia e invenzione, note e ricerche su Cyrano de Bergerac e su altri autori,* Milan, 1967.

Faguet, Emile, *Dix-huitième siècle: études littéraires,* Paris, 1980.

Febvre, Lucien, *Le problème de l'incroyance au XVIe siècle: la religion de Rabelais,* Paris, 1942.

Florida, R. E., *Voltaire and the Socinians,* SVEC 122 (1974).

Geffriaud Rosso, Jeannette, *Montesquieu et la féminité,* Pisa and Paris, 1977.

Ginevra e l'Italia, edited by Delio Cantimori and others, Florence, 1959.

Gouhier, Henri, *La pensée religieuse de Descartes,* Paris, 1924.

Gunny, Ahmad, 'Montesquieu's View of Islam in the *Lettres persanes*', SVEC 174 (1978), 151–167.

Guy, Basil, *The French Image of China before and after Voltaire,* SVEC 21 (1963).

Haase, Erich, *Einführung in die Literatur der Refuge: Der Beitrag der französischen Protestanten zur Entwicklung analytischer Denkformen am Ende des 17. Jahrhunderts,* Berlin, 1959.

Harcourt Brown, W.: see Brown, W. Harcourt.

Harth, Phillip, *Contexts of Dryden's Thought,* Chicago, 1968.

Hazard, Paul, *La crise de la conscience européenne (1680–1715),* 3 vols., Paris, 1935.

La pensée européenne au XVIIIe siècle de Montesquieu à Lessing, 3 vols., Paris, 1946.

Henderson, G. D., *Chevalier Ramsay,* Edinburgh, 1952.

Jehasse, Jean, *La Renaissance de la critique: l'essor de l'humanisme érudit de 1560 à 1614,* Saint-Étienne, 1976.

Julien-Eymard d'Angers: see d'Angers, Pierre-Julien-Eymard.

Kirkinen, H., *Les origines de la conception moderne de l'homme-machine: le problème de l'âme en France à la fin du règne de Louis XIV (1670–1715),* Helsinki, 1960.

Knapp, Richard G., *The Fortunes of Pope's ESSAY ON MAN in 18th Century France,* SVEC 82 (1971), 79–122.

Kot, Stanislas, 'Le mouvement anti-trinitaire au XVIe et au XVIIe siècle', *Humanisme et Renaissance,* 4 (1937), 16–58, 109–156.

'L'Influence de Servet sur le mouvement anti-trinitaire en Pologne et en Transylvanie', in *Autour de Michel Servet et de Sébastien Castellion,* edited by B. Becker, Haarlem, 1953.

Kra, Pauline, *Religion in Montesquieu's Lettres persanes,* SVEC 72 (1970).

Krauss, Werner, 'Fontenelle und die "Republik der Philosophen"', *Romanische Forschungen,* 75 (1963), 11–21.

Fontenelle und die Aufklärung, Munich, 1969.

Kristeller, P. O., 'Le mythe de l'athéisme de la Renaissance et la tradition française de la libre pensée', BHR 37 (1975), 337–348.

Labrousse, Elisabeth, *Pierre Bayle,* 2 vols., The Hague, 1963–1964.

'Note sur Jurieu', *Revue d'histoire et de philosophie religieuse* 58 (1978), 277–297.

Lachèvre, Frédéric, *Mélanges,* Le libertinage au XVIIe siècle, VII, Paris, 1920.

Lanson, Gustave, *Histoire de la littérature française,* Paris, 1895.

Voltaire, Paris, 1906.

Origines et premières manifestations de l'esprit philosophique dans la littérature française de 1675 à 1748, Revue des cours et conférences, 16–18 (1907–1910); reprinted New York, 1973.

'Questions diverses sur l'histoire de l'esprit philosophique en France', RHLF 19 (1912), 1–29, 293–317.

Laporte, Jean, *Le rationalisme de Descartes,* Paris, 1945.

Lavicka, Jan, '"L'Espion turc", le monde slave et le hussitisme', *XVIIe Siècle* 110 (1976), 75–92.

Lechler, Gotthard V., *Geschichte des englischen Deismus,* Stuttgart and Tübingen, 1841; reprinted with introduction and bibliography by Günter Gawlick, Hildesheim, 1965.

Lenoble, Robert, abbé, *Mersenne ou la naissance du mécanisme,* Paris, 1943.

Lovejoy, Arthur O., 'The Parallel of Deism and Classicism', *Modern Philology* 29 (1931–1932).

The Great Chain of Being: A Study of the History of an Idea, Cambridge, Massachusetts, 1936.

McBurney, McKee: see after Mauriac.

Maigron, Louis, *Fontenelle, l'homme, l'œuvre, l'influence,* Paris, 1906.

Manuel, Frank E., *The Eighteenth Century Confronts the Gods,* Cambridge, Massachusetts, 1959.

Margolin, J. C., 'Libertins, libertinisme et "libertinage" au XVIe siècle', in *Aspects du libertinisme, supra,* pp. 1–33.

Mariéjol, Jean-H., *La Réforme et la Ligue: L'Edit de Nantes (1559–1598),* Histoire de France depuis les origines jusqu'à la Révolution, edited by E. Lavisse, 9 vols. in 18, Paris, 1900–1911, Vol. VI, Pt I (1904).

Martin, Henri-J., *Livre, pouvoirs et société à Paris au XVIIe siècle (1598–1701),* 2 vols., Geneva, 1969.

Martino, Pierre, *L'Orient dans la littérature française au XVIIe et au XVIIIe siècle,* Paris, 1906.

Mason, Haydn T., *Pierre Bayle and Voltaire,* Oxford, 1963.

Mason, Sheila M., *Montesquieu's Idea of Justice,* The Hague, 1975.

Masson, Pierre-Maurice, *La religion de Jean-Jacques Rousseau,* Paris 1916.

Maurens, Jacques, *La tragédie sans tragique: le néo-stoïcisme dans l'œuvre de Pierre Corneille,* Paris, 1966.

Mauriac, François, *Voltaire contre Pascal,* Paris, 1929.

McBurney, William H., 'The Authorship of the "The Turkish Spy"', PMLA 72 (1957), 915–935.

McKee, David R., *Simon Tyssot de Patot and the Seventeenth-Century Background of Critical Deism,* Baltimore, 1941.

Mercier, Roger, *La réhabilitation de la nature humaine (1700–1750),* Villemonble (Seine), 1960.

L'Afrique noire dans la littérature française: les premières images, XVIIe – XVIIIe siècles, Dakar, 1962.

Mesnard, Pierre, 'La pensée religieuse de Jean Bodin', *Revue du seizième siècle* 16 (1929), 77–121.

Meylan, Henri, 'Bèze et les Italiens de Lyon (1566)', BHR 14 (1952), 235–249.

'Pierre Viret et les libertins, d'après *L'Intérim (1565)',* in *Aspects du libertinisme, supra,* pp. 191–198.

Mirabaud, Paul de, and Léon-Frédéric Le Grand, *Notice sur J.-B. de Mirabaud,* Paris, 1895.

Monod, Albert, *De Pascal à Chateaubriand: les défenseurs français du Christianisme de 1670 à 1802,* Paris, 1916.

Mornet, Daniel, *Les origines intellectuelles de la Révolution française, 1715–1787,* Paris, 1933.

298

Mühll, Emanuel von der: see Von der Mühll.

Naves, Raymond, *Voltaire, l'homme et l'œuvre*, Paris, 1942.

Niderst, Alain, *Fontenelle à la recherche de lui-même*, Paris, 1972.

Oake, Roger, 'Montesquieu's Religious Ideas', JHI 14 (1953), 548–560.

O'Higgins, James, S.J., *Yves de Vallone: The Making of an Esprit-fort*, The Hague, 1982.

O'Keeffe, Cyril B., S.J., *Contemporary Reactions to the Enlightenment (1728–1762)*, Paris, 1974.

Orcibal, Jean, *Jean Duvergier de Hauranne, Abbé de Saint-Cyran, et son temps (1581–1638)*, Les origines du Jansénisme, II–III, 2 vols., Paris, 1947–1948.

Palmer, R. R., *Catholics and Unbelievers in Eighteenth-Century France*, Princeton, 1939.

Perkins, Merle L., 'Civil Theology in the Writings of the Abbé de Saint-Pierre', JHI 18 (1957), 242–253.

Perrens, F. -T., *Les libertins en France au XVIIe siècle*, Paris, 1896.

Philips, Edith, 'Le Quaker vu par Voltaire', RHLF 39 (1932), 161–177.

Pinot, Virgile, *La Chine et la formation de l'esprit philosophique en France (1640–1740)*, Paris, 1932.

Pintard, René, *Le libertinage érudit dans la première moitié du XVIIe siècle*, 2 vols., Paris, 1943.

'Problèmes de l'histoire du libertinage, notes et réflexions', *XVIIe Siècle* 127 (1980), 131–162.

Pomeau, René, *La Religion de Voltaire*, Paris, 1956.

Popkin, Richard H., *The History of Scepticism from Erasmus to Descartes*, revised edition, Assen, 1964.

Potts, Denys C., 'Saint-Evremond and Seventeeth-Century *libertinage*', unpublished D. Phil. thesis, University of Oxford, 1962.

'Desmaizeaux and Saint-Evremond's Text', *French Studies* 19 (1965), 239–252.

Préclin, E., and E. Jarry, *Les luttes politiques et doctrinales aux XVIIe et XVIIIe siècles*, Histoire de l'Eglise, fondée par A. Fliche et V. Martin, XIX, 2 vols., Paris., 1955–1956.

Rébelliau, Alfred, *Bossuet historien du protestantisme*, second edition, Paris, 1892.

Rétat, Pierre, *Le Dictionnaire de Bayle et la lutte philosophique au XVIIIe siècle*, Lyon, 1971.

Robertson, John M., *A Short History of Freethought Ancient and Modern*, third edition revised and expanded, 2 vols., London, 1915.

Robinet, André, 'Malebranchisme et Régence', in *La Régence*, papers given at the Colloque sur la Régence, Aix-en-Provence, 24–26 February 1968, edited by H. Coulet, Paris, 1970, pp. 263–275.

'Boulainviller auteur du "Militaire philosophe"?', RHLF 73 (1973), 22–31.

Roelens, Maurice, 'Lahontan dans l'*Encyclopédie* et ses suites', in *Recherches nouvelles sur quelques écrivains des Lumières*, edited by Jacques Proust, Geneva, 1972, pp. 163–200.

Roellenbleck, Georg, *Offenbarung, Natur und jüdische Überlieferung bei Jean Bodin*, Gütersloh, 1964.

Rosenberg, Aubrey, *Tyssot de Patot and his work, 1655–1738,* The Hague, 1972.

Nicolas Gueudeveille and his work (1652–172?), The Hague, 1982.

Rossi, Mario Manlio, *Alle fonti del deismo e del materialismo moderno,* Florence, 1942.

La vita, le opere e i tempi di Eduardo, Lord Herbert di Chirbury, 3 vols., Florence, 1947.

Rotondò, Antonio, 'Calvino e gli anti-trinitari italiani', *Rivista storica italiana* 80 (1968), 759–784.

Rousseau, André-M., *L'Angleterre et Voltaire,* 3 vols., SVEC 145–147 (1976).

'Naissance d'un livre et d'un texte: les *Letters concerning the English Nation*', in *Voltaire and the English, infra,* pp. 25–46.

Sabrié, J. -B., *De l'humanisme au rationalisme: Pierre Charron,* Paris, 1913.

Schlegel, Dorothy B., *Shaftesbury and the French Deists,* Chapel Hill, North Carolina, 1956.

Schneider, Gerhard, *Der Libertin: Zur Geistesund Sozialgeschichte des Bürgertums im 16. und 17. Jahrhundert,* Stuttgart, 1970.

Shackleton, Robert, *Montesquieu: A Critical Biography,* Oxford, 1961.

'La religion de Montesquieu', in *Actes du congrès Montesquieu, supra,* pp. 267–294.

Simon, Renée, *Henry de Boulainviller, historien, politique, philosophe, astrologue, 1658–1722,* Paris, n.d. [1939].

Spink, John S., *French Free-Thought from Gassendi to Voltaire,* London, 1960.

Starobinski, Jean, *Montesquieu par lui-même,* Paris, 1963.

Steinmann, Jean, *Richard Simon et les origines de l'exégèse biblique,* Paris, 1960.

Stephen, Sir Leslie, *History of English Thought in the Eighteenth Century,* 2 vols., London, 1876.

Storer, Mary E., 'The Abbé Raguenet, Deist, Historian, Music and Art Critic', *Romanic Review* 36 (1945), 283–296.

Stromberg, Roland N., *Religious Liberalism in Eighteenth Century England,* Oxford, 1954.

Strowski, Fortunat, *Pascal et son temps,* 3 vols., Paris, 1907–1908.

Ternois, René, 'Saint-Evremond et Spinoza', RHLF 65 (1965), 1–14.

Tocanne, Bernard, *L'Idée de nature en France dans la seconde moitié du XVII siècle,* Paris, 1978.

'Aspects de la pensée libertine à la fin du XVIIe siècle: Le case de Claude Gilbert', *XVIIe Siècle* 129 (1980), 213–224.

Toldo, Pietro, 'Dell' *Espion* di Giovanni Paolo Marana e delle sue attinenze con le *Lettres persanes* del Montesquieu', *Giornale storico della letteratura italiana* 29 (1897), 46–79.

Torrey, Norman L., *Voltaire and the English Deists,* New Haven, 1930.

The Spirit of Voltaire, New York, 1938.

Toynbee, Arnold, *An Historian's Approach to Religion,* London, 1956.

Troeltsch, Ernst, *Der Deismus,* in *Gesammelte Schriften,* 4 vols., Tübingen, 1922–1925, Vol. IV (1925).

Van Tieghem, Philippe, 'La "Prière universelle" de Pope et le déisme français au XVIIIe siècle', RLC 3 (1923), 190–212.

Venturi, Franco, *La jeunesse de Diderot (1713–1753),* translated from the Italian by Juliette Bertrand, Paris, 1939.

Vernière, Paul, *Spinoza et la pensée française avant la Révolution,* 2 vols., Paris, 1954.

Voltaire and the English, Transactions of the Oxford Colloquium held at the Taylor Institution from 26 to 28 May 1978, SVEC 179 (1979).

Von der Mühll, Emanuel, *Denis Veiras et son Histoire des Sévarambes 1677–1679,* Paris, 1938.

Wade, Ira O., *The Clandestine Organization and Diffusion of Philosophic Ideas in France from 1700 to 1750,* Princeton, 1938.

Studies on Voltaire, with some unpublished papers of Mme du Châtelet, Princeton, 1947.

Walker, D. P., 'The *Prisca Theologia* in France', *Journal of the Warburg and Courtauld Institutes* 17 (1954), 204–259.

The Decline of Hell: Seventeenth-Century Discussions of Eternal Torment, Chicago, 1964.

The Ancient Theology, London, 1972.

Wickelgren, Florence, *La Mothe le Vayer, sa vie et son œuvre,* Paris, 1934.

Wilbur, Earl Morse, *Socinianism and its Antecedents,* Vol. I of *A History of Unitarianism,* 2 vols., Boston, 1945–1952.

Williams, George Huntston, *The Radical Reformation,* Philadelphia, 1962.

Wirth, Jean, '"Libertins" et "épicuriens": aspects de l'irréligion au XVIe siècle', BHR 39 (1977), 601–627.

Yates, Dame Frances, *Giordano Bruno and the Hermetic Tradition,* London, 1964.

The Rosicrucian Enlightenment, London, 1972.

Young, D. B., 'Libertarian Demography: Montesquieu's Essay on Depopulation in the *Lettres persanes'*, JHI 36 (1975), 669–682.

Zanta, Léontine, *La Renaissance du stoïcisme au XVIe siècle,* Paris, 1914.

Zeller, Eduard, *The Stoics, Epicureans and Sceptics,* translated by O. J. Reichel, revised edition, London, 1879.

INDEX

No references are given for material of a purely bibliographical nature, nor for the Appendix. Page-references include the notes on the relevant pages.

302